Sports Marketing Europe

The Legal and Tax Aspects

Sports Marketing Europe

The Legal and Tax Aspects

edited by

Ian S. Blackshaw

and

Gillian Hogg

Foreword by Richard W. Pound, Q.C., Vice President of the I.O.C.

1993

Kluwer Law and Taxation Publishers
Deventer · Boston

This book is intended as a general guide and not as a substitute for detailed legal advice on any of the topics discussed.

Library of Congress Cataloging-in-Publication Data

Sports marketing Europe : the legal and tax aspects / edited by Ian S. Blackshaw and Gillian Hogg.
p. cm.
ISBN 9065446788
1. Sports—Law and legislation—Europe. 2. Sports—Taxation–Law and legislation—Europe.
I. Blackshaw, Ian Stewart. II. Hogg, Gillian.
KJC6063.S66 1993
343.4'0855796—dc20
[344.03855796] 93—5893
CIP

ISBN 90 6544 678 8

Table of Contents

Preface

by Ian S. Blackshaw

In this book, believed to be the first of its particular *genre*, we have endeavoured to provide a general overview and point of first reference on the various legal aspects of the increasingly important subject of sports marketing in Europe. Although sports marketing is a relatively new 'Industry' in Europe, it is a developing one. With the advent, on 1 January 1993, of the single integrated market of the European Community, coupled with the projected enlargement of the Community, as well as the increasingly global and regional nature of the opportunities for the commercialisation and marketing of sports events, we believe the timing of this book could not be more opportune.

Starting with and using the UK as a basis for comparison, we cover not only the member countries of the European Community, but also the countries of the European Free Trade Association and several of the countries in the former East European block, including the Russian Federation, part of the newly created Confederation of Independent States, which traditionally have been, and continue to be, actively involved in international sports events as promoters and participants. Incidentally, the Czech Republic has just introduced a total ban of advertisements on tobacco products. We also cover the subject of broadcasting, an essential ingredient of sports sponsorship, as well as the fiscal and EC aspects. To complete our *tour d'horizon* of our subject, we also include an account of the activities of the Court of Arbitration for Sport.

As far as possible, we have endeavoured to provide a non-technical and practical coverage of our subject, in the hope that this book will not only appeal to lawyers, but also to sports administrators, businessmen and the many others who are, in one way or another, engaged in the organisation, staging and exploitation of sports events in Europe. Whilst this book is not intended to be an encyclopaedia, we have, however, endeavoured to be as comprehensive as possible. We have also endeavoured to point out some of the pitfalls and traps for the unwary and share some of our know-how and experience in this field of opportunity.

On behalf of my co-editor and myself, I should like to express my sincere thanks to the publishers, especially to Karel van der Linde of Kluwer Law and

Taxation Publishers, Dick Pound of the IOC for contributing the Foreword, and the other distinguished contributors, as well as the partners of Bird & Bird and my secretary, Joyce Foster, for all their efforts and co-operation in this undertaking.

In conclusion, I dare to hope and believe that this book will prove to be a useful contribution to the understanding and development of the sports marketing industry in Europe, which, I also believe, offers so many exciting and valuable opportunities for the creative, enterprising and tenacious, both now and in the future.

Ian S. Blackshaw
Field Fisher Waterhouse
London, 1 January 1993

Foreword

by Richard W. Pound, Q.C.[1]

Less than a generation ago, the idea of publishing a work of this nature would have been, if not unthinkable, at least so far ahead of its time that no publisher would have given it serious consideration. Yet, today, the field of sports marketing has become a major sub-speciality within the *genes* of marketing and one of the highest profile marketing efforts in modern society.

The excitement, suspense, challenge and media attention surrounding sports create an ideal marketing focus for commercial enterprises wishing to bring local, national and world-wide attention to their products and services. The potential to be identified with challenge, competition, success, excellence, winning and 'star' athletes creates almost irresistible opportunities for such enterprises. The images of sport are current, exciting and often dramatic.

In the result, what was a fledgling concept within our lifetimes has become a thriving industry and one which shows signs of growing even more in the foreseeable future. An enormous range of talent has been brought to bear on sports marketing. When once the leading edge of sports marketing was a discreet mention of a sponsor's name in a poorly printed and edited programme distributed at the event and of a signboard near the playing field, today's sports marketing covers the full range of marketing techniques. Indeed, sports market-

1. Richard W. Pound is a Senior Partner in the Firm of Stikeman, Elliott (Montreal, Toronto, Ottawa, Calgary, Vancouver, New York, London, Hong Kong), a member of the Bars of Quebec and Ontario, a Chartered Accountant, a member of the Court of Arbitration for Sport, the Juridical Commission of the International Olympic Committee and the IOC Executive Board. He is the Chairman of the IOC Commission for New Sources of Finance, the IOC Television Negotiations Committee and the Co-ordination Commission for the 1996 Olympic Games. He is responsible for the direction of the IOC's marketing programme, the 'TOP Programme', and is Chairman of its Marketing Co-ordination Committee. He has lectured extensively on legal matters in Canada and at McGill University. He is the Editor-in-Chief of *Doing Business in Canada*, a three volume loose-leaf service, Editor and author of *Tax Case Notes*, Editor of 'Legal Notes' for *CGA Magazine* and Associate Editor of *Canada Tax Cases*. He is a member of many professional associations.

ing has invented new techniques which have subsequently been adopted within other types of marketing.

If, however, sports marketing can be said to have come of age, such transition has not been without complications.

The practice of sport and the scope of sporting activities have expanded beyond all predictions over the past century. What once was practised in school playgrounds as part of a programme for general physical health and recreation has expanded to regional, national and international competitive sport. Even Pierre de Coubertin, the ambitious renovator of the modern Olympic Movement, could have had no conception of what he was about to unleash on the world when he called for the Congress of Paris in 1894, founded the International Olympic Committee and re-instituted the Olympic Games in Athens two years later.

Prior to that time, organised sport was parochial, at best; even the rules for many sports were still in the process of becoming standardised. Many of the sports which are now practised on a world-wide basis were either not yet 'invented' or were in an uncertain infancy. The precocious impetus toward international competition was still awaiting the means to travel efficiently and the development of a reliable spirit of internationalism. Many of the societies and political systems which are important factors in the societies and political systems which are important factors in our modern world had not yet emerged. The social systems which recognised sport as a vital factor in many aspects of society had not yet been developed. Once this recognition occurred, the growth became geometric in proportion. Today, sport is a significant element of society, touching, in one way or another, almost every member of the community. It has, in addition, a significant economic impact on society.

As sport increased in importance and influence within the community, commercial enterprises in those societies which had a significant private sector, began to perceive the values of being identified with sport and of the competitive advantages which might be derived from association with this growing phenomenon. They began to support such activities in a financial manner, in return for some visible identification. Such investment had a certain eleemosynary component, to be sure, but commercial entities organised on any meaningful scale have a limited ability to spend money (often shareholders' money) on charitable endeavours. The objective of a business investment is to produce a return on that investment. How, then, could the investment in sport generate a return; how could it be translated into increased revenues?

While there are many elements of science involved in marketing, it would be illusionary to describe it as an exact science. There is a considerable amount of art and intuition attaching to any marketing programme. But, in the scientific portion of the recipe, the disciplines of market analysis, programme design, measurement and financial control must be observed, at the risk of misadventure. In particular, an analysis must be made of the nature of the activities to be undertaken, the rights of each of the parties and the legal matrix against which rights will be granted, obligations assumed and activities undertaken. In the early days of commercial involvement in sport, there was very little with which to be concerned in this regard. A programme mention or a signboard was not a major undertaking. It was easy to deliver upon promises made.

Such simplicity no longer exists.

That said, no value judgement is made which suggests that the evolution from simplicity to the complexity of modern times is undesirable. It is merely an observation of an undeniable fact of life. Sport itself has changed radically from the original school or community level to the international activity it now represents. The athlete in organised sport at the national or international level has changed from the so-called amateur to, in many cases, a full time employee (or quasi-employee) of a sports club, federation or even the State. Certain rights have come to be recognised as belonging to the athlete. Others belong to the club or federation. Some belong to 'umbrella' international organisations.

The internationalisation of sport brings into play the application of different systems of law and the need to sort out, in many circumstances, which law should apply and in which jurisdiction any actions relating to sports matters should be determined in case of dispute. The range of issues to be considered in a sophisticated sports marketing programme becomes apparent with even a cursory glance at the table of contents of this work. So important is the study of the growing scope of legal issues affecting sport that the International Olympic Committee has taken the unprecedented step of offering to endow a Chair at the Université de Lausanne's Faculté de Droit. The range of marketing skills, negotiating abilities and legal knowledge required to design and implement any such marketing programme is formidable indeed.

This work does not purport to deal with the design of the marketing programme *per se.* That is to say, it does not approach the matter of sports marketing from the perspective of what the marketer hopes to accomplish with the sports marketing effort. The objectives of such programmes can be varied and multi-purpose. These objectives could be to expand brand awareness, to add to or create a corporate image, to move into a new product or service line, to provide an internal focus for staff, to enter new territorial markets, to 'position' a product or service in the marketplace and many other possibilities. The authors and contributors have taken for granted that the programme and its objectives have been defined; their focus is upon the ability to 'deliver' that programme in the context of the many legal issues which surround the business objectives of the plan.

Different societies respond to the issues inherent in sports marketing in their own fashion. The systems of law differ from country to country, depending upon, for example, whether the common law tradition of deriving the general principle from specific precedents or the civil law tradition of deciding the particular case based upon the general principle enacted in a Code is followed. The economic systems in place in a particular country will also condition the legal response to marketing issues. The same is true with respect to the nature and role of the media in a given society. Is, for example, advertising permitted in all media? What are the limitations on advertising statements which can be made? Must there be independent research before advertising claims can be made? Can there be 'exclusive' arrangements made within an industry or product category? To what extent can agreements be enforced, once they are made? Are there alternatives to the general courts as a means of resolving disputes which may arise?

This work attempts to provide a brief catalogue of the situation in each of the countries included within its scope. Such a catalogue is an indispensable starting point in the understanding of the legal framework against which a marketing programme must be evaluated and implemented. One must first have an appreciation of the legal system in the country. This holds true whether the programme is local or international. The applicable legislation must be identified and studied to know the parameters of what is possible and, perhaps more important, what is *not* possible.

Essential to any marketing programme is the extent of legal protection in the jurisdiction for intellectual property. Almost every sports marketing programme is based on ideas, proprietary information and product or corporate identification. Are such matters capable of protection within a particular jurisdiction? Such protection can take the form of trademarks, copyright, registered designs, legislation dealing with unfair competition, special legislation directed at or in favour of specific institutions or marks and legislation implementing international treaties. Whatever it may be, the implementors of any marketing plan must be certain to identify such matters, since it is fundamental to the grant of any right that it be possible to grant the right. By the same token, the nature and extent of the applicable legislation will determine the degree of exclusivity that can be granted and the ability to protect what has been granted.

Essential as well is to know the structure within which rights exist and can be granted. The structures, especially international sport structures, are complex and it is not always easy to determine exactly which organisation owns or controls which rights. Since doubt may exist, it is virtually standard practice for the grantor of the rights to represent and warrant that it has the right to enter into the necessary agreement(s). Any such provision carries with it significant legal implications and it would be reckless to proceed with any such agreement without a considerable degree of confidence that the rights both exist and can be granted. One of the first responsibilities of any legal advisor in such circumstances must be to trace the derivation of the rights which are granted.

This may be quite simple in the case of specific legislation; it may be quite difficult where the rights may have been derived from other organisations. A case in point might be a world championship organised locally under the ultimate authority of an international sports federation, which has assigned certain marketing rights to the local organising committee. Have such rights been adequately conveyed to and vested in the local organising committee? Are there any reservations of such rights on the part of the international federation? Are there residual rights retained by the international federation which might have the effect of diminishing the rights of the local organising committee? For example, the local organising committee may have full marketing rights for sponsors, but the international federation may retain the television rights to the event and have agreements with respect thereto which could conflict with exclusive marketing rights granted by the local organising committee.

Even the registered trademark of an organisation may not be determinative of the ability to grant exclusive rights. Trademark legislation is normally very technical and generally limits the rights attaching to intellectual property to a limited range of products or services. This, coupled with a reluctance on the part of courts to encourage restrictive or exclusive ownership, often leads to a trademark being only partially effective or even of falling into the public domain if all the technicalities and formalities prescribed by the legislation are not scrupulously observed.

Since visual identification is crucial to almost every marketing programme, it is vital to ensure that the visual elements of the sports organisation are fully and effectively protected. The same is true of the name or description of the organisation or event.

The objective of any agreement relating to sports marketing should be to provide the best possible value for the marketing partner. The greater the value provided, the more valuable the rights will become. Anything which dilutes the value of the rights will substantially reduce the value of the association with the sports organisation. This applies not only to the ability of the organisation to grant definitive rights in the first instance, but also the ability and willingness of the organisation to protect the rights which it may have granted. While aggressive actions to protect such rights are sometimes misunderstood by the media, they are by no means misunderstood by the marketing partners of the organisation, which not only appreciate such efforts, but also are increasingly demanding that they be undertaken.

It is a good measure of the success of sports marketing programmes that there is quite often an effort by rivals of the marketers to engage in parasite programmes, which are designed to feed off the programmes of their competitors, without contributing to the sports organisations or athletes involved. An increased vigilance is required to prevent such 'parasite' marketers from poisoning the well and firm action is necessary to expose instances of such activities to the public. The nature and degree of response can be tailored to suit the occasion and the degree of intentional culpability attached to the parasite activity. Where the action is based on lack of understanding, it is often sufficient to bring to the attention of the party that there has been an infringement, whereupon the activity can be brought to an end on an amicable basis. Where it is deliberate or continuing, a public denunciation of the parasite marketer may undo all the advantage sought to have been gained by the infringer and create a negative perception against it. In the final analysis, there is resort to the courts to obtain injunctive and other remedies.

Few areas which have an impact on sports marketing can match the field of broadcasting for complexity and importance. The importance applies both to the dissemination of the sport to wider audiences that can be accommodated in the stadia and to the opportunity to increase the revenues to the organisation over and above those derived from admission tickets. Television, as a medium, is unmatched in its ability to make millions, even billions, of people virtually part of the action. It is immediate, dramatic and compelling. Properly done, it can educate as well as merely show the event and can allow spectators to see even more than they would have had they been physically present at the event. Little wonder, therefore, that one of the most important marketing tools has been television.

This is a rapidly changing landscape, particularly in Europe, as it evolves from a system of essentially State-owned broadcasters to one which includes commercial broadcasting enterprises, whose costs are supported by commercial advertising on a scale not heretofore seen in Europe. There will be many implications for sports organisations who are in a position to control the television rights to their events. There are some pitfalls to be avoided, to be sure, but the net effect as the next few years unfold in Europe should likely be an increase in the level of financial support which can be generated by sports organisations as State-owned and commercially supported broadcasters compete for programming inventory.

Broadcasting contracts are complicated and require considerable expertise and experience to craft properly. Much has been written on such matters, but if anything should be borne in mind in particular, it is the description of what is granted to the broadcaster and what is retained by the granting organisation. There is often a tendency to regard the event as having been 'sold' to the broadcaster when a television agreement has been executed. Few organisations seem to realise that, in time, the residual rights may become as important as the original rights granted at the time of the event. This is especially true where the event is annual or ongoing and attracts a regular following among the public. The ability to provide archival material for promotional and revenue-generating purposes should never be overlooked and steps should be taken to retain or re-acquire control of such material.

Some disputes are inevitable when complicated contracts are entered into for varied and diverse rights. Speedy and reliable resolution of such disputes is essential, since on many occasions the delays involved are both short and critical. It is open to question whether the ordinary courts are equipped to meet the needs of sophisticated parties to such agreements. The court processes tend to be slow and cumbersome and there may well be no expertise of the type needed to best resolve the dispute. Parties should, therefore, give serious consideration to the alternatives available to obtain a speedy and knowledgeable result once a dispute has arisen. Arbitration is, perhaps, the most reliable. This work contains a chapter on the Court of Arbitration for Sport, established by the International Olympic Committee as an independent tribunal for dealing with sports matters. The members of this court, who are prepared to act as arbitrators, have extensive legal backgrounds and are familiar with sports matters, which helps raise the level of understanding brought to the study of any dispute. Arbitration is being studied with a view to making it compulsory with respect to disputes within the Olympic Movement.

This Foreword would be incomplete without some observations on the new situation within the European Community, much of which will mature beginning in 1993. Much of the underlying philosophy and the administrative interest within the EC may have serious adverse implications for sports organisations and their involvement in marketing programmes. The free circulation of goods and the marking of such goods could dramatically affect the ability of many sports organisations to raise the revenues necessary for their existence within their jurisdictions. Great care needs to be taken to ensure that the development of the EC concept does not destroy the institutions which have evolved to meet the needs of sport and which implement sports programmes and activities. It is by no means clear that the implications of the EC on such institutions have been fully appreciated by the administrators of the EC and the European Commission itself, although the political interest of the EC as such in sport has been demonstrated by the many efforts and considerable cost of obtaining a presence at both Olympic Games celebrated in 1992.

This work is a welcome addition to the body of literature in the field of sports law and should provide a most useful summary of many of the major issues to be considered by sports administrators, marketing executives and professional advisors.

Montreal, December 1992 Richard W. Pound, Q.C.

Editors

IAN BLACKSHAW, a former partner of Bird & Bird, is now a partner in the Intellectual Property Department of the Law Firm of Field Fisher Waterhouse, London, Brussels and Beijing, where he specialises in Sports Sponsorship, Merchandising and Marketing. Educated at the Universities of London and Madrid, he is a Solicitor of the Supreme Court. A former Vice President – Legal Affairs of the ISL Marketing Group, based at their headquarters in Switzerland, Ian Blackshaw has also held senior corporate legal appointments for several multi-nationals in the UK and in Europe, including Coca-Cola and RJR Nabisco. A member of the Institute of Sports Sponsorship and also the International Bar Association, he has written several books and many articles on international business law and is a correspondent of the *European Business Law Review*.

GILLIAN HOGG, educated at Birmingham University, is an Assistant Solicitor with the Law Firm of Bird & Bird, London and Brussels, where she is a member of the Sport Media and Entertainment Group. She has written a number of articles on advertising and media law. Bird & Bird is the UK founder member of Sport-Link Worldwide, the global alliance of sports lawyers with representative firms in all major markets throughout the world.

Contributors

MANUEL P. BARROCAS is, together with Henrique S. Pereira, a member of the Lisbon Bar and senior partner in the Lisbon Law Firm of M.P. Barrocas & Associados.

ATILLA BOGSCH, senior partner of the Law Firm of Bogsch & Partners, Budapest, is a member of the Hungarian Bar. Educated at the Eötuös Loránd University of Budapest, where he is a Visiting Professor, he is Chairman of the Copyright Experts' Body.

JACQUES BUEKENHOUDT, of the Law Firm Hoffmann, Lebrun, Jaspar, and Lamoureux, Brussels, is a member of the Brussels Bar. Educated at the Universities of Brussels (Belgium), Edinburgh (Scotland) and Georgia (USA), he is the author of several articles on EC and Commercial Law and a member of the Société Belge des Auteurs et Compositeurs de Musique ('SABAM') and a founder and board member of the European Lawyers Association ('ELA').

ROBERTO CAPURRO, a Partner in the Law Firm Capurro, Marchini, Michetti, Roj and Tomassini, Milan, is an Advocate of the Italian Supreme Court. Educated at the University of Genoa (Italy) and the John Marshall Law School of Chicago (USA), he is a member of the Board of Directors of several Italian subsidiaries of multi-national companies.

LARRY CHRISFIELD, a senior tax partner in the UK practice of the International Accountancy Firm Ernst & Young, based in London, is the founder and chairman of the Firm's UK Entertainment and Media Group and European Entertainment Network. A member of the Editorial Board of *Entertainment Law Review*, he has written and lectured widely on UK and international taxation matters related to the entertainment industry.

SONIA CORTÉS is, together with Rosa Mariá Muñoz, a member of the Barcelona Bar Association and a partner in the Barcelona Office of the Spanish Law Firm of Mullerat & Roca.

IMRE CSIGI, senior Partner of the Law Firm of Csigi & Gulyáls, Budapest, is a member of the Hungarian Bar. A former head of the Legal Department of the State Youth Sports Office, he is also Legal Advisor to the Hungarian Sports Association and the Hungarian Association of Boxers.

GUY HARLES, a Partner in the Law Firm Arendt & Medernach, Luxembourg, is a council member of the Luxembourg Bar. Educated at the Universities of Luxembourg, where he is Professor of Business Law, and Strasbourg, he is a member of the Board of Directors of several Luxembourg companies.

JAN HOLMBERG, of the Law Firm Lagerlöf & Leman, based in Gothenburg, is a member of the Swedish Bar. Educated at the University of Lund, he is a member of the International Young Lawyers Association.

JEAN-LOUIS JASPAR, of the Law Firm Hoffmann, Lebrun, Jaspar & Lamoureux, Brussels, is a member of the Brussels Bar. Educated at the Universities of Brussels (Belgium) and Georgia (USA), he is the author of several articles on Commercial Law and a member of the Royal Leopold Club.

SVEN KLOS, of the Law Firm Nauta Dutilh, Amsterdam, is a member of the Netherlands Bar and was educated at the Universities of Amsterdam (Netherlands), Paris (France) and San Diego (USA).

THOMAS KLOOZ, associated with the Law Firm, Töndury Wyss Uhl, Zurich, is a member of the Zurich Bar. Educated at the Universities of Zurich (Switzerland) and Miami (USA), he is a former Vice President and Legal Counsel of the ISL Marketing Group, Lucerne. He is a member of Sport-Link Worldwide.

JAN THOR KROYER, of the Law Firm Amaliegade No. 22, Copenhagen, is a member of the Danish Bar. Educated at the University of Copenhagen, he has practised in Greenland and held a corporate appointment with Maersk Drilling of the A.P. Mollen Group.

JAN LUNDBERG, a senior Partner of the Law Firm Lagerlöf and Leman, based in Stockholm, is a member of the Swedish Bar. Educated at the University of Stockholm, he is a member of the Board of Directors of several Swedish subsidiaries of multi-national companies and also of the IBA and AIPPI.

MARTIN MAISNER, a Partner of the Law Firm, Balastik, Fiala, Profous & Spol, Prague, is a member of the Czechoslovak Bar. Educated at the Charles University of Prague, he is the author of several articles on Financial and Commercial Law and a member of the American Chamber of Commerce in Czechoslovakia.

ERNEST J. MARGETSON, senior partner of the Law Firm Matheson Ormsby Prentice, Dublin, is a Solicitor of the Supreme Court of Ireland. Educated at Trinity College, Dublin, he is a former President of the Incorporated Law Society of Ireland and an Arbitrator for the International Chamber of Commerce in Paris.

DIRK-REINER MARTENS, a member of the Munich Bar, is a senior partner in the firm Beiten Burkhardt Mittl & Wegener, Munich, a founder member of Sport-Link Worldwide representing Germany. Educated at the Universities of Munich, Hamburg and Paris, he is also the Deputy Secretary-General of the International Basketball Federation ('FIBA') and a member of the Court of Arbitration for Sport.

NICOS MOSCHOS, educated at Athens University, is a member of the Law Firm Bahas, Gramatidis and Associates, Athens.

ROSA MARIÁ MUÑOZ is, together with Sonia Cortés, a member of the Barcelona Bar Association and a partner in the Barcelona Office of the Spanish Law Firm of Mullerat & Roca.

PHILIPPE NETTO is a member of the Paris Bar and the Paris Office of the French Law Firm of Gide Loyrette Nouel.

HENRIQUE S. PEREIRA is, together with Manuel P. Barrocas, a member of the Lisbon Bar and a partner in the Lisbon Law Firm of M.P. Barrocas & Associados.

ANDRZEJ ROGÓYSKI, of the Law Firm of Wandgórski & Partners, Warsaw, is a member of the Polish Bar. Educated at the University of Warsaw, he is a former Legal Adviser of the pharmaceutical firm, 'CEFARM', and a former Under-Secretary of State at the Ministry of Building and Construction.

TOM SCHUBERT, a Partner in the Law Firm of Roschier-Holmberg & Waselius, Helsinki, is a member of the Finnish Bar and admitted to practise as a Judge. Educated at the University of Helsinki, he is a member of the IBA.

GILBERT SCHWAAR, senior Partner of the Law Firm Baumgartner, Schwaar, Wellauer, Diserens, Lausanne, is a member of the Lausanne Bar. Educated at the University of Lausanne, he is the Secretary General of the International Olympic Committee Court of Arbitration for Sport, based in Lausanne. Author of a number of articles, he is also the Secretary of the Swiss Sports Law Association, the Chairman of the Swiss Motor Sport Court and a member of the Swiss Arbitration Association.

JOHANNES SIGURDSSON, a partner in the Law Firm of Adalsteinsson & Partners, Reykjavik, is a member of the Icelandic Bar. Educated at the Universities of Iceland and Virginia (USA), he is the author of a number of books and articles on Icelandic Law.

HANS E. SKIRSTAD, a Partner in the Law Firm of Bull, Lochen, Skirstad & Co., Oslo, is a member of the Norwegian Bar. Educated at the Universities of Oslo (Norway) and Delaware (USA), he is a member of the Board of Directors of several Norwegian subsidiaries of multi-national companies. Co-author of a Book on *Products Protection Law*, he is a member of the Norwegian Association for Copyright Law.

ROBERT STARR, of the International Law Firm Salans Hertzfeld & Heilbronn, is a resident senior partner in the London Office. Educated at the University of Chicago and North-western in the States, Aix-Marseilles in France, and the Graduate Institute of International Studies in Geneva, he is a member of the Illinois and District of Columbia Bars and admitted to practise before the US Supreme Court. A prolific author of books and articles, he is co-editor of Butterworth's *Central and East European Business Law Bulletin*, and also Chairman of the East-West Trade and Investment Committee of the American Chamber of Commerce in the UK. Salans Hertzfeld & Heilbronn are a founder member of Sport-Link Worldwide, representing the CIS.

HOWARD M. STUPP, Director of Legal Affairs of the International Olympic Committee, Lausanne, Switzerland, is a Canadian Lawyer. Educated at the Universities of McGill, Montreal and Simon Fraser, Burnaby, in both Law and Engineering, he is a former member of the Canadian Olympic Wrestling Team and several times Canadian Senior Open Wrestling Champion and Pan American and Maccabiah Games Wrestling Gold Medalist.

WLODZIMIERZ SZOSZUK, of the Law Firm of Wadyáski & Partners, Warsaw, is a member of the Polish Bar. Educated at the University of Warsaw, he is a former Legal Advisor to 'ICL' in Warsaw and the author of *Protecting Author's Copyright in Poland*.

AHMET TEKELI, of the Law Firm Ahmet Tekeli, Istanbul, is a member of the Istanbul Bar. Educated at the University of Lausanne (Switzerland), he is Legal Adviser to and a member of the Board of Directors of several Turkish subsidiaries of multi-national companies. A founder member of the Turkish American Business Association, he is the author of a number of articles on Financial and Commercial Law.

SIMON TOPPING, educated at Oxford University and a member of the English Bar, is the resident lawyer in the Brussels Office of Bird & Bird, and a member of the firm's Sport Media and Entertainment Group.

ARTHUR WOLFF, a member of the Vienna Bar, is the Principal of the Arthur Wolff Law Office, Vienna. Educated at the University of Vienna, he is the author of many articles and the co-author of several books on international business transactions, technology transfer and licensing and computer law. He is also an international arbitrator.

Introduction

by Ian S. Blackshaw

Representing 2.5% of world trade, of which an estimated 4.1 billion dollars are spent annually on sponsorship, sport is big business. Although the promotion, sponsorship, merchandising, other commercialisation and marketing of international and national sports events is well established in the United States, sports marketing in Europe is a relatively recent phenomenon. Nevertheless, it is also fast becoming an increasingly popular form of commercial expression and corporate communication in Europe, notwithstanding the recession and the difficult economic and trading conditions prevailing in so many European countries.

The collapse of communism and the moves from centrally planned and controlled to market economies and the active promotion of private enterprise are also providing many opportunities for commercialisation of sport and sports events in Eastern Europe. In this connection, the role of corporate sponsorship, in particular, is growing in importance and taking on a new significance and dimension.

As this burgeoning new 'industry' of sports marketing becomes more established throughout Europe, the techniques and 'products' more sophisticated and the price of rights packages even higher, the expectations and demands of promoters, sponsors, suppliers, merchandisers and marketers are also increasing. In particular, sponsors are becoming more demanding in the range of rights and commercial opportunities offered to them and more insistent on their complete and timely delivery. This is leading to an increase in disputes and claims arising out of the commercialisation of sports events. The prestige attached to being an official sponsor of a major international sports event, such as the Olympic Games, and the enhancement that this brings to the image of a company and its products or services has also given rise to the phenomenon of 'ambush marketing'. This occurs where a company improperly and unfairly claims a commercial association or relationship with such an event. Needless to say, this does not go down well with either the organisers or the official sponsors, who have paid substantial sums for the privilege of associating themselves and their products and services with the particular event. In the celebrated Ryder Cup Hospitality Case in the UK in 1989, for example, the court granted the organisers of this prestigious golf tournament an injunction restraining the defendants from passing off any business, services or goods offered by them by using the name 'Ryder Cup' in such a way as to suggest that they were authorised to provide hospitality or tickets for this event. Surprisingly, the injunction did not extend to the use of the name 'Ryder Cup' whatsoever, which appeared in the corporate name of one of the defendants, namely, 'Ryder Cup Hospitality Ltd.'. The policy of the IOC on unfair marketing practices of this kind is quite clear and strict: a letter is sent to the Chairman/Chief Executive of the offending company demanding the withdrawal of the claim (usually made as part of an advertising campaign), coupled with the threat, in the event of failure to do so, of informing the world media, at a specially convened press conference, that the company concerned is not, in fact, an official sponsor or otherwise associated with the event and has not paid any fee to support any such claim. If this extra-judicial approach fails, the matter may be referred to the court. During the Albertville Winter Olympics in February 1992, for example, Visa (the official credit card for the Games) successfully obtained an injunction, in the Paris High Court, restraining American Express from engaging in an 'ambush marketing'-based comparative advertising campaign. American Express was also fined US $26,000 for an unauthorised use of the 'Olympic Rings' symbol. The need for effective dispute resolution, therefore, is growing too and is covered in this book. In this connection, the work of the Court of Arbitration for Sport, set up by the International Olympic Committee in 1985 and described in this book, is increasing and fulfilling a well-identified need for a quick, amicable and confidential process of settlement of such disputes. Other forms of Alternative Dispute Resolution (ADR) are also becoming popular for the resolution of sports marketing disputes and are also examined in this book.

The increasing coverage of sports events by television (recent statistics show that sport accounted for over 85% of programme exchanges within 'Eurovision') and the technological development of and demand for videos and films is also having an impact, both commercially and legally, especially in relation to demands for exclusivity. In this connection, the EC Commission has been taking an active interest in sports generally (as set out in the 'EC Policy on Sport' document of 31 July 1991) and in the subject of exclusivity in particular, much to the apparent opposition and discomfort of the international sports federations and bodies as well as of the European Broadcasting Union, which incidentally has just agreed to pay US $250 million for the exclusive European broadcasting rights for the 1996 Atlanta Summer Olympics. We deal with these and other European Community issues in the Chapter on EC Aspects. In this connection, it should be noted that Denmark has now, at the second attempt, ratified the Maastricht Treaty and the UK and Germany are also expected to do so in the autumn of 1993. Furthermore, the EEA Convention has also now been ratified by all the EFTA countries, with the exception of Switzerland, with an effective date of 1 July 1993. Finally, as regards EC matters, a 'common position' has now been agreed by the EC Council on the proposed EC Directive on the coordination of certain rules concerning copyright and neighbouring rights applicable to satellite broadcasting and cable re-transmission, and modified EBU rules on Sports Television Programming have been exempted by the EC Commission.

Another important aspect of television coverage, which we also deal with in this book, is the developing opportunities in Europe for sponsorship of the television coverage of sports events, as opposed to the sponsorship of the events themselves. The value and associated problems of such sponsorship was well illustrated by the sponsorship of the television coverage of the Rugby Football World Cup in the UK in the Autumn of 1991 by Sony, which was perceived by the general public to be the sponsor of the event itself, much to the annoyance of Heinz, one of the official sponsors of the event, which had paid much more for this (?) privilege.

With the phenomenal increase in the prices charged for rights packages already mentioned – for example, a 'TOP' Sponsor of the Olympics is paying around US $40 million for sponsorship, on a global exclusive product/service category basis, of the 1996 Summer Games in Atlanta, USA – the incidence of tax is also becoming increasingly more significant and important to events organisers/rights holders and sponsors alike. This important subject and the need and opportunities for tax planning and minimisation are also covered in this book.

Another topic of practical concern is the increasing control by Governments and also by self-regulatory bodies over advertising and promotions, both of which are an essential ingredient in any sponsorship or merchandising deal. In this regard, the problems of the tobacco, alcohol and pharmaceutical industries come particularly to mind. In France, for example, the new Anti-Tobacco Law, which, amongst other things, prohibits advertising through sponsorship by tobacco companies and brands of sports events, has caused some problems for the 1993 Formula One Grand Prix in France. This follows a £3.7 million fine, imposed in December 1992 by a particularly zealous anti-smoking Judge in Brittany, on the Canon Williams Renault Formula One Team for allowing the 'Camel' name and logo to be displayed on their cars during French television coverage of the Japanese and Australian Formula One Grand Prix. In each of the Country Chapters, we devote a section to this important subject of advertising restrictions.

Likewise, public and product liability issues are also an increasing focus of attention amongst sports administrators and marketers. Tragedies such as the disasters in the stadia at Heysel (Belgium), Hillsborough (England) and Bastia (Corsica) have highlighted and illustrated the range and extent of exposure to legal liability, criminal as well as civil, as well as the need for appropriate precautions and insurance coverage. In addition, the EC Product Liability Directive of 1985, which has introduced into the European Community – and also elsewhere in Europe (for example, in Austria) – a no-fault basis of responsibility for damage caused to persons and property by defective products, must also be taken fully into account when organising, staging and marketing a sports event. All these matters are covered in each of the Country Chapters.

At the heart of any sports marketing programme are the event marks, logos, mascots and other intellectual property rights, including copyright, which can be commercialised and merchandised, providing a substantial income for sports administrators and marketers alike. The nature, protection and exploitation of these intellectual property rights is also covered in this book, as is also the complementary subject of unfair competition. In this latter connection, particular attention may be drawn to the peculiarly Scandinavian institutions of the Consumer Ombudsman and the Market Court/Council, which are described in the relevant Country Chapters. These institutions can be useful for fighting, in particular, cases of 'ambush marketing'.

The basis of all sports marketing deals is contract and various aspects of this subject are examined and compared, including letters of intent, preliminary agreements, standard contract terms, options and pre-emption rights, the latter being a particular feature of sports marketing arrangements.

As will be seen from the Table of Contents, this book also covers many other matters of commercial and legal interest to sports administrators and marketers alike, as well as their professional advisers.

The law of sports marketing is still, in many parts of Europe, in an embryonic stage and, as the sports marketing industry develops, so also will the legal concepts and practice in this field. Generally speaking (Spain being a notable exception), there are no specific laws on sports marketing in Europe, and in some countries (particularly in Eastern Europe), sponsorship is still a somewhat obscure and undeveloped concept. Nevertheless, sports marketing is developing throughout Europe at a phenomenal rate and providing opportunities for creativity and inventiveness, not only for sports administrators and marketers, but also for their legal, tax and other advisers and consultants.

This book can only provide a general introduction to the subject, and appropriate professional guidance, therefore, should be sought on any specific aspects.

Generally speaking, the law and practice in this book is stated as at 1 January 1993, according to the sources available at that date.

SPORTS
MARKETING

United Kingdom

by Ian S. Blackshaw
and Gillian Hogg

1. Sports Marketing – A Business

The sports industry in the UK is larger than the agricultural, chemical and motor industries and, according to a 1986 study, the estimated direct annual spend on sports-related activities amounted to £4.4 billion. This includes £770 million on shoes and clothing, £690 million on sports goods and £530 million on participation. The study also found that sport accounted for 376,000 full-time paid jobs, without taking into account numerous part-time and voluntary jobs generated by the industry.

Sports marketing now plays an important part in the communication and marketing programmes of many corporations throughout the UK. It is estimated that out of the millions of pounds spent on marketing each year, two thirds goes to sports marketing. This growth has been due, in part, to the advances of television and marketing techniques associated with television. As a wider range of sports events is shown on television, so the attraction and opportunities for sponsors has increased. Today many local, national and international sports events staged or viewed in the UK are funded through sponsorship. For example, the various soccer leagues attract much of their financing through sponsorship and the grant of other commercial opportunities and rights, including television rights. The teams themselves are also sponsored.

The rapid growth of the sports marketing industry is reflected in the amounts spent on sports sponsorship in recent years: in 1971, £2.5 million, in 1982, £84.7 million, and in 1988, over £200 million. The total amount spent on sports sponsorship is now running at around £250 million per annum. One example of how sponsorship packages have escalated in value is test cricket: in 1977 the Cornhill Insurance Company paid £1 million to sponsor test cricket in the UK for 5 years; now that amount is paid for just one year's sponsorship.

2. The UK Legal System

The United Kingdom consists of four geographically separate countries: England, Wales, Scotland and Northern Ireland. The legal systems in England and Wales are the same, but the laws governing Scotland and Northern Ireland differ in certain respects. From a practical point of view, the law which applies in England and Wales is most relevant and this discussion will centre on that system.

The English legal system is essentially a common law system, consisting of judge-made law (case law) supplemented by Acts of Parliament (statute law). Case law creates the system of precedents which future judges are generally bound to follow, unless one case can be 'distinguished' from another. Some areas are regulated not by laws in the strict sense of the word, but by self-imposed regulations. The UK advertising industry is one such example. European Community Law, a further source of UK law, is becoming increasingly important in the field of sports marketing and takes precedence over UK law where there is a conflict on the same subject.

The UK legal system is peculiar in that there are two legal systems which operate in parallel – law and equity. The system of law is the strict legal system, which operates according to the letter of the law, i.e. statute or case law, and the system of equity is super-imposed on this to ensure that court proceedings produce 'fair' results. The rules of equity are found in a series of 'maxims' and their interpretation and application are generally at the discretion of the court. In addition, equity provides a number of specific reliefs, for example, orders for specific performance and injunctions. Equity and common law are applied alongside one another in the same courts, with equitable principles taking precedence in the event of any conflict.

3. Applicable Laws

There is no one particular body of law specifically applicable to sports marketing. Instead, there are a number of different general laws, including statute, case law and self-imposed regulations, which apply to different aspects of sports marketing.

Essentially, the relationship between the parties involved, whether they are sponsor and sponsored, TV company and rights holder or licensor and licensee, is governed by contract, and, under the freedom of contract doctrine, the parties are free to make whatever bargain they like. Contracts are subject to certain principles of contract law dealing with such matters as formation and interpretation. In addition to standard contractual requirements, there are a number of specific elements which need to be included in the contract to reflect particular aspects of sports marketing.

4. Intellectual Property Rights

From a legal point of view, intellectual property rights constitute the chief component of any sports marketing programme. For example, in a merchandising programme connected with an international sports event the creation and protection of the intellectual property rights is of crucial importance to the licensor and licensee. 'Commercial opportunities' (e.g. franchising, display and pouring rights) are largely protected by the general law.

The intellectual property rights most relevant are trademarks and copyright. In addition, a body of English case law, known as 'passing-off', prevents unfair competition, particularly in relation to business reputation and goodwill.

4.1. Trademarks

The UK is a signatory to the Vienna Treaty, Madrid Agreements, and the Paris Convention on Trademarks. The national law is governed by the Trademarks Act 1938 as amended by the Trademarks (Amendment) Act 1984. The 1938 Act allows registration of a 'Mark', defined as a 'device, brand, heading, label, ticket, name, signature, word, letter, numeral or any combination thereof',[1] applied to goods, whereas the 1984 Act extends registration to a mark (as defined above) applied to services. The mark may be registered in Part A of the register, provided it is adapted to distinguish goods or services with which the proprietor is connected from those with which he is not. This requirement of distinction is more stringent than the requirement for registration in Part B of the register, where the mark need only be capable of distinguishing the goods or services of the proprietor. Essentially, the difference is that the mark must be more distinctive for a Part A registration.

Registration in Part A is preferable to a Part B registration, as it affords the mark greater protection. For example, a mark which has been registered in Part A for 7 years will be deemed valid, whereas a Part B mark will still be open to challenge after 7, or more, years of registration. It is expected that, with the implementation of the EC Directive on Trademarks, the distinction between Part A and Part B of the UK register will disappear.

The UK is a signatory to the Nice Agreement on the International Classification of Goods and Services of 1957.

Once the mark has been registered, the registered proprietor is given the exclusive right to use the mark in relation to his goods or services, and use by any other person of that mark, or one which is confusingly similar, will be an infringement. An interlocutory injunction can be obtained in the courts to prevent a trademark infringement, and, should the infringement have already taken place, the proprietor can obtain a permanent injunction to prevent further infringements and/or claim relief for either damages or an account of profits.

1. Section 68(1) Trade Marks Act 1938.

The mark is initially registered for 7 years, and thereafter may be renewed, indefinitely, for further periods of 14 years.

The mark may be removed from the register if it was not registered with a *bona fide* intention, or if it is not used for five years in relation to the goods or services for which it was originally registered.[2] For this reason, if the proprietor is not using the mark himself, but is licensing the right to use the mark, the licensee may need to enter into and file a registered user agreement. The licence agreement must contain some quality control requirements, since a mark may also be removed from the register if it has been used improperly, i.e. lost its distinctive quality[3] (i.e. become generic) or has become deceptive.[4]

In respect of well-known marks, the proprietor may make defensive registrations of the marks in classes in which he would not normally use the mark.[5]

'Trafficking' in trademarks is, however, forbidden by statute.[6] In the case of 'Holly Hobbie' TM[7] the courts held that the mark must relate to a genuine business and not simply to the business of licensing the right to use the mark.

4.2. Copyright

The UK is a signatory to the Berne Convention on Copyright and the national situation is governed by the Copyright Designs and Patents Act 1988 and case law.

Copyright exists automatically, without the need for registration, in literary, dramatic, musical and artistic works, sound recordings, films, broadcast and cable cast and published editions. The duration of the copyright is generally the lifetime of the author plus, in the case of literary, dramatic, musical or artistic works, 50 years from the date of the author's death, or 50 years from the date the recording or broadcast was made or the film released.[8] In the case of published editions, the duration is 25 years from the date of first publication.[9] EC proposals are currently under consideration to provide longer periods of protection for owners of copyright and neighbouring rights.

The copyright is owned by the author or the publisher. The definition of the author varies according to the type of work. For example, with films, the author is defined as the 'person for whom the arrangements necessary for the production of the film are undertaken'.[10] With literary, dramatic, musical or artistic works, it is the person who creates the work.[11] With literary, dramatic, musi-

---

2. Section 26 Trade Marks Act 1938.
3. Section 32 Trade Marks Act 1938.
4. Section 11 Trade Marks Act 1938.
5. Section 27 Trade Marks Act 1938.
6. Section 28(6) Trade Marks Act 1938.
7. 1984 R.P.C. 329 (HL).
8. Sections 12, 13 and 14 Copyright Designs and Patents Act 1988.
9. Section 15 Copyright Designs and Patents Act 1988.
10. Section 9(2) Copyright Designs and Patents Act 1988.
11. Section 9(1) Copyright Designs and Patents Act 1988.

cal or artistic works made by a person in the course of his employment, the copyright will be owned by the employer.[12]

Copyright is infringed by copying, publishing, adapting, performing in public, broadcasting, cable casting, renting copies to the public and making a facsimile typographical arrangement.[13] Precisely what constitutes an infringement in each case depends on the type of work involved. Infringement may be primary or secondary: a primary infringer is a person who commits an infringing act himself, and a secondary infringement exists where someone instructs or authorises another to commit the infringing act.

A copyright owner can seek relief against an infringer in the courts in the form of an injunction to prevent an infringement and/or an action for damages or an account of profits. There are a number of defences which may apply, the most relevant being the defence of 'fair dealing' as set forth in Section 29 of the Copyright Designs and Patents Act 1988.

Authors enjoy certain moral rights, including the right of paternity and the right not to have their work subjected to derogatory treatment. Such rights, which last as long as the copyright in the works concerned, may be waived.

All such waivers and assignments of copyright must be made in writing, otherwise they are not valid.

4.3. Unfair Competition

Passing-off is the term given to the common law tort (civil wrong) of gaining an unfair advantage by capitalising on another's reputation by promoting goods and services as those of another. To constitute passing-off there must be:

- a misrepresentation;
- goodwill (reputation in the course of trade); and
- resultant damage.[14]

The person whose likeness has been used may seek redress in the courts in the form of an action for damages. The judgment of Lord Diplock in *Erven Warnink BV* v. *J Townend & Sons (Hull) Ltd*,[15] provides a useful summary of the issues relevant to passing-off. Where trademarks are unregistered, passing-off is an appropriate means of protecting rights and reputation by preventing unauthorised association with the established international sports event.

12. Section 11(2) Copyright Designs and Patents Act 1988.
13. Section 16 Copyright Designs and Patents Act 1988.
14. *Reckitt & Coleman Products Ltd* v. *Borden Inc and others* [1990] All ER 873 HL.
15. [1980] RPC 31.

4.4. Registered Designs

Parts III and IV of the Copyright Designs and Patents Act 1988 provide protection for a design considered novel for a period of 15 years from registration. Design means 'features of shape, configuration, pattern or ornament applied to an article by any industrial process or means, being features which in the finished article appeal to and are judged solely by the eye, but does not include a method or principle of construction or features of shape or configuration which are dictated solely by the function which the article to be made in that shape or configuration has to perform.'[16]

5. The Contract Generally and Preliminary Agreements

5.1. Preliminary Agreements

It is common business practice to enter into a preliminary agreement or heads of agreement before preparation of the principal contract. It is generally difficult to enforce an agreement of this type, as it amounts only to a bare promise which does not satisfy the elements necessary for a binding contract, nor usually are the parties intending to create legal relations (a further requirement; see later). Hence, such preliminary agreements cannot be sued upon.[17] Letters of intent are viewed in a similar light.

5.2. Intention to Create Legal Relations

The parties to the contract must intend to create a legal relationship. In the case of commercially motivated contracts of the kind involved in sports promotion and marketing, the chances are that such intention will be present. However, if consent to enter into the contract by one party was obtained by duress, undue influence, fraud, innocent misrepresentation or whilst the party was drunk, the contract may be voidable by that party.

5.3. Offer and Acceptance

Under English law, a contract is formed once an offer, supported by consideration, has been unconditionally accepted by the person to whom it was made. In practice, there is usually a series of negotiations, so that the offer is made and accepted in part and also met with a counter-offer. There are a number of technical case law rules, which can be applied to decide exactly when the offer

16. Section 1(3).
17. Various case law supports this, for example, *Balfour* v. *Balfour* [1919] 2 KB 571 CA.

was accepted, but generally the offer is deemed accepted when the parties have each indicated that they are content with the terms of the contract. To avoid premature inference of acceptance, the correspondence accompanying draft contracts should be headed 'subject to contract'.

5.4. Consideration

As noted above, for a contract to be valid, there must be some 'consideration' or benefit flowing between the parties. Consideration has been defined[18] as some right, interest, profit or benefit accruing to one party or some forbearance, detriment, loss or responsibility given, suffered or undertaken by the other at his request. Consideration which took place before the contract was signed is not good consideration, and it must be of some value, although it need not be adequate in the sense that it can be merely nominal. For example, £1 is often used in certain transactions as the consideration. Other examples of consideration are wide and include: the assignment of a contract, the guarantee of a loan, entering into a contract with a third party and a promise to render a future service. Mutual promises can constitute good consideration and in respect of documents executed under seal (i.e. signed, sealed and delivered) consideration is presumed.

5.5. Form and Execution

For the contract to be valid it need not be in writing, unless there are special formal requirements, such as an assignment of copyright, which must be in writing.[19] There are no particular execution requirements. For example, the document need not be signed or initialled on each page. However, where it has been amended in manuscript, the amendment should be initialled by all parties, because the presumption is that all amendments have been made *after* signature unless the contrary intention appears. The continental practice of signing or initialling each page is advisable as this avoids any omission(s) and/or substitution(s) after signature. When the contracting parties are companies, the contract should be executed by one of the officials of the company, such as the director or secretary; this creates a presumption that the document has been properly executed by the company regardless of whether the internal organisation of the company actually gave such authority.

18. *Currie* v. *Misa* (1875) LR 10 Exch 153.
19. Section 90(3) Copyright Designs and Patents Act 1988.

5.6. *Void and Illegal Contracts*

A contract may be perfect in terms of form, agreement and consideration, but if it offends against the policy of the law then it will be invalid. For example, a contract to commit a crime or a tort (a civil wrong) will not be enforced by the courts. In addition, contracts which offend against public policy will be invalid. This includes contracts which have an immoral subject matter, or are in restraint of trade. In the case of *Greig* v. *Insole*,[20] which arose out of the *Packer* cricket affair, the court held that cricket authorities could impose restraints on players but that the restraints must not be too wide or unreasonable. In this instance, a test and county ban was held to be too wide. See also *A. Schroeder Music Publishing Co Ltd* v. *Macaulay*[21] where a copyright licence was set aside as its effect was to tie up the copyright with one person who was under no obligation to use the proprietary rights.

A contract will also be void if it was entered into by mistake. The mistake must be fundamental, such as the identity of the contracting parties, or the existence of the subject matter of the contract[22] and not mere commercial error. At law, the contract will be void, but in equity the courts may order rectification or rescission. If one party to the contract was misled by the other, that is, there was a misrepresentation, then that innocent party may be able to repudiate the contract depending on whether the misrepresentation was fraudulent or not.[23] If the misrepresentation was not fraudulent, the innocent party can only seek the alternative remedy of damages.

The Unfair Contract Terms Act 1977 makes void all contractual clauses which exclude liability for death or personal injury caused as a result of negligence by one party.

Contractual clauses which impose penalties and forfeitures are often void. If the clause is an agreement of liquidated damages, then it will be acceptable. *ECGD Universal Oil Products Co*[24] sets out guidelines for distinction between the two.

In some instances the courts will strike down a contract which is unconscionable, in that one party has extracted an extortionate bargain owing to an inequality of bargaining power. In the case of *Lloyd's Bank* v. *Bundy*,[25] the defendant, an elderly farmer, and his only son had been customers of the plaintiff bank for many years. The defendant guaranteed the overdraft of his son's company offering his farm as security. Eventually, the bank sought possession of the farmhouse, but an appeal by the defendant was upheld. Due to the possible loss by the defendant of his sole remaining asset, and the lack

---

20. [1978] 1 WLR 302.
21. [1974] 1 WLR 1308.
22. *Bell* v. *Lever Bros Ltd* [1932] AC 161.
23. Misrepresentation Act 1967 and *Hedley Byrne & Co Ltd* v. *Heller and Partners* [1963] 2 All ER 575 HL.
24. [1983] 1 WLR 399.
25. [1975] 2 QB 326.

of independent advice, it was held that there was a breach by the bank of its fiduciary duty of care and an exercise of undue influence.

With sports marketing contracts, these instances may be of relevance in relation to ticketing and possible exclusion of liability under the terms and conditions of admission to a particular sports event.

5.7. *Privity*

Under the 'privity of contract' doctrine only the parties to the contract may acquire rights, incur obligations and sue and be sued on it. It is important, therefore, that all persons directly involved in the arrangements are made parties to the contract to ensure, amongst other things, delivery of the rights.

Not only may a third party not sue on the contract, but a third party will not be directly liable under the contract. This creates problems when some element of the contract is reliant on the actions of a third party. The problem is often overcome by including a clause to the effect that one party will procure or cause that the acts are performed or that a third party will perform (or refrain from doing) a certain act. Obligations of this sort should be reinforced by 'back to back' obligations in the agreement with the third party. Alternatively, the clause may state that one party will use its 'best endeavours' to perform a certain act. 'Best endeavours' must be interpreted in the context of the contract, but courts have held that the obligated party is bound to take all steps in his power which are capable of producing the desired result.[26] In other cases it was held that the party must do everything that was known to be usual, necessary and proper for the success of his endeavour; that he must do all that can be reasonably expected; and that 'best endeavours' does not mean 'second-best endeavours'.[27]

Beyond the best endeavours obligation, the party may give a warranty or the term may be a condition of the contract. If a warranty is given, the party giving it will be liable for damages in the event that it is breached. If the term is a condition, its breach enables the other party to repudiate the contract and/or claim damages. The right of repudiation must be exercised promptly, otherwise it may be lost (being an equitable remedy, claimants must not 'sleep' on their rights).

Occasionally the parties include a penalty provision should one of them breach a particular term of the agreement. In so far as such a clause is simply a penalty ('*in terrorem*'), it is unenforceable in the UK; however, if it merely amounts to a genuine attempt to estimate in advance the amount of damages that would result from such a breach, then it is enforceable. This is known as a 'liquidated damages' provision. See also under Void and Illegal Contracts at p. 12 above.

26. *IBM United Kingdom Ltd* v. *Rockware Glass Ltd* [1980] FSR 335.
27. *Sheffield District Railway Co* v. *Great Central Railway Co* (1911) 27 TLR 451.

5.8. *Interpretation*

A number of basic rules have developed governing the interpretation of contracts as follows:

- *contra proferentum* rule, whereby any exclusion or restriction is interpreted against the person seeking to rely on it;
- words are given their simple or plain meaning;
- the apparent intention of the parties will be used to aid interpretation.

5.9. *Frustration*

A contract will be deemed to have been frustrated in some extreme event which prevents the contract from being performed.[28] Examples of such events are those out of the control of either party, such as earthquakes, floods and other natural disasters. Rather than rely on these legal principles, the parties usually include in the contract a comprehensive *force majeure* clause, which provides that the contract is frustrated in specified circumstances which are set out in detail.

5.10. *Breach of Contract*

The contract will be breached if either party does not comply with its terms. The consequences of a breach will depend on the contract term that has been breached. In the majority of cases, it will amount to a claim for damages. However, if the term is a condition, the contract may be repudiated. This is also the result if the breached term amounts to a fundamental contract term, i.e. one that goes to the 'heart' or 'root' of the contract.

6. Standard Contract Terms

The following issues should be included in, or considered when preparing, any contract related to sports marketing:

6.1. *Applicable Law*

The contract should expressly state which law is to be the applicable law. The parties have freedom to choose which law applies. In the absence of choice,

28. See the Law Reform (Frustrated Contracts) Act 1943.

the contract is governed by the law of the country to which the contract is most closely related.[29]

6.2. *Definitions*

Include a clause which defines the terms which are specific to the contract. The defined terms should then be used with capital letters. If the definitions are introduced by the word 'means' then other meanings for that word are excluded; however, if they are introduced by 'includes' then the natural or usual meaning also applies.

6.3. *Recitals*

The recitals are used to aid understanding of the contract. If recitals are included in a deed, the parties can be held to them. Recitals may also be used to interpret the contract where the meaning of its principal contents are unclear.

6.4. *Parties*

The full names and addresses of the parties should be included, and, where the party is a company, its registered office, address and the number under which it is registered at the Companies Registry, as a company can change its name, but not its number.

6.5. *Implied Terms*

Certain terms are implied into the contract by the use of specific words or phrases. For example, in relation to an assignment of copyright, if the assignor assigns as 'beneficial owner' there are certain 'covenants' implied into the contract: the assignor has a right to assign and will not later challenge the assignment or interrupt enjoyment of the right; the right is free from incumbrances; and the assignee will do such further acts as are necessary to protect the title.[30] Certain meanings may be implied in relation to a particular industry or which result from a previous course of dealings between the parties. The court may imply terms into the contract if it appears that, from the conduct and intention of the parties, they should have been included. Where the contract relates to the sale of goods, the Sale of Goods Act 1979 implies certain terms, for example, that the goods are of merchantable quality and suitable for their

29. Article 4, Contracts (Applicable Law) Act 1990, which enforces the Rome Convention of 1980.
30. Law of Property Act 1925, Section 76.

purpose. Similarly, the Partnership Act 1890 implies certain clauses into partnership agreements, such as that the partners are equally responsible for the debts of the partnership and will share equally in the profits. These assumptions can be overridden by express provisions to the contrary.

6.6. Legal Relationship

The contract should contain a clause that the parties are not entering into a joint venture or partnership. Such a relationship has particular legal consequences and may be inferred from a course of dealing between the parties arising out of the particular business arrangement in a sponsorship situation. The existence of a partnership in the UK is a question of fact, and not necessarily governed by the presence or absence of a written agreement.

6.7. 'Force Majeure'

The circumstances in which the performance of a contract may be suspended for a period of time or indefinitely need to be defined and the consequences spelled out in the contract. In the event of a *force majeure* situation, it is usual to provide that, if the situation continues for a certain period of time, either party may terminate the contract.

6.8. Address for service

It is useful to include a clause giving details of how (e.g. by fax) the parties may serve notice on each other and at what address, together with other instructions as to the issue of copies of such notices.

6.9. Reputation

A contract which relates to a major sports event or sports body should contain a clause that the licensed party or sponsor will do nothing which might bring the sport, its organising committee, federation or sponsors into disrepute or disrespect. In addition, this obligation should be required from all sub-licensees. The performance of the contract should also be made subject to the constitution or rules of the sports body concerned, for example, the IOC Charter.

6.10. 'Social Conventions'

Public appearance, endorsement and promotion contracts often contain provisions that the party will do nothing to offend against public morals or social conventions. Interpretation of such a clause is difficult and relying on it as a possible ground for termination would also be uncertain. Further, such a clause may be held to be void for uncertainty. However, the clause may prove useful, at least for practical commercial leverage purposes.

6.11. Royalties and Accounting

Very specific details need to be included relating to royalty rates, payments, penalties for non-payment or late payment (e.g. interest) and accounting. In particular, the date on which payments should be made must be expressed and the licensee should be liable to account to the licensor. See further under 'Financial Terms' at p. 24.

6.12. Books Open to Inspection

Where royalties are payable, the licensee should be required to keep books recording sales and any other relevant commercial/financial data, and these books should be open to inspection and audit by the licensor on reasonable notice.

6.13. Termination

The grounds for termination should be spelled out, differentiating between remediable and non-remediable breaches and termination with or without notice. For example, a breach of any material terms or failure to make agreed payments on time would allow the 'innocent' party to terminate without notice. In the case of trademark licences, any challenge by the licensee of the validity of the trademark should entitle the licensor to terminate the contract immediately.

Provision should be made for the consequences of termination. For example, where the agreement is a merchandising agreement, the market place must be cleared of merchandise within a specified period of time, and the licensee must be given a period of time to dispose of all unsold products, after which they should be delivered up for destruction. In addition, the rights should revert to the rights-holder and there should be a time limit during which all outstanding fees and royalties should be paid.

7. Different Types of Business Arrangements

7.1. Sponsorship Agreement

There is no special body of law governing the sponsorship relationship. Instead, the arrangement is governed by contract whereby the sponsor is granted certain rights and opportunities in return for his financial sponsorship and other obligations.

In general, there are no specific restrictions as to who may sponsor an event. However, under the Voluntary Agreement between the Government and the Tobacco Industry, initially entered into in 1977 and subsequently updated, certain restrictions on tobacco sponsorship have been imposed. For example: spending on sponsorship has been frozen at £5 million; advertising signs within the scope of TV coverage must contain health warnings; the word 'cigarette' must not be used; when the event is televised there must be fewer promotional signs; no sports must be sponsored whose audience is predominantly under the age of 18; and sets for small arena sports must not use a combination of colours which resemble cigarette products.

As to advertising on television and otherwise, there are restrictions on advertising of alcohol, pharmaceuticals and certain other health products. Potential sponsors, whose products fall within these categories, should bear this in mind, especially if intending to complement the sponsorship with a general advertising campaign. In particular, the timing of any television broadcast should be considered. The 'water-shed', beyond which advertising and programming guidelines are less restrictive, is generally defined as 9 p.m.

The EC anti-competition rules may be of relevance according to the circumstances. See 'EC Competition Rules' at p. 404. Likewise account should be taken of UK competition law, particularly the Restrictive Trade Practices Act 1976. Although most sponsorship arrangements grant exclusivity in relation to product categories, they are not usually totally exclusive, encouraging rather than restricting trade. However, the rights-holder should be aware of the common law 'restraint of trade' doctrine which makes a contract in restraint of trade void. For example, in *A Schroeder Music Publishing Co Ltd* v. *Macaulay*,[31] the court held a contract void in that the copyright in music, which had been assigned to the defendant, was not required to be used and the rights were thus effectively sterilised. The House of Lords was influenced by the disparity of bargaining power between the parties.

7.2. Merchandising

Again, this subject is covered by contract and not by any specific law. The licensor and licensee should consider the laws of copyright and trademarks as these intellectual property rights are most commonly central to merchandising arrangements.

When trademarks are being licensed, the licensee should seek proof of registration to ensure that the licensor has the rights to license. However, with copyright, which is not protected by registration, the licensee will require warranties from the licensor that he owns the copyright and will indemnify the licensee in respect of any third party claims for any copyright infringement(s).

31. [1974] 1 WLR 1308.

Where the trademark owner (licensor) is allowing another (licensee) to use his trademarks on goods, the licence agreement should contain quality control provisions. If the licensed article is defective and causes injury to a member of the public, the trademark proprietor may be liable for that harm under the EC Product Liability Directive.[32] See further under 'EC Competition Rules' at p. 404.

7.3. *Endorsements*

Endorsements must be genuine. Under the Trade Descriptions Act 1968,[33] the giving of false descriptions or indications amounts to a criminal offence. A false approval amounts to the same thing. Implying that you are an official supplier to the Royal Family or suggesting that your product or service is endorsed by a member of the Royal Family is also an offence. The British Code of Advertising Practice is also relevant in relation to event, service or product endorsements.

Use of the Royal Arms or any mark resembling the Royal Arms is forbidden without specific permission.[34]

Although there is no specific right to privacy in the UK, endorsements by individuals should only be used with their consent, as use without consent may amount to defamation, passing-off or a breach of the individual's proprietary rights. In *Tolley* v. *Fry*,[35] for example, there was held to be defamation when a person's likeness was used in an advertisement without his consent. The rationale for this defamation was that the golfer's amateur status could be jeopardised by the advertisement which carried with it an implication that the golfer had received payment for it.

The Copyright Designs and Patents Act 1988[36] gives the person who, for domestic and private purposes, commissions the taking of any photograph or the making of any film, the right not to have copies of the work issued to the public. Care should be taken, therefore, to ensure that, by promoting an event or organisation by means of endorsement, the promotion is not in breach of this statutory provision.

32. Council Directive of 25 July 1985 on the approximation of the laws, regulations and administrative provisions of the Member States concerning liability for defective products. No. L 210/29.
33. Section 3(1).
34. Section 61 Trademarks Act 1938.
35. [1931] A.C. 333.
36. Section 85.

7.4. *Commissioning Agreement*

Time should be expressly made of the essence in a contract for the production of a logo, emblem, design or advertisement. In such case, if the commissioned party does not meet the deadline, the contract may be repudiated. This may be preferable to suing for breach of a contract, for example, for the commissioning of stadium perimeter advertising boards, premiums and event merchandise.

The agreement should include an assignment in writing of copyright in the 'work' from the designer, who is the 'author' of the work and, therefore, the copyright owner, to the commissioning party. The 'author' should also waive his 'moral rights' in the work.[37]

The commissioning party should require warranties and indemnities from the designer so that the design can be used without fear of any third party challenges or claims. The designs should be registered as trademarks and also, if possible, protected as registered designs.

7.5. *Concessions/Franchises*

Where a party is granted the exclusive concession/franchise to supply, for example, soft drinks at a particular sports event, this is again a matter of contract, in which the scope and other terms and conditions should be clearly defined.

In particular, the contract should contain warranties in favour of the concessionaire/franchisee that the venue (e.g. stadium) will be 'clean', i.e. free of competitive products and advertising. Such warranties should be supplemented by indemnities and a right to terminate the contract in the event of their breach.

7.6. *Film and Video*

Where the contract is a commissioning contract for the production of a film or video, time should be made of the essence, and the producer should be obliged to adhere to a pre-determined budget and/or seek prior cost approval at certain defined stages of production.

The agreement should contain an express assignment in writing of the copyright from the film or video producer to the event organiser, sports federation or rights holder. There is no presumption of assignment. In addition, the 'author' (i.e. producer) should waive all his 'moral rights' in the film or video, and obtain all other releases and assignments from other persons with rights (e.g. performance rights) in relation to the film or video. Corresponding warranties and indemnities should also be given, as well as a right of termination in case of breach.

---

37. Section 87 (1)–(3) Copyright Designs and Patents Act 1988.

A licence to use related trademarks will also be required, and quality control provisions should be included.

7.7. *Public Appearances*

Failure to show by the individual, e.g. sports personality, should be expressly made a fundamental term of the contract enabling the other party to terminate the same. Alternatively, a best endeavours clause may be used.

If necessary, payments may be made to the sports personality's management company, or as benefits in kind, so as not to affect his or her amateur status. There are also taxation implications. See under 'Taxation Aspects' at p. 434.

7.8. *Suppliership*

The event organiser may grant rights to a company or firm to be the 'official' product or service supplier to a particular sports event, for example, official soft drink or official credit card. The sponsor will also require the exclusive right to supply his goods or services at the event, hence the venue will need to be 'clean' of competing products or services and related advertising. See further under 'The Venue' at p. 29.

8. The Rights

In relation to the organisation, staging, management, promotion and exploitation of an international sports event a variety of rights is available to potential sponsors, suppliers, merchandisers and licensees. A brief comment on the legal nature and effect of the principal examples of these rights follows.

8.1. *Options*

The event organiser or sports body may grant an option in relation to the various marketing and commercial rights. The option constitutes an offer which cannot be revoked without the grantor being in breach of the contract. The terms and conditions under which the option can be performed, including time limits, must be carefully defined, especially as regards 'matching options'.

8.2. *Pre-emption*

A pre-emption right amounts to an offer of first refusal, that is, if a rights holder is considering licensing a particular right or entering into a certain commercial arrangement, a first opportunity of acquiring that right will be offered to the pre-emptive rights holder.

The grant of the right of pre-emption is not a positive offer in the same way as an option: the duty is negative in that the grantor may not contract with any third party unless he has first offered to do so with the grantee. In certain circumstances, the grantor is prevented from refusing the grantee's offer at one price and then accepting a third party offer at a higher price.

In addition, the parties may enter into a 'matching' agreement whereby the party granted the right of first refusal may, in the event that his offer is not accepted by the rights holder, be given the right to match the offer of a third party.

As with options, the terms of the grant and the conditions of exercise of rights of pre-emption, in particular the time limits for exercise, should be carefully defined in the agreement.

8.3. Exclusivity

The rights granted may be exclusive, shared with the grantor, or shared generally. The word 'exclusive' denotes that the right may only be exercised by the grantee; 'sole' means that it may be exercised by the grantee and the grantor; 'non-exclusive' means that the right may be exercised by the grantee, the grantor and any other party with the grantor's permission. Again, this is a matter for clear definition in the agreement.

Exclusivity also raises questions of national and EC competition law, as to which see further at p. 404.

8.4. Copyright Licence

Copyright can be split according to term, territory, product class, media and form. It cannot, however, be split in the same term, product class, media and form within one territory.

Provision should be expressly made in the agreement for the rights to revert back to the licensor following termination of the contract.

The licensee should also ensure, if the licensor is not the creator of the 'work', that the licensor has the copyright to license, that is, that it has been properly assigned from the 'author'. The licensee will, therefore, require a warranty and indemnity from the licensor that he owns the copyright and will indemnify the licensee against any copyright claims by any third parties.

8.5. *Trademark Licence*

Under EC competition law, any undertaking not to challenge the validity of the licensors' trademarks is contrary to Article 85(1) of the Rome Treaty. See further at p. 404.

The licensee cannot be prevented from challenging the trademarks under UK Law,[38] so the agreement should contain a provision that should the licensee challenge the marks, the licence will automatically come to an end. In addition, the licensor may need to include a provision that the licensee will execute a registered user agreement.

The licence will usually include a provision that the licensee will use the trademark in a certain format. That is, it will ensure that the representation of the mark is as true as possible, that the correct colours are used, and so on. This is important for the licensor in ensuring that the value, reputation/goodwill, and validity of his trademark are maintained and fully protected.

The licensee will most likely insist on warranties from the licensor that he owns the trademark and will indemnify the licensee in respect of any third party claims.

Consider also product liability mentioned under 'Merchandising' at p. 18.

8.6. *Territory*

The rights can be divided according to geographical territory, but the licensor should be aware of the UK and EC Competition Rules on territorial restrictions. The agreement may require registration under the UK Restrictive Trade Practices Act 1976 and notification under Article 85(1) of the Rome Treaty. As regards EC competition rules, the distinction between 'active' and 'passive' sales outside the territory should be particularly noted. See further under 'EC Competition Rules' at p. 404.

8.7. *Media*

The intellectual property rights can be split according to media and product category. For example, the same material might exist as a film or video and a broadcast. Equally a trademark might be licensed separately for use on clothing or on a book cover.

8.8. *Product and Service Categories*

In arranging sponsorship of a major sports event, it is usual to structure the sponsorship so that a sponsor will be the exclusive sponsor for a particular

38. Section 18(2) Trademarks Act 1938.

product category, such as soft-drinks, computer equipment, or running shoes, or exclusive sponsor for a particular service category, such as airlines or hotels. The product or service category will need to be carefully defined, so that, for example, it is clear whether 'soft drinks' includes mineral water, and 'beer' includes non-alcoholic beer.

8.9. Duration

The term of the agreement should be expressly defined and there should also be an express provision for earlier termination in specified circumstances, such as failure to pay the sponsorship fee or royalties on time.

8.10. Post Termination

The licensor should expressly provide in the agreement that the rights should revert to him following termination and that any outstanding stock of the licensed product is returned. The licensee may also be required to clear the market place of unsold stock. It is unlikely that the event organiser or licensee could prevent the other party from doing similar business in the future in a competing field, for example, sponsoring a different event or producing and distributing videos for alternative championships. Such a restriction would be in restraint of trade and, therefore, open to challenge. It would also be anti-competitive under EC competition rules.

However, such a non-compete clause is usually enforceable during the existence of the contract and, if used, should therefore be so limited.

8.11. Accreditation

The event organiser and the sponsor/marketer should also consider accreditation rights. These are the rights of entry for such things as corporate hospitality to different sections of the stadium or arena which is under the control of the event organiser. The rights that are being granted should be specified and accreditation passes issued accordingly.

9. Financial Terms

The financial terms of the deal, whether consideration is flowing from the rights holder or event organiser to the commissioned party or from sponsor to event organiser, should be clearly defined in the contract.

Where royalties are payable, the following points should be considered:

- period of payment;
- on what will the royalty be calculated;
- will an amount be allowed for marketing and promotion expenses before the royalty percentage is calculated;
- what is the currency of obligation and currency of payment;
- how will the exchange rate be calculated;
- who will pay the costs of transmission of the money;
- will interest be payable on late payments (where interest is payable on late payments, this should be expressed in such a way so that it does not constitute a waiver of any other remedies for breach of the contract, including termination);
- a right to inspect the accounting records and the right to have the accounts audited, with the licensee paying for the audit should it reveal an underpayment of royalties.

Some of these points are also relevant where payments are made in a form other than royalties, e.g. lump sum payments (sponsorship fees).

The right of set-off applies unless expressly excluded by the terms of the contract.

Interest for late payment should be reserved and the rate fixed in the contract, otherwise the common law rate of 15% would apply.

Where payment is in a form other than money, that is 'value in kind', such as the supply of computerised time-recording equipment or attendants' clothing, the amount and value and other terms of contribution should be carefully spelled out in the contract.

The payment should be expressed to be made net of all withholding taxes and other deductions. If the organising body is a charity this should be particularly considered. As to fiscal matters generally, see further under 'Taxation Aspects' at p. 424.

10. Insurance Aspects

Insurance will be required to cover a number of contingent liabilities, namely:

- Public liability insurance – to cover claims from members of the public over defective premises, see further under 'Venue' at p. 29.
- Cancellation – some insurance companies offer insurance covering cancellation of major sports events, which otherwise could prove very expensive to the organisers, sponsors and others commercially associated with them. Likewise, the premiums for such insurance cover can also prove very expensive.
- Intellectual property rights – it is useful to take out insurance to cover claims made by third parties over intellectual property rights. In many cases such insurance may be taken out by the commissioned designer, film or video

producer, in which case all relevant parties will need to be named in the policy.

- Product liability insurance – to cover claims made by members of the public relating to injury caused by defective products. Such liability may arise as a result of the use of trademarks on merchandise.

11. Advertising and Promotion

11.1. Advertising Controls

UK advertising is governed by voluntary regulations, statute and case law. The regulations, which are found in various Codes of Practice, form the basis of control and, although statute and case law do play a part, there is little difference in content between those sources and the Codes of Practice.

Non-broadcast advertising (e.g. print media) is governed by the British Code of Advertising Practice, presided over by the Committee of Advertising Practice and the Advertising Standards Authority. Broadcast advertising is governed by the Code of Advertising of the Independent Television Commission ('ITC') and the Code of Advertising of the Radio Authority. There is an additional Code which covers television programme sponsorship. Radio programme sponsorship is covered in the Radio Code.

The main theme running through the Codes is that advertisements must be 'legal, decent, honest and truthful'. Beyond that, the restrictions tend to be specific and relate to certain product types, times of broadcast and other matters.

11.2. Tobacco Advertising

The most obvious restrictions relevant to sports marketing are those which relate to tobacco advertising. An event may be sponsored by a tobacco company, subject to certain limitations, but tobacco products may not be advertised on television or radio. There are also restrictions on television coverage of tobacco sponsored events. These are contained in the Voluntary Agreement between the Government and the Tobacco Industry.[39] See p. 18 above.

11.3. Programme Sponsorship

The new area of programme sponsorship is also relevant to sports marketing. The ITC Code on Programme Sponsorship specifically allows sponsorship of

39. *Re* Voluntary Agreement on Tobacco Products' Advertising and Promotion and Health Warnings. September 1991. Revised 1 January 1992.

the television coverage of sports events and this may be by one of the major sponsors of the event itself. The sponsorship of the 1991 Rugby World Cup by Sony helped to establish the phenomenon as a successful marketing avenue. The Code is in line with the EC Directive on Television Broadcasting.[40] The basic principles set out in the Code are as follows:

1. Any television programme may be sponsored unless it is a news or current affairs programme.
2. No sponsor is permitted any influence on either the content or the scheduling of a programme.
3. Any sponsorship must be clearly identified at the beginning and/or end of the programme.
4. No promotional reference to the sponsor, or to his product or service, is permitted within the programme sponsored.
5. No programme may contain within it any promotional reference to any other product or service.
6. No programme may, without the consent of the ITC, be sponsored by any person whose business consists, wholly or mainly, in the manufacture or supply of a product, or in the provision of a service, which is not acceptable for television under the Advertising Code.
7. Product placement is prohibited.

11.4. Affinity Marketing

With affinity marketing and other direct marketing activities using a customer or client list, the parties should be aware of the restrictions of the Data Protection Act 1984 and the British Code of Advertising Practice. Amongst other things, the Act requires those who electronically store data of a personal nature, such as names and addresses, to comply with certain rules of good practice. For example, the data user may need to be registered, should obtain the data fairly and will be restricted as to what he can do with it.

11.5. Agencies

The advertising agency handling the promotion of the event will require a licence to use the intellectual property rights of the organiser or rights holder in the advertisements. In addition, the copyright of any advertisements designed by an agency should be assigned to the commissioning party.

40. 89/552/EEC of 3 October 1989.

11.6. Ancillary Advertising

If the advertising relates to advertising a video or film connected with an event or its organisers, the advertiser or video producer will require a separate consent to use excerpts from the video or film in advertising. Similarly, with advertising merchandise associated with the event, even if its production and sale has been commissioned by the event organiser, the commissioning agreement should contain an authority to advertise the products in a pre-determined manner.

11.7. Advertising in the Official Programme

An event organiser or sports federation may commission an official programme, book, or yearbook and may sell advertising space in such publications. In addition, a sponsor may sponsor the programme or the book itself. Such rights should be defined and documented.

11.8. Comparative Advertising

Comparative advertising is permitted in the UK subject to certain restrictions found primarily in the British Code of Advertising Practice. The Code states that comparisons must deal fairly with competitors and must not aim to mislead; they must make clear with what the product being advertised is being compared; any claims must be capable of being substantiated; the advertisement must not simply highlight selected advantages. The Department of Trade and Industry Code on Price Indications should also be observed, as should the law on trademarks, copyright and passing-off.

Attention should also be paid to possible claims for trademark infringements when the products compared are protected in some way by trademark registrations.

11.9. Defamation

The advertiser should also be aware of the common law torts (civil wrongs) of defamation and trade libel, which provide relief for a person whose personal or business reputation has been lowered, in the eyes of the public, by the statements of another. These laws restrict the use of comparisons and unauthorised endorsements in advertising.

11.10. 'Ambush Marketing'

The phenomena of 'ambush marketing' and other unfair marketing practices, which create a false association between the advertiser and the sports event or sports federation, can be prevented by use of trademark law and the law against trespass (see 'The Venue' below). If necessary, an injunction can be obtained from the court to prevent a proposed trademark infringement. Beyond these methods of protection, there is little that can be done in the UK to prevent 'ambush marketing'. However, there seems to be a trend in the courts towards extending the doctrine of 'passing-off' to a wider range of unfair competition situations in the future.

11.11. Airspace

Advertising in the airspace may only be restricted by resorting to the common law tort of trespass; see 'The Venue' below. However, some sports charters, such as the IOC Charter, specifically exclude the use of airspace above the event for advertising or otherwise.

12. The Venue

The following points should be considered.

12.1. Public Liability

The event organiser will need to ensure compliance with the health and safety rules and local authority rules relating to construction of the stadia, fire regulations, public safety and so on. Failure to do so will result in fines from the local authorities. With some events (e.g. football), it is a requirement that the stadia are all seating. This can be checked with the relevant governing body, for example, the Football Association.

Under the common law tort of negligence, which imposes a general duty of care on the organiser, the organiser will be liable to members of the public if he is found not to have exercised that duty of care. He will be liable for any loss or damage caused to any person who might foreseeably have suffered loss. So, for example, if the organiser fails to comply with required safety checks and a spectator, or sports person, is injured as a result, the organiser will be liable. The Occupiers Liability Act 1957 reinforces this common law doctrine.

The case of *Alcock* v. *Chief Constable of South Yorkshire*,[41] which followed the Hillsborough football tragedy, held that a negligent party may be liable for

41. [1991] 3 WLR 1095.

nervous shock, although the sufferer was not present at the actual scene. In this case, the family and friends of those killed at the football ground successfully sued the police for nervous shock caused as a result of watching live television coverage of the event. The organiser should consider insurance to cover such claims.

The organiser may try to limit public liability by expressly excluding liability on the admission tickets. The Unfair Contract Terms Act 1977 limits the effect of such exclusion clauses, so that the organiser cannot exclude liability for personal injury or death. Where possible, the organiser should pass on the liability to sub-contractors, for example, the company responsible for erecting the seating, providing the safety barriers, manufacturing or installing stadium perimeter boards, and obtain corresponding indemnities from them. In addition, the doctrine of contributory negligence enables the sued party to argue that the injured party was also partly responsible for the injury.

12.2. Control

The stadium will generally be under the control of the event organiser, who will hire or lease it from the owner for a specific occasion and specific period of time. The organiser is thus in lawful possession and, therefore, able to restrict access and grant accreditation, parking and other passes. Being in possession, the organiser will be responsible for security of the stadium and will be able to discharge this responsibility through hiring an appropriate security firm or using the stadium owner's security personnel.

The event organiser needs to define precisely the area of the venue, which will be under its direct control and police this area. This will involve ensuring that unauthorised camera crews do not find their way into the grounds, or that competing sponsors do not launch 'ambush marketing' campaigns at the venue. Such activities can be prevented through the common law offence of trespass. The offence of trespass covers a number of different actions, including setting foot on land, riding or driving over it, pulling down or destroying anything attached to it (this includes advertising hoardings), and erecting or causing to be erected anything which invades the airspace over the land. In order to do these things lawfully, a person would require consent, either express or implied, e.g. through acquiescence. 'Ambush marketing' initiatives can also be prevented through an action for trademark infringement or passing-off.

The airspace above the property is only safe from trespass to a limited extent. Aircraft which fly over a property at a height above the ground which, having regard to the wind, weather and all the circumstances is reasonable, are not guilty of trespass. Should the aircraft continually circle a property at a low height this may amount to a trespass. This catches advertising balloons and light aircraft which fly over the venue pulling advertising streamers.

An action for trespass should be brought by the person who was, or is deemed to have been, in lawful possession of the land at the time of the trespass. This is likely to be the event organiser. The action is brought in the High Court and the remedy is damages.

The event organiser will need to ensure that the location, existence, and running of the event do not cause a public nuisance. For example, that the event does not create an excessive amount of noise or pollution which has a serious detrimental effect on 'neighbours'. Nuisance is a tort for which an organiser may be liable in damages.

The event organiser will also need to consider the provisions of the Sporting Events (Control of Alcohol) Act 1985 and the, currently proposed, Amendment Act 1992. The Act imposes restrictions on the sale and admission of alcohol in certain sports grounds.

12.3. Sponsor Access and Protection

Event sponsors may have been granted certain exclusive display rights, supply rights and pouring rights, and they will want to be sure that the venue is free from competitors who might sell similar products or services. This can be achieved by contract and also through the law of trespass. However, where the stadium has a 'tied' arrangement with a competitive supplier, the organiser may have to negotiate a release from it to keep the competitive supplier away during the staging of the particular event. The organiser should be aware of potential problems under competition law which exclusive arrangements may trigger.

As part of a normal sponsorship package, an organiser will offer corporate hospitality facilities and space for stands, tents and promotional arrangements. Sponsors will need to satisfy themselves that there are no existing conflicting contractual arrangements.

Sponsors, their employees and guests will require accreditation passes to enable them to have access to the venue and make full use, according to their contractual rights, of the various facilities available. Sponsors will require access for themselves and their contractors to the venue to erect display boards and advertising hoardings and also to dismantle them after the event. These are matters for careful negotiation and inclusion in the respective sponsorship agreements.

13. Dispute Resolution

When a dispute arises between the parties it will most likely be in relation to the performance, or non-performance, of the contract, or an infringement of intellectual property rights. There are a number of remedies to provide the innocent party with some form of redress. The remedies can be pursued in the courts, which are generally time consuming and costly, or the aggrieved party may consider extra-judicial remedies through arbitration or alternative dispute resolution (see 'Alternative Dispute Resolution' at p. 34).

13.1. Court Action

An action would be brought in the High Court, either the Queen's Bench Division or the Chancery Division, depending on the subject matter of the dispute. Proceedings would be issued and there may be a number of interim appointments with the court before a date is set for the trial. Proceedings may be instigated by a foreign plaintiff, in which case some form of security for costs may be required by the court. Service of papers outside the jurisdiction will require the 'leave' of the court. Depending on the complexity of the dispute, the trial may take between one and five years before it is listed. The complexities of the High Court procedure are covered in detail in 'the White Book'.[42]

Specific performance and injunctions

An order of specific performance is an order forcing a party to a contract to perform the act it agreed to perform in accordance with the precise terms of the contract. An injunction is an order restraining a party from doing a specific act and often relates to intellectual property rights. An injunction may be made in the interim stages of proceedings, that is before the matter is heard at the trial. In such cases, the court may require an undertaking in respect of costs from the plaintiff, and will only make the injunction if there appears to be some real case to answer. If the potential harm that would be caused by the injunction to the defendant is great, the court may not grant the injunction. In *American Cyanamid* v. *Ethicon*[43] Lord Diplock set out the following rules for deciding whether an interlocutory injunction would be granted: there is a good arguable case; damages would be inadequate for the plaintiff; damages would be adequate for the defendant at trial should the final decision go against the plaintiff; and the balance of convenience must be in favour of the plaintiff.

The granting of injunctions and specific performance is discretionary. Failure to abide by the terms of either order amounts to a contempt of court, for which the offender may be liable to imprisonment, a fine or sequestration of funds.

Action for an agreed sum

This is a simple action to recover money due under the contract and which has not been paid. The amount due is usually a specified amount and a judgment can often be obtained by a short-cut method under Order 14 of the High Court Practice Rules without the need to conduct a full trial. Once a judgment has been obtained, there are a number of ways in which the sum can be recovered, including a charge over property or an order to put the company into liquidation. Interest at the court rate is payable on court judgments.

42. Supreme Court Practice.
43. [1975] FSR HL.

General and consequential damages
Damages are generally measured as the amount necessary to put the innocent party into the position he would have been in had the contract not been breached. This may include damages that were consequential, but will exclude damages that are too remote. In some agreements the parties include clauses limiting the measure of damages, calculating the expected damages, and/or excluding claims for consequential loss.

Legal costs
Costs are in the discretion of the court, but they usually 'follow the event', that is to say, generally the costs of both parties are paid by the losing party.

If the court feels that the plaintiff, although successful, has behaved unreasonably, the judge may award costs to the losing party.

There is often a dispute as to the amount of costs that are reasonable and this can be settled by a process known as 'taxation'. In most cases, even though the winning party is awarded his costs, he will not recover them in full, but is more likely to recover a sum more equal to 75% of the total.

13.2. Arbitration

Arbitration is available as an alternative to court action. The arbitration body applies legal principles and rules to settle the dispute and the finding, or award, is legally binding on both parties. In the absence of an express provision in the agreement, the question of which law applies to the arbitration is resolved in the same way as with a court action.

The parties must agree to go to arbitration and this agreement is usually contained in the contract which governs their relationship. A written arbitration agreement of this sort is governed by the Arbitration Acts.[44]

If there is an arbitration agreement in existence between the parties and one of the parties pursues an action in the courts, rather than observing the arbitration agreement, the other party may apply to the court for a 'stay' of the court proceedings. Where the arbitration agreement is non-domestic in nature, the court is obliged to stay the proceedings. Such a stay gives the arbitration procedure chance to work, but it does not preclude the court making orders ancillary to the arbitration.

There are various rules which apply to decide the identity of the arbitrator, and the court has power to appoint the arbitrator, where necessary.

There is a right to appeal an award of the arbitrator to the court on the basis of a question of law. However, such an appeal may only be brought with the consent of the other party or with the leave of the court.

There is an implied promise in every arbitration agreement that the parties will comply with the award, failing which the award may be enforced in the same way as an order of the court.

44. Arbitration Act 1950, Arbitration Act 1975 and Arbitration Act 1979.

The arbitrator has the power to make an award as to costs which he considers appropriate; any clause in the arbitration agreement to the effect that the parties will each pay their own costs is void.

The UK is a party to the New York Convention on the Reciprocal Recognition and Enforcement of Foreign Arbitral Awards of 1958. It is common practice in the UK to refer disputes to arbitration by either the London Arbitration Court or the International Chamber of Commerce Arbitration Court in Paris.

Reference to arbitral awards being binding is acceptable under the Arbitration Act 1979[45] and only in exceptional cases of an appeal on a point of law can an arbitration award be challenged in the ordinary UK courts.

13.3. Alternative Dispute Resolution

In view of the delays, complexities and expense of litigation through the ordinary courts, and also the increasing technicality of arbitration procedures, litigants and their lawyers have sought, in recent times, to mitigate these effects by following alternative forms of dispute resolution ('ADR').

These forms include conciliation and mediation procedures and appointment of *ad hoc* 'mediators' to act as experts (not arbitrators) in the settlement of disputes. Clauses in sports sponsorship and merchandising agreements are often found providing for the settlement of all kinds of technical disputes by 'experts', for example, the President for the time being of the International Amateur Athletic Federation ('expert determination').

Other forms of ADR include 'good faith' clauses to resolve disputes amicably in good faith and a timely manner, failing which either party may terminate the agreement.

The practice of ADR is developing and new forms are being devised to settle and resolve all kinds of contractual disputes in a creative, efficient and cost-effective manner, such as 'mini-trials'.

45. Section 52.

SPORTS
MARKETING

Austria

by Dr. Arthur Wolff

1. Sports Marketing – A Business

In Austria, sports marketing and sports sponsorship, in particular as a commercial marketing route, have existed for quite a number of years. In connection with sports that attract a large audience to a sports event itself (e.g. football) or where the event is viewed by large numbers of viewers on TV (e.g. football, tennis, ski competitions) or gets wide coverage in the print media, various industries, and in particular the sports goods industry, are very keen on sponsoring such events and/or participating teams, individual athletes and sportsmen and women. Thus, although no figures are available, it is quite clear that considerable sums are spent on sports marketing and sponsorship.

2. The Austrian Legal System

Austria is a union and consists of nine states, the capital, Vienna, also being a state. The legal system is a civil law system. Most of the laws relevant for business in general are federal law, which is enacted by the Parliament.

The courts are either 'ordinary' courts with jurisdiction over all civil (including commercial) disputes and criminal cases, or 'special' courts, the most important being labour courts with jurisdiction over labour disputes. The procedural rules to be followed by the courts are federal law. Subject to certain restrictions, a decision of a court of first instance may be appealed to a superior court and its decision appealed, in turn, to the Supreme Court. A party may – and in many cases, especially in more important matters – must be represented in court by a lawyer.

3. Applicable Laws

There are no particular laws in Austria specifically applicable to sports marketing. Thus, the general rules of different laws apply, in particular the rules relating to contracts under the General Civil Code, in so far as the contractual relationship between the parties involved is concerned. According to the principle of 'freedom of contract' the parties are free to determine and agree what terms they want to include in a contract and to shape it at their discretion, subject to rules of mandatory provisions of law. For an international contract, this 'freedom of contract' includes the possibility to agree on the law applicable to the contract. Such a choice would be upheld by the Austrian courts to the extent that there is no violation of public policy (*'ordre public'*).

4. Intellectual Property Rights

Whatever form the sponsorship takes, it will require a carefully constructed and worded contract and particular attention should be given to the intellectual property rights, which – as *the* means to protect it – constitute the core of a sports marketing programme.

The intellectual property rights most relevant in this context are trademarks and copyright. Regarding the protection of goodwill and business reputation and against confusion, the Law against Unfair Competition can be an important supplement to these rights.

4.1. Trademarks

Austria adheres to the Paris Convention on the Protection of Industrial Property and the Madrid Trademark Agreement. The national law is embodied in the Trademarks Protection Act ('Markenschutzgesetz'; 'MSchG'). Case law has an influence not usual in other fields of law. Both trademarks and service marks may be registered.

Marks may, in particular, consist of a name, word, and – provided that they can be read as a word – of a combination of letters, a picture ('device') or any combination of such or a distinctive shape ('three-dimensional marks'), such as the Coca-Cola bottle, provided the shape does not result from the function of the product.

Section 12 of MSchG affords protection also for names, including company marks, against unauthorised use even if they are not registered as trademarks.

Marks are registered with the Patent Office. Austria being a signatory to the Nice Agreement on the International Classification of Goods and Services of 1957, an application for registration must follow this classification. The application is not examined as to prior rights of marks that might be identical or confusingly similar to the mark applied for. The law does not provide for a third-party opposition procedure. The duration of the term of protection of a mark is ten years and it may be renewed indefinitely for periods of ten years each by payment of the renewal fees.

The registered owner of a mark has the exclusive right to use the mark in relation to the goods and services covered by the registration and to enjoin third parties from using such mark or a confusingly similar mark for the same or similar goods or services. He may also claim damages from an infringer.

If a mark has not, to a reasonable extent, been used within five years from registration, anybody may file an application to remove it from the register.

The licensing of marks is permitted. Use of the mark by a licensee is imputed to the mark's owner (licensor) and enures to his benefit, i.e. is sufficient to constitute use for purposes of the user requirement.

A licence may be recorded in the trademark register but this has no effect against third parties. There are no legal requirements that a trademark licence contain provisions as to quality control or similar matters. Since licensing agreements are not covered by a particular body of law, the parties are free to include in their licence agreements any provision they wish within the confines of mandatory general law. Care should be taken, in particular, that Austrian and EC/EEA competition rules are not violated.

In particular, owners of well-known marks frequently register marks in classes in which they would not normally use the mark ('defensive marks'). In view of the user requirement, such registrations should be re-registered prior to the expiration of the five years 'grace' period, as otherwise they may be cancelled upon any third party's application.

4.2. Copyright

Austria is a party to the Berne Convention and the Universal Copyright Convention. National copyright law is governed by the Copyright Act ('Urheberrechtsgesetz'; 'UrhG').

Copyright protection is afforded to works of literature and art (the latter comprising musical, cinematographic and artistic works), provided they are 'original' intellectual creations.

Such works are protected by copyright law as soon as they have been created and made perceptible to the human senses, i.e. independent of any formalities. No registration or deposit of the work or a copyright notice is required. The general term of protection is 70 years from the date of the author's death. Films are protected for 50 years from the making of the film.

Pursuant to Section 78 of the Copyright Act a picture (likeness) of a person (e.g. photograph) may not be publicly exhibited or otherwise published without the depicted person's consent, if his/her legitimate interests are violated thereby.

The author has certain 'moral rights' and the exclusive economic rights in his work, in particular the right to copy, publish, distribute and adapt his work. He may obtain injunctive relief against an infringer, including a preliminary injunction. Other remedies include an action for damages. Infringing items may be seized and destroyed.

Copyright as such is not transferable, but the author may waive his moral rights and grant licences under his economic rights.

4.3. Registered Designs

Austrian law makes no distinction between utility models and designs nor is there any protection of utility models outside patent law. The Austrian Design Protection Act of 1990 protects only outward appearance. Design protection is supplemented by other statutory provisions. For example, the design of an object may enjoy copyright protection. In exceptional cases, it may be granted trademark protection and imitation of a competitor's products may violate fair competition law.

Austria is a member of the Locarno Agreement establishing an International Classification for Industrial Designs.

A design protected under the Act 'is any prototype (*Vorbild*) for the appearance of a commercial product'. It may be a two-dimensional illustration as well as a three-dimensional object. A requirement for registration with the Patent Office or a Chamber of Commerce is that the design must be new. The term of protection is five years and the registration can be renewed twice for further periods of five years each by payment of the renewal fees. The owner has the exclusive right to produce, distribute, offer or use products that are identical or confusingly similar to the design or sufficiently similar. Remedies for infringement include injunctive relief (including a preliminary injunction) and an action for damages.

4.4. Unfair Competition

The Act against Unfair Competition ('Gesetz gegen unlauteren Wettbewerb'; 'UWG') prohibits the following, which may be relevant to sports marketing:

- any conduct in the course of business for purposes of competition that offends *bonos mores* ('general clause'; Section 1 UWG);
- deceptive statements in the course of business for purposes of competition concerning business matters ('deceptive advertising'; Section 2 UWG). Under this provision, for example, misleading advertising (such as misleading references to testimonials or endorsements or a non-existent association with a sports event) may be prosecuted;
- the unauthorised use in the course of business of, *inter alia*, a name, firm name, the special designation of a business or enterprise or a trademark in a manner which may cause confusion with the name legitimately used by another ('protection of commercial designations'; Section 9 UWG). Thus,

under this provision not only registered but also unregistered trademarks and other designations or names may be protected.

Any competitor (including, of course, the injured party, if any) may obtain injunctive relief (including a preliminary injunction) and has an action for damages.

5. The Contract Generally and Preliminary Agreements

5.1. Preliminary Agreements

Frequently prior to the contract proper a 'memorandum of understanding', 'heads of agreement' or a 'letter of intent' is signed. While these are usually not intended to create legal relations, they may be binding, if they are not carefully drafted (see below at 5.2).

5.2. Intention to Create Legal Relations

A contract being a legally binding agreement between the parties, the parties must intend to create a legal relation. As the agreements being entered into in connection with sports marketing and sponsorship are commercially motivated, there can normally be no doubt that the parties intend to establish a binding legal relation which, according to the principle of freedom of contract, they are free to shape as they see fit (see above at 3).

5.3. Offer and Acceptance

As a rule, a contract is formed when the offer of one party has been unconditionally accepted by the other party. Problems may arise in particular if the negotiations are conducted and agreement is reached by the exchange of correspondence or if, in personal negotiations, agreement is reached step by step and no careful record is kept of the discussions, as it may be difficult to determine at which point in time agreement was reached on what. This may occur, for example, where there is a series of offers and counter offers. The practice familiar, for example, to English lawyers to negotiate and draft contracts 'subject to (formal) contract' may be of some help to avoid this problem.

5.4. Consideration

Austrian law does not require a 'consideration' or benefit flowing between the parties, i.e. a performance and counter performance, as a requirement for a contract being valid.

5.5. Form and Execution

No special formalities need to be observed for contracts relating to sports marketing and sponsorship. There are also no special execution requirements, but in the case of companies being parties to a contract, care should be taken that it is signed by a person having statutory representation authority or a representative duly authorised by a power of attorney.

5.6. Void and Illegal Contracts

One of the essential elements in a valid contract is that there must be a genuine consent between the parties. This consent may be vitiated by the following factors:

- mistake;
- misrepresentation;
- illegality.

Where one of these factors exists in relation to a contract, there can be no true consent and the contract may be rendered void or voidable.

A contract may be void if its making, performance or purpose contravenes a statutory prohibition, the intention of which was to invalidate the contract. It is not very likely that such a situation would arise in connection with sports marketing or sponsorship contracts, with the exception of clauses excluding or unduly limiting liability or unduly restricting one party. Such clauses may be attacked by the party affected as being void. In particular, where an intellectual property licence is involved, a restrictive clause may violate national or EC/EEA competition rules.

A contract is not void, but *may be voidable* by the courts upon the mistaken party's initiative, if it was entered into by mistake and such mistake is fundamental and either was caused or should have been realised by the other party or was clarified before the other party acted in reliance on the contract. The mistake is fundamental if the mistaken party would otherwise not have entered into the contract or, if so, on different conditions, for example, where the mistake related to the identity of the subject matter of the contract or its existence (e.g. that the trademark being the subject matter of the licence has been registered) or to the identity of the other party, a rather remote possibility.

A non-fundamental mistake does not make the contract voidable; the court may only order rectification.

A mistake caused by fraudulent misrepresentation makes the contract not only voidable but the innocent party may also claim damages.

5.7. *Privity*

The relationship created by a contract may be described as 'relative', as only the parties to it may acquire rights and incur obligations under it. It is, therefore, important that all parties intended to acquire rights or to perform obligations under the arrangement contemplated are made parties to the contract or, in the case of a third party's actions being required for the implementation of the contract, that one party to the contract undertakes (to use best efforts) to procure from or cause the third party to act or refrain from acting as required.

5.8. *Interpretation*

The basic rules on the interpretation of contracts are:

- words are to be understood in their plain and literal meaning, subject always to evidence of a usage adding to or varying their usual meaning;
- words must be interpreted in their context and according to the parties' intention to be gleaned *from the whole* of the contract;
- unclear and ambiguous words and phrases will be interpreted against the party using them.

5.9. *Frustration and Force Majeure*

A party to a contract not performing it properly is generally liable for breach of contract. If, however, late or non-performance is due to an *external* event unforeseeable and unavoidable (by reasonable means) in its consequences, i.e. due to *force majeure*, the party affected may be released from liability for late or non-performance and the contract terminated or its performance suspended. This concept of *force majeure* is somewhat related to, but not identical with the concept of *frustration* in *common law*. The general law not being entirely satisfactory in this respect, it is best to spell out exactly in the contract what the parties intend should happen in such an event, that is to define carefully *force majeure* and the extent to which foreseeability, fault and lack of control enter into the situation and to specify the consequences and effects.

5.10. *Breach of Contract*

If a party to a contract does not comply with its terms, in other words, is in breach of contract, the other party may claim specific performance and damages and, depending on the type of breach and contractual stipulations, terminate the contract. As frequently it may be quite difficult to determine or even prove damages, the parties often agree to assess the damages at which they rate a breach of contract by one or both of them and introduce their assessment into the terms of the contract by way of a 'liquidated damages' clause.

6. Standard Contract Terms

The standard contract terms that should be included in or considered when preparing a contract related to sports marketing are more or less the same as the ones set forth in the Chapter on the United Kingdom. In addition, the following clauses would be standard:

- a warranty clause setting out the scope of any required warranty and the consequences of its breach;
- a clause providing for amendments or other changes of the agreement to be made in writing;
- a clause providing for dispute resolution either by certain specified state courts or by arbitration, either *ad hoc* or, more commonly, under the auspices of a national or international arbitration institution.

7. Different Types of Business Arrangements

7.1. Sponsorship Agreement

Sponsorship is a form of marketing whereby the sponsor contributes to, or underwrites, the cost of staging an event, or the cost of a participant in a prestigious event, or the cost of an individual competitor or a team under a periodic agreement, in return for the grant of marketing or promotion rights by the sponsored party entitling the sponsor to promote his image and products in connection with the event.

As no particular body of law governs such an arrangement, the parties are, in principle, free to shape their contractual relationship as they see fit. As to restrictive terms, national and EC/EEA competition rules may have to be considered.

As to advertising on television or otherwise, there are certain restrictions, in particular, regarding advertising of cigarettes, alcohol, pharmaceuticals and certain other products. This area is in a state of flux, as in view of Austria's application for membership of the EC, the legislator is *already now* adapting existing and enacting new legislation to conform to EC rules. Also the EEA Treaty has some impact in this respect.

Cigarette advertising must contain health warnings and is not allowed on radio and TV. Advertising for pharmaceuticals must contain a caution referring to the use instructions to doctors or pharmacists as to possible negative side effects.

7.2. Merchandising

When a sponsored party owns and organises a successful high profile event, there can be great potential in linking the promotion of the event name and logo with the sale of suitable merchandise and the granting of merchandising licences under rights relating thereto (usually trademarks or copyright) may thus be very lucrative.

The terms of the licence of such rights will constitute the core of the arrangement and should cover all questions usually dealt with in a trademark and/or copyright licence agreement.

As there is no particular body of law governing such agreements, the parties are, in principle, free to agree on the terms and conditions of the arrangement as they see fit. As to any restrictive terms of the licence, national and EC/EEA competition rules may have to be considered.

7.3. Endorsements

Endorsement is the promotion of a company's product by means of the personal recommendation of an individual, who is sufficiently well known and respected to influence the purchasing patterns of the consumer public.

A false approval may be prosecuted under Section 2 of the Act against Unfair Competition (see above at 4.4).

An endorsement by an individual without his/her consent may, depending on the circumstances, amount to defamation. The use of a person's likeness without his/her consent may be prosecuted under Section 78 of the Copyright Act (see above at 4.2). This is to be distinguished from a photographer's or the commissioning party's exclusive economic rights in such photograph under Section 74 of the Copyright Act. In the promotion care should be taken that such rights are not infringed.

7.4. Commissioning Agreements

In contracts for the production of logos, designs, advertisements, or event merchandise, time should expressly be made of the essence, which would allow the commissioning party to end the contract if the time limits are not respected without having to give the other party a grace period for performance. This would, of course, not prejudice any claim for damages for breach because of non-performance.

Copyright itself not being assignable under Austrian law, the contract should make it clear that all 'economical rights' of the author (e.g. designer) in the work are licensed to the commissioning party and that 'moral rights' of the author are waived.

The usual warranties/indemnities against infringement of third parties' rights should be included.

7.5. Franchises

Franchising not being covered by a particular body of law, it is a matter of contract. As to intellectual property rights the parties should address in sufficient detail the question of trademark and know-how licences and in particular termination provisions in connection with them.

7.6. Film and video

The situation regarding commissioning contracts for the production of a film or video is rather similar to the situation in the UK.

7.7. Public Appearances

Again, the situation is quite similar to that in the UK.

7.8. Supplièrship

Also regarding supplierships the situation in Austria is similar to that in the UK.

8. The Rights

A brief comment on the legal nature and effect of certain rights, often the subject matter of agreements relating to sports marketing, follows.

8.1. Options

The legal nature and effect of options under Austrian law is similar to the position outlined in the UK.

8.2. Pre-emption

Also regarding pre-emption rights (rights of first refusal) the situation in Austria is quite similar to the one in the UK.

8.3. Exclusivity

Under Austrian law, 'exclusive' and 'sole' rights must be distinguished, although frequently the unwary attributes to the term 'exclusive' the notion of 'sole' right: 'exclusive' means that the right may be exercised only by the grantee, excluding also the grantor, whereas a 'sole' right does not exclude the grantor.

8.4. Copyright Licence

Under Austrian law, the copyright as such may not be transferred. Therefore, the author may only grant licences under his 'economical rights' and waive, but not licence, his moral rights. The licence may be exclusive, sole or non-exclusive and be split according to the category of the rights (e.g. only for copying or distribution), territory, product class, media.

Copyright licence agreements not being subject to special legal rules, the parties may freely agree on their terms and conditions, which, in the licensee's interest, should include, in particular, a warranty of copyright ownership or authority to licence and indemnities.

8.5. Trademark Licence

Certain aspects of a trademark licence under Austrian law were already outlined above at 4.1. Such licences not being governed by a particular body of law, the parties are free to agree on the terms and conditions, but may have to consider national and EC/EEA competition rules.

8.6. Territory

Intellectual property rights may be divided according to territory, but national and EC/EEA competition rules should be considered.

8.7. Media

Intellectual property rights may be split as to product category and media.

8.8. Product Classes

The situation being similar in Austria, reference is made to the chapter on the UK.

8.9. Duration

Reference is made to the chapter on the UK, as the situation outlined there is similar to that in Austria.

8.10. Post Termination

The comment in 8.9 above also applies to Post Termination.

8.11. Accreditation

The comment in 8.9 above also applies to Accreditation.

9. Financial Terms

9.1. Sponsorship

The sponsor's obligations to the sponsored party in return for the rights granted are primarily the payment of money or the supply of goods or services, but may extend to other kinds of assistance for the benefit of the event and the organisations. The cash fee to be agreed between the parties may either represent the anticipated shortfall in income related to the expense of running the event or an amount the sponsor is willing to pay for the privilege of being a sponsor. In the first case, the sponsor may wish to stipulate a maximum liability for the income shortfall, meaning that the sponsored party would be wholly responsible for the outstanding balance. Where a 'contribution to cost' sponsorship payment is to be made, the agreement should set out how the 'cost' is to be calculated. Instead of paying a cash fee, the sponsor may agree to pay directly for the cost of providing goods or services, again to a specified amount. Each party will have to calculate carefully the sums of money it is willing to commit respectively which it requires before reaching an agreement, which will set forth details on how the fee shall be calculated, if it is not an agreed fixed fee, and how it shall be paid, which will depend on several factors, including the cash-flow needs of the sponsored party. The agreement should also set out the terms and conditions for cancellation of the sponsorship and repayment of the fee or part thereof.

9.2. Merchandising

When a sponsored party owns and organises a successful high profile event, there can be great potential in linking the promotion of the event name and logo with the sale of suitable merchandise. The financial return to the sponsored party is a royalty paid by the licensee upon sales of licensed merchandise. The royalty may be a fixed rate or percentage royalty and the parties will agree in detail on the provisions usually found in licence agreements (e.g. foreign currency aspects, sliding scale royalties, royalty advances, minimum royalties, accounting and so on).

9.3. Endorsement

While merchandising income is based upon a royalty on sales of the products merchandised in association with the name of a personality, the remuneration of a personality in consideration for the endorsing of a product will not be a royalty on sales of the product, but a fee to be agreed. This fee may be a flat sum or it may have a potential increase structure calculated upon a greater than normally anticipated sales level of the endorsed product.

9.4. Interest and Set-off

If no rate of interest for payments in arrears has been agreed, the creditor may by law claim interest at 4 percent or – between merchants – at 5 percent per annum. Under the head of damages, interest may be claimed at a rate corresponding to the rate the creditor has to pay for any overdraft or other credit facility.

Unilateral set-off is expressly allowed by law, but in practice often specifically excluded in a contract.

10. Insurance Aspects

It would be prudent to consider taking out insurance in particular against the following contingent liabilities:

- Products liability: where a claim because of damage or injury caused by a defective product marketed with a licensed trademark is not unlikely under Austrian products liability law a trademark licensor may, under certain circumstances, be liable.
- Public liability: to cover claims from members of the public for damages or injury caused by defective premises. Such insurance may be a prerequisite for the permission to organise the event.
- Cancellation: to cover the more often than not very high costs and expenses resulting from the cancellation of a major event.

11. Advertising and Promotion

11.1. Advertising Controls

Advertising controls and restrictions in Austria are rather limited. The most important are set out in the following.

11.2. Tobacco Advertising

Any tobacco advertising in Austria is required to contain a health warning. Tobacco products may not be advertised on radio or television.

11.3. Alcoholic Products Advertising

There are no general restrictions on advertising of alcoholic products. However, spirits may not be advertised on radio or television.

11.4. Pharmaceutical Products

Advertising of pharmaceutical products may not be misleading as to their properties or effects and must contain a caution referring to the use instructions to doctors or pharmacists regarding possible negative side effects.

11.5. Programme Sponsorship

No particular body of law governs programme sponsorship. Pursuant to Section 26 of the Media Act ('Mediengesetz') product placement on television must be identified as advertising, if directly or indirectly paid for, as it would otherwise constitute 'hidden' advertising and may also violate Section 1 of the Act against Unfair Competition (see above at 4.4).

In view of Austria being a signatory to the EEA-Treaty and its application for EC membership, it is likely that the EC Directive on Television Broadcasting will be transformed into Austrian law in the near future.

11.6. Comparative Advertising

Comparative *price* advertising is expressly permitted under Section 2(1) of the Act against Unfair Competition, provided that is not misleading and does not violate Section 1 (see above at 4.4). According to case law, comparative *quality* advertising is also permitted, subject to the same restrictions.

11.7. Misleading Advertising and Defamation

As to misleading advertising, see above at 4.4. The use of unauthorised endorsements in advertising may constitute misleading advertising and, depending on the circumstances, amount to defamation (see above at 7.3).

12. The Venue

In particular, the following points should be considered regarding the venue for a sports event:

12.1. Control

As the situation in Austria is quite similar to the one in the UK, reference is made to the chapter on the UK.

12.2. Sponsor Access and Accreditation

The position in 12.1 above also applies here.

12.3. Public Liability

As an event organiser owes a general duty of care to the public, he may be liable for any damages caused by his failure to exercise that duty of care, for example, when he makes no proper safety checks and somebody is injured as a result. Furthermore, he will need to comply with federal and local rules as to public safety, construction of stadia, fire regulations and so on.

The law on standard contract terms makes it difficult to exclude the organiser's liability (e.g. on tickets), which may, if at all, only be excluded in the case of slight negligence. Whenever possible, he should pass on the liability to sub-contractors.

13. Dispute Resolution

In practice, many contractual disputes are solved by direct negotiation. However, in contrast to *domestic* contracts, where the local national court system will have jurisdiction, unless the parties have agreed to arbitration, parties to *international* contracts need to agree on what will happen if a dispute arises.

13.1. National Courts

Parties occasionally designate a national court as the forum for resolving disputes. However, in international contracts it is unlikely that the same national court will be acceptable to both sides and that the courts of a third, neutral country, are likely to be appropriate. Furthermore, in such a situation the judgment of a foreign court may not readily be enforceable in the country where enforcement is sought. If enforcement of a foreign judgment is sought in Austria and enforcement is not assured under a bilateral or multilateral convention, the judgment will be enforced only if reciprocity exists. These factors show why most international contracts contain arbitration clauses.

If an Austrian court has jurisdiction (regarding the Austrian court system, see above at 2) and depending on the cause of action, the remedies may include, in particular, injunctive relief (including preliminary injunctions), and an action for damages, including consequential or liquidated damages. In principle, the losing party must reimburse the winning party's legal fees as determined by the court on the basis of a statutory schedule.

13.2. Arbitration

Subject to agreement of the parties, most commercial and private law matters are arbitrable under Austrian law. Arbitration may be *ad hoc* or conducted under the auspices of an arbitration institution in accordance with its rules.

For *domestic* arbitration, the most important institutions are the Chambers of Commerce in the various states of Austria.

Regarding *international* arbitration, the Austrian institution administering international arbitration is the 'International Arbitral Centre of the Federal Economic Chamber Vienna' in accordance with its 'Rules of Arbitration and Conciliation'. More frequently the parties resort to ICC arbitration.

Austria adhering, *inter alia*, to the New York Convention on the Recognition and Enforcement of Foreign Arbitral Awards, enforcement of awards in accordance with this Convention is assured in Austria.

13.3. Alternative Dispute Resolution

Although more and more widely used in many countries, alternative forms of dispute resolution ('ADR') are only slowly gaining acceptance in Austria, also for disputes arising from international contracts. Of the various forms of ADR, conciliation, mediation and experts' opinions are used. Mini trials are almost unheard of. In connection with sports marketing agreements, often experts' opinions are relied on in accordance with an express contractual stipulation to settle technical disputes through expert determination.

Belgium

by Jacques Buekenhoudt
and Jean-Louis Jaspar

1. Sports Marketing – A Business

The development of sport and its consequences for the economy have led to the creation of a huge 'sports market'. Besides television rights, other sources of revenue have emerged, thanks to patrons, sponsors and other forms of commercialisation. Sports sponsoring is achieved daily by the media. Businesses have discovered a new possibility for transmitting their messages to their potential clients. The reasons for involvement on a sporting level are varied: improving the name, maintaining an image, supporting promotional activities.

For the sponsor, the sponsored activity is part of the company's marketing communication plan, placed at the level of mass communication. The company can manipulate different elements, for example, *the place* – that is the way in which the product, by means of different channels, reaches the consumer –, *the product* (or the services), *the price*, *the promotion*.

In marketing strategy these elements are known as 'the four Ps', and mixed marketing is the term used to indicate the simultaneous presence of all these elements. Sports sponsoring is part of promotion.

The sponsor's objectives can concentrate on the effort to increase the brand's reputation, to improve the image, or even, to create goodwill.

In Belgium, sponsoring has become a very important part of the financing of many clubs or federations, including the National Olympic Committee.

In 1985, the Belgian Sports Sponsoring Association was set up. This non-profit organisation comprises mainly professional sponsors who claim that: 'The Sponsor accomplishes a "social educative duty".'

2. The National Legal System

The Belgian legal system, as in most European continental countries, is based on a written Constitution, various Codes (e.g. Civil and Commercial Codes) and also Acts of Parliament.

However, readers should bear in mind that Belgium has engaged in the process to federalise with the result that in many areas the powers to legislate have already been transferred from the central State to the Communities (French, Flemish and German) or the Regions.

European Community Law prevails over domestic regulations and has also become an essential source of Belgian law in all matters covered by the Treaty. It should, therefore, be considered while dealing with the various legal aspects of sports marketing.

The Belgian judicial system may be generally defined as a two level courts system – first instance and appeal – capped with the Supreme Court ('Cour de Cassation'). Courts are specialised according to the nature of the dispute and categorised into Small Claims Local Courts, Civil, Commercial or Labour Tribunals and the Courts of Appeal.

3. Applicable Laws

There are no statutory provisions specifically applicable to sports marketing, but instead, as in the UK, a diversity of legal instruments, including statutes, various provisions of the Civil or Commercial Codes and case law applies.

As in the UK, under the freedom of contract doctrine the parties are free to make whatever bargain they wish. According to the Civil Code and, subject to general principles of contract law, for example, dealing with its formation, interpretation, enforcement, and compliance with public policy, the provisions of the agreement will be considered as the 'law of the parties'.

4. Intellectual Property Rights

4.1. Trademarks

Belgium is signatory to a number of international instruments such as the Paris Convention,[1] the Madrid Agreement,[2] the Vienna Treaty[3] and the Nice Agreement regarding the International Classification of Goods and Services.[4]

The national law in Belgium is governed by the Benelux Convention, signed on 19 March 1962, containing the Uniform Benelux Law on Product Trade

1. Ratified by the Belgian law of 5.7.1884 (Belgian *Official Journal* of 6.7.1884), last amended in Stockholm on 14.7.1967, implemented by the Belgian law of 26.9.1974 (Belgian *Official Journal* of 29.1.1975).
2. Ratified by the Belgian law of 13.6.1892, Belgian *Official Journal* of 31.8.1892.
3. Ratified by the Belgian law of 14.2.1962 (Belgian *Official Journal* of 14.7.1965), last amended in Geneva on 13.5.1977 and implemented by the Belgian law of 15.5.1984 (Belgian *Official Journal* of 22.5.1985).
4. Belgian *Official Journal* of 14.7.1965, last amended by the Belgian law of 15.5.1984, published in the *Official Journal* of 22.5.1985.

Marks that came into force on 1 January 1971.[5] One must also take into account a few remaining provisions of the Belgian domestic law of 1 April 1879, as amended by the Royal Decree of 29 January 1935.[6]

The scope of the Uniform Benelux Law has been extended to trademarks related to services by the Protocol, signed in November 1983, which came into force on 1 January 1987.

One generally refers to the Benelux Convention as the 'Uniform Law'. Article 1 defines a trademark as 'any denominations, drawings, seals, letters, numerals, forms of products or packagings and all other signs used to distinguish the products of a company'.

The exclusive right to use the mark is granted to the owner subject to the prior registration thereof. However, the registration will not confer any right if the use of the mark is misleading for the public about the nature, composition, content, qualities or origin of the product. A misleading trademark will be declared void.

The application is made on a special form, either in French or the Dutch language, to the Benelux Office of Trade Marks ('Bureau Benelux des Marques') located in The Hague or to one of the national administrations. The application made in one of the three Benelux countries automatically extends the protection to the others. The 'Bureau Benelux' is also competent to process the application for international registrations based on the Madrid Agreement.

In practice, the application is very often filed by specialised patents or trademarks agents, who also carry out the search of anteriority and assist the applicant in relation to the classification.

The publicity of applications and further registrations are organised by two means. First, by the Registry which mentions all the applications, whether Benelux or international, which are accessible to the public (in Brussels, The Hague and Luxembourg). Second, by the *Recueil des Marques – Benelux Merkenblad*, which is the monthly publication of the 'Bureau Benelux' and contains indications regarding all Benelux or international applications.

Under the Benelux Convention, no application can be rejected *ex officio* and no procedure is organised to oppose the application. The courts have exclusive jurisdiction to arbitrate any dispute in relation to the Uniform Benelux Law, including the competence to declare a registered trademark void.

When the registration is completed, a certificate is delivered to the applicant.

The protection is granted for 10 years and is renewable for similar periods indefinitely. The protection may be cancelled if the trademark has not been used within 3 years of the application for registration or if its use has been interrupted for more than 5 years.

Any transfer, assignment or licensing of a mark must be made in writing and recorded in the Registry.

5. Benelux Uniform Law, signed in Brussels on 19.3.1962, amended on 10.11.1983 (Belgian *Official Journal* of 30.10.1986).
6. Belgian *Official Journal* of 8.2.1935.

In case of any infringement, the Uniform Law provides legal remedies to any person having an interest, including individuals, companies or other moral persons, for example, consumer associations and the public prosecutor.

4.2. Copyright

Belgium is a signatory to the Berne Convention on Copyright, whilst at the national level copyright is governed by the Belgian Law of 22 March 1886. A thorough reform is planned and a draft proposal is currently under discussion by Parliament.

Belgium is also a signatory to the European Agreement of the European Council of 22 June 1960, as amended on 22 January 1965, in relation to the protection of television broadcasting, ratified by the Belgian Law of 14 January 1968.[7]

Although some conditions of the Benelux Convention on Trade Marks could provide some protection,[8] copyright law usually secures the protection of designs and models.[9]

Copyright exists automatically and is not subject to any registration and remains for the lifetime and fifty years after the author's death. However, authors can secure their copyright by registering their work with specific bodies, e.g. the 'SABAM' ('Société Belge des Auteurs et Compositeurs de Musique').

Unlike French Law, for instance, Belgian law does not formally require that an assignment of copyright should be effected in writing. However, as the Code of Civil Procedure states that any disputes in copyright matters are of the exclusive competence of the Tribunal of First Instance, a civil jurisdiction, and, as the Civil Code states that in civil matters the existence and terms of a contract made for a consideration in excess of 15,000 BF must be evidenced in writing, it is obvious that most of the copyright assignments require a written form.

Unlike the UK and as in many 'civil law' countries, in Belgium moral rights are the author's non-transferrable 'birthrights' which cannot be sold, assigned or waived.

In case of infringement of copyright, redress may be obtained in the form of a summary injunction or an action for damages in tort.

7. Belgian *Official Journal* of 6.3.1968.
8. Article 21 of the Benelux Convention.
9. Benelux Court of Justice, case 85/3, *Screenoprints* v. *Citroën Nederland*, 22 May 1987, *Journal des Tribunaux*, 1987, p. 570.

4.3. Unfair Competition

Unfair competition and trade practices are governed in Belgium by the Law of 14.7.1971, as amended by the Law of 14.7.1991[10] in relation to Trade Practices and Consumer Information and Protection.

The law prohibits any act contrary to fair practices in commercial matters by which a trader prejudices or attempts to prejudice the business interests of one or several other traders or attempts to prejudice the interests of one or several consumers.

A professional trader has the obligation to provide in 'good faith' the consumer with fair and useful information in relation to the characteristics of the product or the service offered.

Unfair competition is regarded as constituting an unlawful trade practice.

According to Belgian case law, the use of an unlawful trademark or a misleading advertisement to promote a product will be considered as being an unfair trade practice.

Infringements of the 1991 Trade Practices Law give rise to civil actions in tort for damages and, in certain cases, to criminal prosecution. In addition, the law provides a special remedy for the victims, either competitors, traders or consumers having a personal interest, in the form of a summary procedure before the President of the Commercial Court. This action is designed to allow the plaintiff to obtain an injunction whereby the court will order a trader to stop infringing the law or committing unfair trade practices, subject to an automatic fine if the trader does not immediately comply with the terms of the injunction.

5. The Contract Generally and Preliminary Agreements

In many cases, the conclusion of a contract is preceded by contacts, talks, negotiations and the drafting of working papers. The legal effects of those preliminary stages deserve some comments.

In principle, letters of intent or preliminary agreements cannot be considered as generating contractual obligations.

Following the common saying that 'as long as one does not agree on everything, one does agree on nothing', negotiators have the right to break off the negotiations as part of the freedom of trade. As a temper to that principle, the breaking off of negotiations might, according to the circumstances – for instance, if made in bad faith – give rise to an action in tort seeking damages.

Option rights may be granted. The option is considered as an unilateral contract as it imposes obligations only upon the promisor. The promisee will be bound only if he exercises the option. The option must be exercised within the time limit stated in the contract.

---

10. Belgian *Official Journal* of 29.8.1991. The Act came into force on 29 February 1992.

The principles of the law of contracts in Belgium are to be found in the Civil Code. To be valid, the contract needs to satisfy four requirements: the intention to create legally binding obligations; the capacity to do so; a consideration; and a lawful cause.

The contract is not required to be made in writing to be valid. In commercial matters its existence may be evidenced by any means legally admissible, including eye witnesses. However, in civil matters, the existence and the terms of a contract made for a consideration in excess of 15,000 BF can only be evidenced by a written instrument.

A contract may be void in case of error on the substance or lack of consent, as well as where it was made for an unlawful purpose, or for a cause found to be against public policy.

In principle, according to the privity of contract doctrine, a contract is only effective as between the parties and does not create rights or obligations towards third parties. However, a third party who in full knowledge helps one of the parties to breach the contract might be held liable for damages in tort.

Interpretation, frustration or breach of a contract are governed by the relevant provisions of the Belgian Civil Code. However, any agreement should contain specific clauses regarding those issues and be drafted in accordance with the commercial and financial requirements of each contractual situation.

Under Belgian law, the parties may freely choose the law under which their contract shall be governed, subject to public policy or compliance with mandatory statutory regulations.

If the parties do not express any specific choice, the contract will be governed by 'the proper law of the contract', that is to say, the law with which the contract presents the closest links.

In that respect, Belgium is a signatory to the Convention of Rome of 19 June 1980 in relation to the law applicable to the contractual obligations, which came into force on 1 April 1991 (Belgian *Official Journal* of 16.4.1991).

The parties should put in the contract a special clause to determine which court shall have jurisdiction over their possible disputes. In that respect, they should consider the provisions of the Brussels Convention of 23 September 1968, as amended in Lugano on 16 September 1988, on jurisdiction and the enforcement of judgments in civil and commercial matters,[11] in particular Articles 5.1, 16.4, and 17 (prorogation of jurisdiction).

6. Standard Contract Terms

Factual and legal issues that should be carefully considered when negotiating and drafting a contract related to sports marketing in Belgium do not basically differ from those in other countries, except for those designed to comply with domestic regulations, whether national or regional.

11. JO L 319 of 25.11.1988.

The standard contract terms will cover, amongst other issues, the identification of the parties (companies, clubs, federations or committees, consortium of sponsors, advertising companies, non-profit organisations, individuals); the purpose and duration (a single event, one or several sports seasons, an indefinite period of time);[12] the rights and obligations of the parties; the *intuitu personae* clause and the prohibition to transfer or assign the contract; the territory; the financial terms (lump sum, payment of royalties, assistance 'in kind', accounting, audit of accounts, conditions and period of payments, penalties); exclusivity clause; liability towards partner(s) as well as third parties; insurance provisions; advertising and promotion (including TV, radio, video, film); secrecy and confidentiality during and after termination; protection of the image and reputation of the sponsor; termination; breach of contract, rescission and penalties provisions; the *force majeure* clause; the address for service; applicable law; dispute resolution.

As regards the protection of the image and reputation of the sponsor, it has been held in *SA Proserv-City* v. *SA Herz Europe* that the 'sponsored party has a duty to abstain from any act or statement that might prejudice the image of the sponsor or the sponsored event'.[13]

When drafting their agreement, sponsors and sponsored parties should pay close attention to the regulations of the relevant national or international sports governing bodies. For instance, the Belgian Cycling Federation does not authorise a change of sponsors during the professional cycling season. Following its Charter, the International Olympic Committee holds the negotiations with television networks for royalties to the athletes and defines which are the intellectual rights to be protected. However, on various recent occasions, the monopoly of these bodies to rule the sports disciplines has been successfully challenged.

In the *Belgian Public Radio-TV Institutes/Union Royale Belge de Football Association (URBFA)* v. *KV Mechelen Football Club and VTM* (a private TV broadcasting company) case, the club had granted by contract to VTM the exclusive rights in relation to the live transmission of the UEFA Cup match against Eintracht Frankfurt. The public radio and television institutes (BRT/RTB) and URBFA tried to oppose the enforcement of the contract on the grounds, first, that according to its own regulations, the URBFA had the exclusive competence to authorise the retransmissions of football matches; second, that there was a 5 year agreement between BRT/RTB and the URBFA, whereby the latter conferred on the public networks the exclusivity of broadcasting football matches.

12. The experience shows that unless they are made for a specific event, e.g. a professional cycling race, the majority of sponsorship contracts are made for a rather short term to face the incertitude regarding advertising return and sporting fortune of the sponsored party. The contracts are seldom made for more than 3 years.
13. Tribunal of Commerce of Brussels, 14.6.1989, *Revue de droit commercial Belge*, 1990, p. 421.

The President of the Tribunal of First Instance of Brussels held, in a summary order, that the club retained its property rights over the venue, including the assignment of the broadcasting rights, and that the disputed 5 year agreement was a *res inter alios acta* and consequently could not be used against the club.[14]

In *Markakis* v. *Fédération Royale des Sociétés de Basketball*, the same Tribunal held that Community law, in this case Articles 7 and 48 of the Treaty, prevails over any regulations of national federations or sports bodies.[15] A similar decision has been reached in *Bosmans* v. *Football Club Liège*.[16] The case is still pending a preliminary ruling before the European Court of Justice in Luxembourg.

7. Different Types of Business Arrangements

It is not possible within the scope of this chapter to consider all kinds of sports marketing arrangements available to the parties.

The most common agreements however include sponsorship, where the sponsor provides financial support or assistance in kind in return for different rights, licensing and merchandising, related to the use of intellectual or industrial property rights; and suppliership, granting to the sponsor the exclusive rights to supply specific products or services and advertising himself as the 'official supplier'.

As previously stated, sports marketing is not governed in Belgium by any particular statutory instrument. The terms of each agreement, including rights, obligations and liabilities of the parties, should be carefully detailed in the contract.

8. The Rights

A great variety of rights are available to sponsors, suppliers or licensees in connection with the organisation or the support of sports events. As regards Belgium, the examination of dozens of agreements reveals that in many cases contracts in relation to sports marketing are very brief and do not cover more than 3 to 5 typed pages. Coupled with the fact that these agreements are usually made for a short term, it seems that mutual confidence between sponsors and sponsored parties is a key issue in sports marketing. However, a few rights deserve a short comment.

---

14. Summary Order, 15.3.1989, *Journal des Procès*, 24.3.1989, p. 29.
15. Summary Order of 14.9.1992, not yet published, referring to European Court of Justice judgments in *Walrave* of 12.12.1974 (case 36/74) and *Dona* of 14.7.1976 (case 13/76).
16. Civil tribunal of Liège, summary order, *Jurisprudence Liège Bruxelles Mons*, 1990, p. 1442.

8.1. Pre-emption

Upon termination of the contract, the sponsor should always ensure, by a special provision, his priority right of renewal.

8.2. Copyright and Trademark Licence

The owner of the copyright, trademark, logo or design gives the right to use them in consideration of royalties. The sponsor should check if the purpose of the licence deserves legal protection. Otherwise, there is no point in paying royalties. For instance, it is very dubious that logos like 'Mexico 86' or 'Euro 92' could give rise to any legal protection.

8.3. Advertising Rights

For the sponsor, advertising and promotion rights are of the essence of the agreement. The obligations of the sponsored in relation thereto should be drafted in every detail. This could cover the nature of advertising available to the sponsor (newspapers, radio and TV, magazines, programmes); the technical issues (e.g. placement in the stadium of a 30 metres long panel in front of the TV cameras); and the quantum of advertising (e.g. the sponsor logo must appear at least 5 seconds or 5 times on TV in any broadcasting hour, the sponsored must advertise the event by displaying at least 200 posters where the logo of the sponsor appears).

9. Financial Terms

Considering the different types of sponsorship agreement possible and the wide variety of situations that one could come across, the financial terms should be clearly defined in each particular contract.

According to the Civil Code, damages for late payment of monies are limited to legal interest subject to a prior notice to the debtor. It is, therefore, essential to introduce specific penalty provisions in the contract stipulating a higher interest rate applying automatically and without notice of late payment, without prejudice to other remedies, including a claim for further damages.

Penalties for late or default of payments may be expressed in terms of an automatic percentage of the overdue balance.

As the Belgian Civil Code provides for the automatic offset of the mutual debts when two persons are indebted towards one another, the right of set-off should be expressly excluded by a special provision in the contract, if it is not to apply in a particular case.

It should be stressed that there are no exchange control restrictions or limitations on capital flow in Belgium. A declaration to the Belgo-Luxembourg Exchange Office is the only requirement.

Potential sponsors should bear in mind that, according to the Belgian Income Tax Code, expenses and charges are not deductible in so far as they exceed unreasonably the professional needs. Deductible expenses are those that are 'made or borne for the purpose of acquiring or retaining taxable income'.

On the other end, contributions received by the sponsored shall, in principle, be considered as a taxable income, unless it could be absorbed by the cost of the organisation of the sponsored event. As an exception, the Belgian law exempts income received by sporting clubs in relation to the renting of advertising spaces inside their premises!

Therefore, it is often advisable to set up a non-profit organisation under Belgian law which shall be in charge of the organisation of the event and which shall collect the sponsors' contributions.

10. Insurance Aspects

Sponsors generally do not insure their public liability, but usually they transfer this task to the organiser. The organiser will insure the event and, of course, reinsure 95% of the risk with a reinsurance company (generally Lloyd's).

However, all foreseeable liabilities that an organiser, sponsor, licensor or licensee, merchandiser or any other party may incur in relation to the venue should always be carefully considered while negotiating a sports marketing contract.

Under Belgian law, in tort the organiser of a sports event is liable towards the public for their safety and security. To satisfy this obligation, he would be required to exercise the standard of care of the *reasonable person*. According to the circumstances, his liability may be either contractual (e.g. towards a paying spectator) or in tort (towards the public in general).

Amongst insurable contingencies are several strict liabilities in tort, including the liability of the owner for defective premises, or default of maintenance, and the liability of the organiser/employer for damage caused to the public by an employee.

Defective product liability may also arise from sponsorship, licensing or merchandising agreements. Belgium has implemented the 85/374/EEC Directive on Liability for Defective Products by a Law passed on 22 March 1991.

Without going into the details of the respective advantages of the different legal grounds for liability available, under Belgian law the plaintiff has the choice to base his claim either on the strict liability created by the Directive, or on the common liability in tort, without prejudice to possible contractual liability.

Unlike the strict liability for defective products under the EEC Directive, contractual liability or common liability in tort may be expressly waived, except in the case of wilful fault.

11. Advertising and Promotion

Public advertising was originally governed by the Belgian Law relating to 'Trade Practices' of 14 July 1971, which has been completely amended by the Law of 14 July 1991.

The Law defines advertising as being 'any communication having as its direct or indirect purpose to promote the sale of a product or a service, wherever it is made and whatever means of communication are used'.

The Law also prohibits any communication that contains indications, affirmations or representations that may be misleading as regards the identity, nature, composition, origin, quality, method of manufacture or characteristics of a product. The terms of the prohibition have been directly inspired by the 84/450/EEC Directive of 10 September 1984 relating to the approximation of the laws, regulations and administrative provisions of Member States concerning misleading advertising, that came into force on 1 October 1986.[17] Belgium failed to take necessary measures to implement the Directive in time and was brought before the EC Court of Justice in Luxembourg on the basis of Article 169 of the EEC Treaty.[18]

Commercial advertising on public radio and television networks was authorised for the first time in Belgium in 1987.[19]

Belgium being in the process of federalisation, the competencies to legislate on radio and television matters have been transferred to the French, Flemish and German Communities. In the process, the Law of 6 February 1987 has been amended, *inter alia* by a Decree of the Flemish Community of 21 June 1991, a Decree of the French Community of 19 July 1991, and by the German Community of 16 February 1990.[20]

These statutory instruments include special provisions that govern the sponsoring of radio and television programmes in line with the Directive 89/522/EEC of 3 October 1989.[21]

Broadcast and non-broadcast commercial spots are subject to a variety of statutory restrictions considering the nature of the product/service advertised. There is a general prohibition to advertise tobacco products, drugs and medica-

17. EEC *Official Journal* L 150 of 19.9.1984, p. 17.
18. Judgment of the European Court of Justice of 16.11.1989, Case 360/88, *Commission* v. *Belgium*, *Recueil de la Jurisprudence de la Cour de Justice*, 1989, p. 3803.
19. Law of 6.2.1987 and Royal Decree of 3.8.1987, in relation to the radio and television distribution networks and to the conditions of inserting commercial advertising into TV and radio programmes, public or private. In the same respect, local radio stations (short waves) are governed by a Royal Decree of 20.8.1981.
20. See also the Decree of the French Community of 17.7.1987 relating to audiovisual matters, the Arrêtés of the Executif of the French Community of 21.11.1989 and 3.5.1991 fixing the conditions of commercial advertising on radio and television, and the Arrêté of the Executif of the Flemish Community of 31.7.1990 establishing the Advertising Code.
21. Directive relating to radio and television broadcasting activities, OJ L 298, 17.10.1989, p.23. The Directive has not yet been passed into Belgian law.

tions on radio and television.[22] Other restrictions concern products and services, for example life insurance, cars, education by correspondence, cosmetics, alcohol, foodstuffs.

Comparative advertising is allowed, subject to strict conditions, since the Trade Practices Law of 1991.

12. The Venue

The sports event is not as such directly linked to the sponsorship agreement although certain aspects of the venue are likely to affect the agreement or the situation of the sponsor.

From the sponsor's point of view, the main concerns are, first, to ensure that he shall not bear any liability for the happenings and, second, that his contractual rights will be enforced.

12.1. Public Liability

The event organiser is responsible for the organisation of the venue and compliance with the relevant regulations issued by the sports ruling bodies, either national or international, and the national authorities of the country where it takes place.

Under the Belgian Civil Law on tort, the organiser will be liable for damage or personal injuries sustained by third parties resulting from his fault, negligence or lack of precaution. In addition, when personal injuries are sustained, the organiser faces criminal liability under the Belgian Criminal Law.

In Belgium, however, the responsibility for the sports event is not only vested in the organiser but may be jointly and severally shared with other persons or relevant bodies, including national or local authorities involved in the organisation of the venue, for example, the Fire and Police Departments.

These principles have been highlighted after the tragedy of the European Cup final between Liverpool and Juventus Turino in 1985. In the *Heysel Stadium* case,[23] criminal charges were brought not only against several board members of the Belgian Football Federation and the UEFA (as organisers), but also against officers of the Gendarmerie and the Police Departments who were in charge of ensuring the safety and the security of the public inside and outside the stadium.

22. Royal Decree of 5.3.1980 (Belgian *Official Journal* of 14.3.1980). See also the Commercial Advertising on Radio and Television Code passed by the Flemish Executif of 31.7.1990 (Belgian *Official Journal* of 14.12.1990).

23. Criminal Court of Brussels, 28.4.1989, *Journal des Tribunaux*, 1989; p. 697; Court of Appeal of Brussels, 26.6.1990, *Journal des Tribunaux*, 1991, p. 106; Supreme Court of Belgium, 16.10.1991, not yet published.

Accordingly, the sponsor should be wise and include in the agreement a provision clearly stating that he takes no part in the organisation and cannot be held liable therefor. This provision should be carefully drafted according to the particular circumstances of each situation.

12.2. Control

The compliance with safety and security measures in relation to the venue is basically a matter for the responsibility of the event organiser.

The passive measures involve the respect of a wide range of statutory instruments and administrative regulations regarding the specifications, equipments and fittings of the stadium or the premises where the event takes place. Shaken by the Heysel Stadium tragedy, Belgium has been very active since 1985 in regulating safety and security in stadia.[24]

The active measures are basically vested in the organiser and the police forces which are responsible for the safety and the security of the public on the premises and their vicinity during the event.

Belgium is also a signatory to the 'Convention européenne sur la violence et les débordements lors de manifestations sportives et notamment de matches de football', signed in Strasbourg on 19 August 1985.[25]

Although this matter is not directly related to the sponsorship agreement, the contract should contain a provision stating that if the sponsored party fails to comply with all relevant statutory or administrative requirements, the sponsor shall be entitled to rescind the contract.

A problem that essentially arises in relation to open stadia is that of the control and the use of the airspace above the installations. Under Belgian law, the basis of property rights has not changed since 1803, when Napoleon issued the Civil Code. Article 553 states literally that 'the ownership of the soil involves the ownership of the above and the underneath'. This assumption has to be moderated. The owner certainly has the right to use the immediate airspace above his property and to oppose intrusions or trespasses. He could, for instance, seek an injunction to prevent a tower crane from swinging over the property.

In practice, the right to use the immediate airspace is significantly limited by administrative and statutory regulations, including a Royal Decree of 13 February 1989 fixing the airspace general regulations, which also govern flights of (advertising) balloons, and a Royal Decree of 30 June 1989 in relation to flights of light aircraft pulling advertising streamers. Actually, the use of the

---

24. See Royal Decree of 17.7.1989 fixing prescriptions in relation to the protection of spectators against fire and panic during sports events in '*à ciel ouvert*' installations and also the Manual regarding Security in Football Stadia, issued by an Advisory Commission, last updated in 1991.
25. Ratified by the Law of 18.4.1989 (Belgian *Official Journal* of 7.10.1990).

airspace, in most cases, will be subject to an authorisation by the Minister of the Aeronautical Administration and the Local Authorities.

12.3. Sponsor Access and Protection

Under the sponsorship agreement, the sponsor is usually granted different types of rights in relation to the venue.

A first type concerns the access of the sponsor to the event. As a part of the agreement the sponsor will be offered a number of business or official seats, VIP parking spaces for its own staff members, guests or clients.

The sponsor will also reserve the access to and use of the organiser's facilities (restaurant, conference room, press centre).

Other kinds of right more directly related to the advertising and the promotion of the sponsor's products and services may be secured by specific provisions in the sponsorship agreement (e.g. promotional displays).

The sponsor shall ensure by a specific provision the right to have free access to the organiser's facilities during the event in order to control the enforcement of the contract and the respect of its contractual rights.

13. Dispute Resolution

13.1. Court Action

An action would be brought in the Court of First Instance, either the civil or the commercial section, depending on the nature of the dispute or the exclusive competence that might be set by the law (e.g. in matters related to copyright).

In principle, the Belgian Civil Procedure Code still allows the court to require, under certain conditions, a deposit from foreign plaintiffs to cover the costs. This provision, however, has been deprived of most of its effects by the The Hague Convention of 3 January 1954 on civil procedure and the Brussels Convention of 23 September 1968, as amended in Lugano on 16 September 1988, on the jurisdiction and the enforcement of judgments in civil and commercial matters.[26]

The procedure is initiated by the service of a writ of summons upon the defendant.

The procedure is divided into two parts. At the first stage, the parties lodge their pleadings at the court and disclose their files containing the documents relied on in support of them. In some cases, the court may appoint experts to report on factual or technical evidence. After the preparatory written procedure has been completed, the court must fix a date for the oral procedure, the second stage. Usually, in civil and commercial matters, the oral procedure consists of

26. Articles 17 and 18 of The Hague Convention and 45 of the Brussels Convention.

one single hearing in which the lawyers sum up factual, technical and legal issues involved in the dispute.

Legal costs
Unlike in many other countries, costs are not in the discretion of the court and only part of them is paid by the losing party.

Usually, the court must 'tax' the costs of the writ of summons, the sums paid to the expert(s) and a lump sum set by the law (less than £200 in first instance!) which is totally inadequate to compensate the expenses incurred by the successful party for the purpose of the proceedings, in particular, the lawyer's remuneration.

The outcome, therefore, of the proceedings, is often very disappointing and financially sore for the 'successful' party, who will never really be compensated.

13.2. Arbitration

Very often, sponsors and federations will prefer to submit their disputes to arbitration, for reasons of confidentiality and to avoid the excessive duration of court actions.

Unless expressly excluded (e.g. actions directly related to the Benelux Uniform Law on Trade Marks), the parties are free to resolve their disputes by arbitration, whether they are related to patent, copyright, licensing, franchising or sponsoring matters.

Belgium has translated into its Judicial Code the provisions of the Uniform Law attached to the European Convention on Arbitration Matters, signed in Strasbourg on 20 January 1966.

The arbitration agreement must be evidenced by a written instrument. There is no appeal based on the facts or merits available against the award. A court can only declare the decision of the arbitrator(s) void in limited cases, for example, in cases of violation of public policy or the rights of the defence. The court also has jurisdiction to authorise the compulsory enforcement of the award.

Belgium is a signatory to the New York Convention of 10 June 1958 on the Recognition and Enforcement of Foreign Arbitral Awards, approved on 5 June 1975, and to the European Convention on International Commercial Arbitration, signed in Geneva on 21 April 1961, approved on 19 July 1975.

The Czech Republic

by Martin Maisner

1. Sports Marketing – A Business

Czechoslovakia[1] traditionally has a very strong sports background and tradition. The most popular sports are soccer, ice hockey, volleyball, tennis, skiing, rallying, car and motorcycle races.

Sports marketing, as a business, is a relatively new feature in the Czech business environment. The business structure of the Czech Republic started to develop after the political changes of 1989, as a result of which the ability to privately own and to start private businesses developed rapidly. The newness of sports marketing as a business is certainly connected with the problem that sports and sports clubs for the last 42 years were organised under the authority of the Union of Czechoslovak Sports, which was governed by the Communist Party and treated and managed in accordance with the political needs of the Communists. It meant, in practice, that some of the sports were paid substantial sums for their performance, because the development of such sports was in accordance with the plan of the Government, Party and the Association of Sports. Other sports suffered, because they did not receive any donations from the State.

Since the 'Velvet' Revolution, the situation has changed substantially. Under present circumstances, the State, in the midst of economic reform, has no funds to donate to all branches of sports activity on a substantial level and, in fact, is not willing to do so. Sports clubs are transforming themselves into specific legal entities, varying from limited liability companies, co-operatives, and joint-stock companies to associations established under the Civil Code, and such entities behave in the new business environment in Czechoslovakia according to the rules relevant to their legal form.

---

1. The nation-state of Czechoslovakia no longer exists. However, since both the Czech Republic and Slovakia have inherited much of their legislation from the former Czechoslovakia, the term continues to be used in this Chapter. Much of this Chapter, therefore, is also valid for Slovakia.

Although the Czech and Slovak Federal Republic have split into two independent or semi-independent sovereign States, no major changes in legislation or development in the States has ensued.

2. The National Legal System

The Czech legal system is based on a codified civil law system. Current legislation finds its source in Austrian legislation from before 1918. It was modified during the period between the World Wars, then substantially modified during the so-called 'socialist period of development' and, after 1989, modified hopefully for the last time according to Western European standards. Except for some local specialities, the Czech legal system is comparable to the Austrian or German legislation.

Legislation is generally divided into four basic codes: Penal (Criminal) Code, Civil Code, Commercial Code and Labour Code. Other areas are regulated by separate laws. Procedural rules are found in the Civil Procedural Order, the Criminal Procedural Order, the Administrative Procedural Order and the Civil Construction Procedural Order.

The legislative procedure and system is being amended and refined continuously. Approximately 600 new laws are passed by the Parliament every year and there are still areas which require substantial legislative attention.

2.1. The Court System

The court system in the Czech Republic consists of three basic types of court: the so-called ordinary courts dealing with ordinary civil law plus criminal law; the commercial courts, newly established on the ruins of the so-called State Arbitrary Body, deciding business affairs; and the system of military courts dealing with servicemen and special criminal charges. On a vertical level, the courts are divided into District Courts, Regional Courts, and the Supreme Court. Ordinary courts begin at the district level, and commercial courts begin at the regional level.

The Czech Republic has a one-appeal system, which means the decision of the first instance court is not final, but one can seek an appeal in a court of higher level. In the event that the first instance court is the District Court, following the appeal proceedings at the second instance court the appellant may be given an extra chance to appeal to the Supreme Court. Except for these regular appeal procedures, there are several instruments of so-called irregular means of revocation, but these are not relevant to sports marketing.

Trials are administered and ruled by single professional judges elected and nominated for life by the Parliament, upon the proposal of the Ministry of Justice. No jury system operates. However, criminal cases and selected civil cases are decided by a tribunal composed of one professional judge and two non-lawyer judges.

Personal presence at the court is required, at least at the beginning of the proceedings, where each party has to present a personal statement before the court. During the proceedings each party may be represented either by a professional lawyer or by any third person. Professional legal services are rendered by the Czech Bar Association (members of the bar are called 'advocates') and the Chamber of Commercial Lawyers (members are called 'commercial lawyers'). Although these two associations have agreed to merge before the end of 1994, currently they represent two options of professional legal representation. The basic difference is that commercial lawyers cannot represent clients at higher courts and their activity is limited to 'commercial and adjacent disputes'. As mentioned above, any party may be represented by any third person, even without a legal education (except in cases of criminal defence), provided that such representation is on a non-paid basis.

2.2. Sources of National Law

The only permitted sources of national law are Acts and Bills passed by the Parliament or Parliaments. The courts decide upon the law, which is written and published, and the law itself contains rules for its interpretation. However, no civil law system gives an entire coverage for all available variation. For that purpose, the decisions of the Supreme Court are published as precedents: they are not the source of the law but are recommended rules of interpretation.

In the environment of the Federal State containing two Republics with their own legislative procedures, there were several degrees of legislation. The main and most powerful were Constitutional Acts, governing most important issues of the State. These Acts were considered to be part of the Constitution and a backbone of the legal system. The other sources of law were the following: Acts of the Federal Parliament; Federal Government Rulings; Acts of the Czech or Slovak Parliament (Called Czech or Slovak National Council); Republic Government Rulings; and Procedural Rules of the Ministry. Municipalities and local authorities had limited legislative powers derived from the basic legislation, but the basic rule is that the law of lower force (i.e. passed by a lower legislative body) cannot amend a law of stronger force.

After dissolution of Czechoslovakia into the Czech Republic and the Slovak Republic, the situation regarding the previous legislation is that all legislation, including federal laws, remain in legal force unless amended by the legislative bodies of the new Czech or Slovak Republics. New amendments apply only in the territory of the respective Republic.

3. Applicable Laws

There is no special legislation concerning marketing in general or sports marketing in particular. This area of activity and its legal regulations depend on the position and legal form of the entity involved. In the Czech situation there might be substantial differences depending on whether the entities involved are established according to the Civil Code or the Commercial Code. In any case, this kind of activity is governed by the general applicable laws since no special regulation(s) exists.

For sports marketing, both the Civil Code and the Commercial Code may apply. The basic difference for the application of these Codes is whether the contractual relationship covers only entrepreneurial entities, or if individuals with no commercial status are involved at any level.

One other possibility is that one party of the contract is a foreign legal entity. In such a case, parties have the right to choose foreign law as a governing law. Such a contract will be deemed to be fully valid and enforceable under Czech law.

4. Intellectual Property Rights

4.1. Trademarks

In the Czech Republic there is specific legislation in this area based on the fact that the Czech Republic is a signatory to the Vienna Treaty, the Madrid Agreements, and the Paris Convention on Trademarks.

The basic legal protection of a duly registered trademark is for a period of ten years. The owner of the trademark has the right to renew the protection for further periods of ten years, provided that the owner applies for the further period in the last year of the existing period of protection.

The authority responsible for the registration of trademarks cannot register as a trademark:

(a) only the plain name or a picture of the product;
(b) only the official name or a general geographical name or description;
(c) a false or misleading name or marking;
(d) a trademark identical to an already known trademark;
(e) the name of a protected plant or protected animal;
(f) labelling, the use of which may be against public favour;
(g) labelling, the use of which is contrary to the international obligations of the Czech Republic; and
(h) a trademark containing the official name of the State, authority, or the name or a portrait of a person other than the applicant.

The application for registration of a trademark may be submitted only through a Czech licensed lawyer or patent agent.

There is no such requirement for trademarks which will remain protected for the registered period even though not used.

4.2. Copyright

The Czech Republic is a signatory to the Berne Convention on Copyright. Therefore, Czech legislation is in union with the international treaties and is more or less comparable to EC standards.

Under this legislation an 'author' enjoys both assignable and non-assignable ('personal') authorship rights. Non-assignable authorship rights are:

- right to be named as an author;
- right to the integrity of the work; and
- right to be fairly compensated for the work.

The only assignable authorship rights are the right to use the author's work and the copyright. Basic protection is during the life of the author and 50 years after his death (in the case of co-authorship 50 years after the death of the last surviving author). In case the work was published during the last 10 years of the protection period, the protection is prolonged to a period of 10 years from the date of publication. Anonymous and pseudo-anonymous works are protected for a period of 50 years from their publication. Film works are protected for a period of 10 years. Articles and works presented in compilations and magazines are protected for a period of 10 years. Photographs are protected for the period of life of the author plus ten years after his death.

4.3. Registered Designs

Registered designs are protected for a period of 5 years, which can be prolonged twice for the same period each time.

4.4. Unfair Competition

In the area of unfair competition, the Czech Republic does maintain a slightly different position. Czech competition law is more or less simple and not particularly restrictive. The reason for this is that, as there is nearly no competition in the country, it is necessary to adopt some rules of competition law simply to encourage the people to enter into competition. The rules of unfair competition are stipulated by the Commercial Code, where unfair competition is deemed to be such conduct that is contrary to the standard practices of competition and that may be detrimental to other competitors or consumers.

Unfair competition is deemed to be a prohibited activity and the Commercial Code distinguishes between the following types of unfair competition:

(a) false advertising;
(b) deceitful description of goods and services;
(c) contributing to mistaken identity;

(d) parasitic exploitation of a competing company's goods or reputation;
(e) bribery;
(f) discrediting;
(g) disclosure of business secrets; and
(h) endangering consumers' health and environment.

After the basic legislative changes, the Agency for Commercial Competition has been established with the main task of applying an antitrust and anti-monopoly protection and developing some rules for enforcement. In the period of transition from a centrally planned economy with a majority of monopoly producers, to a market economy with healthy competition, this Agency has not made a great impression, probably because its powers are more formal than real and its staff is not at a high level.

5. The Contract Generally and Preliminary Agreements

According to the basic provisions of both the Commercial and Civil Codes, a contract is a manifestation of will interpreted according to the intention of the acting persons. Contractual freedom is the basic rule, provided that specific provisions of the law which cannot be altered by the agreement of the parties are followed. The will must be free and true and the person must act under three conditions:

(a) under no oppression or force;
(b) the legal act to be performed as indicated has to be clear and expressed accordingly, without any possibility of misinterpretation;
(c) the manifestation of will, which includes terms and expressions which may lead to interpretations, shall, if in doubt, be interpreted to the disadvantage of the party which used the said terms in negotiations first.

The basic elements crucial for the validity of a contract are as follows:

(a) Each of the parties must be described in the correct form and with the correct terms. For example, if there is a name of a sports club or a company and the address or legal form is wrong, such party may be deemed non-existing and the entire contract void.
(b) Each of the parties must be represented by an empowered person. A signature made by an apparently non-empowered person shall be deemed void and non-binding.
(c) The nature and substance of the contract must be clear and precisely expressed. The requirement of all legal acts is that they must be clear and exact. Legal acts which create an obligation which is not definable and not exact enough shall be deemed void.

Regarding the specific steps of an agreement, the first step will be the verification of existing legislation enabling the parties to create a preliminary agreement, if such preliminary agreement includes at least the substance of the future contract. The Commercial Code itself describes several types of contracts. For the purpose of sports marketing, we presume that a licensing contract, contract for work, mandate contract or commission agent contract, and to a certain extent a brokerage contract, may be used in this area.

In addition to these types, which are described in the Commercial Code, any party is empowered to conclude even such a contract which is not regulated as a certain type. However, should the parties not sufficiently identify the subject matter of their obligation then the contract shall be deemed void.

It is not necessary to deal with all aspects of law in each contract. Such things as interpretation of the law, breach of contract, liability for damages and *force majeure* are described in the Civil and Commercial Codes and, except for parties who wish to apply more rigid rules such as conventional fines and special liabilities, it is advisable to stay with the regulations of the Commercial Code.

Any agreement is created by an offer and its acceptance. Both parts may be in one deed or in two parts. Although written form is not necessary, it is definitely not advisable to make contracts other than in writing.

6. Standard Contract Terms

Since sports marketing is a relatively new activity in the Czech Republic, it is not possible to identify any standard terms. Sports marketing in the Czech Republic means all forms of sponsorship and financing of sports activities based on any relationship parties can imagine. The only limits are the rules generally applied by legislation, which means that no contract may be contradictory to the wording of the Commercial and Civil Codes and have as its intention the violation of third parties.

7. Different Types of Business Arrangements

7.1. Sponsorship Agreement

The most frequent arrangement for sports marketing in the Czech Republic at present is a sponsorship agreement. This is an 'innominate' contract, which is a type not specifically named in the Commercial Code. In such a contract, both parties are absolutely free to specify their mutual liabilities as they wish. The variety of current sports sponsorship contracts is extremely wide, because the needs differ so much between, for example, a tennis player being sponsored and the sports club having several sponsors and dealing with ten to fifteen types of sports activities. Sponsorship agreements of different forms and substance are the basis and main vehicle of sports marketing in the Czech Republic.

7.2. *Concessions/Franchises*

Franchise agreements are not specifically regulated by Czech legislation and the parties therefore have a considerable degree of contractual freedom.

8. The Rights

In general, there are no limitations concerning application of specific rights in the discussed agreements. However, it is advisable to keep in mind that, when structuring the deal, any waiver of future rights shall be deemed invalid and no person can legally bind a third party by the contract.

Options are not mentioned in Czech legislation. There is no restriction on granting an option, if this is created by agreement. In practice, it is advisable to use forms such as preliminary agreements, with one party having obligations, and the other having rights. This structure has the same effect as an option and is regulated by the legislation.

9. Financial Terms

The Commercial Code provides that 'penalty' interest for late payment can either be specifically agreed in the contract or calculated according to the formula of 'bank interest' plus 1%.

10. Insurance Aspects

For a long time, the only insurance company in Czechoslovakia was the State Insurance Company. With the privatisation of the insurance business, the market starts to be competitive and there are some new possibilities. In case the entities involved, either at the sports venue or in related marketing activities, are duly registered commercial entities, they have a duty to maintain a mandatory insurance for liability for damages caused by their activity to third parties.

In case the entire situation is based on a Civil Code relationship, the insurance coverage must be individually designed according to the particular circumstances.

The general approach of Czech legislation concerning liability for damages is as follows:

- general liability on a 'fault' basis (actual damage occurring plus breach of duty plus direct relationship between the breach and the damage);
- liability for damages caused by the operation of the business towards third parties on a 'non-fault' basis (based on the fact that each entrepreneur has a general duty to prevent damages), which liability is covered by a mandatory insurance; and
- criminal liability, which may occur by negligence of, for example, the organiser or an owner of the stadium causing a situation of 'public danger' (danger of death or serious health injury for at least 7 persons or danger of damage of a large financial amount), which liability is not insurable.

11. Advertising and Promotion

There is no specific regulation concerning advertisements related to sports with a restrictive effect. We can say that the only restrictions to the disclosure and display of advertisements and announcements are dealing with general rules of permitted and unpermitted subjects.

Currently, there is no ban on advertising of tobacco, alcohol and pharmaceuticals under Czech law. The only restrictions imposed are due to the regulations of international sports associations and federations, which impose their own restrictions on specific venues through their members.

12. The Venue

Rules concerning the organisation and staging of a sports event at a venue vary according to who is the owner of the facility and what are the relationships between the entities involved (owner, organiser, participants, municipality). Sports venues are organised in several ways and the difference is substantial.

Basically, the most regular case is that the owner of the stadium is the sports club which organises the venue and concludes related contracts with all the participants and media. In such cases, the liability of the club for maintaining and following all fire regulations, local legislation and damages caused to third parties by and during the event is unquestioned.

In case the organiser, owner and participants are in different positions, it is necessary to develop a system of mutual liabilities and obligations stipulated by mutual contracts.

13. Dispute Resolution

A particularly important subject in regard to the Czech Republic is dispute resolution and enforcement of the corresponding award. All courts in the Czech Republic are overworked because of the number of disputes and the limited number of judges. The period between filing a claim and the hearing in court is from two to three years and parties cannot expect their dispute to be resolved earlier than three to four years.

The current problem is that arbitration voluntarily applied between the parties is not permitted in the Czech Republic and such arrangements are not legally binding. The laws permitting arbitration between Czech and foreign entities is permitted because in such cases the parties have a right to choose foreign applicable law. The Czech Republic has surprisingly long experience in arbitration (Arbitration Court of the Czech Chamber of Commerce), because in the past Prague was one of the few places acceptable both for Western and USSR parties.

The question of the execution of judgments and awards is even worse than the court proceedings themselves. In the case of enforcement of foreign court judgments or arbitration awards, one has to follow the same procedures as in a court case.

The costs of court proceedings (including legal costs in a sum based on a calculation derived from the value of the dispute) are paid by the losing party. The amount may be modified at the discretion of the court. However, both parties have a right of appeal against any ruling on the legal costs.

SPORTS
MARKETING

Denmark

by Jan Thor Kroyer

1. Sports Marketing – A Business

From the start of the more organised sports, that is, the holding of rallies and competitions, prizes have been awarded to the winners. Such prize giving is not only of value to the one who receives it, but also to the giver, who gets his name mentioned, his product marketed in a positive way, and thus gets publicity. This form of marketing has existed for many years.

On the other hand, the concept 'sponsoring' has only been known for about 30 years, but only in the last 10 years has it gained a foothold, because of, amongst other things, the foundation of the 'TEAM-DANMARK Sportsmarketing' eight years ago.

'TEAM-DANMARK Sportsmarketing' is part of the institution 'TEAM DANMARK', which is backed by a majority in the Danish Parliament, the 'Folketing', and which was established in 1983 in order to encourage the development of élite sports in Denmark. Every year 'TEAM DANMARK' supports directly between 400 and 500 Danish athletes and implements, increases the capacity of and correlates common measures within élite sports. The sports marketing department was established at the wish of athletes. It handles the sale and marketing of arrangements and special unions under the Danish Sports Federation. Formerly, there was merely general advertising and the above mentioned prize sponsoring, but experience has shown that an active sports marketing pays well for both parties.

'TEAM DANMARK' is financed in various ways. Two thirds of the financing is provided by the Ministry of Cultural Affairs by way of receipts from the state football pools ('tips') and the numbers game ('lotto').

The remaining third must be earned by 'TEAM DANMARK' and the athletic sports themselves, and this is done in co-operation with sponsors, as well as through the sale of television rights to sports events.

One of the advantages of sports marketing is precisely that sports, to a high degree, express something dynamic, and, generally, they are associated with strong young people. Companies that previously had an old-fashioned image can profit from profiling themselves through sports.

It is still very important to find out which section of the population the product has as potential customers. It is also interesting to look into their lifestyle and their choice of sports, and then, subsequently, stake on this particular field.

Furthermore, the concept 'company sports' has become very popular in Danish workplaces during the last 30 years. The concept itself is not new but, because of the wish to join today's 'health wave', a development has taken place within sports. Company sports is a benefit to the individual employee, who will often be offered a more favourable price than he could obtain elsewhere, and, furthermore, it may strengthen the social relations in the workplace. Outwardly, the company can strengthen its image by profiling itself through sports which will picture the company as dynamic and active and unconsciously affect the attitude of the customers towards the company and its products.

Likewise, sports for the handicapped are sponsored by 'TEAM DANMARK'. Here attempts are made to help élite handicapped teams.

Additionally, Denmark has a second TV channel which is financed by commercials. Sports deliver a very high number of viewers and are, therefore, a must for a TV station financed by commercials.

This has sharpened the interest of the many companies for sports marketing and has conversely increased a broad part of the population's knowledge of these companies.

2. The National Legal System

The Danish legislative system is founded on statutes, subordinate legislation and circulars.

Statutes are passed in the Danish 'Folketing', whereas subordinate legislation is issued by a minister or other administrative authority. It is common to these rules that they are legally binding for everybody, authorities as well as private bodies and individuals.

Likewise, circulars are issued by the administrative authorities, but these are exclusively 'directive' and can, to a certain extent, be applied as principles of interpretation of statutes and subordinate legislation.

The Danish civil courts system is organised into 82 jurisdictions, each with a District Court. There are two High Courts and one Supreme Court. The High Courts are courts of first instance in important cases and courts of appeal for the District Courts. The Supreme Court hears both appeals directly from the High Courts and from the District Courts, when special leave to a third instance is given.

Case law and trade practice play a certain role, but are subordinate to the actual legislation.

Furthermore, EC law plays a more and more important role in Danish law, and is, to a large extent, directly applicable in Denmark.

In Denmark, the Consumer Ombudsman also plays an important part in the world of advertising and marketing. According to the Act on Marketing, the Consumer Ombudsman has authority in disputes regarding violations of good marketing practices.

Pursuant to Section 15 of the Act on Marketing, the Consumer Ombudsman must supervise and control that violations of the principles of good marketing practices do not occur. This can be done either by the Consumer Ombudsman handling cases on his own initiative, or in consequence of complaints or applications made by others. The sanctions available include the issue of injunctions, a substantial encroachment on the freedom of action of the parties involved.

Furthermore, one is entitled to request an advance statement from the Consumer Ombudsman as to whether or not the planned marketing measure will be in accordance with the principles of good marketing practices. Such advance statements are legally binding.

In practice, the activities of the Consumer Ombudsman are most significant in connection with cases where there is a clear and strong interest in the protection of consumers.

In other types of cases, in which the parties involved are not individual consumers, the parties will often not address the Consumer Ombudsman but go directly to the courts, the court of arbitration or the independent boards or tribunals available within the particular field.

3. Applicable Laws

In Denmark, there is no special legislation governing the rules on marketing and sponsoring. The most important legislation is, therefore, contained in the following Acts: Act on Contracts and other Legal Transactions within the Area of Law of Property of 8.5.1917, No. 242; Act on Marketing of 14.6.1974, No. 297; Act on Competition of 7.6.1989, No. 370; Act on Radio and Television Trade of 15.6.1973, No. 421; Act on Copyright of Literary and Artistic Works of 31.5.1961, No. 158; and Act on Trade Marks of 11.6.1959, No. 211.

To a large extent, the Law on Contracts applies as many agreements on sponsoring will be concluded by agreement between the parties.

In Denmark, taxation plays a substantial part in advertising and sponsoring. Expenses for advertising gifts are basically fully deductible.[1] The tax authorities suspect that unlimited allowances in relation to advertising and sports could mean a difficult delimitation towards real hobby activities.

The starting point, the Tax Assessments Act s. 8(A), has, accordingly, been restrictive. Lately, it has become more popular to contribute to culture and sports and the development tends towards the necessity of such contributions in order to maintain the desired athletic level. Hence, practice has advanced

1. Act on Taxation of Income and Property s. 6(a) and the Tax Assessments Act s. 8(1).

in such a way that, in general, the sponsor contribution may be allowed for in the income where the value of advertising is considered to be in direct connection with this. However, it is presumed that the identity of the sponsor clearly appears from the advertisement, display works or in any other way.

To obtain tax allowances, it is a condition that the sponsor's personal or political interests are not cultivated.

4. Intellectual Property Rights

4.1. Trademarks

Trademarks belong to the oldest disciplines of intellectual property rights and today they carry a strong international mark because of the extensive foreign trade.

Trademark rights protect the actual trademarks only and can, in principle, retain their monopoly forever.

Trademark rights may be obtained either through registration or commercial use. The latter is not subject to any specific provisions as to the intensity of use or time limits, and, in principle, the trademark right can be obtained in just one day.

In principle, trademark rights are everlasting, as they are not subject to any time limits.

In case one chooses to register the trademark, the concept of an obligation to use still does not exist in Danish law within this area. Therefore, so-called formal registrations can be effected, i.e. the registration of a trademark which is not used. In practice, the courts have been inclined to limit this. The protection of products by formal registration – particularly in connection with the establishment of the criteria for confusion (mistake) – is not considerable in this situation.

A registered trademark right is subject to renewal every 10 years and can be renewed for a 10-year period each time.

As mentioned above, a trademark right can also be based on commercial use. As a starting point – also in this connection – the commercial use is not subject to any time limits. The rules applying to the obligation to use are somewhat different from the rules applying to registered trademarks, as the acquisition of the actual right is connected with the factual use.

In case the commercial use of the trademark definitively ceases, so does the protection, which means that others are free to use the trademark. On the other hand, the protection shall not cease in connection with an accidental or temporary cessation of use. The final decision as to whether or not the cessation of use is definitive will be made by the courts.

4.2. Service Marks

For the registration of a service mark in Denmark, a written application must be submitted to the Patents Office.

The application must state the classes under which registration is requested. The Danish Ministry of Industry has issued Order No. 799 of 6 December 1991, with supplement, in which are enumerated all classes of trademarks. The service marks are comprised by classes 36-42.

The above-mentioned classes describe in detail what is comprised by the stipulations. Class 42 contains the overall stipulation so that all services may be registered by service marks. The Patents Office has to approve the application.

4.3. Copyright

The Danish Act on Copyright dates back to 1961 and was subjected to later amendments.

There are no registration requirements for the acquisition of copyright, and thus the legal protection commences without regard to form. The right is acquired as soon as the work is made. However, it is a requirement that it shall appear as a 'work'.

The limits for the copyright concept 'work' are not well-defined, but there are certain quality requirements for the copyright work. The requirement concerns not the usual quality decided by taste, but the character of the work. The basic condition is that the work is original, that is, originating in the author himself as produced in a personal, creative effort.

In Denmark, no requirements exist for the use of the copyright, neither regarding Danish nor foreign products. Denmark is a member of the Berne Convention, which does not contain any requirements as to form.

In relation to advertisements, copyright has an exceptional position. Formerly, there were special rules regarding advertisements, but, according to the rules in force at the present time, advertisements are to be judged in pursuance of the general rules in force. The relevant form of protection is, therefore, of a legal competitive nature in the form of applying the rules on unfair competition.

4.4. Unfair Competition

Unfair competition means the obtaining of an advantage by exploiting another person's market position, for example, by marketing one's own products in the same way as another's product or similar to it. Section 1 of the Act on Marketing prohibits unfair competition.

Three requirements must be fulfilled before there is unfair competition:

- there is a possibility of confusion (mistake);
- the other party has a good market position;
- there is evidence of loss.

Formerly, the starting point regarding comparative advertising was that this was not allowed. However, today this form of advertising is allowed, primarily because, when practised in a correct manner, it can be an effective means of informing the group of consumers to whom it is addressed. There are no rules of law governing the area, but there are requirements that the advertising made must be correct, relevant and loyal. The information provided must be truthful and refer to data which may easily be verified, and all relevant points must be included so that nothing is left out for the sake of one's own advantage. Furthermore, other products must not be disparaged.

Within the field of price advertising, comparative advertising is fully allowed when the products involved are identical or uniform.

4.5. Design Rights

The concept originates in the textile industry and their tapestry weavers of the late Middle Ages and protects the shape and configuration of the article, not its technical function.

The Danish rules in force on design rights date from 1970 and have been made on the basis of a Nordic co-operation.

Design rights lay down that the individual countries' legislations shall be strictly limited to their own territories, which is why protection in Denmark is only provided for designs registered in Denmark.

The acquisition is formal, and a written application must be submitted to the registration authorities: in Denmark, the Patents Office.

In the above-mentioned fields, the most important global Conventions are the Paris Convention ('Convention de Paris pour la protection de la proprieté industrielle') of 1883 with amendments and the Berne Convention ('Convention de Berne pour la protection des oeuvres litteraires et artistiques') of 1886 with amendments. The countries which have ratified these Conventions constitute a so-called union for the protection of the intellectual property rights, that is, patents, designs, trade marks and copyright. Denmark has been a union member almost from the start, from 1894 of the Paris Convention and from 1903 of the Berne Convention.

5. The Contract Generally

Basically, Danish law has no formal requirements as to the making of a contract. The rules have been codified in the Contracts Act (Act on Contracts and other Legal Transactions within the Field of Law of Property of 8.5.1917,

No. 242), and contracts may be made both orally and in writing. For apparent legal reasons, it is recommended that contracts be made in writing. Furthermore, the actual content of the contract must be specified to such an extent that the contract creates rights for the parties in such a way that they cannot be disputed.

Natural and legal persons can be parties to a contract. A legal person's contracts may, however, be entered into by a representative of the entity concerned.

The below-mentioned rules also apply where one of the parties simply wants to express an intention of making a contract.

Danish law is founded on generally acknowledged principles on the making of an offer and acceptance.

5.1. Offer and Acceptance

A contract between two parties is entered into on the making of an offer and the other party's subsequent absolute acceptance of that offer. The offeror is bound by his offer until:

(a) expiry of the time limit for acceptance;
(b) a reasonable time has expired should no time for acceptance be prescribed;
(c) the offer is refused (or accepted with supplements, restrictions or reservations which do not comply with the original offer).

As mentioned above, the offeree must accept the offer within a reasonable time, or it will be held to have lapsed.

5.2. Invalidity

As mentioned above, there are no general requirements as to the contents of a contract.

However, it shall not contain any unlawfulness, for example, criminal actions.

Furthermore, a contract will be declared void where it has been entered into by mistake. For instance, where it has been entered into between the wrong parties.

Invalidity can also be claimed where a party's violent conduct or threats thereof has resulted in any declarations of intent.

Neither will the contract be of any legal effect where any of the parties have concealed any substantial facts regarding the entering into of the contract and thereby obtained the acceptance of the other party.

5.3. Power of Attorney

Contracts may also be entered into by an agent. As a rule, powers of attorney assume two forms: (a) general agent; and (b) *ad hoc* agent.

The actions of the agent made within the limits of his authority shall be binding on the principal towards a third party to the same extent as if he himself had entered into the contract.

5.4. Interpretation

In cases of doubt, a contract must be interpreted by the courts. The courts emphasise both the linguistic interpretation of the contract and the presumed intentions of the parties at the time of making the contract.

5.5. Breach of Contract

Breach of contract occurs where one party does not fulfil the obligations imposed on him under that contract. The consequences of a breach of contract depend to a large extent on the form of the breach and on the contents of the contract. In most cases, the result will be a claim for damages for the loss which the breach has inflicted on the other party.

5.6. Frustration and Force Majeure

The Danish Act on Contracts contains no *force majeure* stipulations which may form the basis of a possible termination of contracts, including sponsoring contracts.

However, according to common principles of Danish Law, it is possible to avoid liability for non-fulfilment in cases of impossibility and *force majeure*.

6. Standard Contract Terms

In spite of the lack of any requirements for the formation of the contract, there are certain important requirements which should be taken into account in the formation of sponsorship contracts:

- contracting party;
- rights;
- obligations;
- term;
- termination;
- terms of payment;

- the settling of disputes by arbitration (in international contracts, which country's rules of law are to be applied);
- trade sovereignty;
- option(s); and
- limits for co-operation.

7. Different Types of Business Arrangements

Basically, only imagination sets limits as to how to enter contracts and about what. Amongst others, it is possible to advertise through the use of brands, general display works, clothes brands, the mentioning of a name in a TV commercial, open-air advertisements, the possibility of sponsoring of prizes and so on.

7.1. Sponsorship Agreements

The typical sponsorship agreement in Denmark implies that the sponsoring company – depending on the amount involved – may obtain:

- its name on one or more team shirts;
- its name on signs when playing home matches;
- advertisement through loudspeakers;
- possible use of some of the club members for special arrangements;
- advertisements in programmes;
- marketing aimed at club members.

Smaller amounts paid would involve, for example, the conclusion of a sign or an advertisement in the club programme.

7.2. Merchandising and Endorsements

These agreements depend upon the will and commercial needs of the parties.

8. Financial Terms

The price and the financial part of the agreement on the whole should be fixed at the signing of the agreement.

A guideline for the fixing of the price could be supply and demand, particularly in cases of a sports arrangement, which is to be shown on TV. Here it is often easier to fix the price, and, in general, ceiling prices will be established.

Fixing the price in connection with smaller groups, sports unions and local sports is more difficult. Thus attention should be given to the following:

- spectators;
- readers of newspapers, in which logos appear;
- customers attending the activity in shops/shopping centres;
- local environment;
- personal prestige; and
- price level in the area.

Naturally, many factors should be taken into account when fixing the price, but it is always a good idea to fix the prices at a minimum which will make it easier to sell the products and thus maintain the sellers' spirits.

Furthermore, it is recommended that the contract lays down the final price, time for payment and a possibility for a later adjustment of the price.

9. Advertising and Promotion

In Denmark, there are limits as to who can act as a sponsor in the above-mentioned fields.

It is the wish of the Danish authorities to regulate advertisements for alcohol and tobacco on the grounds of the health risk connected with an excessive use of these goods.

The National Consumer Agency has issued certain directions regarding the marketing of alcoholic beverages. These came into force on 1 January 1991. The basic rule for the marketing of these products is that special attention should be exerted regarding both the means of advertising and the contents, shape and use of the advertisement. Marketing must not – directly or indirectly – appear obtrusive, provocative or in any other way persuasive in wording, language or choice of pictures. The purpose of these very restrictive advertising rules is to urge the consumer to be sensible and responsible in his use of alcoholic beverages. Furthermore there are special restrictions regarding advertisements that primarily address the young. Marketing must not take place through commercials specially connected to sports nor in any sports and athletics magazines. The consumption of alcohol must not, under any circumstances, be connected with any positive thing or anything worth striving for.

Regarding tobacco, an agreement has been made between the tobacco industry and the Ministry of Health on the marketing of tobacco products. Under this agreement, the tobacco industry is under an obligation to provide all consumer-orientated advertisements with warnings that smoking is unhealthy and to state the contents of tar and nicotine in every cigarette. Like alcohol, tobacco must not be marketed in commercials for young people, nor in magazines that address the young. Nor shall any idols or similar persons be used in tobacco commercials. Where the tobacco industry – or rather a wholesaler or a distributor – does not comply with this agreement, the industry is under an obligation to stop the delivery of tobacco to the wholesaler or distributor concerned.

Special rules apply to radio and TV programme sponsoring. Companies producing or selling beer, wine, alcohol, tobacco and pharmaceuticals may not be sponsors. Apart from local radio, programmes must not be sponsored by any employers' associations, trade unions, political parties or religious movements. News programmes may not be sponsored at all.

10. Public and Product Liability

EC membership has resulted in Denmark passing an Act on Product Liability (Act No. 371 of 7.6.1989). This Act only applies to producers and intermediaries and has no direct influence on the sports marketing area.

Considering non-contractual actions, a sponsor will only become liable according to the principle of negligence.

Sponsoring the winning team will normally bring the highest publicity. This, however, has no importance in considering liability for non-contractual actions.

As an exception, product liability could, however, occur through the sponsoring of athletes' clothes and shoes, which have an unforeseen defect, where the sponsor is a producer or intermediary.

11. Dispute Resolution

As mentioned above in 'Standard Contract Terms' at p. 84–85, it is very useful that the parties on entering a contract agree on the steps to be taken in connection with a breach of contract.

In sponsorship agreements and other agreements it is wise for the parties to agree to settle any disputes by an amicable solution. A dispute being settled by arbitration or in court is probably the worst advertisement a sponsor could get.

Where an amicable solution cannot be obtained, it is recommended to settle the dispute by arbitration to which the public has no access and to bind the parties to professional secrecy and loyalty, for example, sanctioned with penalties.

Professional persons can act as arbitrators and special rules regarding the hearing of the arbitration, for example, the time limit for the award, may be settled in the agreement.

In general, the settlement of disputes by arbitration is not cost-saving for the parties concerned.

Litigation arising out of intellectual property rights may also be settled by arbitration.

Through Denmark's accession to the Brussels Convention of 1968, which took effect from 1 November 1986, it has become easier to enforce a foreign judgment. Danish courts base their execution upon the foreign judgments without re-examination of the case, provided that the foreign judgment bears an endorsement of execution from the foreign court.

SPORTS
MARKETING

Finland

by Tom Schubert

1. Sports Marketing – A Business

The lack of exact figures and comprehensive statistics makes it difficult to evaluate the exact size of the sports industry or sports marketing industry in Finland.

Nevertheless, it may be stated that sports marketing has existed in Finland for quite some time and is becoming increasingly important. Especially in areas of sports which attract a large public, such as the national ice hockey league, or sports in which Finland has enjoyed international success, such as rally driving, the sums spent on sports marketing may be estimated to be considerable.

2. The Finnish Legal System

The Finnish legal system has developed in close connection with other Scandinavian countries, i.e. Sweden, Norway and Denmark. Especially the influence of Swedish legislation has been of great importance due to Finland's union with Sweden for more than 700 years. Because of extensive legislative co-operation between the Scandinavian countries since several decades the Finnish legal system of today is basically the same as in other Scandinavian countries. The legal system in Finland is based on the principle of the rule of law and the general European legal traditions, including the powers of the ruler, the rights of the citizens and the sanctity of law.

The judicial power in Finland is exercised by independent and permanent courts of law. The court system and jurisdiction is based on the division of courts into the general courts of law, administrative courts and special courts.

The general courts of law are the courts of first instance, the courts of appeal and the Supreme Court. All the matters that have not by law been expressly submitted to the special courts or administrative courts fall under the jurisdiction of the general courts of law.

The personal presence of the parties in the court is usually not required in civil matters and the parties are often represented by advocates or attorneys-at-law. A party appearing in court does not need to be represented or assisted by an advocate, but he may appear without counsel or be represented or assisted by a layman. In practice, however, legal proceedings are usually handled by professional lawyers. The members of the Finnish Bar Association are called 'advocates' or 'attorneys-at-law' and the competence of the members and their practice is supervised by the association. An advocate is required to have a law degree and a several years practical experience in the field.

3. Applicable Laws

As regards applicable laws, the Finnish situation is rather similar to that of England. It should, however, be noted that in Finland case law does not play nearly as important a role as in England.

4. Intellectual Property Rights

From a legal point of view, intellectual property rights constitute the main component of any sports marketing programme; in, for example, a programme connected with an international sports event the creation and protection of the intellectual property rights is of crucial importance to the licensor and licensee.

4.1. Trademarks

Exclusive rights to a trademark can be obtained either by registration, or also without registration if the trademark reputation has been established. The exclusive rights can be maintained ten years from registration, and the registration can be renewed for like periods. The application for registration of a trademark can be submitted only through a Finnish agent.

Finland is a signatory to the Paris Convention on Trademarks and the Nice Agreement on the International Classification of Goods and Services of 1957.

4.2. Copyright

A person who has created a literary or an artistic work has the copyright therein. With certain limitations, copyright shall include the exclusive right to control a work by producing copies thereof and by making it available to the public. A special law to copyright on photographs grants, with certain exceptions, the photographer an exclusive right to make copies of a photograph produced by him, and to exhibit it publicly until the end of the 25th year after the year in which it was first published.

Finland is a signatory to the Berne Convention on Copyright.

4.3. Registered Designs

Finnish law provides for the protection of designs for a period of five years from the date of application for registration. The registration may be renewed for two additional five-year periods.

Finnish law provides also for the protection of utility models for a period of four years from the date of application for registration. The registration may be renewed for one additional four-year period.

Under Finnish law protection is granted to the design of a product, provided that the design fulfils the criteria of creativity and novelty, and differs distinguishably from the existing designs. Protection is given to the design, not to the product itself.

Protection is furthermore granted to the technical solution (invention) that materialises in the design or structure, or in combination thereof, of a product, provided that the criteria of novelty and the level of invention are fulfilled, and that the invention differs from what is known by the date of application.

4.4. Unfair Competition

Finnish law prohibits the use of unfair business practice or otherwise incompatible conduct towards another tradesman in business activities. Main types of cases involving such practice or conduct relate usually to:

- misleading advertising;
- imitation;
- denigration;
- comparison advertising;
- promotional offers, free gifts;
- reference to testimonials or endorsements in advertising;
- exploitation of goodwill; and
- confidentiality obligations.

5. The Contract Generally and Preliminary Agreements

The Finnish situation relative to the basic contractual principles is fairly similar to that of England, although case law is not an important factor in the Finnish legal system.

Note, however, that under Finnish law there need not be any consideration or benefit flowing between the parties for a contract to be valid. Also, it should be noted that under Finnish law even the assignment of copyright need not be in writing.

Under Finnish law a contract may be invalidated, for example, on the basis of the fact that the signature on the document has been forged or that a contracting party was minor and thus lacked the capacity to enter into the contract. Other grounds making the contract voidable are, for example, the fact that one contracting party has forced the other into a contract, applied fraud in the inducement, or availed himself of the distress, lack of understanding or dependent position of the other party.

In case any of the above means have been applied by a third party, the contract is voidable if the other contracting party was or should have been aware of the use of such means. However, where grave duress has been applied by a third party, this may be invoked even against a contracting party acting in good faith. A further ground resulting in the contract being subject to invalidation is the fact that the contract was concluded under such circumstances that it would be degrading and dishonourable to invoke the contract and it must be assumed that the other contracting party was aware of this.

Finnish law further provides that, in case a contractual term is unreasonable, or in case the result of the application of a contractual term would be unreasonable, such term may be modified or ignored by a court of law. In case such modification would make the contract as a whole unreasonable, the contract may be modified also in other respects or be invalidated.

The 'privity of contract' doctrine is not as such applicable in Finland. Although a third party may not, under Finnish law, incur obligations or be sued upon a contract, such third party may acquire rights (e.g. by transfer of rights made by one of the contracting parties) and thus sue upon the contract.

In case the contract is unclear and where it cannot be interpreted based upon the earlier practice in the dealing between the contracting parties, trade practice or non-mandatory provisions of law, the interpretation shall be made based upon the so called general principles of contract law. The mutual intention of the parties must be taken into account when interpreting a contract. If an expression has been used in a meaning different from normal practice and the parties agree thereon, their joint understanding shall be decisive. Otherwise, the interpretation is made in accordance with the meaning a 'reasonable person' would accord it. Even the behaviour of the parties during the negotiations and after the conclusion of the contract shall be paid attention to. A general principle of interpretation is that the drafting party shall bear the risk in case of unclear conditions (*in dubio contra stipulatorem*).

As regards frustration and breach of contract, the Finnish situation is fairly similar to that of England.

6. Standard Contract Terms

As regards standard contract terms, the Finnish situation is fairly similar to that of England. Naturally, the English Acts referred to are not applicable in Finland but the corresponding Finnish law applies.

7. Different Types of Business Arrangements

7.1. Sponsorship Agreement

There is no special body of law governing the sponsorship relationship. Instead, the arrangement is governed by contract whereby the sponsor is granted certain rights and opportunities in return for his financial sponsorship and other obligations.

7.2. Merchandising

The Finnish situation relative to merchandising is fairly similar to that of England. However, Finland is not yet a member of the EC and thus EC Directives do not as such apply.

7.3. Endorsements

It should be noted that the use of endorsements by individuals without their consent may even amount to defamation, insult or invasion of privacy, the penal scale for which varies from fines up to two years' imprisonment, depending on the gravity of the violation.

7.4. Commissioning, Franchises, Films and Videos and Suppliership

As regards commissioning agreements, franchises, films and videos, public appearances and suppliership, the Finnish situation is rather similar to that of England.

8. The Rights

The Finnish situation relative to the rights granted in the different agreements is fairly similar to that of England, with the exception of the EC and UK competition rules which are not applicable. However, similar rules apply in Finland.

9. Financial Terms

As regards financial terms, the Finnish situation resembles that of England.

10. Insurance Aspects

The Finnish situation relative to insurance is rather similar to that of England.

Furthermore, it may be noted that, under Finnish law, when arranging exhibitions, races or similar public events where the health or property of spectators, officials or third parties may be in danger, the obtaining of a liability insurance may be set as a prerequisite for the granting of a permission to arrange the event. Where races with certain motor driven vehicles or horses are arranged the obtaining of an insurance is always a prerequisite for the granting of a permission to arrange the event.

11. Advertising and Promotion

11.1. Advertising Controls

Finnish advertising is governed by voluntary regulations, statute and case law. International codes, such as those issued by the ICC, play an important role in the creation of guidelines and in forming of the case law resulting from the Market Court rulings (only and final instance). In the Government Bill for the Act on Unfair Trade Practice, there is even an indirect reference to established international voluntary codes of practice as guidelines in the application of the Act which is mainly of a general nature and does not deal with details.

In addition, there exist codes of practice regarding advertising through specific media, such as TV and radio (the advertising principles of the Finnish Commercial TV company, MTV Oy, and the frame agreement on sports mass communication between the Finnish Broadcasting Corporation and the Finnish sports federations) as well as roadside advertisements (the agreement between the members of the Finnish Exterior Advertising Association).

Furthermore, there are regulations and statute laws governing advertising of specific products, such as tobacco, alcoholic and pharmaceutical products.

11.2. Tobacco and Alcohol Advertising

The advertising and marketing of tobacco products and alcoholic beverages when it is aimed at the consumers is prohibited under Finnish law. Exempt from such prohibition are foreign printed publications the primary aim of which is not to advertise tobacco products or alcoholic beverages.

12. The Venue

12.1. Control

The Finnish situation regarding control is rather similar to the English one, with the exception of the enactments mentioned in the Chapter on the UK.

12.2. Public Liability

Under Finnish law, the organiser, under its general duty of care, will be liable to members of the public. If the organiser is found not to have exercised that duty of care, it will be liable for any foreseeable loss or damage caused to any person. Thus, for example, if the organiser fails to comply with required safety checks and a spectator, or sportsman, is injured as a result thereof, the organiser will be liable.

13. Dispute Resolution

13.1. General and Special Courts of Law

Proceedings in general courts of law are by far the most common way of dispute resolution in Finland, despite certain disadvantages compared with arbitration, such as the slowness of the proceedings and the uncertainty of the expertise of the court. Proceedings in general courts of law are initiated by the claimant whose summons is served by a 'summoner' to the defendant.

The enforcement of the rulings of a general court outside Finland is currently possible in the Nordic countries only, whereas enforcement in other European countries will become possible in line with the Lugano Convention.

Certain special courts worth mentioning are the Market Court, which deals with questions relating to unfair competition, and the Helsinki City Court, which is a general court of law, but has exclusive jurisdiction in industrial property rights matters, as well as in copyright matters relating to radio and TV.

13.2. Arbitration

Most commercial and other private law matters which may be settled by agreement are arbitrable under Finnish law. The question of damages in connection with a criminal suit may also be submitted to arbitration. The condition that it must be allowed to settle the matter in question by agreement excludes arbitration in settlement of, for example, certain commercial matters, such as patent, trademark and antitrust matters, in part or in whole. There are no requirements with respect to the parties particular to arbitration.

In order to initiate the proceedings, according to the Finnish Arbitration Act, the claimant must give the respondent a written notice of arbitration, setting forth the questions with respect to which an arbitral award is requested.

The parties are free to arrange for the choice or appointment of any number of arbitrators. Failing a decision by the parties in this respect, the Act provides for three arbitrators, one chosen by each party and a chairman chosen by the two arbitrators.

In spite of the obvious advantages (expedience, expertise, no possibility to appeal) connected with arbitration proceedings, such proceedings have disadvantages, perhaps the most remarkable being the cost factor. Arbitration proceedings are, as a rule, far more expensive than proceedings in general courts of law.

Finnish arbitral awards are enforceable outside Finland in accordance with the New York Convention.

France

by Philippe Netto

1. Sports Marketing – A Business

Could Baron Pierre de Coubertin, who witnessed the emergence of the first professional sports and stressed his belief in the necessity of developing the concept of amateur sports by alluding to the 'social aspect' of sport, even have imagined the dynamics and extravagance created today by the inter-play between the world of sport and the liberal economy?

Sport now attracts investments and merchandise and sports related activities represent an annual expenditure of about 30 billion francs. The number of occupations related to the 'sports profession' can be estimated at more than 50,000 (professional sports people, trainers, teachers, sports club organisers), not to mention all those who voluntarily take part in countless sports associations.

While sporting events have tapped the interest of a great many individuals for many years, a logical development, albeit more recent, is that the media have latched on – mainly with the explosion of television – and the increasingly sophisticated advertising techniques which encourage more and more firms to participate directly in sports as sponsors.

As sports sponsoring produces an eminently positive image, this is a favoured method of communication among many firms at every level. The amounts spent on sports sponsorship were estimated at 5 billion francs in 1990. In order to ensure that the planned operation will succeed, whenever a firm decides to sponsor an event or to engage in any other communication strategy, it must necessarily take into consideration the rules of French law which are summarised in this chapter.

2. The French Legal System

2.1. Territoriality

French law applies to the following territories: Metropolitan France, including Corsica, Overseas Departments (Guyane, Guadeloupe, Martinique, Réunion, Saint Pierre et Miquelon), Overseas Territories (Polynesie Française, Nouvelle Calédonie et dependences, Terres Australes et Antartiques Françaises, Wallis et Futuna). Mayotte Island has the special status of territorial collectivity ('collectivité territoriale').

2.2. Legal Sources

The law of France is a codified system, principally based on five original or Napoleonic Codes: Civil Code, Code of Civil Procedure, Commercial Code, Code Penal and Code of Criminal Procedure.

These rules are today defined not only by the competent national authorities (Parliament, Government), but also particularly by the European Community institutions, which play an increasingly important role.

The Constitution and the legislation have also recognised and consolidated the existence of local authorities (*collectivités locales*) (*communes*, *départements*, *regions*) which are legal bodies governing areas of varying scope, and particularly the organisation of sporting events.

2.3. The Role of Sports Federations

Alongside State or local law should be emphasised the importance of laws laid down by sports activities themselves and developed by sports federations.

These are private organisations which offer a public service. They may sometimes be endowed with prerogatives of public power. They have regulatory and disciplinary power over clubs affiliated to them and their licensees.

More generally, State-approved federations have the particular task of promoting education through sports activities, developing and organising sporting events and issuing licences or federal titles.

2.4. Structure of the Court System

The French legal system comprises two sets of parallel but independent court systems: the administrative jurisdiction (*système administratif*) and the judicial system (*système judiciaire*).

The *système administratif* has jurisdiction in matters of administrative law arising within the executive branch and between individuals and the executive. Administrative courts are divided into three levels of jurisdiction. The lowest level consists of Administrative Tribunals or *Tribunaux Administratifs*. The second level is the *Cour Administrative d'Appel* which has been in effect since January 1989, and has jurisdiction over appeals from the lowest level. The highest level, the *Conseil d'Etat*, hears some appeals against decisions of administrative tribunals, appeals against decisions of the second level and also has original jurisdiction for appeals against ministerial decisions based on breach of the rule of law or *ultra vires*.

The *système judiciaire* has jurisdiction in criminal, civil and commercial matters. Disputes arising between individuals and between the executive and individuals in such matters are dealt with by the *système judiciaire*.

Within the *système judiciaire* with respect to courts of original jurisdiction, the *Tribunal de Grande Instance* has jurisdiction when no other court expressly is competent to hear a case. The Commercial Court is the most significant court with express and specific jurisdiction.

The judicial system has three levels of jurisdiction: courts of original jurisdiction or first instance courts, courts of appeal and the *Cour de Cassation* which is one of the French supreme courts.

The first instance courts and the courts of appeal are competent in respect of facts, as well as in respect of legal issues, while the *Cour de Cassation* can review a case only on the basis of a mistake of law by the lower courts.

3. Applicable Laws

There is no specific body of legislation governing all sports marketing related activities.

Consequently, subject to observing the general principles of contract law, in theory the parties have wide scope to determine the contents of their agreements.

However, many specific laws must be observed where particular transactions are entered into, for example, Act No. 87–571 of 23 July 1987 on the development of sponsoring and patronage, the various laws governing advertising, or the provisions of the legislation governing trademark law.

4. Intellectual Property Rights

Most sports marketing agreements are governed by a number of aspects of intellectual property law because the purpose of such agreements is to reinforce the brand image of a product or firm. Thus, according to the case in question, the following laws have to be observed: trademark law (4.1), copyright law (4.2) and design and models law (4.3).

4.1. Trademarks

France is a signatory to the Paris Union Convention (20 March 1883), the Madrid Agreement (14 April 1891), the Treaty of Vienna and the Nice Agreement (15 June 1957). Under domestic law, the subject matter is governed by the provisions of Act No. 91–7 of 4 January 1991 governing manufacturing, commercial and service trademarks.

This Act applies to products and services and lists in broad terms the signs and symbols which may be chosen as a trademark, including names (patronymic names, geographical names . . .), representational signs and symbols (labels, stamps . . .) or sound signs.

However, legal protection only extends to signs which are available (i.e. to the exclusion of signs belonging to and used by a third party to describe identical products or services) and distinctive (the distinctive quality of a sign or symbol is relative and is assessed on the basis of the product or service it is used to describe at the time of registration of the trademark).

Once the trademark is registered, whether in person or by an agent, at the INPI (Institut National de la Propriété Industrielle) or with the Clerk of the Commercial Court (Greffe du Tribunal de Commerce) for the area of domicile and the authorities have fully examined the contents thereof, it is automatically registered in the National Register of Trademarks and published in the BOPI (*Bulletin Officiel de la Propriété Industrielle*).

Registration in the above manner confers the benefit of trademark protection on the sign or symbol for 10 years, which is renewable for similar periods indefinitely as from the date on which the application is filed.

However, any interested party may apply to the court for a ruling that the right to the trademark is lost by reason of failure to exploit the same for a continuous period of 5 years.

4.2. Protection of Copyright

Protection of copyright is governed by the rules contained in the Berne Convention (1886), the Geneva Convention (1952) and the Rome Convention (1961) as well as the Copyright Act No. 57–298 of 11 March 1957.

The 1957 Act recognises an automatic property right in favour of the author of any creative design. Some sporting activities, therefore, come within its sphere of application (figure skating, martial arts, advertisements using a sportsman's brand name . . .).

Copyright, which is established by proving precedence of the work, vests in the author of the work (i.e. under whose name the work is disseminated) or in his representative editor. Where the work is governed by the rules of industrial and commercial property and has been created by a salaried employee during the exercise of his duties, it vests directly in the employer.

The author of a work enjoys property rights over the work (moral rights) and property rights over the material constituents of the work (patrimonial rights).

Moral rights are not subject to any limitation period and may be bequeathed to one's heirs. They give the author control over the destiny of his work. Patrimonial rights (right to exhibit the work, right of reproduction, right to assign rights) expire 50 years after the calendar year of the author's death.

Full or partial reproduction of a work without the author's consent is punished as the major offence of counterfeit and is a tort, which may give rise to the payment of compensation, as well as confiscation of the infringing product.

4.3. Protection of Designs and Models

France is the only European country which fully recognises protection available in 2 distinct legal areas:

- failing registration, the 1957 Act: copyright protection, as set out above, is conferred on original designs or models;
- where registered, the Act of 14 July 1909 governing designs and models: a 25-year protection, renewable once, is granted from the date of registration: 'to all novel designs, all novel plastic forms, all industrial articles which can be differentiated from like products, either by a distinct and recognisable configuration conferring a novel feature, or by one or more external effects which confer on it its own novel appearance'.

5. The Contract Generally and Preliminary Agreements

Article 1108 of the Civil Code lays down four essential requirements for the valid formation of a contract: the parties undertaking an obligation pursuant to the contract must consent to it; the parties must have the capacity to contract; there must be certainty as to the subject matter of the contract; the contract must have a real and legal purpose.

Once a contract has validly been formed, it must be duly performed. Otherwise, any breach of the contract may entail sanctions.

5.1. Preparation of the Contract

5.1.1. The various preparatory documents

More and more frequently, the conclusion of a contract is preceded by preparatory documents, governed either by prior negotiations or preliminary agreements. Moreover, the terminology is very varied and covers a great difference in scope of legal commitment resulting therefrom.

The parties must, therefore, take great care to establish their respective obligations, i.e., whether they are merely undertaking to negotiate (in good faith) or whether they intend there and then to determine the main components of the future agreement.

In any event, case law holds that liability rests with the party who untimely or abusively breaks off negotiations. Such party can be ordered to compensate the co-contractor for the loss suffered as a result of breaking off negotiations.

5.1.2. Unilateral promise to contract (option)
An individual, the promisor, firmly undertakes to enter into a particular contract with another, the promisee, but only where the latter requests that he do so within a specified time period. The unilateral promise therefore confers an option on the promisee for a certain duration. When the promisee exercises the option, the contract is formed without any further undertaking on the part of the promisor.

5.1.3. Preference agreement (Pacte de préférence) (Right of Pre-emption)
The preference agreement is a preliminary agreement which may involve any type of contract. One of the two parties to the preference agreement, the promisor, thus undertakes, in the event that he should decide to enter into a particular transaction, to give the other party to the agreement, the promisee, the right of first acceptance. Unlike the unilateral promise to contract, when the promisor enters into the agreement, he is only undertaking to give preference to the promisee in the event that he, the promisor, should decide to enter into the particular transaction. As it is an obligation to do something, should the promisor fail to perform the agreement, he is ordered to pay damages to the promisee.

5.2. Offer and Acceptance

The meeting of offer and acceptance denotes the meeting of minds of the parties and hence the moment of formation of the contract.

However, it must be a perfect meeting of minds and where the offer is accepted with some reservations, this is deemed to be a counter-offer and not an acceptance (Cour de Cassation, Civil Division, 12 March 1985).

Acceptance may be made by any standard means of communication (letter, fax, telex, telegram), the principle being that the contract may also be formed orally. However, where it is manifested in writing and signed by the parties, this constitutes firm proof, which is sometimes required by law, particularly where the undertaking is made by a person with no commercial expertise and where the amount in issue is more than 5,000 francs (Art. 1341 of the Civil Code).

5.3. Capacity

Under Article 1123 of the Civil Code, any person may enter into a contract unless expressly prohibited from doing so by statute. There are three categories of persons so prohibited: minors; those prohibited by order of the court; and those prohibited from entering into certain types of contract.

5.4. Certainty of Subject Matter

Pursuant to Articles 1126 and 1127 of the Civil Code, every contract must involve either the transfer of some form of property, or an obligation to do or refrain from doing something. The subject matter of a contract may also be the use or occupation of property, without the transfer of titles.

Any contract must specify the scope of the obligation of the parties. In this respect, the type of goods which are the subject matter of the contract must be specified, but the quantity need not be, provided that the quantity is determinable. Objects which have not yet come into being may be the subject matter of a contract.

The price to be paid under the contract for the benefit conferred must also be specified, or the method by which it may be determined must be expressed.

Failure to stipulate the subject matter of the contract, or the price to be paid for it, automatically renders the contract null and void.

5.5. Valid and Real Purpose of the Contract

Article 1134 of the Civil Code requires that each obligation contained in a contract has a real and lawful purpose ('cause'). In essence, this means that the party undertaking an obligation under the contract must have a legitimate and lawful interest or purpose for so doing. The provision thus avoids completely sham obligations and contracts with illegal aims. This notion of 'cause' which can be complex to understand, is completely different from the common law concept of 'consideration' and cannot be compared to it, even if particular examples coincide.

'Cause' can be considered to be the reason for which a party undertakes an obligation. In a sales contract, therefore, the reason for the vendor's undertaking to transfer title is the money that he will receive. In a unilateral contract (e.g. a promise or a donation, which can be an enforceable contract under French law), the cause for the transfer may be that the transferor wishes to please the transferee or that he wishes to divest himself of the property.

The notion is complex, but rarely causes problems in practice, except in relation to sham or illegal agreements.

5.6. Void and Illegal Contracts

Where the above conditions for the formation of the contract are not observed, the contract will be void. It will also be void in the event of fraud (5.6.1), violence (5.6.2) or mistake (5.6.3) which tarnish the consent given.

5.6.1. Fraud

A fraud (‘*dol*’) is any act carried out with the deliberate intention of misleading the other contracting party. Fraud is in contrast to mere ignorance of a fact, or unintentional failure to communicate that fact to the other party, which cannot amount to a ‘*dol*’.

Mere silence, if accompanied by an intention to deceive, may amount to a ‘*dol*’.

The ‘*dol*’ may normally only be perpetrated by a party to the contract. However, the agent of a contracting party may commit a ‘*dol*’. Further, a third party’s fraudulent act, subsequently ratified by the contracting party, may be sufficient to amount to a ‘*dol*’ (Cour de Cassation, Chambre Commerciale, 25 March 1974).

In order to end contractual liability, the ‘*dol*’ must have induced the other party to enter into the contract or to agree to terms to which it would not otherwise have agreed.

Where the victim of the ‘*dol*’ would not have entered into the contract but for the ‘*dol*’, then the contract is voidable and the victim may claim rescission of the contract or damages, or both. The limitation period for claims based on ‘*dol*’ is 5 years (Art. 1304 of the Civil Code). Where, without the ‘*dol*’, the victim would have entered into the contract, but on different terms, then he may only claim damages.

‘*Dol*’ will never be inferred, but must be proved.

5.6.2. Duress

The following acts may constitute duress: physical violence; threats of violence; or the threat of legal proceedings, if their use would amount to an abuse of process. However, French law does not recognise the concept of economic duress.

An act which amounts to duress may emanate from third parties.

Duress is operative where it is the effective cause of the victim’s apparent consent.

A contract entered into under duress is avoidable only at the instance of the victim (Art. 1117 of the Civil Code). The limitation period for an action based on duress is 5 years (Art. 1304 of the Civil Code).

5.6.3. Mistake

A mistake may operate to void a contract when the mistake concerns either the substance of the contract or the identity of the contracting party where that is a condition of the contract (Art. 1110 of the Civil Code).

For a mistake to be capable of voiding a contract, it is essential that the party concerned would not have contracted but for that misapprehension. Furthermore, the victim of the mistake must show that he is not responsible for the mistake.

5.7. Relative Enforceability of Contracts, Obligations as to Ends and Means, Penalty Clauses

Article 1165 of the Civil Code provides that contracts are only enforceable between the contracting parties and that they must not harm third parties and must only be of benefit to third parties in exceptional cases. Thus, the parties are sovereign but only with regard to each other.

The extent of this principle of relative enforceability does, however, need to be specified: while the contract may neither harm nor advantage third parties by giving rise to obligations which either burden or favour them, *third parties are nonetheless obliged to acknowledge the existence of the contract which is binding upon them.*

Moreover, contracts providing for obligations to do something (e.g. sponsorship agreements), obligate the parties to define the purpose thereof on the basis of whether the obligations relate to ends or means. The former, which require the obligor to achieve a specified end, involve *de facto* the liability of the defaulting party (except in the event of *force majeure*). The latter require the obligor to act with maximum care and attention. However, he will only be held liable where he has failed to act with all due care and it is up to the obligee to prove such failure.

The parties to the contract may sometimes include a penalty clause. Such provisions are recognised as valid under French Civil law (Art. 1126 of the Civil Code). However, the clause must expressly indicate that the purpose thereof is to compensate loss caused by failure to perform the contract. The amount of compensation must not be excessive; where it is excessive, the judge may reduce it (Art. 1152 of the Civil Code). Finally, the circumstances in which the clause may be invoked must be clearly defined.

5.8. Performance and Breach of Contract

Article 1134 of the Civil Code sets out three consequences of a valid contract:

- the terms agreed between the parties have the force of law;
- they may not be revoked or varied except with the consent of both parties;
- the terms must be performed in good faith.

When the terms of a contract as drafted do not accurately reflect the intention of the parties, the court has the power to vary the terms in order to reflect that intention. The following principles are applied:

- intention takes precedence over form;
- when two clauses are inconsistent, the handwritten term takes precedence over the printed term;
- written terms should not obstruct the spirit of the agreement;
- in case of doubt, a term is always interpreted in favour of the debtor;

– the court may not subsequently vary a term which accurately reflects the intention of the parties without their consent.

In general, failure to perform an obligation under the contract does not entitle the victim to invoke self-help remedies. Thus, in the event of breach of contract, where the contract does not have a termination clause, it is necessary to go before a court to obtain the termination of such contract. The nature of the contract and the nature of the breach dictate the remedies available. Delay in performance only amounts to a breach if time has been of the essence, or if the victim has given reasonable notice that he requires timely performance.

However, the party who has suffered the breach may either suspend the operation of the contract, if the contract expressly allows this, or may refuse to carry out his obligations under the contract (*exception non adimpleti contractus*). This is an exception to the general rule prohibiting self-help remedies.

5.9. Unfair Competition

Unfair competition (*concurrence déloyale*) is a tort, developed by case law from the basic fault concept of Article 1382 of the Code Civil, that any person whose fault in act or omission causes damage to another is obliged to compensate such damage. Torts of this special type include: denigration of competitors; creation of confusion by using trademarks, symbols, wrappings or containers imitating those of competitors; claiming falsely to be a purveyor to government or particular persons or to be holder of prizes or medals; copying of advertisements or catalogues of another in a manner calculated to deceive the public; manipulative use of famous trademarks or products to attract clients and sell competing items to them; bribing or inducing employees of another to leave their employer or to reveal trade secrets or otherwise injure their employer. Fraud need not be shown: negligence or fault is sufficient.

Objective and scientifically based criticism of a product for the purpose of informing the public and not of denigrating the product is not deemed to be unfair competition.

6. Different Types of Business Arrangements

This section is designed to list and describe those contracts most likely to be necessary for sports marketing ventures. It is, therefore, not intended to be exhaustive.

6.1. Sponsorship Agreements

Sponsoring is a method of advertising based on financing a sporting, cultural or audiovisual activity . . . and designed to associate such activity in the mind of the public with the sponsor's trademark. Sponsors of sporting activities undertake to finance, at least partially, the organisation of a competition or the participation of a sports person.

As there are no overall regulations, the parties are at liberty to agree terms between themselves. The resulting contract is complex and may be drafted using provisions from advertising contracts, loan agreements, business contracts or employment contracts. Consequently, rather than just relying on the type of legal transaction used, the parties must make every effort to set out the specific details of both their intentions and obligations.

Generally, it is up to the sponsor to provide the financial or material means. For his part, the sponsored individual undertakes to provide certain services: for example, to prepare himself thoroughly for the competition and to observe the sporting ethics; to use the event as an opportunity for exposing the sponsor's trademark; to advertise the sponsor's trademark during interviews; and to participate in cocktails, conferences and other autographical sessions planned by the sponsor.

As sponsoring arrangements link the image of the sponsor and that of the sponsored individual in the mind of the public, there should also be a non-competition clause covering competing activities regarding both the sporting event itself and the post-termination period.

The penalty for breach of an obligation is usually termination of the contract. The parties provide for the restitution of equipment and money upon expiry of the contract.

Sponsoring arrangements are also governed by the rules pertaining to a number of specific contracts. Thus, as it is a form of advertising, sponsoring, like any advertising agreement, is subject to the restrictions governing advertising notices as set forth in the 29 December 1979 Act relating to advertising, signs and pre-signs and to the restrictions and prohibitions on advertising laid down by law in a number of specified areas (e.g. tobacco or alcohol advertisements).

As sponsoring arrangements frequently involve lending equipment, it is in the sponsor's interests to make provision in the contract for the determination of liability therefor as set forth in Article 1891 of the Civil Code governing loans for use, and to include in the contract a provision for restitution of the equipment at the end of the competition/event.

Similarly, if it is clear that the sportsman is patently subordinate to the sponsor, the judge may interpret the arrangement as an employment contract which would mean that the sportsman would automatically be entitled to the protected status of a salaried employee (social security, collective bargaining agreements, compensation in the event of breach).

6.2. *Commercial Representation*

This is an arrangement whereby a professional acts as a manufacturer's representative with the task of distributing the latter's products. This technique can therefore easily be adapted to the distribution of sports industry products.

Representatives may be employed either as commercial agents (*mandat commercial*) or under a commissioning contract. However, this practice appears to be on the wane because the fact that the representative acts on behalf of the manufacturer but in his own name conceals the manufacturer (or the tradesman) and his trademark from the public eye.

The other possibility is for representatives to act under a *mandat civil* pursuant to a commercial agency agreement (*contrat d'agence commerciale*) (see the 25 June 1991 Act). The agent then has the permanent task of negotiating and, as the case may be, concluding contracts, and carrying out matters entrusted to him in the name and on behalf of the manufacturer, tradesman or another agent.

6.3. *Film or Video Production Contracts*

Where parties enter into a contract for the production of a film or video, they should include among other provisions regarding the length of time necessary to complete filming, a provision as to the total budget granted and the consequences of exceeding such budget. The parties should also resolve any problems as to copyright. Thus, any firm wishing to sponsor a film has to call on the services of a professional producer. Furthermore, save for an express provision in the contract, the rule is that no right of exploitation may be transferred to the sponsor (see the provisions below).

6.4. *Contracts for the Exploitation of Copyright*

Apart from being subject to the rules of general contract law, contracts for the exploitation of copyright are governed by the provisions of the 1957 Act (see section 4.2 above). The extent of the rights transferred must, therefore, be rigorously defined as regards both reproduction and performance of the work.

Similarly, although the author may transfer an entire part of his rights over his work, he may not transfer all rights over his future works.

Moreover, performance, publishing and audiovisual production contracts must be recorded in writing, as must free authorisations to perform. Proof of a contract may only be established against the author by evidence in writing (Cour de Cassation, Civil Division, 6 November 1979).

6.5. *Trademark Licences*

Trademark licences are contracts under which the right of exploitation is granted to a third party in consideration of royalty payments. Moreover, several separate licences may be granted in order to allow exploitation of the mark for different categories of products/services or during various different sporting events.

Other restrictions may be placed on the rights of the licensee, for example, on the type or duration of exploitation or territorial limitations under the licence. The licensee, therefore, undertakes to exploit the trademark, to pay royalties and observe certain obligations relating to the quality or presentation of the product(s) covered by the licence.

The licensor must be the owner of the trademark and, as such, be in a position to guarantee quiet enjoyment of its rights to the licensee and thus ensure protection and renewal of the trademark for the entire duration of the licence. Where a third party disputes the right of exploitation of the trademark, the licensee may join the licensor as a party to the proceedings.

7. Standard Contract Terms

Generally speaking and also in sports marketing, the following are the main clauses to be included in a contract between the parties.

7.1. *The Parties*

The contract must describe clearly the identity of the parties by stating their names and addresses and, where one of the parties is a company, its registration number with the Trade and Companies Register, together with the name of the individual who has authority to commit the company.

7.2. *Recitals*

The recitals set out the extent to which each of the parties commits itself on the basis of its capacity.

7.3. *Definitions*

If desired, the contract may include by way of a specific clause the definitions of terms used in the contract to describe the property rights referred to therein, the event or show in respect of which the contract is concluded, the advertising techniques envisaged as part of the contract and so on.

7.4. Purpose

The object of this clause is to specify the subject matter of the agreement between the parties. See p. 103 above.

7.5. Financial Terms

Generally speaking, the purpose of the price clause is to determine and specify the price in a sales contract or contract for services.

The financial terms of a sports promotion agreement (sponsoring a sports person or a competition) with the payment of lump sums, royalties or other commissions must be rigorously and precisely defined taking particular account of the following aspects:

- dates of payment;
- taxable base of sums paid;
- amounts to be imputed to this base;
- determination of rates of exchange;
- provisions relating to the taxable base and to the calculation of interest.

Where the payment is made in kind, provisions should be included to cover the construction of equipment, the funding thereof and guarantees deriving therefrom.

Similarly, it is normal practice in sponsorship agreements to link the payment of premiums or bonuses to the performance of the sports person or his position in the competition on set dates.

Moreover, under the provisions of Article 31 of Order No. 86–1243 of 1 December 1986, which provide that 'any purchase of a product or any provision of services for a professional activity' must be invoiced, any invoice 'must bear the name of the parties and their address, the date of sale or provision of service, the quantity, the precise description and the unit price exclusive of VAT of the products sold and services rendered together with any reductions, rebates or refunds which are due in principle and are calculable in figures at the time the sale is effected or the service is provided, whatever the date of payment'.

7.6. Duration of the Contract

The contract may be of fixed or indefinite duration (sponsorship agreements are often concluded for a specified event, i.e. the sports person's participation in a competition or a series of tests).

In the case of fixed duration, expiry of the term automatically terminates the contract, subject to the terms and conditions of renewal thereof, if any. In the case of indefinite contracts, they may be terminated by one of the parties at any time generally by giving notice sufficiently far in advance. Abrupt termination of the contract, failure to give adequate notice, wrongful termination, or intent to harm the other party, obliges the wrongdoer to compensate the other party.

In both cases, the parties must use their best endeavours to alleviate the consequences of the breach by non-competition clauses, taking back stocks or restitution (e.g. trademark licences and sponsorship agreements).

7.7. Respective Obligations

Great care must be taken to ensure that the clauses setting out the mutual obligations of the parties properly define the extent thereof.

Furthermore, in addition to the obligations arising under the type of exploitation envisaged by the contract, it is possible to provide for additional obligations such as:

- Obligation to inform. Where the contract provides for a substantial collective effort by the parties, for example, a licence contract, the licensee has a duty to keep his licensor informed of his activities. Thus, the licensee shall grant the licensor a right of inspection and control over his exploitation by submitting to the licensor his inventory, his financial statements and the details as to the installation of his sales point.
- Exclusivity by category of products. Where the sponsor takes part in the organisation of a sports competition, he frequently requests in consideration thereof exclusivity of sponsorship within his category of products/services. Care should, therefore, be taken to define the obligation thereby placed on the organiser or the sponsored sports person and the extent of the category of products.

7.8. Penalties for Breach of Obligations

This clause provides for the consequences of failure by either party to perform its obligations. Generally speaking – and sometimes on the basis of how far the obligation in question was decisive in inducing the other party to enter the contract – the other party may either rescind the contract on the stated terms and conditions or demand payment of lump-sum compensation (penalty clause).

Thus, for example, sponsorship agreements may provide for the following violations to result in rescission of the contract:

- Public appearances. This obligation is by definition inherent to sponsorship agreements. The sponsored individual thereby undertakes to participate in cocktails, autographical sessions, conferences and so on. Failure to honour such obligation will result in rescission of the agreement. Detailed provisions should also be made for the timetable of such appearances and the funding thereof by the sponsor.

- No counter-advertising. Particularly in sponsorship agreements, the sponsored individual shall undertake neither to make nor cause to be made any declaration which may damage the trademark or professional services provided by the sponsor. The sponsored individual would be held liable in the event of such behaviour and it would bring the contract automatically to an end in accordance with the terms and conditions set forth in the deed.

7.9. Breach of Contract Clause

There are three possible ways in which contracts providing for lasting collaboration between the parties may be terminated: time (see section 7.6 at p. 110), fault (which will affect the transaction by application of contractual liability) and amendment of the main elements of the contract (which may cause the contract to lapse or terminate). As mentioned briefly earlier, the contract may make provision for termination on any grounds: taking back of stock, restitution of signs and distinctive logos, and compensation as the case may be. Similarly, non-competition clauses may also be included provided that they comply with domestic and European Community rules. However, separate provision should be made for non-competition provisions to cover the period of performance of the contract.

7.10. Applicable Law

The Rome Convention of 19 June 1980 relating to the law governing contractual obligations provides that 'the contract is governed by the law of the parties' choice'. However, it goes on: 'where no governing law has been chosen, the contract is governed by the law of the country with which it appears most closely related'.

7.11. Force Majeure

Save where the law makes express provision for the applicability and effects of *force majeure*, the parties are free to determine the constituent elements thereof. Furthermore, the parties should make provision for the effects of *force majeure* on the outcome of the contract to cover the scenario where such an event of *force majeure* causes extensive disruption of performance of the contractual obligations.

7.12. Schedules

The purpose of the schedules is to assist comprehension and construction of the contract by describing the products or works (timetable of sporting events concerned, list of trademarks, designs or models used) which are the subject of the contract or by exhibiting the relevant administrative authorisations or documents of proof.

In order to avoid disputes as to the contents thereof, it is recommended that they be signed by the parties on the same terms and conditions as the contract itself.

8. Advertising and Promotion

8.1. Applicable Rules

There are no regulations governing this area in its entirety. It is, therefore, governed by agreements between the parties, case law decisions and a mosaic of legislation. We shall mention Act No. 92–60 of 18 January 1992 on comparative publicity, Act No. 91–32 of 10 January 1991 on the anti-tobacco and alcohol campaign (amending Act No. 76–616 of 9 July 1976), Act No. 86–1067 of 30 September 1986 and Decree No. 92–280 of 27 March 1992 (which incorporates the provisions of the EC Council Directive of 3 October 1989) on advertising and audiovisual sponsoring, and Articles 44 and 45 of Act No. 1193 of 27 December 1973 on misleading advertising.

As a rule, one may freely engage in advertising, and more specifically sports advertising, provided that it is neither false nor of a type likely to induce mistake; that it does not constitute an act of unfair competition or counterfeit; and that it does not infringe binding legislation, particularly that relating to public health and safety.

Particular rules apply depending on the medium used (audiovisual advertising), the nature of the products (alcoholic drinks, tobacco, health products), or the contents of the advertised message (comparative publicity, advertising by means of a person's image).

8.2. Tobacco Advertisements

As from 1 January 1993, pursuant to the 10 January 1991 Act, it will be illegal to advertise, directly or indirectly, tobacco or tobacco products through any medium whatsoever.

The above prohibition will also apply to any free distribution of tobacco products and any sponsoring arrangement the purpose of which is to publicise or advertise directly or indirectly tobacco or any derivative products.

8.3. Alcohol Advertisements

This is governed by the 9 July 1976 Act as amended by the 10 January 1991 Act.

Thus, one may freely advertise drinks containing less than 1.2 degrees of alcohol. However, advertisements of drinks containing more than 1.2 degrees of alcohol are subject to substantial restrictions regarding the advertising medium and contents. Thus, any form of direct or indirect advertising of alcoholic drinks is forbidden on sports grounds and on television.

Similarly, sponsoring is forbidden where the purpose or effect thereof is the direct or indirect advertisement of alcoholic drinks.

8.4. Television Sponsoring

Some sponsorships of television programmes are forbidden under the provisions of the 27 March 1992 Decree; these are sponsorships of newscasts and political programmes and sponsorships by firms mainly producing or selling alcoholic drinks and tobacco products.

Otherwise, television programmes may be sponsored. Sponsored programmes must then identify the sponsor who must exercise discretion. The 1992 Decree provides that:

'1. The sponsor must not influence the contents and programming thereof in any way which may adversely affect the editorial independence of the company or television service or render the editors thereof liable.
2. They must not encourage the purchase or hire of products or services of the sponsor or a third party and in particular they must not contain promotional references specific to such products or services.
3. They must be clearly identified as such at the beginning or end of the sponsored programme.
   One may identify the name of the sponsor, the tradename, the corporate name, the business sector, the trademarks or distinctive signs or symbols which are usually associated with the sponsor, such as the sign, logo or sound symbol. It is forbidden to use any advertising slogan and to present the product itself or its packaging.
   However, where a games or competition programme is being sponsored, samples of the sponsor's products or services may be freely distributed to individuals provided that no advertising message is thereby communicated.
4. During the sponsored programme and the introductory titles, reference to the sponsor must be brief and discreet and must be limited to mentioning the contribution made by the sponsor who can only be identified using the means referred to in 3. above.'

8.5. Advertising Agencies

Where an advertising agency is given the task of promoting an event, it is entitled to copyright over its advertising designs. The contract with the advertiser (organiser of the event) provides for the rights of exploitation of the design to be transferred to the advertiser.

8.6. *The Advertisement of Films Shot at Sporting Events*

The advertisement of films is subject to obtaining the same authorisation to exploit as cinematographic films. Authorisation is delivered by the Ministry of Culture after a decision is made by the Commission monitoring cinematographic films.

Provisions for the publicity of this type of film could be included in the transfer of the exploitation rights set forth in the contract between the film producer and the agency or advertiser.

8.7. *Advertising and Official Events*

Sports federations frequently pass regulations restricting advertising during competitions falling within their jurisdiction. Failure by their members to observe these rules is penalised by disciplinary sanctions.

For example, the French Tennis Federation stipulates that the advertising boards placed around the courts must be black and green.

8.8. *Comparative Publicity*

Authorised by Act No. 92–60 of 18 January 1992, comparative publicity must comply with the terms and conditions laid down by this legislation. Failure to comply therewith will result in an order for damages and the application of criminal sanctions.

Advertising may henceforth compare goods or services by using the trademark, the corporate name, the name, the brand name or the sign of other manufacturers. Such comparative techniques are only legal where the following conditions, in particular, are met:

- The advertisements must be faithful, accurate and not of a type likely to induce mistake on the part of the consumer.
- The advertisements must be limited to an objective comparison which may only concern the main, significant, relevant and verifiable features of goods or services of the same type and available on the market.
- Any comparison of prices must concern like products, sold on the same terms and must indicate the period during which such prices are maintained by the advertiser.
- Comparative advertisements may not feature on tickets for entry to shows or to places open to the public.

8.9. Right of Portrayal

Advertising designs are restricted by the rights of the person (*droits de la personnalité*) (Article 9 of the Civil Code). Use of a sport person's photograph without his or her consent is deemed to be interference with his or her private life and is forbidden as such (Court of Appeal of Paris, 3 April 1987).

Where the portrayal is accompanied by unpleasant commentaries which are damaging to the sports person's reputation, proceedings in defamation may be taken against the advertiser.

9. The Venue

The organisation of a sporting event may raise difficulties relating to the necessary authorisations (9.1), possible liability of the organisers (9.2) and the authorities (9.3) concerned, particularly regarding protection of sponsors.

9.1. Necessary Authorisations

It is necessary to obtain authorisation from the competent federation and sometimes from the administrative authorities before organising a sports competition.

Authorisation by the federation is granted where the organiser observes the obligations laid down by the regulations of the federation relating in particular to the running of the competition and the liability of the organiser in respect of matters of law and order.

This authorisation is particularly crucial because, once obtained, the federation automatically acknowledges the planned competition and failure to obtain such authorisation prevents the member athletes of the federation from taking part in the event (unless they can obtain an individual exemption).

Administrative authorisation is compulsory for the organisation of three categories of sporting events: namely, those taking place on public grounds; those concerning closed circuits motor vehicle contests; and boxing events. It is granted on condition that various pre-determined conditions are met, namely: the organiser must take out an insurance policy; bear the costs of policing the event; and be a member of a group, governed by the 1 July 1901 Act, which has been in existence for at least 6 months and is affiliated to a federation.

The sports premises and equipment used for sports competitions only rarely belong to the organiser. Most belong to the local authorities. The organiser obtains the use thereof by entering into a contract for the use of public grounds.

9.2. Responsibilities of the Organiser

The organiser must first comply with national and local regulatory requirements governing the correct running of shows, publicity notices, public health and safety and possibly the construction of the stadium. The organiser must also observe the particular rules of the event (compulsory number of seats for certain football matches).

As the organiser assumes a general obligation to ensure safety and to use his best endeavours, he may be held liable in civil proceedings (liability in tort or contract) for any damage inflicted on an individual during an event.

In order to obtain compensation on the basis of civil (or administrative) liability, the plaintiff must show a sufficiently direct causal link between the act giving rise to the damage and the damage sustained. Once the act giving rise to the damage is proved, compensation is ordered to cover the entire loss.

In order to limit the scope of this liability, the organiser may be tempted to include clauses limiting liability. However, it should be emphasised that these clauses may not be used to cover personal injury (Cour de Cassation, Chambre Civile, 2 August 1950).

However, the organiser may be better advised to use other means of reducing the burden of his liability: by invoking fault on the part of the victim or the liability of a third party, an agent, a co-contractor or the authorities.

The organiser may also be held liable for damage caused to the neighbourhood during the competition on the basis of unreasonable interference with the right to quiet enjoyment (e.g. 'loud and frequent noises coming from a rifle range' – Cour de Cassation, Chambre Civile, 13 January 1972).

The organiser may also face criminal liability, particularly where he opens a drinks bar in an area in which it is forbidden to sell drinks because it is too close to a stadium (Tribunal de Grande Instance Quimperè, October 1979). Temporary refreshment bars set up within the confines of the stadium appear to be forbidden in principle by Article 147 of the Code des Débits de Boissons.

However, it has become common practice to break this rule and judges turn a blind eye to it. Most stadia are confident of receiving a financial contribution from such refreshment bars.

9.3. Powers

The organiser has the benefit of a right of use over the grounds where the competition takes place and is, therefore, free to determine the terms and conditions of entry and access thereto (granting accreditations and passes).

He should also ensure that contracts of exclusivity are performed. He will keep an eye out generally to make sure that sponsors of the competition are not disadvantaged by the presence of their competitors at the event and that they are able to promote their interests on beneficial terms.

As regards the many problems linked with the performance of the contracts of exclusivity relating to televised broadcasts of sporting events, reference should be made here to the 'Code of Good Conduct' adopted on 22 January 1992 following a round-table discussion between the television authorities and the sports organisations called by the Conseil Supérieur de l'Audiovisuel ('CSA').

The CSA is an independent authority which, pursuant to Act No. 89–25 of 17 January 1989, has the task of safeguarding the free exercise of audiovisual communications on the terms and conditions laid down by this Act.

Thus, the CSA adopted the following principles which are intended to safeguard the public's right to be informed:

- those television channels which do not have exclusive coverage of the sporting event may broadcast short extracts thereof free of charge in their news programmes and regular news bulletins;
- sports programmes run by a channel which does not have exclusive coverage may include short extracts of the broadcast in their programme in consideration of a fair payment;
- film crews of a broadcaster not having exclusivity are freely entitled to entry to a sporting event for the purposes of showing a recorded broadcast limited to regional programmes;
- henceforth, no provision for an exclusivity clause for interviews may appear in contracts between sports people and broadcasters.

With the consent of all the parties to the discussions, this Code is expected to incorporate more and more provisions with a view to ironing out all the remaining difficulties.

10. Dispute Resolution

Any difficulty encountered by the parties, which will particularly and frequently be problems connected with performance of a contract or liabilities following damage, may first be brought before the courts (10.1). Furthermore, the parties may mutually decide to refer the matter to domestic or international arbitration (10.2). Finally, brief mention should be made of the alternative procedures available, namely conciliation and settlements between the parties (10.3).

10.1. Court Proceedings

According to the case in question, court proceedings may be commenced either before the administrative courts or before the judicial courts. A number of years will elapse between the time of filing the summons, which denotes the beginning of the proceedings, and the execution of the final decision rendered.

This is due to the inherent complexity of the matter, the length of time taken to prepare the case for trial and to the exercise of rights of appeal and also the time necessary to enforce a judgment.

This is why, in urgent cases, a number of special procedures, summons and ex-parte applications (ordonnance en référé, ordonnances sur requête), are available for bringing the matter before the first and second tier courts (court of appeal).

10.1.1. The référé order

In general, *référé* orders may only be applied for in urgent cases. The standard of urgency has been assessed in a flexible way by French courts and is a question of fact, not of law. As a result, the Cour de Cassation does not hear appeals on this issue.

At the request of the applicant, the President of the Court may, therefore, grant an injunction in order to prevent imminent damage (*dommage imminent*), or to stop an illegal action. It is within the President's discretion to decide whether damage is imminent.

Moreover, the order granted may not cover a 'serious dispute'. In such a case, the President will not grant the injunction but will send the parties back to the court to settle the dispute.

10.1.2. Ex-parte orders (ordonnance sur requête)

Ex parte orders are made without notice to the defendant. An individual refers the case to the President by means of an unilateral application. This power is specifically provided for, *inter alia*, in relation to attachments (*saisie-arrêté*) and charging orders (*saisie conservatoire*).

This action may be used when, in case of extreme urgency, it is undesirable for the defendant to be informed of a forthcoming decision.

The party against whom an *ex parte* order has been issued may apply to the judge who issued the order to have it reversed. Such a procedure results in a hearing with both parties in attendance. For instance, in the event of an application for an attachment or charging order, a creditor may request an *ex parte* order so as to avoid any depletion of the debtor's assets; if it is granted, the debtor will then be entitled to contest it.

10.1.3. Legal costs and expenses

During the proceedings, each party pays for its costs. As a rule, at the end of the proceedings, the party losing the case is ordered to bear all the costs. But the court may consider that the winner should bear all, or a part, of the costs.

Costs consist of fees incurred in conducting the case (expert witnesses' fees, lawyers' fees).

However, it should be noted that lawyers' (*avocats*) fees, fees for legal specialists or professors' opinions and a party's travelling costs are not considered as costs. However, if the court considers it inequitable that a party should pay for its fees and costs, the judge may compel the other party to pay a portion thereof (Nouveau Code de Procédure Civile – NCPC – Art. 700).

The amount which a party requests of the judge depends on the stage and duration of the proceedings. In practice, a sum ranging from 5,000 FF to 700,000 FF is usually requested, but judges do not often grant such an indemnity.

If a plaintiff or a defendant is deemed to have abused his right to resort to legal action, he might be ordered to pay the costs or a civil fine or damages. This is the consequence of the 'abuse of right' theory. When a party to proceedings is liable for any wrong suffered by the other party, he has to compensate usually up to 50,000 FF for any damage caused.

10.2. Arbitration

Arbitration is also binding on the parties. It is an attractive alternative to cumbersome court proceedings.

The NCPC provides for two sets of arbitration rules: one governing domestic arbitration, and the other governing international arbitration. Great liberty is accorded to the parties to formulate their own rules and procedures.

10.2.1. Domestic arbitration

An agreement to arbitrate may arise by virtue of either a written clause contained or referred to in the contract between the parties (an arbitration clause, stipulating that the arbitration is to be used to settle any dispute arising out of the contract) or an agreement referring the matter to arbitration once litigation has commenced.

In both instances, the agreement must expressly set forth either the name of the arbitrator or arbitrators or the method by which the arbitrators are to be appointed. Failure to comply with the foregoing formalities renders the arbitration clause or agreement void (NCPC, Arts. 1442, 1443 and 1448).

An arbitration clause that purports to resolve a matter, which is within the exclusive jurisdiction of the courts, is void. In French domestic arbitration, an arbitration clause is only valid in commercial matters (Commercial Code, Art. 631).

If legal proceedings are instituted in respect of a matter which is already being arbitrated, the court should decline jurisdiction. It should also decline jurisdiction where a dispute is subject to arbitration but where arbitration has not yet been commenced, unless the arbitration clause is manifestly void (NCPC, Art. 1458).

As far as the conduct of arbitration is concerned and subject to certain fundamental rules (e.g. respect of the right to a defence), the parties are free to provide for their own procedure.

The arbitration award takes immediate effect, subject to any appeal. However, enforcement by means of specific performance or injunction (*exécution forcée*) is only available if the arbitration decision has received an *exequatur* (order of enforcement). The *exequatur* must be granted by the High Court

(Tribunal de Grande Instance) for the area in which the arbitration award was made (NCPC, Art. 1477). No appeal lies from an order granting an *exequatur*.

10.2.2. International arbitration
The other set of arbitration rules apply to international arbitrations. The rules of international arbitration are more liberal than those governing domestic arbitration. An arbitration is deemed to be international when it deals with matters pertaining to international commerce (NCPC, Art. 1492).

Moreover, the parties are free to follow their own rules of procedure and to specify the applicable law to govern the procedural aspects of the dispute. The parties may, in fact, agree to apply one particular law to govern the procedure. If they fail to stipulate the rules of procedure to be applied to the arbitration, the arbitrator may decide on the appropriate procedure.

The arbitrator applies the law stipulated in the arbitration agreement, failing which he applies whichever law he considers appropriate. In either case, he must consider commercial practice and custom (NCPC, Art. 1496).

International arbitration awards are not automatically recognised in France. Two conditions must be fulfilled before they are recognised: the existence of the award must be proved by the production of certain documents and the award must not be manifestly contrary to French international public policy in order to get an *exequatur*, which has to be applied for at the Tribunal de Grande Instance.

A decision refusing to recognise or to grant an *exequatur* of a foreign international arbitration award may be appealed but only in limited circumstances (NCPC, Art. 1502).

10.3. Alternative Dispute Resolution

10.3.1. Conciliation procedure
The parties are free at the outset of the initial contract or at the beginning of the dispute to agree to use their best endeavours to reach a conciliation with or without the intervention of a mediator of their choice before taking the matter to the State courts or referring it to arbitration.

If there is a favourable outcome to conciliation proceedings (the parties may follow the conciliation regulations laid down by certain private bodies) and the agreement includes mutual concessions, it must be performed in the same way as a settlement.

10.3.2. Settlements
Article 2044 of the Civil Code defines settlements as 'a contract whereby the parties put an end to a dispute which has arisen or prevent the occurrence of a future dispute'. It must be in writing.

Settlements are contracts. Apart from the rules expressly applicable thereto (Civil Code, Art. 2044), settlements are governed by the general rules applicable to any contract.

Like judgments, settlements are final and must be performed in accordance with their specific provisions; failing this, an application may be made to the court for enforcement.

SPORTS
MARKETING

Germany

by Dr. Dirk-Reiner Martens

1. Sports Marketing – A Business

Sport is of major importance in the Federal Republic of Germany. 19 million citizens belong to one of the 68,000 sports clubs of the Deutsche Sportbund.[1] The preservation of health and physical fitness is the main reason for their sporting activities; furthermore, sport is a hobby and is practised just for fun and company.[2]

The value of production of sports, leisure and camping goods in 1991 amounted to approximately DM 5.37 billion. DM 1.75 billion was attributable to exports and DM 3.71 billion to imports. Apart from the manufacture of sports products, a lucrative market for sporting services has developed with an estimated value of DM 50 billion.[3]

The modern media rank very high in the propagation of sports. High payments are required to ensure the transmission licences. For example, UFA paid US $91 million for the transmission rights of the Wimbledon tennis tournament to be transmitted worldwide on 'RTL Plus'. However, in general, it is not easy for German private television stations to prevail over their State-run competitors at a national and European level, since State-owned institutions have the benefit of relatively high revenues at their disposal when bidding for exclusive transmission rights of sporting events.

Indeed, all parties involved seem to benefit.

The *organisers* of sporting events receive funds not only by way of royalties but also through sponsors who are interested in the success of an event.

The *media* follow various routes of funding ranging from traditional advertising to product placement and the admission of sponsors to the programmes.

In particular, the *manufacturers* have a distinct interest in that their products are identified with top-ranking athletes who act as important advertising media.

1. G+J-Branchenbild, *Sport*, position as at January 1992, p. 1.
2. *Loc. cit.* p. 8.
3. *Loc. cit.* p. 1.

Their remuneration reflects the scarcity of this group, which often includes household names.

The interlocking of sports and commercial interests in Germany has led to the development of new marketing ideas and techniques, such as the purchase of whole football clubs, the marketing of whole sporting events up to comprehensive financing of top-ranking athletes.

2. The German Legal System

Commercialisation of sport seems to go hand in hand with an increase in disputes. There is, generally speaking, no specific judicial system for sports disputes as they are usually brought before the established courts of the country.

The court system of Germany is based on the German Constitution (*Grundgesetz*).

The highest German court is the Federal Constitutional Court which may also override acts of the legislature.

It is, however, the civil courts which primarily deal with sports matters. The local courts have jurisdiction in disputes, which involve a value of up to DM 6,000 (*Amtsgericht*); any dispute of higher value is to be brought before the district courts (*Landgericht*). In principle, there are two further instances: the Regional Appeal Court (*Oberlandesgericht*) and the Federal Supreme Court (*Bundesgerichtshof*), the highest civil court. In special matters, such as the granting of public transmission rights or the recognition of the nonprofit-making status of sports clubs, the administrative courts have jurisdiction.

3. Sources of Law

In contrast to the legal system of the common law countries, such as the United Kingdom, German law is generally based on codified law.

The highest ranking source of law in private law is the Constitution (*Grundgesetz*) of the Federal Republic of Germany, followed by statutory legislation of the federal government and, then, statutory legislation of the individual regions. International treaties, which have been properly ratified and promulgated, are part of the domestic law and are equal to Federal statutory law. Although ranked below parliamentary statutes, statutory instruments (delegated legislation) are, in practice, important, as they usually deal with technical details not regulated in the statutes themselves. The lowest source of statutory law is to be found in the bye-laws of municipalities. The customary law ranks equal to the statutory law, but is generally of minor importance, unless it concerns trade customs and conventions. In the absence of an express agreement between the parties these can play a decisive role in litigation.

Although the parties are generally free to negotiate the contents of their agreement, German law contains a number of mandatory provisions, which have to be taken into account when drafting a contract. Outstanding examples are the provisions relating to unfair competition and copyright. Such law may not be modified by the contractual parties.

There is no special codification of 'sports law'. Not surprisingly, rules and regulations concerning sports marketing are, therefore, contained in a number of individual laws.

Contracts governed by German law tend to be significantly shorter than, for example, those governed by English or American law, as the parties rely more readily upon a comprehensive body of statutory rules for the drafting, interpretation and performance of a contract such as the Civil Code (*Bürgerlichesgesetzbuch*) and the Commercial Code (*Handelsgesetzbuch*). The Civil Code consists of a comprehensive set of rules regulating the contractual relations between the parties. These rules are supplemented and sometimes modified by rules contained in the Commercial Code.

Statutory provisions of particular relevance to sport relate to the rules on intellectual property rights and on unfair competition. They serve to balance the need for the protection of the holder of intellectual property rights on the one hand and a need for the preservation of fair competition on the other hand. In practice, these different interests conflict, as the case law illustrates. Patents, utility models, registered designs and copyrights are protected by various statutes on intellectual property. The brand name and the name of a company, as well as its trademarks and logos, are further protected by the law against unfair competition (*Gesetz gegen den Unlauteren Wettbewerb*).

4. Intellectual Property Rights

The success of a sports product depends first and foremost on its quality, but increasingly on well targeted marketing. Public awareness mainly depends on its 'signalling effect' towards the customer. The customers are to recognise and classify the sports product by way of a brand name, a slogan, a particular design or other form of distinction. The protection of the holder of intellectual property rights against any competitors violating such rights can be fundamental to the success of a marketing campaign. The following will give a brief account of the current legal framework protecting the holder of intellectual property rights.

4.1. The Trademark Law

The rules on trademarks are laid down in the Trademark Act of 2 January 1968, as amended on 23 April 1992.[4]

4. Sections 1, 11, 64 I Copyright Act.

A prerequisite for the protection of a trademark is its registration in the Trademark Register.[5] The trademark owner is protected, initially, for a ten year period, but may apply for an extension of the term by another ten years.[6]

The trademark law protects the owner against the use of identical marks or similar marks if such similar marks are capable of being confused with the registered marks. The owner, who seeks to protect his trademark, must register as soon as possible, since the priority principle 'first come first served' applies. The owner of a registered trademark has a right to have any subsequent registration of such trademarks struck off.

The use of trademarks is freely assignable. It may be assigned to third parties without having to transfer the business to which it relates.[7] This serves both parties. The assignee may wish to use the trademark commercially to improve the marketing of his product, whilst the assignor and owner of the trademark obtains a royalty for granting its use.

The owner of a trademark or the name of a company has a right to compel any third party to refrain from affixing such name or registered trademark to his goods, packaging or advertising brochures, price lists, business letters, recommendations, invoices and the like.[8] The presentation of a product can be protected in much the same manner.

4.2. Copyright

The rules on the protection of copyright were codified in 1965, and further strengthened by amendments in 1990.

German copyright law provides protection for any immaterial intellectual work which enters into the material world so that it can be used by a third party (in a material or immaterial form). Copyright protected works cover, *inter alia*, literary work (including speeches), works of music and graphic art, photographs and films.

The copyright is a proprietary right which is effective without being registered. Once the work has been created, the creator's intellectual and personal relations to the work and his use of the work are protected.

The creator has an exclusive right to exploit his work in a tangible form (reproduction, distribution, exhibition) and in an intangible form (lecture, performance, presentation, transmission, communication by means of visual and sound records, communication of broadcasts).[9] The term of protection expires 70 years after the death of the 'author'.[10]

5. Section 97 *et seq.* Copyright Act.
6. Version of 7 June 1909 (*Federal Law Gazette*, p. 499) as amended on 17 December 1990 (*Federal Law Gazette*, p. 2840).
7. Section 9 Registered Designs Act.
8. BGH NJW 1990, p. 1235.
9. Sections 1, 11, 15 *et seq.* Copyright Act.
10. Sections 1, 11, 64 I Copyright Act.

The right of use may be assigned to third parties. The creator's personal right remains, however, with the creator.

The right of use is transferred by means of licence agreements. The licence concerning these rights may be limited as to territory, time or contents.

The owner is entitled to forbearance and compensation in the event of a wrongful use of these rights. In deviation from the usual rules on the assessment of damages, the aggrieved party may claim the profit of the infringing party in lieu of lost earnings. In case of reproduction of protected works, the beneficiary is entitled to destruction or transfer of the reproductions.[11]

4.3. The Act against Unfair Competition

The Act against Unfair Competition came into force in 1909 and has undergone various amendments, largely in connection with the Act Concerning Consumer Credits and the Act concerning the Change of the Civil Procedure Code and other Acts dated 17 December 1990.[12]

Section 1, which is the central and most comprehensive provision of the Act against Unfair Competition, prohibits any breach of good conduct and behaviour for the purpose of competition.

The Act sanctions, *inter alia*, misleading advertising, camouflaged advertising, sensational advertising, restraint of advertising, certain forms of comparative advertising and direct or indirect participation in third party's infringements.

In sports advertising one of the main concerns seems to be the problem of camouflaged advertising. Therefore, sponsoring and product placement have to be checked as to their compliance with the respective inter-state broadcasting agreements between the stations, which specifically cover this point. As a rule, advertising must be separated from the display of sports events. If, during the transmission of, for example, a football match, the name of the sponsor or the emblem or trademark of a company were to be shown in an eye-catching manner, the rules against unfair trading would be infringed. The question is whether the advertising effect was deliberate and thus avoidable or simply incidental. The unfairness of such action would lie in the deception of the spectator, who may not consciously recognise the advertising effect of the product placement.

4.4. The Law of Registered Designs

Not all designs are capable of being protected. Protection is restricted to intellectual-aesthetic designs, which are commercially exploitable, for example,

11. Sections 97 *et seq.* Copyright Act.
12. Version of 7 June 1909 (*Federal Law Gazette*, p. 499) as amended on 17 December 1990 (*Federal Law Gazette*, p. 2840).

designs and graphics, such as mascots, and the design of products. The rights under the copyright law and those under the law of registered designs have equal status. However, the design has to be registered with the Patent Office to be effective. The term of design protection may not exceed 20 years.[13]

5. The Contracts and Preliminary Agreements

5.1. Preliminary Contract

Preliminary contracts, commonly known as 'heads of agreement', may be a preferred option for negotiating parties, who already agree on essential parts, but wish to postpone the main agreement on detail to a later date. This preliminary contract usually gives either party the right to specific performance, that is, to the conclusion of the main agreement. The parties must, however, have reached agreement on all essential elements of the contract so that the content of the main contract is already determinable.[14]

5.2. The Conclusion of the Contract

The making of a contract in the area of sport does not pose any particular legal problems. The parties to a contract are free to make their own arrangements, provided, however, they do not conflict with mandatory statutory provisions.

The contract is made by offer and acceptance of the parties (Section 145 *et seq.* of the German Civil Code); this can also be effected orally or by conduct, if no written form is required by law and the parties have not agreed otherwise. Non-compliance with the required form of a legal transaction results in the invalidity of the transaction but may be remedied by performance.

Contracts may be concluded by the principals or their respective representatives (Section 164 *et seq.* of the German Civil Code). The representative has to disclose to the other party his proxy-status in such a manner that he is clearly acting on behalf of a particular principal; such intention may be inferred from the circumstances.[15] In the event of invalid representation, the contract is provisionally invalid until approved by the representative. In the event that the agency is not disclosed, the contract is made with the 'undisclosed agent'. The principal may, however, retroactively approve the contract by stating so to the other party and, by doing so, become a party to the contract, unless the original party to this contract ('undisclosed agent') is 'of the essence' to the other party.

---

13. Section 9 Registered Designs Act.
14. BGH NJW 1990, p. 1235.
15. Palandt-Heinrichs, BGB, 51st ed., Section 164 marginal No. 1.

5.3. Consideration

The validity of a contract is not dependent on consideration. However, gifts must be executed by notarial deed in order to be binding. If the arrangement is a mere act of courtesy (*Gefälligkeit*), without any consideration or other benefit in money's worth, the parties may lack the intention to create a legally binding agreement. Although such situations may arise in the area of non-commercial sport, this would be unusual in professional sport.

In the event of the non-performance or faulty performance of a contract by one party, the other party to the contract is entitled to claim damages or to rescind the contract.

5.4. Form and Execution

Where written form of a document is required the document must be signed by the parties personally. The signature must be affixed to the same document, unless each party signs the document which is intended for the other party (exchange of contract). If a copy of the contract is signed and sent by facsimile this does not comply with the requirement of written form.[16]

5.5. Void, Voidable and Illegal Contracts

A contract is void if it infringes statutory rules, which are intended to protect one or both parties to the contract. A contract is voidable if one party wilfully threatens or deceives the other or if one party enters into a contract by a false perception of essential facts.

Legal transactions may be *contra bonos mores* if they restrict the economic freedom of one party in such a manner that the party loses its self-determination or if a powerful position or monopoly position of one party results in the claiming of, for example, excessive prizes or excessive contractual penalties.

Licensing agreements of sports trademarks sometimes infringe the rules against unfair competition and may be ineffective if they are capable of unduly influencing market conditions. In the event of cross-border trading such conduct may also constitute an infringement of Articles 85 and 86 of the EC Treaty.

5.6. Privity of Contract

In principle, contracts are effective only between the contracting parties and do not grant any contractual rights to third parties. There are, however, exceptions where a contract is of a protective nature in favour of a third party. A third party does not acquire a right to claim the main performance, but is

16. Ffm NJW 1991, 2154.

covered by the duty to exercise proper care and protection. A third party may assert damages in contract in the event that these obligations are infringed.

In certain circumstances, an agreement between two football clubs to allow the transfer of a football player also creates rights on the part of the player concerned.

In the case of a contract to the benefit of a third party, the third party directly acquires an enforceable right to claim performance by the other contractual party.

5.7. Interpretation

Any contract has to be interpreted in good faith by taking customs and conventions into account.

Under German law, it is not so much the letter of the word but the real intentions of the parties which determine the construction of a contract. Statements must in cases of ambiguity be interpreted in conformity with the law so as to avoid the ineffectiveness of a legal transaction. If the contract itself does not provide an unequivocal interpretation, it may be construed by reference to the hypothetical intentions of the parties to the contract.[17]

The rules of codified law, however, take preference over the construction by reference to the parties' hypothetical intentions.

5.8. Frustration and Force Majeure

The doctrine of frustration does not normally play a part in the area of sports law, with perhaps one exception. Due to the unification of Germany and the demise of the State of East Germany, it is arguable that some contracts had to be adjusted to the new circumstances. The doctrine of frustration takes into account any unforeseen change of circumstances. One may distinguish between the objective and subjective element of a transaction. The objective element relates to those circumstances which are objectively required for the contract to be continued as a reasonable arrangement between the parties. The subjective element consists of certain expectations of both parties by which both parties were guided when making the contract.[18]

Only a substantial change, however, justifies a contract to be frustrated. Even the demise of East Germany as an independent State does not necessarily imply a substantial change of circumstances in a private contractual arrangement. If such material change can be established, the contract has to be adjusted to the changed conditions. Only if the continuance of a contract cannot be reasonably

17. BGH (Federal Supreme Court) 9, 278.
18. Larenz, Section 21 II, quoted by Palandt-Henrichs, German Civil Code, Section 242, marginal No. 122.

expected by a party, the contract partner is granted a right to terminate, or withdraw, from the contract as a whole.

5.9. Breach of Contract

5.9.1. Damage caused by delayed performance

It often occurs that sports events are delayed by reason of weather conditions or non-appearance of players, defects in satellite transmission or other technical problems. Sometimes one party to a contract can be blamed, sometimes none, occasionally both. The Civil Code tries to cater for all of these circumstances. In the event of one party being in default of his performance, the other party is entitled to claim compensation for the damage incurred as a result of the delay. If the other party is no longer interested in specific performance, he has a right to claim full compensation or withdraw from the contract as a whole. Prior to that, the aggrieved party must normally fix a deadline and threaten to repudiate the contract or to claim damages for non-performance unless the other party performs on time.

5.9.2. The impossibility of performance

If the performance of the contract becomes impossible, due to the fault of one party, the aggrieved party may claim damages. Alternatively, he may withdraw from the contract.

If the performance becomes impossible and none of the parties to the contract bears responsibility for it, the aggrieved money debtor may forfeit consideration. If compensation is however paid by a third party to the money debtor e.g. on the basis of an insurance policy, the other party is entitled to receive such funds. If payment has already been made he may reclaim the monies on the basis of unjustified enrichment.

5.9.3. Defective or partial performance

One of the most frequent breaches of contract occurs as a result of a party's defective performance. The German Civil Code covers such cases in special provisions relating to the special nature of a contract, such as the purchase contract and performance/success related agreements. Quite surprisingly, the Civil Code does not contain a general provision on defective performance which would cover all those cases not covered by the special provisions mentioned. It was left to the courts to develop the concept of what is now known as 'positive breach of contract'. The following concentrates on the defective performance of probably the most frequent classes of contract: the contract of sale/purchase and the success/performance related contract.

If the seller sells a defective product, the buyer has a right to either rescind the contract or to reduce the purchase price to allow for its reduced value. If the subject-matter of the purchase lacks a warranted specification upon the passing of the risk, the purchaser may claim damages as if the contract was not performed at all (Section 463 of the German Civil Code).

Under the law concerning success/performance related contracts, the customer has a right to subsequent improvement and, if this fails, a right to damages (Section 633 *et seq.* of the German Civil Code) apart from the right to rescind the contract or reduce the agreed price.

6. Standard Contract Terms

6.1. Choice of Law

The parties are free to choose the law which is to govern the contract (Article 27 of the Introductory Act to the German Civil Code). It is, however, recommendable to agree expressly on a choice of law to avoid ambiguities. Furthermore, the choice of law may be limited to some parts of the contract to cause a splitting of the proper law of the agreement. If no choice-of-law clause is included in a contract, it is the law most closely connected with the contract which applies (Article 28 of the Introductory Act to the German Civil Code).

It should be noted that the accrual, validity, contents and effects of intellectual property rights is governed by the law which applies to the intellectual property right itself. Thus, the parties are restricted in their general right to choose the law of their own preference.

6.2. Definitions

As under English law, the terms used in a contract should be defined to avoid ambiguities. In the German tradition of legal drafting, however, the definitions are not put at the beginning of the contract but occur when they first arise in the contract. There is, however, a trend to adopt the Anglo-American method of legal drafting.

Furthermore, German statutory law consists of many statutory definitions which usually apply if the parties do not include their own definitions.

6.3. Use of Rights

Usually, the parties who wish to transfer intellectual property rights determine the scope of their application. It is recommended to define clearly the use, that is, the period of time allowable, the persons permitted, the location and the nature and purpose of the use.

As long as the restrictions do not intend to distort competition or create unfair competition the parties are free to agree on any form of application.

6.4. Warranty Rights

The owner of the property rights normally warrants that the rights are unencumbered. Otherwise, the parties to the contract describe the encumbrances in detail.

6.5. Royalties and Accounting

In the absence of express agreements on royalties, payment methods and contractual penalties statutory provisions assist in filling such gaps, albeit to a limited extent. It is thus advisable to agree expressly on above all the amount, time and currency of payment. If the creditor requires payment on a certain date, he must ensure in the contract that the obligation has to be fulfilled on that day, in order to take into account considerable delays between performance and payment in cross-border money transactions.

6.6. Books Open to Inspection

The licensor is usually granted a right to demand information and a right to submission of accounts at regular intervals. Moreover, it is common for the licensor to be granted a right to inspect the relevant books of the licensee. In the event of disputes concerning the amount of fees and/or royalties it should be further agreed that an independent auditor commences an audit.

There is often a dispute as to who is to bear the costs for such inspection, and the clauses vary considerably. Generally, the costs are normally borne by the person calling for it. In case of irregularities discovered, such costs should, however, be recoverable, and provisions should be made in the contract to that effect.

6.7. Termination

If agreements are entered into for an indefinite period of time, a clause of ordinary termination, subject to a period of notice, should be included. German law always allows for the immediate or extraordinary termination of a contract if a party commits a material breach. It is prudent to stipulate the reasons or circumstances which allow the parties to terminate at short notice. A party may, for instance, wish to be released from the contract if there is a substantial change of management or shareholding structure of the other party.

If a licence agreement also concerns the delivery of products, provisions should be made for a final accounting. Arrangements ought to be made concerning the destiny of unsold products, at the date of the termination of the contract, and the payment of fees relating to those products.

6.8. Authentic Text

Contracts are often drafted in different languages. It should be determined which contract is to be the authorised version and which is considered to be a mere translation. It should be made clear that the authorised version is relevant in the case of any ambiguities.

6.9. Venue, Arbitration Court and Law of Procedure

Each licence agreement ought to include a court venue and jurisdiction clause; alternatively, an arbitration clause. The venue clause has to meet the requirements of Section 38 *et seq.* of the German Civil Procedure Code.

7. Different Types of Business Arrangements

7.1. Sponsorship Agreements

There is no special legislation relating to sponsorship agreements. In general, a sponsorship agreement consists of a combination of different individual standard contracts which are subject to the rules governing the individual classes of contract. It is, thus, often unclear which special statutory provisions are to apply if the parties fail to stipulate all the relevant terms in the contract.

The interest of a sponsor is focused mainly on events which attract a large number of spectators or viewers. The sponsoring of broadcasts is regulated in Section 3 VII of the RfStV, which generally permits any sponsoring, provided it does not serve the economic interests of the sponsor or any third party. In the event that not the broadcast is sponsored but the event which is to be transmitted, No. 4.2 of the ARD Guidelines concerning the Separation of Advertising and Programmes permit such promotion if and to the extent that there is an overriding interest in the programme and that the independence of the structure of the programme is not affected.[19] The advertising of tobacco products on television is, however, prohibited.

At the same time, the parties are to observe the rules on competition and intellectual property rights.

7.2. Merchandising

This area is not uniformly regulated either. It is governed by individual provisions in the copyright and trademark laws.

19. Baumbach/Hefermehl, *Wettbewerbsrecht* (Law on Competition), Section 1 of the Law against Unfair Competition, marginal No. 41.

The EC Directive on Product Liability has been incorporated into national law by the introduction of the Product Liability Act. Pursuant to Section 4 of the Product Liability Act the liability has been extended also to those persons who create the impression that they are the actual producers (e.g. licensors).

7.3. Commissioning Agreements

If goods or other articles, which serve advertising purposes, are supplied by third parties, it should be ensured that the intellectual property of third parties may only be used if there are corresponding rights agreed. Otherwise, there is the risk that third parties may claim the remedy of forbearance. If rights are created which are capable of being registered such registration is recommended.

7.4. Franchises

Franchise agreements are mixed agreements. They are agreements in which the franchisor grants the franchisee a franchise right for the purpose of supplying certain goods or services in return for direct or indirect financial remuneration. To date, there are no homogeneous statutory provisions concerning this type of contract. The leasing of rights constitutes the core of the contract.

A franchise agreement has to be delimited from exclusive dealer agreements, licence agreements, agency agreements and from the existence of corporate relations.

Franchise agreements must give due regard to the German and European cartel law.

7.5. Film and Video

If films and videos are produced, the principals have to take great care that copyrights and trademarks of third parties are not infringed. If persons are portrayed, the Artistic Copyright Act (*Kunsturhebergesetz*) must be complied with. Pursuant to Section 22 of the Artistic Copyright Act, the privilege as to one's own image is protected by law in various ways. The distribution and publication of the portrayed person requires the latter's consent, which, however, is considered to be given if he receives remuneration for being portrayed. This protection continues for a period of ten years after the death of the portrayed person and can be enforced by his heirs.

7.6. Supply Agreements

If a party is both a sponsor and a producer or supplier of goods, he usually seeks to ensure that his products are frequently used during the sports event and that products of third parties may only be presented in co-ordination with the sponsor. Respective guaranties and warranties are to be agreed. Again, anti-competition practices may infringe national and EC competition rules.

8. Specific Rights and Agreements

The parties may wish to secure their legal positions prior to the conclusion of the main contract. There are a number of possibilities to achieve such an objective.

8.1. Options

An option is the right to bring about a contract by unilateral declaration if it is exercised. The option right follows from a contract, which is subject to a condition precedent, and which becomes absolute/unconditional by the statement of option.[20] The option holder may bring about the contract by exercising the option although there is no obligation to exercise the option. If the option is not exercised within a certain period it usually lapses. It is recommended to specify the duration of the option, the option price, the amount of an option premium and the terms of the option, in particular, to designate the contractual party who shall receive the notice concerning the exercise of the option, since unilateral declarations of intent requiring communication have to be served upon the correct party. Service shall only be effected if the declaration of intent comes within the control of the addressee of the declaration.

8.2. Pre-emption

A distinction is to be made between a right of first refusal and the granting of a first option.

In the event that a contractual partner is granted a right of pre-emption, the contractual partner may exercise this right only if the obliging party has concluded a contract with a third party pursuant to Section 504 of the German Civil Code. If exercised the obliging party may, however, agree with the third party on a right of rescission.[21] This is appropriate, since otherwise the third party may claim damages vis-à-vis its contractual partner. Detailed arrangements have to be made between the parties.

The agreement on a first option entails the obligation to inform the person entitled to such an option about the offers made by other potential buyers and to request his decision to conclude the contract in priority over the other

20. Federal Supreme Court 47, 391.

21. Palandt-Putzo, BGB, vor Section 504 German Civil Code, marginal No. 13.

potential buyers. The principle of first option is mainly an obligation to submit an offer to the person entitled to a first option. The infringement of such an obligation may trigger claims for damages. The right of a first option may also be designed in such a way that it has the effects of a right of first refusal.

It is also possible to grant to third parties a right to enter into an already existing contract. This leads to a *subrogation* with the legal effects of an assignment of claim pursuant to Section 398 *et seq.* of the German Civil Code and an assumption of debt pursuant to Section 414 *et seq.* of the German Civil Code.

These rights are not very clearly regulated by law. Detailed agreements, therefore, have to made as to how these rights may be exercised and under what circumstances.

8.3. Exclusivity

The granting of an exclusive right may have adverse implications under the rules on competition. Any exclusivity has to comply with the decisions of the European Court of Justice interpreting Articles 85 and 86 of the EC Treaty. Section 20 of the German Law against Restraints of Competition permits the restriction in the use of patents, utility models and in licence agreements provided they do not affect the statutory protected rights of the holder of the intellectual property. Similar rules apply to contracts concerning the transfer or the use of inventions, manufacturing processes and designs, which are not protected by statutory law. Pursuant to Section 20 III of the Law against Restraints of Competition, however, an application for a licence can be made to the German Cartel Office, which is granted provided the economic freedom of action of the buyer or licensee or another enterprise is not unduly restricted by the licence agreement.

8.4. Copyright Licence

Copyright, as an intangible property right (but not the author's personal rights) may be assigned to third parties. Ordinary and exclusive rights of use may be granted pursuant to Section 31 of the Copyright Act. The non-exclusive right of use entitles the holder to use this right apart from the author himself; an exclusive right to use entitles the holder to use the copyright to the exclusion of the author (Section 31 III of the Copyright Act).

It should be pointed out that the non-exclusive right to use, granted by the author prior to the granting of an exclusive right of use, remains valid vis-à-vis the holder of the exclusive right unless provided otherwise between the author and the holder of the non-exclusive right of use (Section 33 of the Copyright Act).

Copyrights may be limited as to territory, time or contents (Section 32 of the Copyright Act).

8.5. Trademark Licence

The right established by the registration of a trademark can be assigned or transferred to third parties irrespective of the transfer of the business enterprise (Section 8 I of the Trademark Act). Such registered right may, however, be asserted against third parties only if the transfer of the trademark has been recorded in the Trademark Register (Section 8 II of the Trademark Act).

8.6. Territory

Although the holder of an intellectual property or a copyright right may determine how his rights shall be used, the provisions of Articles 85 and 86 of the EC Treaty and the indemnification regulations have considerably restricted the parties' freedom to exercise their rights.

8.7. Product Classes

The organiser may grant to certain sponsors the right to provide exclusively certain classes of products, and the precise definition of the products concerned is advisable so as to avoid definition problems at a later stage.

8.8. Duration

The contractual parties are generally free to determine the duration of their contractual relationship. It is, however, prudent to stipulate the circumstances which would allow the parties to terminate the contract.

8.9. Post Termination Agreements

Clauses which restrict or prohibit competition after the termination of a contract are questionable as they equally infringe the German and European law of competition.

In practice, it is difficult to assess the damages caused by an unlawful termination of the contract. To facilitate the proof of such damages, it is wise to agree on the payment of lump-sum damages ('liquidated damages').

8.10. Financial Terms

Fees are either based upon fixed fees or on a percentage of the turnover. Other arrangements are possible.

The date of the accrual of a claim is to be defined either by reference to the calendar date, or to certain events, such as, for example, delivery of the product, receipt of the customer's/licensee's payment. The payments are usually net payments; it should be expressly provided who has to bear the direct and indirect taxes on the fees. Payments effected in foreign currency may incur exchange risks so that the parties should consider as to how such exchange rate risks can be minimised.

Payments in foreign currencies may also be secured by dealings in futures and options. There are several possibilities of how to structure the covering costs. The currency laws of the respective States must, however, be adhered to.

In the event of delay it may be agreed that the contractual partner in default has to pay interest at a certain rate.

9. Insurance Aspects

Certain contingencies (e.g. event cancellation) and certain public and product liabilities may be covered by insurance and appropriate provisions included in the sponsorship and merchandising agreements (e.g. who pays the premiums).

10. Advertising and Promotion

In Germany, advertising is subject to comprehensive regulation. Consumers as well as competitors are protected mainly by Sections 1 and 3 of the Law against Unfair Competition.

The German Civil Code is applicable to the extent to which it serves to fill any gaps in special statutory provisions. Of particular reference is the protection of names (Section 12 of the German Civil Code) and the protection of an enterprise against interference (Section 823 sub-section 1 of the German Civil Code).

In view of its wide application, Section 1 of the Law against Unfair Competition is by far the most important provision. It covers the following aspects:

10.1. Inaccurate Self-Appraisal

Advantages or benefits, which are praised, must be true. If a competitor can successfully prove the incorrectness of the statement, the advertising will be deemed to be anti-competitive and subject to legal remedy.

10.2. Camouflaged Advertising

Public and private radio and TV broadcasters must clearly separate advertising from the rest of their programmes. The programme must be independent and guarantee the neutrality in relation to competition in a free market.

Sponsoring should be exercised in a way that it restricts advertising effects on TV to the greatest possible extent. The programmes may not serve the economic interests of a particular sponsor or a third party.

In respect of product placement the principle of the separation of advertising and programmes should also be adhered to, since otherwise the television viewers are misled about the advertising nature of the programme.

The person responsible for this action is liable for an act of unfair competition.

10.3. Violation of Special Provisions

Section 22 of the LLMBG provides that radio advertising for cigarettes, tobacco products, which are similar to cigarettes, and tobacco products, which are essential for the production of cigarettes is strictly prohibited.

Section 22 sub-section 2 of the LLMGB limits advertising in other areas.

Further special regulations, such as the Act concerning Advertising in Medical Care of 18 October 1978, the Medical Preparations Act, Section 46 of the Wine Act, which relates to wine, liqueur wine, sparkling wine, wine-containing beverages and brandy made from wine, also severely restrict advertising.

In addition to the statutory restrictions the tobacco industry has concluded voluntary self-restraint agreements.

Advertising may not be done with athletes and prominent persons. There are international standards of conduct relating to advertising practice, which have been used by the International Chamber of Commerce in Paris, as well as Guidelines of the Zentralausschuß für Werbewirtschaft (Central Committee for the Advertising Industry), issued by the Bundesverband Deutscher Zeitungsverleger e.V. (Federal Association of German Newspaper Publishers).

10.4. Subliminal Advertising

Advertising, which is done in a way that the spectator cannot recognise the fact that it is advertising, is prohibited.

10.5. Telephone Advertising

Telephone advertising is allowed subject to the law of competition if the person who is called has agreed to it either expressly or implicitly. Any 'cold calls', therefore, are prohibited.

10.6. Comparative Advertising

Comparative advertising is prohibited, if it contains statements which cannot be proved to be true (Section 14 of the Law against Unfair Competition). It may be admissible if there are sufficient reasons for it and if the competitor is thereby not unreasonably discriminated. Acknowledged exemptions are any comparison of systems, counter-offensive advertising, as well as any comparison as to information and development.

10.7. Taking Advantage of the Reputation of a Third Party to Recommend One's Own Products

Hidden imitation of the advertising of a third party, by taking advantage of its good reputation, in particular, of its advertising value, is considered as unfair; the same applies to exploiting the good repute of a third party's product or performance, if it is used as a blueprint for one's own advertising.

10.8. Advantage by Violation of the Law

This concerns, in particular, infringements of special statutory provisions, such as the Foodstuffs Act relating to tobacco advertising.

Section 3 of the Law against Unfair Competition prohibits deceptive advertising, which includes, deceptive statements concerning the quality, characteristics and effects of the products; inaccurate descriptions; unwarranted assumption of protective rights; fraudulent misrepresentation concerning the geographic origin, the manufacturing origin of the product, the manner of production and the manner of supply of the product; and the existence of awards, memorial coins, honourary deeds and letters of recognition.

An offence may be defended by the right to a forbearance granted by Section 3 of the Law against Unfair Competition. A claim for compensation follows from Section 3 in connection with Section 13 sub-section 4 No. 1 of the Law against Unfair Competition.

11. The Venue

11.1. Control

The organiser of a sports event has a right of possession in the premises in which the event takes place.

He derives his right from his contract with the owner or another possessor. The organiser may exercise his right also through possessory servants (*Besitzdiener*). Pursuant to Section 855 of the German Civil Code, a possessory servant exercises the actual control over an object on behalf of the organiser.

Possessory servants of the organiser are, in general, his employees, for example, security guards.

Furthermore, the organiser has the right to grant access to the premises. He must, however, do so to all persons with whom he has assumed contractual relations and whose performance is only possible by physical presence at the event, for example, the TV crews who have been granted licences.

If the organiser refuses to grant access without good reason, he would be in breach of contract, which would give rise to a right of damages against the organiser.

The right of possession also gives the organiser the right to defend himself if there is an unlawful interference with his mentioned rights (Sections 858 and 859 of the German Civil Code). Any person who turns the possessor out of his possession or interferes with his quiet possession, acts unlawfully, unless he is allowed to do so by law (Section 858 of the German Civil Code). The right to defend himself against such interference is granted both to the possessor and the possessory servant. Accordingly, a security guard has a statutorily protected right to remove intruders, troublemakers or hooligans from the premises.

Furthermore, the organiser has a claim for compensation against the intruder, since the right of possession is protected under the German law of tort (Section 823 of the German Civil Code). Thus, the organiser is capable of suing the intruder to enforce his claims.

If several parties jointly organise an event, they are jointly liable (Section 866 of the German Civil Code).

If the organiser is also the owner of the premises, he is entitled to all absolute rights arising under the law of ownership and to all related protective rights.

11.2. Public Liability

The organiser may be under a duty to maintain safety of the premises, as risks may be created through the opening of the event to a larger group of spectators. Generally, a person who creates a risk must take the necessary measures to protect third parties.[22] Only those measures have to be taken which the spectators could reasonably expect to be taken. In principle, safety measures have to be taken only for the admitted spectators and not for unauthorised users, because they do not belong to the group of protected persons.[23]

However, the organiser must take reasonable steps to ensure that unauthorised access is avoided or, at least, made difficult. He may otherwise still be liable for injuries sustained by a minor who gains unauthorised access.

All persons who commit a tortious act by reason of their negligence are jointly and severally liable.

22. BGH NJW 1977, 1457.
23. BGH NJW 1985, 1076 *et seq.*

11.3. Access and Accreditation

As part of the possessory or proprietary rights the organiser may regulate who actively may participate in the event and how access is to be granted to individual groups (e.g. sponsors).

12. Dispute Resolution

Disputes may either be settled by resort to the ordinary courts of law or by arbitration through a court of arbitration.

12.1. The German Court System

The German court system distinguishes between the following types of courts: in civil matters, the proper venue is the ordinary courts of law; in employment law matters the labour courts have jurisdiction; disputes involving a public law matter must be brought before the administrative courts; and criminal matters are dealt with in the criminal courts. There are other special courts, such as the tax court and social security court, which can sometimes be of importance in this area of legal practice.

12.2. Civil Jurisdiction

The civil courts comprise local courts (*Amtsgericht*); district courts (*Landgericht*); regional appeal courts (*Oberlandesgericht*); and the Federal Supreme Court – Civil Divisions – (*Bundesgerichtshof*). Local courts have jurisdiction up to a value in action of DM 6,000 (inclusive) (Section 23 S. 1 No. 1 of the Judicature Act). All other civil disputes have to be dealt with in the competent district court. The regional appeal court is the appellate court for judgments rendered by the district court; only in special cases is it concerned with judgments passed by the local court (Section 119 I of the Judicature Act).

The Federal Supreme Court is competent, *inter alia*, for appeals on points of law against judgments of the regional appeal courts. The Federal Supreme Court, however, only finds on points of law: it is not a trial court on questions of fact.

12.3. System of Administrative Courts

Pursuant to Section 40 of the Rules governing Administrative Courts, the administrative courts have competence in public law disputes, which are not of a direct constitutional nature. Even in sports law such a public law dispute may arise if, for example, lease agreements between an organiser and the owner of the premises, where an event takes place, have to be judged according to public law, or if a dispute arises concerning the obligations of the organisers under public law to the municipality or government. For example, parachuting events are subject to strict safety conditions, which form part of public law.

As a rule, a matter may be brought before the administrative courts only if extra-judicial administrative proceedings have been exploited.

The administrative court system comprises a two-tier appeal system with the administrative courts, where proceedings always commence, the Administrative Appeal Courts and the Federal Administrative Court, which is the highest court in administrative law matters.

12.4. Appeal on a Constitutional Issue/Constitutional Complaint

A constitutional complaint may be lodged against judgments rendered by the court of last resort (Article 93 No. 4a of the German Basic Law), if a civil right has been violated, or if the appellant has been violated in his rights under Articles 20 IV, 33, 38, 101, 103 and 104 of the Basic Law. These civil rights not only apply to natural persons, but also to domestic legal persons, to the extent to which they are applicable to those persons (Article 19 III of the Basic Law).

12.5. Interim Legal Protection

12.5.1. Seizure and Arrest

Pursuant to Section 916 of the German Civil Procedure Code, an application for seizure may be made to the court in order to seize the debtor's movable or immovable property. The decision of the court may be taken *ex parte.* An application for arrest is granted if there are valid reasons for granting the order, that is, reasonable grounds to suspect an imminent frustration of or substantial impediment to attachment.

12.5.2. Interim Injunction

Pursuant to Section 935 of the Civil Procedure Code, interim injunctions can secure the right to specific performance. Pursuant to Section 940 of the Civil Procedure Code, interim injunctions can also determine an interim *status quo* pending a dispute in the main action.

12.6. Damages

If interim injunctions prove to be wholly unjustified and if such measures have been reversed pursuant to Section 926 II of the Civil Procedure Code, or Section 942 III of the Civil Procedure Code, the applicant party must pay damages, according to Section 945 of the Civil Procedure Code.

12.7. Legal Costs

The legal costs in connection with litigious work are laid down in the German Federal Attorney Fees Act (BRAGO). Pursuant to Section 91 I of the Civil Procedure Code, the losing party must bear the costs of litigation. However, only the legal fees and expenses of the attorney-at-law have to be refunded, pursuant to Section 91 II of the Civil Procedure Code. If fee arrangements have been concluded exceeding the statutory fees, the amount exceeding the statutory fees has to be paid by the party concerned.

In addition, the losing party has to pay the court fees.

12.8. Arbitration

Under German law, an arbitration agreement can be entered into by the parties in order to avoid an action being brought before the ordinary courts of law.

Pursuant to Section 1027 I of the Civil Procedure Code, an effective arbitration agreement requires written form according to Section 126 of the German Civil Code. The agreement may only contain those provisions which relate to the arbitration proceedings. If an agreement is part of a wider contract, it must be separated from the contract and has to be signed separately.[24]

A valid arbitration agreement has the effect that an action filed with an ordinary court of law has to be dismissed (Section 1027 of the Civil Procedure Code).

An arbitration award may, however, be thwarted, if a party files its objections in the attachment proceedings, pursuant to Section 1042 II of the Civil Procedure Code, or if a party files an action for rescission, pursuant to Section 1041 of the Civil Procedure Code. An action for the declaration of the non-existence of an arbitration agreement is admissible as long as the requirements of Section 1039 of the Civil Procedure Code are not met.[25]

The Convention concerning the Acknowledgement and Execution of Foreign Arbitrations Awards of 10 June 1958 and the European Convention concerning the International Commercial Jurisdiction of 21 April 1961 have been fully implemented as part of the law of the Federal Republic of Germany. In addition, there are bilateral treaties, for example, the German-U.S. Treaty of Friendship, Commerce and Navigation, dated 29 October 1954, *Federal Law Gazette* 56 II p. 488, Art. VI, which need to be considered.

12.9. Alternative Dispute Resolution

Furthermore, there is the possibility to settle amicably the proceedings through conciliatory bodies which have no statutory powers. If a conciliation clause has

24. BGH 38, 163.
25. Baumbach/Albers, *ZPO*, introduction to 1041–1044, 1.

been agreed upon, conciliatory proceedings must be conducted prior to taking any court action, so as to avoid the action being dismissed.[26] It is, however, perfectly possible for an ordinary court to be given jurisdiction once the conciliation proceedings have come to an end.

26. BGH NJW 1984, 669.

Greece

by Nicos Moschos

1. Sports Marketing – A Business

The Sports Industry in Greece is growing rapidly and is one of the largest business activities in Greece. The annual spending on sports related activities (clothing, shoes and the like) is hard to estimate. However, the large amounts spent on sports marketing reflect the tremendous growth of the sports industry in Greece.

It has been estimated that the amounts to be spent in 1992 on sports marketing will approach 2 billion drachmas, which proves the significance of athleticism for the best promotion of commercial corporations.

The rapid increase of the television transmissions of basketball and football games within the last two years was accompanied by an equal increase in the amounts which networks spend in order to cover a popular sports event. The Greek Television (Elliniki Tileorasi – 'ET') spent about 1.5 billion drachmas in 1992 on showing the games of the National Basketball Championship. The private network Mega Channel has a similar participation in the sports marketing industry.

It must be noted that the wide range of sports events shown on television (730 hours of athletics programmes from October 1991 to March 1992) attracts the interest of sponsors. In 1992 – as well as the previous year – many national and international sports events, especially the games of basketball teams, were funded through sponsorship.

2. The Greek Legal System

The Greek legal system is mainly a codified system. It consists of: (a) the Civil Code; (b) the Code of Civil Procedure; (c) the Penal Code; (d) the Code of Penal Procedure; and (e) the Commercial Code. Of course, there are many areas of legal practice not covered by the above-mentioned Codes, which are regulated by Laws, Presidential Decrees and Ministerial Decisions. The courts do not create law, but simply participate in the proper interpretation and application of the law. There are also some general clauses (such as public order, contractual freedom, abuse of authority) which govern the structure and logic of the Greek legal system.

The sources of law are: (a) the Constitution; (b) laws; and (c) custom. It must be noted that commercial as well as the local customs have an important part to play in the creation of the legal system of Greece.

3. Applicable Laws

There is no specific law governing the area of sports marketing. We can claim that the legislative status of sports marketing consists of general principles imposed by the Civil Code (freedom of contract), general laws regarding different aspects of sports marketing, for example, the sponsorship of television programmes, and, of course, commercial customs (*lex mercatoria*).

The parties are free – within the limits of commercial morality – to define the terms of a contract. The contracts are subject to certain principles of marketing which concern the best promotion of a product through a sports event.

4. Intellectual Property Rights

4.1. Intellectual Property Laws

The development of technology has made possible the re-transmission of a television programme to the most distant areas of the earth.

Intellectual property is closely connected to the rapid development of technology (transmission via satellite). The popularity of international sports events raises the need for their transmission throughout the world. It is understood that the protection of intellectual property rights is of crucial importance in a sports event, covered by a TV network, sponsored by a corporation and transmitted to a large number of countries.

In Greece, intellectual property is regulated by the Law 2387/1920. The national legislation was amended by specific laws on intellectual property (e.g. Law 4301/1929, Legislative Decree 619/1941, Legislative Decree 4208/1961, Legislative Decree 4264/1962). The Civil Code and international conventions (Greece implemented the Berne Convention in 1920 and the Geneva Convention in 1952) are also important sources of intellectual property law. Finally, we have to acknowledge the influence of European Community law on the Greek legal system: for example, Articles 85 and 86 of the Rome Treaty which deal with unfair competition.

4.2. Trademarks

Greece is a signatory to the Paris Convention on Trademarks. The national law is governed by the Law 1998/1939 as amended by the Laws 3205/1995, 164/1975, 1380/83, 1934/1991, 1961/1991 and the Presidential Decree 317/25.9.1992, which implemented the First Directive 89/104/EEC on Trademarks.

Articles 2 and 16 of the Law 1998/1939 gives the proprietor the exclusive right to use a trademark after it has been registered in relation to his goods or services pursuant to the Presidential Decree 317/25.9.1992. Pursuant to Article 1, a trademark is defined as a mark used in distinguishing goods or services. The main requirement set by the law for the registration of a trademark is the distinction of goods and services with which the proprietor is connected from those with which he his not. Any registered trademark is valid for 10 years. This protection can be extended for similar periods indefinitely.

A conflict between two trademarks is regulated by the principle of priority. The exclusive right of using a mark belongs to the one who has registered it first. The proprietor is protected against any trademark infringement by the Penal Code (Article 26 Law 1998/1939) and the Civil Code (Article 281 on abuse of right) as well as by the Law 141 on Unfair Competition.

Whoever desires the registration of a trademark has to file a petition with the Trademark Courts. The courts examine the requirements set by the law and register the trademark. Against this judicial decision a petition can be filed by anyone with a lawful interest.

4.3. Copyright

Greece is a signatory to the Berne Convention. Copyright is exercised by the author or a third person which has undertaken the publication of his work (usually the publisher). Copyright is regulated by Article 57 of the Civil Code ('right of personality'). The right of publishing a literary, musical or artistic work is regulated specifically by Article 13 of Law 2387/1920. In Article 6B of the Berne Convention (as implemented by the Legislative Decree 4264/1962) the author reserves the right to claim the copyright. The Law 1075/1980 provides artists with a severe penal protection (Article 21).

In case of copyright infringement by copying, publishing, performing in public, or broadcasting the owner has the right to ask the courts for recognition of his copyright and relief against the infringer. The protection of copyright is not subject to any time limit.

4.4. Unfair Competition

Economic competition in Greece is regulated generally by the Laws 146/1914 and 703/1977. The common object of both of them – as well as their common logic and philosophy – is the protection of free competition within the framework of a liberal economic system, but, at the same time, the control of its social mission. The Committee for the Protection of Competition has the same objective. The actual law on competition is governed also by general clauses, such as the principle of equality, the principle of truth (Article 3 Law 146/1914), the principle of objectivity. Anyone who commits an unfair competitive activity against a person or a legal entity is obliged to compensate them (Articles 174, 179, 914, 919 of the Civil Code).

5. The Contract Generally and Preliminary Agreements

5.1. Preliminary Agreements

The Greek Civil Code recognises the right of citizens to regulate their legal relations according to their free will (contractual freedom, Article 361 of the Civil Code). The freedom of a person to define or amend its legal relations is due to the economic system of free competition. In business practice, persons enter into a preliminary agreement before signing the final contract (Article 166 of the Civil Code). Such an agreement is legally enforceable: the contracting parties are obliged to sign the final contract. Otherwise, one who fails to sign the final contract can be obliged judicially to do so (Articles 946, 949 of the Code of Civil Procedure).

5.2. Intention to Create Legal Relations

Any contracting party has to declare verbally its intention to commit to a commercial transaction. The Civil Code distinguishes the time during which a contract is signed between negotiations (Articles 197–198 of the Civil Code) and the final contract (Article 185 of the Civil Code). In the sensitive area of competition the intention for legally binding contracting parties plays an important role. However, if the consent of a party to sign a contract is obtained by taking advantage of its need, vanity or lack of experience, then the contract is void.

5.3. Offer and Acceptance

The offer to enter into a contract is a necessary element for the signature of a contract (Article 185 of the Civil Code). This offer has to be clear and concrete. The acceptance is the affirmative answer to the offer (Article 193 of the Civil Code). This acceptance has to be made without reserve (Article 191 of the Civil Code). The coincidence of will of the contracting parties constitutes the contract.

5.4. *Form and Execution*

Pursuant to Article 158 of the Civil Code, a contract has to be in writing only when this is required by law. When the legally required form is not kept the contract is void. When the contracting parties are companies, the contract is executed by an official of each company, usually a person called the legal representative of the company.

5.5. *Void and Illegal Contracts*

Any provision which is against the law is illegal (Article 174 of the Civil Code). Additionally, contracts with an immoral subject or contrary to public order are invalid. Pursuant to Article 178 of the Civil Code, a contract is void when it binds the freedom of a person illegally. A contract will also be void when signed by taking advantage of one's need, vanity or lack of experience (Article 179 of the Civil Code).

A valid contract can be cured and legally recognised if the contracting parties consider its relation to another similar legal contract (Article 182 of the Civil code). For example, a void sale contract can be transformed to a valid recognition of debt. A contract can also be declared void judicially, if the consent of a contracting party is obtained by mistake, fraud or threat (Articles 140, 147, 150 of the Civil Code).

5.6. *Privity*

The 'privity of contract' doctrine is translated into Greek Legislation as the 'relativity' of contracts. A basic element of each contract is the personal connection between the contracting parties. Third persons, as a general rule, are not entitled to acquire rights. However, some contracts include clauses in favour of a third party (Articles 410–414 of the Civil Code). Article 415 of the Civil Code regulates the obligation of a third party to perform a certain act pursuant to the specific terms of a contract.

5.7. *Interpretation*

The interpretation of contracts is governed by a number of principles as follows:

- The intention of the parties is expressed in the contract.
- Good faith (Article 200 of the Civil Code).
- Commercial customs (Article 288 of the Civil Code).
- The exercise of a right is prohibited if it exceeds the limits imposed by good faith or morals or the financial and social purpose of that right.

5.8. Frustration and Force Majeure

A contract is frustrated when a party cannot perform its terms due to facts for which he is not responsible (Articles 198, 330 and 914 of the Civil Code). In certain cases, the frustration of a contract is due to circumstances beyond the human factor (earthquakes, natural disasters, *force majeure*).

5.9. Breach of Contract

A contract is breached when a contracting party does not comply with its obligations, in which case either party can claim damages (Articles 335 and 380 of the Civil Code).

6. Advertising and Promotion

The most important part of competitive activities is covered today by advertising. Advertising is not defined legally. However, we can make a definition through its purpose, which is to introduce a product to consumers. Advertising must serve the need of people to be informed of the market and to decide freely. Pursuant to decisions of the International Chamber of Commerce, advertising which takes advantage of trust or lack of experience of the consumer is illegal.

The most important source of law in connection with advertising is the Law 146/1914 (as amended), which protects fair competition and imposes restrictions in the public interest. According to this law (and its amendments), any false presentation of a product regarding its quantity, origin and the like is prohibited. In compliance with the scope of the Law 146/1914, the Competition Commission ensures the effectiveness of the legal and social restrictions on advertising.

6.1. Restrictions

The Ministry of Health has prohibited (with a number of decisions) the advertising of tobacco products on television and radio. However, the advertising of tobacco products is permitted in magazines and newspapers, under the warning of the Ministry that smoking has a bad influence on health.

6.2. Programme Sponsorship

The rapid increase of television coverage of sports events has attracted the interest of corporations. The Presidential Decree 236/16.7.1992 allows television sponsorship.

6.3. *Intellectual Property Rights*

For any use by an advertising agency of the intellectual property rights of corporations, which sponsor or organise a sports event, a licence is definitely required.

6.4. *Comparative Advertising*

Comparative advertising, whereby people are informed by the media that a product has a lot of advantages in relation to another similar product, is illegal. This kind of advertising informs and does not attract consumers, which is the main purpose of advertising. For that reason, such an advertisement is illegal.

6.5. *Defamation*

Article 12 of Law 146/1914 prohibits the defamation of any person or company by another who is aware of his false statements. Defamation is also punished as a crime by the Penal Code (Article 363).

7. Standard Contract Terms – The Rights

In the specific part of the Civil Code referring to contract law, certain kinds of contracts (sale, leasing, loan) are regulated. There are no specific articles governing the contracts which deal with sports marketing. The freedom of contract doctrine permits the parties to sign contracts, the contents of which are defined freely under the presumption that the chosen terms are not contrary to public order rules (Articles 3 and 174 of the Civil Code). In contracts, such as sports marketing contracts which are not regulated directly by the Civil Code, the applicable law as well as the contract terms are found in similar contracts specified by the Civil Code. Otherwise, the terms will be based on the general principles of the law relating to contracts.

8. Different Types of Business Arrangements

8.1. *Sponsorship Agreements*

The sponsorship agreement is not regulated specifically by the Civil Code, and so the content of such an agreement is covered by the general provisions of contract law. Consequently, the contracting parties are free to define their agreement within the principle of the 'freedom of contract'. In contractual arrangements, the following elements at least must be included:

(a) description of the parties;
(b) the sponsor's obligations; and
(c) the duration of the agreement.

The most significant term in such agreements is exclusivity, which means that the company which sponsors a sports event or the activities of a team, is granted an exclusive association with the event or the team.

Certain products cannot be advertised on radio and television. Pursuant to Ministerial Decisions, tobacco advertisements are strictly prohibited through television and radio. Furthermore, in any advertisement with regard to tobacco the Ministry of Health adds a note with which it warns the people of the bad influence of smoking.

Specific contracts signed to date, which include a social dimension, are ones for the sponsorship of certain sports events not necessarily with a professional character, which, at the same time, present a concrete social, cultural or national subject, such as the Aegean Rally, Beach Volley-Ball, the Basketball League 'Acropolis'. The 3E Company alone has sponsored about 1000 sports events all over Greece. Some companies sponsor programmes with a social target, such as the construction of a stadium or the support of young athletes.

Other modern types of business arrangement are the management of players, the purchase of television rights and the marketing of products. Greek managing companies have already taken international steps by undertaking the marketing of Bulgarian athletic organisations, the founding of joint ventures with commercial and athletic targets in the Ukraine, and marketing for the Olympic Committee of the Ukraine.

8.2. Merchandising

Merchandising agreements are not regulated specifically by Greek law. Specific terms of such agreements may include protection of the marks, obligations resulting from the unauthorised use of a mark and royalty provisions.

8.3. Endorsements

Each sports federation regulates differently the obligations of its members. For example, the Federation of Classic Athleticism considers that the spirit of athleticism limits the opportunities of individual sponsorship. The Basketball Federation permits commercial arrangements with sponsors. The contractual arrangements can only be limited by the personal freedom of the athlete. A compromise between contractual freedom and the personality right is necessary.

8.4. *Franchises*

The organisation of a franchise depends on the will of the contracting parties (contractual freedom doctrine, Article 361 of the Civil Code). A licence requirement for the use of trademarks or copyright is also in this case necessary.

8.5. *Film and Video*

The production of a film or video gives rise to the obligation of the contracting parties to seek a licence from the rights holder. Warranties and indemnities also need to be provided.

8.6. *Suppliership*

The large companies of athletic shoes and clothes (such as Nike, Converse, Reebok) offer to basketball or football teams free clothes, as well as big sums to wear clothes with their title. This applies to a number of athletic sectors, such as basketball, volleyball, football and handball.

The biggest company in the field of athletic clothes and shoes is Nike. This company co-operates with famous athletes of classic athleticism. It has already signed contracts with 100 Greek and foreign basketball players.

8.7. *Commissioning Agreements*

This kind of agreement is a new kind (for Greece) of sports marketing. For the time being, only one company has undertaken the production and exploitation of trademarks (logo, emblem and design) in favour of a famous basketball team. The copyright of such works belongs to the individual designers. The law does not impose a specific form for these agreements, but it is better for their execution to be in writing.

9. Financial Terms

The terms which should be specified in the contracts are the following:

(a) whether payment is to be in advance or not;
(b) whether the payment is to be in instalments or not (usually sponsors in Greece spend a significant amount within a period of time);
(c) the payment method (e.g. cheque or cash);

(d) the relation between payment and the fulfilment of certain conditions (in a sponsorship agreement of a basketball team the sponsoring company has the right to break the contract if the team fails to win the championship).

Additionally, the parties can also agree on the supply of certain goods (e.g. clothes and shoes) or equipment to the other party.

Another very important term: in return for the licence of a team for transmitting its games, television offers an amount of money and free advertising spots, which the sponsoring company can exploit.

10. The Rights

10.1. Options

The rights available to businessmen interested in dealing with sports marketing cannot be defined specifically. The principle of contractual freedom permits potential sponsors or suppliers (the two main types of business arrangement relevant to sports marketing in Greece) to acquire a variety of rights, under the presumption that they are not contrary to the rules of public order. However, a sponsor lays down a lot of requirements in order to assure its investment. Concrete terms focus on the spending of a significant amount within a period of time. The company has the right to negotiate the terms of a new agreement. The content of an option is agreed freely by the contractual parties.

10.2. Exclusivity

There are rights, like exclusivity, which are granted. The scope of exclusivity must be defined specifically in the agreement. For example, a basketball team, sponsored by a big athletics products company, wears exclusively clothes with the title of this company. On certain occasions, a team is obliged to change its name. The new name will be a combination between the title of the company and the name of the team.

10.3. Pre-emption

A pre-emption right is not submitted to any specific rules regarding a sports marketing agreement. However, a pre-emption right could be agreed between the parties. In addition, when a company sponsors the television coverage of an international sports event (e.g. a football game) the title of the company is presented on the television screen during the game.

10.4. Copyright and Trademark Licence

There are no specific rules applied to sports marketing agreements which concern copyright or trademark. The subjects of trademark and copyright licences have already been presented. These matters are governed by the corresponding intellectual property laws.

10.5. Media

The rapid increase of television transmissions of sports events has created a new situation in sports marketing. All the networks spend a large amount of money to obtain the television rights of the Basketball Championship Games, as well as the European Championship Games. According to estimations of sports marketing executives the television transmissions of basketball games have increased by about 40% in 1992 as compared to 1991. The spending for the purchase of television rights for the coverage of popular sports events has been calculated at approximately 1 billion drachmas.

The corresponding intellectual property rights regarding the exploitation of the different media must be provided for in the agreements.

10.6. Product Categories

A lot of sponsorship programmes are based on the exclusive relationship between the sponsor and the event organiser. This means that the product concerned must be exclusively advertised within the entire period of its sponsorship.

10.7. Duration

The length and the grounds for termination of the arrangements must be expressly provided for in the contract.

10.8. Post Termination

Usually terms imposing post-contractual obligations on the parties could be considered to bind the freedom of the parties unreasonably and so any rights, which may be exercised after the expiration of the agreement, must be carefully defined by the parties in the contract.

11. Insurance Aspects

The subject of civil liability is regulated by the Civil Code. According to the Civil Code, the owner of the premises on which a sports event takes place is liable for damages caused in connection with the use of, for example, a stadium, if the accident or the damage is due to inadequate maintenance. The requirement of adequate maintenance is imposed by the good faith principle and commercial custom (Article 914 of the Civil Code).

As to product liability, there are no specific provisions governing this subject. However, the Greek courts have developed a rule according to which the producer of a product is liable for damage caused by a defect in the product. Consequently, the plaintiff can claim damages from the producer. Risks caused by *force majeure* should be covered by insurance.

12. The Venue

All matters related to the venue of the event are regulated by the system of the Civil Code which punishes any breach of a contract when it is due to the responsibility of the organiser. Liability does not exist for actions not due to the responsibility of the organiser (Articles 330 and 914 of the Civil Code for illegal behaviour and Article 198 of the Civil Code for preliminary agreements). Consequently, the organiser will not be liable for any loss or damage which is caused by negligence. If the organiser undertakes contractually an obligation to cover any damage, even if he is not responsible for it, this contract could be declared void and illegal. Parties who perform specific functions at the event (for example, broadcasting organisations) enter into contracts with the competent federations, which provide them with access to the venue.

Sponsors and suppliers having the right of exclusivity for their particular products will require a term in their contracts with the event organisers prohibiting the promotion of competitive products in relation to and during the sports event concerned.

13. Dispute Resolution

13.1. Courts of Law

When a dispute arises it can either be pursued in the courts or agreed by arbitration or settled by an extra-judicial agreement. An action could be brought before a District Court for any dispute of an amount up to 300,000 drachmas. Disputes of a larger amount will be brought in the High Instance Courts. The court action is regulated by the Greek Code of Civil Procedure.

Against a judicial decision an appeal or objection can be exercised. The Supreme Court has the function of deciding on the legal part of decisions issued by the appeal courts. The courts impose the payment of legal costs on the losing party.

There are two kinds of judicial decisions:

(a) those with no binding effect (simply recognising a claim against the defendant); in case of a favourable judgment, the plaintiff converts same into:
(b) one with binding effect which is enforceable.

If someone seeks the issue of a judgment based on the second option he has also to pay a judicial stamp duty plus interest.

Interest on a claim is calculated from the date the petition claiming indemnities for losses and damages is filed in the competent court.

Interim injunctions can be obtained only in urgent cases, in order to prevent a danger which cannot otherwise be prevented (Article 682 of the Code of Civil Procedure).

There are certain legislative provisions which secure the payment of debts by charging property or sealing stores.

13.2. Arbitration

Arbitration is a form of alternative dispute resolution. It is regulated by Articles 867–903 of the Code of Civil Procedure. The arbitration agreement is always in writing. The arbitrators are appointed by the first instance court. The fees of the arbitrators are limited by law (Article 882 of the Code of Civil Procedure). The arbitrators cannot award interim measures (Article 889 of the Code of Civil Procedure). The applicable law in arbitration procedure consists of general clauses of good faith, equity and commercial customs.

An arbitration award can be declared void by a judicial decision if the arbitration agreement is void and is contrary to public policy and morals.

Arbitral awards are enforceable (Article 904 of the Code of Civil Procedure) as well as judgments. Foreign arbitral awards and judgments are declared enforceable by the competent first instance court of the place of residence of the debtor. Foreign arbitral awards contrary to the public policy of Greece or morals are not capable of being declared enforceable (Article 905 of the Code of Civil Procedure).

13.3. Conciliation

Ordinary courts and arbitration are not the only forms of dispute resolution. Litigants usually sign forms of conciliation and extra-judicial settlement, which include terms bilaterally beneficial for the parties.

'Good faith' clauses are often used in practice, but their legal efficacy is questionable.

SPORTS
MARKETING

Hungary

by Dr. Atilla Bogsch
and Dr. Imre Csigi

1. Sports Marketing – A Business

Sports, as a business and advertising possibility, has begun to gain significance in Hungary only in the last few years. The socialist approach to society and the State establishment considered sports, from an ideological point of view, as an activity having a promotional value (as a proof for the incorrect theory of the superiority of socialist society) and not as a part of economic life and market competition to be exploited.

Accordingly, the income deriving from the marketing activity, based on the actual market conditions, also played an insignificant role compared to the other income resources received for sports purposes through other channels (granted by the State in a direct or indirect way). This is clearly shown by the fact that, even under today's circumstances, only half of the income resources derives from business financing (around 6–8 billion forints).

The socialist approach – due to this reason – considered the financing of sports as a task for the State, as a consequence of which the major part of sums reaching sports derived from central or local State resources, but the remaining part was also divided mostly in ways and forms defined and essentially prescribed by the State.

Besides the dominant role of the property of the State, the sponsoring activity was also carried out in the way defined and prescribed by the State and exceeded largely the traditional sponsoring activity. With few exceptions, all sports associations had a so-called basic organ, which, beyond financing the operation of the sports association, maintained the sports institution and secured a working place for the sportsmen, who were formerly amateurs, but essentially professionalists. Beyond this form of support, there existed a financing form which could be considered as advertisement. However, this was of limited importance only as, in an economic system based on the monopoly of State ownership, the effective market economy and market competition were not existing and, consequently, advertising had no perceptible role.

The role of the State could be also be seen in the institutional form of sports, which had an important effect on the character sponsorship and marketing system. Although sports associations operated as legally independent organisations, their actual independence was considerably affected by their connections to the basic organs, as mentioned above, as well as the fact that the organisations were supervised by State management organs. At the same time, the national sports branch associations, directing the individual sports branches, did not have an actual independence either since they operated as the organic unit of the central sports directing organ.

As a consequence of the political meaning and ideological considerations of the success orientation of sports, for a long time even the fact, which is obvious in the Western market-orientated economies, that successful sportsmen have a financial value was not accepted. A significant breakthrough happened only at the beginning of the 1980s, when, although with strict provisions, the 'sale for abroad' of soccer players was permitted.

2. The National Legal System

The legal system of the Hungarian Republic belongs to the so-called continental type. The law is based on strictly codified written regulations. Act No. XI of 1987 on Sources of Law brought a substantial change as regards the sources of law:

- it regulated the hierarchy of sources of law, that is, it fixed what results of codification have an effect binding for everybody (i.e. are to be considered as legal regulations) and what is the hierarchical order thereof.
- on the other hand it regulated the organs of the State and State management organs which have a right of codification (i.e. which may create legal regulations).

Accordingly, the hierarchy of the Hungarian legal regulations is as follows:

- Acts, including the Constitution, regarding which the Parliament has the exclusive right of legislation;
- Law Decrees (enacted before 23 October 1989);
- Government orders;
- Orders of the individual ministers;
- Orders of municipalities.

There are further mandatory regulations which do not have a general binding effect on everybody, but only for a limited circle (e.g., orders of the Secretary of State, instructions, circulars).

In contrast with common law systems, the Hungarian legal system forbids codification by judges; in this sense no precedent law is known. Nevertheless, the Supreme Court exercises a direction on all courts (decision of principle).

Some of its *ad hoc* decisions are binding on the courts; nevertheless, this activity of the Supreme Court is to be considered as a concrete interpretation of the law.

The system of judges passing sentences is based on the ordinary courts (local, county and Supreme Court) and is complemented by labour courts functioning as special courts.

3. Applicable Laws

Political changes at the end of the 1980s have caused, as a consequence, substantial transformations, partly in the organisation system of sports and partly in their financing. The Merger Act and the Law Decree, both of 1989, having a codification form equivalent to the Act relating to the regulation of the operation of sport branch organisations, regulated the right of merger and, within this sphere, also the operation of sports organisations in accordance with European legal principles.

For the sports organisations and sports associations that became independent, the transformation to a parliamentary democracy and market economy has brought favourable changes, as far as the principles are concerned, but they have also faced considerable economic difficulties. Due to the economic recession and the modification of the concept role, the role of the State in sports financing is decreasing. At the same time, however, no group having a substantial capital power has yet developed which could, as a result of its economic significance and in the knowledge of its market interests, perform sports financing tasks.

The sports business can perform its task suitably only under market economy circumstances. Accordingly, up to the present state of the transformation from a State monopoly to a market competition-based economic system, the separate, itemised regulations and the practical forms of sports financing and sports marketing have not been developed yet, all the more since, as mentioned above, on the one hand, according to the previous approach, sports financing was considered as a State task, while on the other hand, the business world has not realised fully the actual possibilities and power of sports business. At the same time the strictly budget, monetary attitude of the economic policy does not support investments in sports with suitable benefits either. Sports financing is supported only within a narrow range, e.g. by tax allowances, and the amounts streaming into sports on a business basis are held substantially back by the State budget.

In this way the major part of the financing and marketing connections of sports is defined not on the basis of strict business considerations but by the traditional faith to a sports club, by sympathy. The group of entrepreneurs developing since the liberalisation of the corporate law in 1988 which permitted individuals to have economic companies – with few exceptions, let's think here of multinational firms, joint ventures in the Hungarian economy – establishes economic relations not on the basis of business considerations but on traditional club sympathy.

As mentioned above, separate regulations of sports marketing have not been developed yet in Hungarian law, so the regulations relating to this field are included in the general economic legal regulations and in spheres other than itemised law, primarily the internal norms of sports branches.

4. Intellectual Property Rights and Unfair Competition

The law of intellectual property is one of the most modern parts of our legal system. The Hungarian civilistic science considers it as a relatively independent field of civil law. This comes from the assurance of the personal rights and the appreciation of creative activity through the legal protection of the intellectual property created.

Intellectual property law is divided to two main parts: copyright and the industrial property law comprising patents, designs and trademarks. Copyright protects creations of art and is valid essentially from the time of the creation of the piece of art, while the other fields protect scientific-technical creations as of the moment of registration with the organisation designated for this purpose.

The Hungarian codification of intellectual property rights took place after the start of international co-operation, which enabled Hungary to follow the latest international trends and developments.

The most important Hungarian legal regulations are:

- Act III of 1969 on Copyright;
- Act II of 1969 on the Patent Protection of Inventions;
- Law Decree 28 of 1978 on the Protection of Designs;
- Act IX of 1969 on Trademarks;
- Act LXXXVI of 1990 on Unfair Competition.

Copyright protection extends to 50 years after the death of the 'author' of the 'work'. There are no special regulations for the protection of 'moral rights'. As to assignment of copyright, the general formulation prescribed by the Civil Code applies, but authorship cannot be transferred.

Hungary is a member of the Paris and Madrid Conventions. Trademarks are registered at the Trademark Department of the Hungarian Patent Office for an initial period of 10 years, and can be renewed for further periods of 10 years indefinitely. If a trademark is not used at all during a period of 5 years, cancellation of its registration may be sought by a third party. However, it should be noted that a single advertisement amounts to 'use' for these purposes.

As to unfair competition, there is a relatively new Special Act, the terms of which are very close to the provisions of similar legislation in Western European countries.

5. The Contract Generally and Preliminary Agreements

The fact that the Hungarian legal system belongs to the German type is also apparent in contract law in relation to the general principles of contracts.

Regulations relating to contracts are included in the Civil Code which also defines the main rules of the individual types of contracts.

5.1. Preliminary Agreements

On the basis of a preliminary contract the parties are obliged to conclude the main contract at a later date. In case of failure to do so, the court may establish the contract at the request of any of the parties. Moreover, it may also define its exact contents in case this can be established according to all the circumstances. Any of the parties may be released from his obligation to conclude the contract if he can prove that:

- he is not able to conclude the contract due to circumstances which have occurred after the conclusion of the preliminary contract;
- the conclusion of the main contract would harm the interests of the national economy;
- due to circumstances which have occurred later the contract could be given up or it could be terminated.

5.2. Offer and Acceptance

Persons who offer to conclude a contract will be bound by their offer, except where the binding character was excluded when making the offer. The person making the offer may decide on thc period when it shall be binding, in the absence of which condition the law shall be applied.

The contract is to be considered as concluded when the declaration of acceptance enters into force: orally, when the other party takes knowledge of same; in writing, when it reaches the other party. Declarations not yet in force may be cancelled.

In case the approval of a third party or the permission of any authority is necessary for the conclusion of a contract, the contract does not come into force until these are obtained; however, the parties are bound to their declarations. Once the approval has been given according to the general rule, the contract becomes effective retroactively.

5.3. Formalities

In the absence of any legal regulation to the contrary, contracts may be concluded either orally or in writing. The formalities of contracts are mandatory and so, in case of failure to observe these formalities, the contract is to be considered as null and void.

The parties themselves may also stipulate formalities, but in this case, by accepting the performance the contract it is to be considered as valid, even if the formalities stipulated by the parties are ignored.

In case the validity of the contract is prescribed by the formalities the cancellation or termination of the contract is valid only if these formalities are met.

5.4. *Termination*

A contract is to be considered as null and void if:

- it is against a legal regulation;
- it was concluded by avoiding a legal regulation;
- it is contrary to 'good faith';
- by misusing the situation of the other party, one of the parties stipulated conditions especially favourable for him.

If there is a great difference between the values of the service and counter-service, without the intention of one party to advantage the other party, the injured party may attack the contract (*laesio enormis*).

Contracts concluded due to error, deceit, and threat can also be attacked.

The following contracts cannot be enforced by the court:

- demands deriving from gaming or betting, except if carried out with State permission;
- demands deriving from promises and credits made especially for the purpose of gaming or betting;
- demands the enforcement of which by State organs is excluded by legal regulation.

Contracts concluded for demands not enforceable by the court are null and void.

5.5. *Force Majeure*

According to the Hungarian Civil Law the circumstances and events constituting *force majeure* need not be defined separately. It is sufficient if in the text of the contract – where the question of responsibility is dealt with – an obvious reference to *force majeure* is made, the contents of which are given by legal regulations and the practice of the judges.

5.6. Breach and Non-Performance

The cases of breach of contract, delay, incorrect performance, refusal of performance or impossibility of performance are regulated in the Civil Code, which lays down common and special rules.

It is remarkable that, in the case of some instances of contract breach, the Civil Code considers the limitation and exclusion of liability null and void.

For liability for breach of contract, as well as for the measure of compensation, the liability for damages caused beyond contract (delictual liability) is to be applied according to the Civil Code, with the provision that, according to the main regulation, no decrease of the compensation is possible.

6. Standard Contract Terms

This is not applicable in Hungarian law in the field of sports marketing.

7. Different Types of Business Arrangements

Business arrangements are of two types in Hungary:

(1) traditional patron, sponsoring support; and
(2) market-orientated public relations and advertising activity.

Traditional patronage is made possible by the relevant regulations of the Civil Code, either in the form of a fund or in the form of a so-called obligation of common interest. A pre-condition for both forms is that beyond publishing the fact of the support they are not allowed to have any subsequent advertising character.

In case of sponsoring support, which already assumes some PR orientation, the valid regulations consider this equal to PR and advertising activity, which means that the support provided in this form belongs to sales falling under VAT. However, as sports fall into the tax-free realm, the tax paid cannot be reclaimed.

8. The Rights

Only general rules are to be applied, as discussed under other points.

9. Financial Terms

There are no special financial terms or tax benefits existing. The general interest rate for delayed payment amounts to 20% per annum. As between economic associations, the interest rate is always changing and, at present, it is 44% per annum.

10. Insurance Aspects

The general rules on insurance apply.

As to product liability, this is only generally covered by the Civil Code, there being no special regulation as yet.

11. Advertising and Promotion

As already mentioned above, business relations are of two types in Hungary: traditional patronage and market-oriented PR and advertising activity.

The main regulations relating to advertising are as follows:

Marketing relationships, based on contracts, do not have any special rules, other than the general ones, which means that like other economic connections they fall under the competence of general contract law included in the Civil Code.

As to the contents of advertising and promotion, several limitations exist, which are discussed hereunder.

11.1. Prohibitions and Limitations by Law

The Act relating to home trade, issued in 1978, regulates in general the individual elements of advertising and promotion and prohibits the advertising of certain products in general. Particularly the advertising of any spirits, tobacco products and medicines is prohibited.

However, due to the growing importance of foreign parties in the Hungarian market, these prohibitions – although the legal regulation is still in force – are not or not fully enforced in practice. Consequently, the advertising activity of companies producing spirits and, although on a smaller scale, tobacco products has also been started in the field of sports.

11.2. Regulations Relating to the Ethics and Norms of Advertising

The system of norms regulating the activity of organisations dealing with advertising, the Advertising Ethics Code, also includes prohibitions and limitations, the individual elements of which are drafted also in the legal regulation relating to market competition. There is a prohibition of advertisements which do not correspond to the actual characteristics of the product, and a prohibition of dumping advertising.

11.3. Sports Branch Regulations and Norms

The most important limitations of sports advertising are presently given by the sports branch regulations, which mostly follow the norms of international sports bodies. These regulations define what size and contents advertisements may have, what promotions may be placed at sports events, and at which sports events advertising is allowed at all.

12. The Venue

No special regulations exist.

13. Dispute Resolution

Hungary has no court experience up to now in the field of sports marketing.

There are two court levels: the first instance courts and the appeal courts. The duty payable in civil litigation at first instance is 6% of the value of the claim, with a maximum of 300,000 HUF; for appeals, the duty is 3% of the value of the dispute. Attorney's fees are generally subject to a maximum of 10% of the value of the dispute, but can also be fixed by free agreement between the client and the attorney.

According to the Hungarian Code of Civil Procedure, a court claim begins with the *demand* of the plaintiff containing the precise claim, statement of facts and supporting evidence. The defendant has the right to argue against the plaintiff's arguments and evidence by filing counter evidence, after which the first trial begins.

There is a Court of Arbitration of the Hungarian Chamber of Economy, with its special rules, and enforcement of court judgments and arbitral awards depends upon multinational and bilateral treaties and agreements. Hungary is a member, among others, of the New York Convention on the Reciprocal Recognition and Enforcement of Arbitral Awards.

Iceland

by Johannes Sigurdsson

1. Sports Marketing – A Business

Sport in Iceland is generally practised at an amateur level, at least officially. The participants have been defined as amateurs since they generally do not get salaries for playing. However, it is a well known 'secret' that the top players are being paid for their efforts. This development, from amateur status to what might be defined as a semi-professional level of sports, is at least partly due to a growth in sports marketing in this area. More money is coming into the sports, so clubs are in a better position to pay for top players.

Sports marketing, which was almost an unknown business in Iceland until a decade ago, has been growing rapidly for the last five to seven years. One explanation of this growth is that the State monopoly on television and radio broadcasting was abandoned in 1986. The competition for good television and radio programmes on sports events has become more intense, since it attracts advertisers and sponsors. The sports associations took the opportunity and raised their prices for broadcasting rights. Since sports marketing is a relatively new business in Iceland and the disposition of money coming into the clubs a kind of a secret matter, no study has been made on the amounts spent in this area.

2. The Icelandic Legal System

It is difficult to place the legal system in Iceland within one of the two major groups of legal systems in Western Europe: common law and civil law. The Icelandic legal system has characteristics of both systems, but generally it has been defined as a civil law system. Many areas are regulated by statutes enacted by Alpingi (the legislative body) and in some fields it has been so for many centuries. Precedents by courts, mainly the Supreme Court of Iceland, play a important role in regulating other areas such as tort and some areas of commercial law.

The legal development in Iceland has been influenced by legal development in the other Nordic countries. The Nordic countries have had a close cooperation in certain fields of legislation. This cooperation has resulted in a certain uniformity of law, for example on contracts, sales, insurance and copyright.

Before the end of 1992 Iceland, as a member of the European Free Trade Association (EFTA), has to make a decision whether it will become a party to the European Economic Area Convention. If Alpingi (Parliament) verifies this Convention, it has to alter statutes in many areas to comply with the Convention's provisions. Moreover, many directives of the European Community will influence the legislation in Iceland in the future, e.g. competition rules.

3. Applicable Laws

Since sports marketing is a relatively new legal area there has been no need to date for special legislation on this matter. General rules on contracts, intellectual property rights and competition are the most important rules that will be applied in this field of business.

The principle of freedom of contract, which is generally accepted in Iceland, leaves it to the parties involved to decide on the content of their relationship. Despite this principle, the agreement made between the parties must take into account some compulsory rules which are applicable on certain issues in this area, for example, certain advertising contracts.

4. Intellectual Property Rights

4.1. Trademarks

The Trademark Act No. 47/1967 provides the rules on registration and protection of a trademark. According to Article 1 of the Act, companies can obtain an exclusive right to a trademark by registration of the mark. Trademark rights can also be obtained without registration if the mark is generally known in a certain field of business and has been established in the market (Article 2).

A registered trademark is protected for ten years from the date of registration and the registration can be renewed for ten years, as often as one chooses (Article 22).

There are no user requirements under Icelandic trademark law.

Iceland is a signatory to the Paris Convention on Trademarks.

4.2. Copyright

Copyright is regulated by the Copyright Act No. 73/1972. Iceland is a signatory to the Berne Convention and the Universal Copyright Convention. The Rome Convention has not yet been ratified, but it is expected that it will be soon.

According to Article 43 of the Act, the general rule is that copyright on literary and artistic works protected under Chapter I of the Act exists for the lifetime of the author and 50 years after his death. Registration of copyright is not necessary for protection of the right.

Copyright protection is based on the principle that a creator of a literary or an artistic work is always the initial owner of the copyright in the work. The author has an exclusive right to make copies of his work and make the work available to the public in its original or changed form. In the absence of a contract, an employer may for his normal activities use works that have been created by the employees in the course of their employment.

An author of a work has moral rights in the work which are protected by the Copyright Act. Article 4 of the Act provides that the author's name shall be properly indicated when his work is being made available to the public. This article also provides that the author has the right to object to any distortion of or other derogatory action in relation to the work, which would be prejudicial to the author's honour and reputation. These rights exist independently of the economic right and can only be waived under exceptional circumstances.

Whilst there are no particular formalities required for an assignment of copyright, in practice, it is advisable to express this in writing, for evidence purposes.

4.3. Designs

Designs are also protected by the Copyright Act of 1972. Similar rules as those mentioned above for copyright are applicable to designs. Designs have to meet two standards to be protected by the provisions of the Copyright Act: they must have a certain effective value and be of an artistic character.

5. The Contract Generally and Preliminary Agreements

5.1. Preliminary Agreements

Preliminary agreements are normally on a verbal basis in Iceland. Since the contents of such agreements are often vague and contain only a declaration of an intention to make a contract it is difficult to enforce such agreements. Such agreements may however have some legal consequences if a party does not adhere to them.

5.2. Establishing a Contract

As mentioned, the principle of freedom of contract leaves it to the parties to decide the content of their agreement. To establish a binding contract between parties some basic requirements must be met. This issue is regulated by the

Act on Contracts No. 7/1936. The provisions of this Act are only applicable if the parties do not decide otherwise in their contract or if a custom provides a different rule. According to Article 2 of the Act, a contract will become binding when the acceptance of an offer has been delivered to the offeror. If no time limits have been put in the offer, it is binding on the offeror until he has cancelled the offer and the cancellation has reached the other party. The offeree must, however, respond to the offer within a reasonable time.

It is normal practice in some areas of contract that an offer and an acceptance decide only the main issues of the agreement between the parties. When such basic agreement has been reached parties sit down and negotiate the details of their contract. If the parties do not agree on the details, it is possible that the basic agreement will not be enforceable. This would be the case if the issue is fundamental for the agreement. Generally the agreement will be enforceable and the disputes on the details have to be solved according to general rules based on interpretation of the agreement already made.

If the agreement the parties are planning to enter into is not in a field of well-established contract customs, which is the case with sports marketing, the parties generally negotiate all details before they enter an agreement. In these instances, the contract becomes enforceable when the parties have signed the agreement.

5.3. Form and Execution

The general rule on contracts does not require the agreement to be in writing. In some areas, statute makes it a condition that an agreement on transfer of rights is made in writing. Despite the general rule most contracts in this area are made in writing, for obvious reasons.

To ensure that the contract will be enforceable against a legal entity it is imperative that the contract is signed by a person that has power to execute such contracts. Normally the general manager of a legal entity has such power. If some other person is signing the contract, on behalf of a legal entity, one has to verify that he has such power, either in writing, or by his status as an employee. Information of this sort can be obtained from the general company registrar or limited liability company registrar.

5.4. Void and Illegal Contracts

Despite the rule of freedom of contract and that no formal conditions have to be fulfilled to establish a contract, the contract must comply with three rules to be enforceable. First, the contract must be decisive on the parties' rights and duties. If the contract is ambiguous on those matters, it is possible that it will not be enforceable. Second, the duties written out in the contract must not be impossible to execute, neither generally nor for the party involved. Third, the terms of the contract must not be unlawful or against public policy.

To be able to enter into a valid contract the parties must comply with the provisions set forth in Chapter III on void contracts of the Contracts Act. The provisions in this Chapter cover such matters as fraudulent behaviour, duress, mistake. One rule that should be mentioned here is in Article 36 of the Act, a provision which was added in 1986. The rule provides that, if a contract term is obviously unfair or against good business practice, it is possible to void the contract or alter its terms. In deciding to apply this rule, one must consider the content of the contract, status of the parties involved, situation when the contract was made and the facts arising after the contract has been made.

5.5. Breach of Contract

If a contract is breached by a party, the opponent has some alternative claims. If the breach is considerable, one can repudiate the contract and claim damages as well. In cases where the breach cannot be defined as considerable, the party has a choice of three remedies. One can claim that the contract should be enforced by its terms: an order of specific performance. This alternative is limited to some extent, depending on the duties stated in the contract. Another alternative is to claim a rebate; and the third is to make a claim for damages.

6. Standard Contract Terms

Since sports marketing is a relatively new concept in Iceland, contract terms in this area are not very well established. The structure and basic contents are similar to that of contracts in other fields. General customs in contracts can, therefore, be used. If the parties do not cover a certain issue in their contract, general rules may be applied to the issue in dispute.

The first thing to mention about standard contract terms is the necessity to define the parties by full name, addresses and identification numbers. If terms in the contract are used in a different manner than usually, it is necessary to define those terms. If this is not done, the ordinary meaning of the word or phrase will be used when a contract term is interpreted. If the parties are trying to reach a special goal with the contract, it is advisable to spell this out in a recital. This may prove useful for interpretation, especially when it is difficult to make concrete provisions in the contract to reach the goal.

The duties and the rights of the contracting parties must be written down very carefully. In this context the agreement should include guarantees from a party, for example, on how many games will be provided or on admission to a stadium. Payments for rights and royalty rates must be spelled out in detail. It is also imperative to decide how it will influence the payments if a duty is only partially delivered. Where royalty payments are part of the agreement, it is necessary to include a clause which gives the licensor the right to appoint an auditor to inspect the books of the other party.

A clause covering a *force majeure* situation should be included, even though general rules on this issue will be applicable if not included in the agreement. Other events not covered by the *force majeure* rule, but which might prevent either party from performing, should be adopted if the parties find it necessary.

Since sport has a special image that needs to be protected – an image of young people, healthy living and body power – it is necessary to include provisions which secure that the business arrangement and the performance of the sponsor or the licensed party will not bring the sports body or event, which is the subject of the contract, into disrepute.

Finally, in international contracts in this area, a clause on applicable law should be part of the contract. The parties can select which nation's law shall apply. Generally, it is advisable to make the law of the country, where one has to pursue one's rights, applicable.

7. Different Types of Business Arrangements

The most extensive field of sports marketing in Iceland is in sponsorship agreements. There are no general restrictions on who may enter into a sponsorship agreement in the country. The relationship between the parties is governed by the contract and no special legislation has been enacted in this area. However, legislation in several areas prohibits advertising of certain goods and services. Such provisions may limit, in certain ways, the content and execution of a sponsorship agreement. Advertising of alcoholic beverages and tobacco are banned. There are severe restrictions also on the advertising of pharmaceutical products. For more detailed information, see Section 12 on Advertising and Promotion at p. 179.

This ban does not necessarily exclude, for example, producers of alcoholic beverages from sponsoring a sports programme. If a producer, for example, produces a beer which contains less than 2.25% of alcohol he can advertise the label of that beer, even though he produces beverages which contain higher alcohol percentages under the same label. In those cases, it may be necessary to mention that it is only the non-alcoholic product that is being advertised. The producer can also sponsor an event under its company name, but special attention must be paid to the terms of such a contract.

It should also be mentioned here that companies that import alcoholic beverages have been sponsoring sporting events for many years.

Sponsorship agreements generally grant the sponsor an exclusivity in the sponsor's field of business. Provisions of this kind are generally accepted. However, if such rights are very extensive regarding time and scope, it is possible that they can be considered to be in breach of some provisions of Chapter IV of the Act on Prices, Competition Restraints and Unfair Business Practice No. 56/1978.

Other kinds of sports marketing, such as merchandising, suppliership, public appearance and endorsement, are also known in Iceland. The same goes for contracts in these fields: they are regulated by the particular contract entered into between the parties. One thing that should be mentioned in this context is that a producer is prohibited from using the national flag of Iceland on his product as a trademark or for commercial purposes.

8. The Rights

To make sports marketing contracts attractive to a sponsor, licensor or some other party, it is necessary to offer a variety of rights to suit the interests of each party.

Generally, the agreement between parties in this field includes a clause which grants the party some exclusivity. This clause may vary from granting a total exclusivity or only in a certain product category. As mentioned, provisions of this kind are generally accepted, but if this right is very extensive it may be considered as a restraint on competition and may, therefore, have to be abandoned. If the exclusivity is only in a certain product category, a dispute may arise concerning how extensive this right is. For example, if a party has been granted the right for sports equipment, the same party might argue that his rights cover sportswear. For this reason, it is necessary to define the scope of the rights very carefully in the agreement.

Another right often used in sports marketing contracts is the right of first refusal. Provisions of this kind give a party a priority to make a contract or to match an offer from a third party. The contract should include provisions on the procedure for the parties to exercise this right. It is advisable to put a time schedule in the contract for making or matching an offer for a new contract. The contract terms should clearly state that this right is only applicable for the next contract after which it will automatically terminate.

The rights granted in sports marketing agreements are often limited to a certain geographical territory. Two or more parties are given the same right(s) but in different territories. Such provisions must state clearly the borders in this context and effects of breaches.

Similarly, copyright and trademarks can be split into different categories. One party can be given the right to broadcast an event and another party the right to sell videotapes of the event. Trademarks can also be licensed to a different party for a different product.

The rights granted in the contract must be limited to some time or alternatively a provision on termination should be included. It is also important that there is a general clause in the contract stating that all rights that have been granted with the contract will go back to the grantor/licensor when the contract has reached its time limit or been terminated.

9. Financial Terms

Financial terms of contracts differ form one contract to another. It should, however, be emphasised that such terms ought to be defined very carefully regarding amount, time of payment and place of delivery.

If a party fails to deliver a payment in accordance with the contract he must pay penalty interest on the amount due. The penalty interest rate varies from time to time and is decided by the Central Bank of Iceland (Act on Interest No. 25/1987). The current rate is 16% per annum.

One specific issue that must be borne in mind when a contract stipulates that each party shall provide service to the other, is that the value of the service should be put into the contract. This must be done since tax authorities may otherwise claim that the service is worth more than the parties had in mind.

10. Product Liability and Insurance Aspects

Even though the image of sport is of a friendly nature, experience has taught us that mass damages may result from sporting events. This is evident in areas such as car racing, boxing and wrestling. One who is organising such an event should take out a policy for public liability.

In a public sports affair, such as a running contest, the participants are often covered by a personal injury insurance. Sometimes such insurance is made an express term of a sponsorship agreement.

An owner of a stadium may be liable for damages caused by some defects of his property. The owner will be made liable if one can prove that he saw or should have seen the defects of the property and did not fix them. For this reason one should take out an insurance for liabilities of this kind.

At the beginning of 1992, the Act on Product Liability No. 25/1991 came into force. This new Act imposes a rule of *strict* liability on producers and distributors of goods. It is advisable, therefore, for parties to agreements in areas such as merchandising and suppliership to consider insurance coverage in this respect.

11. Venue

Generally, the organiser of a sports event will be in control of the stadium where the event takes place. This, however is, a matter of contract between the owner and the organiser. It is necessary to define the area under control in the contract and which party will decide on admission to it. This is important so that the organiser can control admission to the stadium. The owner has generally some right to supervise the area during the preparation for and holding of the event.

12. Advertising and Promotion

Article 27 of the Act on Prices, Competition Restraints and Unfair Business Practice No. 56/1978 provides a general rule on the form and content of advertisements. The provision states that misleading and unsatisfactory information in advertisements is banned. The content of this rule is of a general nature and gives the competition authority flexibility to set standards in these matters. Since the rule is very open for different interpretations one expects that the standards will develop and change from one time to another in harmony with public views and accepted business practice.

The name of the competition authority is now 'Verdlagsrad' but will be changed to 'Samkeppnisrad' if a new Bill, being discussed in the Parliament, will be enacted. If Iceland becomes a party to the European Economic Area Convention, it will be necessary to enact this Bill in order to comply with the terms of the Convention.

In addition to this general rule, there are others that provide more specific standards in certain areas.

Article 16, para. 4, of the Alcohol Act No. 82/1969 bans, without exemption, all advertising regarding alcoholic beverages. This provision does, however, not exclude producers of alcoholic beverages from sponsoring a sports programme as mentioned at p. 176.

In the field of pharmaceutical products there are also restrictions on advertising. In chapter VII of the Pharmaceutical Act No. 108/1984, it is provided that pharmaceutical products may only be advertised in professional magazines and with a direct mailing to professional people. Despite these provisions, pharmaceutical companies may sponsor sports programmes if such sponsorship does not refer to a special pharmaceutical product.

Advertising tobacco is also prohibited according to Article 7 of the Act on Tobacco Protection No. 74/1984. In this provision, both direct and indirect advertising is banned with a very limited exception. It is, however, possible for a producer of a tobacco product to sponsor a sporting event but the terms of the contract and execution must be designed very carefully.

If one is planning direct marketing in the area of sports marketing one has to take into account provisions of the Act on Registration and Handling of Personal Information. According to Article 21 of the Act one must apply for a licence to be able to collect and store data of a personal nature.

13. Dispute Resolution

There are mainly two methods used in Iceland to settle disputes arising from a contract. One is to make a claim before a court and the other to submit the dispute to an arbitration.

13.1. Court Action

Disputes arising out of sports marketing contracts will generally be submitted to a District Court (Héraðsdómur) which is a common civil court of first instance. This court is competent to try claims if the party being sued has a domicile in the jurisdiction of the court. This principal rule on venue applies whether the plaintiff is Icelandic or foreign (Article 32 of the Civil Procedure Act No. 91/1991). In addition to this domicile rule there are others which are applicable, for example, if the parties have been doing a certain kind of business in the jurisdiction of the court.

The average time to try a case before a District Court is somewhere around eight months. Procedure may take a much longer time if there are hearings on the formal side of the case and if the case is very complicated. If there are no disputes regarding the amount of the claim, the procedure may take much less time.

If time is a vital issue for preventing someone from infringing the rights of another party, it is possible to get a temporary verdict from the District Court for injunction or attachment. Generally, the plaintiff in these cases has to provide a security for potential loss of the defendant if the temporary action is taken without merits. These temporary actions must be followed up by a confirmation trial within a week from the verdict.

Decisions of the District Court are subject to appeal to the Supreme Court (Hæstiréttur), the highest court in the country. It may take up to two and a half years to try a case at this level.

As mentioned, the courts can, depending on the claims set forth by the plaintiff, decide that the defendant shall act according to the terms of the contract (specific performance). Alternatively, the plaintiff can get a verdict for rebate or damages.

If a party loses a case in court it normally has to pay the opponent's legal costs (Article 130 of the Civil Procedure Act No. 91/1991). The amount of the costs awarded is at the *discretion* of the court. When deciding this, the court has to determine how much the party has to pay its lawyer for the work on the case. In this context, the courts can get some guidelines from the Bar Association's Legal Fee List. Court awards in this area are often lower than the actual costs of litigation for the party, especially if the case is complicated and the amount claimed is not big.

13.2. Arbitration

Arbitration clauses are often put into sports marketing contracts. The arbitration procedure has several advantages. One is that the procedure may take less time than before a court. Furthermore, parties can decide the procedure and the result will be confidential, which is often of great value to parties in this field of business. The major disadvantage of arbitration is that the costs may be high compared to an action in court, since the parties have to pay the costs of the arbitrators.

The Arbitration Act No. 53/1989 provides general rules on arbitration procedure. Generally, the parties can decide which rules of procedure will be applicable. If the parties do not include provisions on these issues in their contracts, the provisions of the Arbitration Act will apply.

Parties can agree in a contract to submit almost all disputes regarding sports marketing matters to arbitration. This applies to intellectual property rights as well as others. However, it should be mentioned that disputes regarding registration and protection of trademarks are decided by the trademark registrar and a special appeal committee. The decisions of the appeal committee are reviewed by the general courts.

13.3. Alternative Dispute Resolution

In some sports marketing contracts parties include a clause which provides that each party shall designate two or more persons to a committee, which will settle disputes and decide on certain issues which may arise when the agreement is being executed.

Provisions such as those are adopted by the parties for the purpose of resolving disputes in an amicable way. As mentioned, sport has a special image that must be protected and all means should be tried to settle a dispute amicably before the parties take their claims to court.

Republic of Ireland

by Ernest J. Margetson

1. Sports Marketing – A Business

Figures are not available for the money that is spent on sports related activities in the Republic of Ireland but it is very clear that it has been one of the largest growth industries in the last twenty years. Sponsorship now plays a very important part in all areas of sport.

It is fair to say that, initially, sponsorship tended only to exist in professional sports, such as golf and association football. In Ireland, golf was one of the major recipients; in particular, the Irish Open Golf Championship. Because of the amount of sponsorship that was available in other countries throughout the world, Ireland completely lost out on professional tennis. Sufficient funds were just not available, and whilst back in the 1950s and early 1960s many of the worlds leading 'shamateurs' were enticed to Ireland by a payment of generous 'expenses', once professionalism entered the sport there were not sufficient funds. There has been a breakthrough in November 1992 when a small Irish ladies tennis event was sponsored by one of the banks and six of the top women players, who were ranked between 4 and 14, participated in this event, which is now going to become an annual event and no doubt once started now will spread.

It is true to say that it is only in the 1980s that sports organisers took an interest in and were keen to co-operate with various sponsors. It is also true to say that, whilst at first the press was reluctant to report sponsorship, this has now changed and sports reporters happily acknowledge sponsors, taking the practical view that, in fact, sponsorship is news. In Ireland, as probably in many other countries, once the event is an established annual event and where traditionally the name of the event contains the brand name of the product of the sponsor, then there are no doubt great attractions in establishing a long term viable commitment rather than concentrating on maximising one year's support from whatever source on a year by year basis.

2. The Legal System of the Republic of Ireland

The legal system of the Republic of Ireland is a common law system consisting of judge-made law (case law), which is supplemented by the Acts of the Oireachtas or Parliament (statute law). Under the various statutes, power is very often given to the particular minister involved to introduce regulations and these are known as Statutory Instruments.

Ireland became an independent republic in 1922 and, up to that stage, had been governed by the British Parliament. Accordingly, up to the time of independence, Irish law was, in general, identical to the law of England and Wales. On the Declaration of Independence, the existing law was incorporated as part of the law of the Republic of Ireland.

Since then Ireland has developed its own legislation, but it has to a very large extent followed English law, particularly in general areas such as intellectual property, contract, and tort. The legal systems of Ireland and the UK are still linked together to the extent that a reported decision of the High Court or of a Court of Appeal in England has a persuasive influence on an Irish court, and, unless there are some exceptional circumstances, will tend to be followed. Similar to the UK legal system there are the two systems, namely law and equity, which operate together.

Also, as in the United Kingdom, the advertising industry is regulated by self-imposed regulations. There is a Code of Advertising Standards, which contains a set of general rules, which apply to advertising and sponsorship. The Code is administered by the Advertising Standards Authority for Ireland, which was established in 1981. The Authority is a non-profit making limited company and the members of the Board are the Directors of the Company. The Authority is the advertising industry's own watchdog. It is independent of Government and receives no State funding. The principal aim and object of the Authority is stated as follows: 'to promote and enforce throughout Ireland the highest standards of advertising in all media of communication so as to ensure in co-operation with all concerned that no advertising contravenes or offends against these standards, having regard *inter alia* to the Code of Advertising Standards for Ireland'.

Particularly within the scope of the Authority, as in many countries, is the question of tobacco advertising and this is partially dealt with under legislation, namely the Tobacco Products Act 1978 and the regulations made thereunder. Under this legislation there is power to limit the form which advertising associated with sponsored events may take.

3. Applicable Laws

Once again, as in the United Kingdom, there are not any laws specifically applicable to sports marketing. Obviously, to a very large extent, the law which is applicable is the law of contract. Once the agreement between the parties is a valid one under the law of contract and does not infringe any self-imposed regulations, then there is a valid enforceable agreement.

4. Intellectual Property Rights

The intellectual property rights which command the most attention in the field of sports marketing are trademarks and copyright. There is also the area, mainly based on case law, known as 'passing off', to prevent unfair competition.

4.1. Trademarks

In Ireland, the law on trademarks is contained in the Trade Marks Act 1963. Comparison between trademarks statutes of the United Kingdom and Ireland adds weight to a comment made by one of our High Court Judges in which he stated: 'We have thought fit very deliberately to adopt and continue the British Trade Mark system, and, consequently, wherever the laws coincide, it is legitimate and necessary to consult the English decisions from which much help is obtainable in a country where Trade Mark business is very small in comparison with its immense volume across the channel'.

Section 2 of the Act defines a 'Mark' as including 'a device, brand, heading, label, ticket, name, signature, word, letter, numeral, or any combination thereto'. As will be seen, this is identical to the provisions in the UK 1938 Act. The provisions in relation to registration of the mark are identical to the UK provisions. Similarly, having registered the mark, the registered proprietor has identical rights as those in the UK. It is, however, important to note that under Section 15 of the Act, it is provided that neither the proprietor nor the registered user of a registered trademark can interfere with or restrain the use by another of an identical or resembling trademark, where that person or predecessor in title has continuously used that trademark from a date prior (a) to the use of the registered trademark or (b) to the registration of the registered trademark, whichever is the earlier, or object to such a person being put on the register for that identical or resembling trademark on proof of honest concurrent use of his mark.

Similarly, under Section 16, no registration of a trademark shall interfere with (a) any *bona fide* use by a person of his own name or of the name of his place of business or of the name or place of business of a predecessor in business or (b) the use by any person of any *bona fide* description of the character or quality of his goods, not being a description that would be likely to be taken as importing a reference to the registered proprietor.

Section 70 of the Trade Marks Act 1963 gives effect to the State's obligations pursuant to the International Convention for the Protection of Industrial Property of 1883. This Convention was revised in Brussels in 1900, Washington 1911, the Hague 1925, London 1934, Lisbon 1958 and Stockholm

1967 and, under Article 1, the countries adhering to the Convention constitute a Union for the protection of industrial property. Ireland is among the countries which have ratified the Stockholm text of the International Convention. The purpose of the International Convention is not to provide for an international system for the registration of trademarks, but rather to ensure reciprocity of treatment as between proprietors of trademarks in the different States which have ratified the Convention. Apart from the International Convention, the major international treaty affecting trademark rights in Ireland, is, of course, the Treaty of Rome. The combined effect of the provisions of Articles 30–36 inclusive, 85, 86 and 222 of the Treaty and the manner in which these have been interpreted by the European Court of Justice have had a profound effect on the manner in which trademark rights may be used and exercised within the European Community.

4.2. Copyright

The law on copyright is to be found, for the most part, in the Copyright Act 1963 and relevant case law. The Act defines copyright as being the exclusive right to do (and to authorise other persons to do) certain acts in relation to 'work'. In other words, the owner of the copyright in a 'work' has exclusive rights in it, subject to any contrary provisions in the Act. The infringement of any copyright is similar to the position as described in the UK. The general rule, which has emerged from decisions by the courts over the years, is to the effect that any performance which takes place outside the domestic circle is to be regarded as 'public'.

4.3. Common Law Protection

Under this heading is what is known as the 'passing-off' action, which is a tort. In this action, traders can rely on a claim for 'passing-off' when seeking redress against a trade rival who palms off goods and services as those of a *bona fide* trader. In many cases, it is possible to seek redress for trademark infringement pursuant to Section 12 of the Trade Marks Act 1963, where the plaintiff can rely upon a registered trademark, and, additionally, upon a claim for passing off in respect of the defendant's tortious trading not falling within the ambit of Section 12. In such an action, what is sought to be protected is not the property in a particular name or mark, but rather the business goodwill of which the former are only a part. It is important to note that a common law action for 'passing off' can only be brought by one trader against another and not by a member of the public, who may have been deceived into buying the goods or availing of the services of the defendant rather than the plaintiff. The essential ingredients for an action of 'passing off' were laid down by the President of the High Court in an action which was affirmed by the Supreme Court on Appeal in the case C *& A Modes & Anor* v. *C & A (Waterford)*

Limited & Ors (1976, *Irish Reports*, page 198): 'on the authorities, the fundamental ingredients of the action for "passing off" are that the Plaintiff has a name applicable to his goods or business which is known to the public in the area which the Defendant seeks to carry on his business to an extent that the name, brand or mark proposed to be used or being used by the Defendant is likely to deceive and to cause confusion'.

5. Insurance Aspects and Venue

The legal position in the Republic of Ireland in relation to these matters is the same as under English law.

6. Dispute Resolution

As in the United Kingdom, the remedies available when a dispute arises may be through the courts, by arbitration or alternative dispute resolution (ADR).

6.1. Court Action

An action would be brought in the High Court. Proceedings are issued, pleadings are filed and the action is then set down for trial. Almost certainly applications will be made by both parties for an order for discovery. If the plaintiff is a foreign plaintiff, an application can be made for an order for security for costs, but, if the plaintiff carries on business in an EC country which has subscribed to the Brussels Convention, it is very unlikely that security for costs will be granted, unless there are exceptional circumstances. At present, the action will come on for hearing within about twelve months after the setting down of the action for trial, provided no difficulty arises on discovery.

As in the UK, application may be made by one of the parties for an injunction. In determining as to whether an injunction should be granted, the rules as set out by Lord Diplock (cited in the Chapter on the UK at p. 32) also apply in Ireland. In addition, the party who is successful in obtaining an injunction is obliged to give an undertaking to the court as to damages in the event of his being unsuccessful at the trial of the action. These damages would be the losses suffered by the other party because of his inability to carry on with his business or whatever effect the injunction may have had.

The measure of damages is similar to that in the UK.

The position in relation to legal costs is identical to that in the UK.

As Ireland is a subscriber to the Brussels Convention, any judgment of another European Community country is enforceable in the Republic of Ireland.

6.2. Arbitration

The position on arbitration is also similar to that of the UK, as to which, please see pp. 33 and 34. Ireland is also a party to the New York Convention on the Reciprocal Recognition and Enforcement of Arbitration Awards.

6.3. Alternative Dispute Resolution

This concept is new in Ireland, only having come into being in the past twelve months. It is reasonable to forecast that because of the considerable delays in the courts, which are increasing, and also the costs and expenses involved, it would appear that ADR will become very much more popular and will undoubtedly be written as a condition of sports marketing contracts in the future.

SPORTS
MARKETING

Italy

by Dr. Roberto Capurro

1. Sports Marketing – A Business

In Italy, sports marketing is a relatively recent phenomenon which started after the Second World War. It now represents a very significant market sector in terms of dimension and social impact, being second only to that of the United States in terms of current importance and rate of development.

The business aspect of sports derives from the organisation of events and related activities which in themselves generate profit, the production and retail of equipment and sportswear and the sponsoring and advertising activities linked to sport. The growth of this business in Italy is to be attributed to three main factors: the traditional, passionate interest Italians have for sports; the vast press and television coverage available; and the nation's aptitude for fashion and design.

Generally speaking, the Italians prefer a passive rather than an active role in sports, a preference which has contributed significantly to the growth of sponsoring and advertising. The capillary coverage afforded by the press and television – Italy has more sports papers and specialised magazines than any other country and a large number of State and private television networks operating on national and regional levels – is also an important factor.

Finally, if companies under foreign control are taken into account, Italy is one of the leading countries in the production of sportswear.

The combination of these three factors renders advertising and sponsoring highly advantageous to those companies and institutions which operate both directly and indirectly in sports related activities.

2. The Italian Legal System

Italian legislation is based on a system of civil law. The basic rules regulating contractual relations are embodied in the Italian Civil Code which was brought into force in 1942. While many modifications have been made to the Code since its enactment, the section regarding contracts has remained substantially unchanged. However, a number of laws have been added to deal with specific problems deriving from the needs of a developing society, for example trademarks, copyright, factoring, and so on.

Italy is also a party to several international treaties, such as the EEC Treaty and the Convention on Contracts for the International Sale of Goods, which may affect or prevail over national legislation.

As most countries, Italy has not yet developed a body of laws specifically applicable to sports marketing. General rules are therefore applied, but in this field self-imposed regulations are also of paramount importance (in particular, the statutes of sports federations or associations and the 'Codice di Autodisciplina Pubblicitaria' (Code of Self-Discipline in Advertising)).

3. Applicable Laws

The provisions governing the choice of applicable law are to be found in the 'Disposizioni Preliminari al Codice Civile' (Preliminary Provisions to the Civil Code). Article 25 of these provisions states: 'Law governing obligations. Obligations arising from contracts are governed by the national law of the contracting parties, if both belong to the same nation; otherwise by that of the place in which the contract was made. The parties may agree to have their contract governed by the laws of a different foreign state. Non-contractual obligations are governed by the law of the country in which they occur.'

The first two options established in this article can, therefore, be derogated, should the contracting parties decide to apply the laws of a third country. However, there should be a logical connection between the law selected and the transaction, especially when the parties are of the same nationality.

It is possible for the contracting parties to determine indirectly which law will govern the formation of the contract. Article 26 of the Preliminary Provisions to the Civil Code states that the formation of a document, whether it be contractual or not, shall be governed by the law of the country where it is drawn up, or, alternatively, by the law which governs its substance.

The freedom of the parties to choose the law they wish to be applicable to their contractual obligations is confirmed by the EEC Convention of 19 June 1980 on the Applicable Law for Contractual Obligations – promulgated in Italy by Law No. 613, 14 October 1985. This freedom is however limited by Article 31 of the Preliminary Provisions, which states that: '[. .] in no case can the laws and acts of a foreign State, the rules and acts of any institution or entity, or private provisions and agreements be effective within the territory of the State, when they are contrary to public policy and morals.'

4. Intellectual Property Rights

The majority of agreements necessary for the implementation of a sports marketing programme entails the exploitation of intellectual property rights, such as trademarks or copyright.

4.1. Trademarks

The regime regulating trademarks is set forth in the Royal Decree No. 929 of 21 June 1942, which establishes that all new words, designs and/or emblems and logos used to distinguish marketable goods and products may be registered. Protection is also afforded, given certain circumstances, to unregistered trademarks.

Applications for trademark registration must be filed with the 'Ufficio Centrale dei Brevetti' (Central Trademark Office), and, should the trademark be assigned to another party, the transaction must be recorded with the same Office, in order to be enforceable against third parties. Protection against infringements is afforded the trademark from the date on which the application is filed (and not the date of registration) and is effective for twenty years from that date. Renewals are also valid for twenty years and provide continuous protection.

Furthermore, trademarks identifying services also enjoy protection and can be registered (in classes 35 to 42, both inclusive).

Protection lapses if the trademark remains unused for an uninterrupted three-year period, but only if the owner of the trademark is not using contemporaneously other similar trademarks to distinguish the same product.

Italy is a signatory of several international conventions, including: the International Convention on the Protection of Trademarks, known as the 'Union de Paris', last reviewed in London, on 2 June 1934, and ratified by Law No. 1332, 15 December 1954; the Madrid Arrangement for the International Registration of Trademarks, last reviewed in Nice, on 15 June 1957, and ratified by Law 1178, 24 December 1959; and the International Convention regarding the filing of models and industrial designs, known as the 'Arrangement de la Haye', last reviewed in Geneva, on 29 August 1975, and ratified by Law No. 37, 25 January 1983.

4.2. Copyright

Copyright is regulated by Law No. 633, 22 April 1941. This law applies only to Italian citizens and residents; the protection of foreign works is subject to reciprocity unless governed by international conventions (in this connection, it should be noted that the Universal Copyright Convention was ratified in Italy by Law No. 923, 19 July 1956). Under Law No. 633, the creator of an original work in the fields of science, literature, the figurative arts, music, architecture, theatre, cinema, radio and television has the exclusive right to publish and exploit his work. This includes reproduction in any form or manner, public performances, broadcasting, trading, translation and adaptation of the protected works. The rights mentioned above may be purchased, sold, transferred or assigned, independently one from another. The creator and, subsequently, his heirs, has a moral right over his work, i.e. he has the right to be recognised as the 'author' and may restrain anyone from altering his work in a manner he considers prejudicial to his honour or reputation. This right is personal, is not transferable and is not subject to time limitations.

Protection of the economic rights of a work covered by copyright lasts for the lifetime of the author and extends fifty years after his death; in the case of films the protection is valid for thirty years from the date of the first public showing.

Records, photographs and other visual works can be registered in order to secure protection, but in general it is not necessary to register new works. Registration is effected by filing a copy of these works at a special office of the President of the Council of Ministers (or its local branches).

Assignments of copyright must be in writing to be valid.

4.3. Unfair Competition

The Italian Civil Code affords wide protection against unfair competition; Sections 2598–2601 embody the main rules governing this issue. Section 2598 defines acts constituting unfair competition as follows:

'Subject to the provisions concerning the protection of distinctive signs and patent rights, acts of unfair competition are performed by whoever:

(1) uses names or distinctive signs which are likely to create confusion with the names and distinctive signs legitimately used by others, or closely imitates the products of a competitor, or otherwise performs acts which are likely to create confusion with the products and/or activities of a competitor;
(2) spreads news and comments, with respect to the products and/or activities of a competitor, which are likely to discredit said products and/or activities, or treats as his own the positive qualities of the products, activities and/or enterprise of a competitor;
(3) avails himself directly or indirectly of any other means which do not conform with the principles of correct behaviour in the trade and are potentially damaging to the enterprise of a third party.'

Section 2599 establishes that a judgment, which ascertains that certain acts constitute unfair competition, must prohibit the continuation thereof and issue provisions to eliminate the deleterious effects caused.

In Section 2600, the Civil Code states that any person found guilty of performing acts of unfair competition with fraud, malice or negligence (when such acts are ascertained, negligence is assumed) shall be liable to pay damages. The publication of the sentence may also be ordered in such cases.

Other restrictions are contained in the Code of Self-Discipline in Advertising and other self-imposed regulations.

5. The Contract Generally and Preliminary Agreements

5.1. Preliminary Agreements

Under Italian law it is necessary to be particularly careful in distinguishing between documents relating to pending negotiations and letters of intent in general as opposed to preliminary contracts. The former usually imply only the intention of the parties to negotiate in order to reach a binding obligation, the only legal duty of the parties being to conduct the negotiations and behave in good faith.

The legal connotation of preliminary contracts is different. These imply the existence of an agreement already reached between the parties and their obligation, enforceable before the court, to execute the final contract.

Section 2932 of the Civil Code states: 'Specific enforcement of the obligation to execute a contract. If a person who is bound to make a contract does not perform his obligation, the other party, when possible and unless he is barred by the preliminary contract itself, can obtain a judgment producing the same effects as the contract which has not been made.'

5.2. Contracts

As a general principle, Italian law allows contracting parties complete liberty in establishing the terms and form of their business relationship. The Civil Code contains provisions governing general contract principles and provides the general rules applicable to specific types of agreements, including sales contracts and agency agreements, as well as standard terms to facilitate drafting and performance. However, it is possible to modify most norms if both parties are in agreement as to the requisites of contract validity. There are however a few limitations: certain contracts must be evidenced in writing or executed in the presence of witnesses (e.g. in the case of donations) or acknowledged by a Notary Public (e.g. for sales of immovable property). Italian law permits all competent persons to enter into contractual agreements, the only restriction being the obligation to respect public policy and avoid illegal behaviour.

Italian contract law also provides norms to protect parties with less experience or bargaining power. Under Sections 1341 and 1342 of the Italian Civil Code, standard contracts prepared by one party which modify certain provisions of the Code, such as limitations of responsibility, the right to terminate or suspend an agreement, limitations on the right to raise objections, restrictions on relationships with third parties, automatic renewal or extension of the contract, arbitration clauses and choice of forum, must provide for specific written approval of said modifications by the other party, which is usually expressed with a second signature preceded by the approval of each relevant clause. In the absence of this written approval, the provisions have no effect.

5.3. Creation of a Legal Relationship: Offer and Acceptance

Contrary to US practice, contracts, when not executed simultaneously, are considered concluded on the date and at the place that the offeror physically received acceptance, normally the offeror's place of business. This is very important with regard to international contracts as, in the absence of a specific provision to the contrary, contracts are governed by the laws of the country in which they are concluded. The offeror may request specific formalities for acceptance to be valid. Should the terms of an acceptance vary even slightly from those of the offer, it is considered a counter offer.

While the general principle is that parties are free to determine the form of their agreement, and special requirements as to the form and execution of a contract are needed only in special cases, in practice, it is always advisable to execute the contract in writing.

A party, who has entered into an agreement as a result of material error, duress or deception, may request a court to void the document. In the case of material error, this can only be done if the party is in a position to prove that the error was substantial and that the other party was aware or should have been aware of it. An error is considered material when it concerns the nature or the object of the contract, the identity or the essential characteristics and qualities of the obligation and, if relevant, the identity of the other contracting party. A contract can also be voided if an error in law was committed, but only if the error is the sole or predominant reason that moved the party to make the contract.

5.4. Consideration

The concept of consideration is foreign to Italian law, although '*causa*' (cause) is somewhat comparable, albeit vaster in scope. Section 1325 of the Italian Civil Code establishes it as an essential contract requisite.

No satisfactory and complete definition of the concept of '*causa*' has been given, but, in general, it may be described as the 'useful social or economic function of the contract', or to be precise, of the 'type of the transaction considered in general'. The concept of '*causa*' is to be considered as opposed to 'motive', which is the particular reason which stimulated the parties to conclude the agreement (and which is usually not at all relevant). The concern is, in fact, with the function of the transaction and not with the motive. For instance, lease contracts are enforced because they are considered, in the social context, to be worthy of protection. Whether the specific parties executing a lease contract actually have economic and social motives is not relevant.

'*Causa*' is illegal when it is contrary to imperative rules, public policy or morals. A contract without '*causa*' or in which it is illegal, is void.

5.5. Form and Execution

As previously mentioned, whenever special formalities are not required by law, the parties are at liberty to adopt whatever form of execution they prefer. However, if the agreement is in document form, it should be signed or initialled on each page, a practice which eliminates the possibility of substitutions after execution. Furthermore, where amendments to the text have been made in manuscript, such modifications should be initialled by all parties as it is to be supposed that they have originated after execution. If the contract is signed by or on behalf of a corporate or other entity, it is advisable to check that the person acting on its behalf has the authority required to bind that corporation or entity.

5.6. Void and Illegal Contracts

As mentioned in point 5.3 above, a party, who has been induced to enter into an agreement as a result of material error, duress or deception may request the court to void the contract.

A contract without '*causa*' lacks an essential element and is, therefore, void.

Contracts against public policy or order are invalid.

Whenever the law so prescribes, contracts must be executed with the required form.

5.7. Interpretation

Section 1362 of the Italian Civil Code establishes that: 'that which was the common intent of the parties, not limited to the literal meaning of the words, shall be sought in interpreting the contract. In order to ascertain the common intent of the parties, the general course of their behaviour, including that subsequent to the conclusion of the contract, shall be taken into account.'

The following principles are also applicable:

- each clause in a contract is interpreted with reference to the other clauses, attributing to each the meaning resulting from the deed as a whole;
- no matter how general the expressions used in a contract, they can only include the objects as to which the parties intend to contract;
- the contract shall be interpreted in good faith;

- in case of doubt, the contract or its individual clauses shall be interpreted in the sense in which they can produce effects, rather than in that in which they would produce none;
- ambiguous clauses are interpreted according to the general practice in the place in which the contract was executed and, in contracts involving an entrepreneur, ambiguous clauses are interpreted according to the general practice of the place where the business has its main offices;
- in cases of doubt, provisions contained in the standard conditions of a contract or in forms or formularies prepared by one of the contracting parties are interpreted in favour of the other.

5.8. Frustration and Force Majeure

When circumstances outside a party's control prevent said party from fulfilling its contractual obligations, complete or partial relief may be granted from such obligations, depending on the cases. Partial or total impossibility to perform may depend on events varying from natural catastrophes, such as earthquakes and floods, to acts by public authorities or third parties outside the control of the contracting parties.

If performance becomes completely impossible, the contract is terminated and the party involved must restore any benefit already received. If the events impeding performance are temporary, the contract is not immediately terminated and fulfilment is delayed until performance becomes possible. This notwithstanding, if the delay renders the performance useless for either party, due to the nature of the performance required or the type of obligation, the contract will be terminated.

In the case of partial impossibility and provided the obligation which cannot be performed is not essential to the agreement, the contract maintains its validity, but the benefit accruing to the party failing to perform is reduced proportionately.

Furthermore, contracts to be performed over a period of time or at a later date, such as supply agreements or licence agreements, may be rescinded if performance has been rendered excessively onerous by extraordinary and unforeseeable events. If occurrence of such events falls simply under commercial impracticability, this will not exonerate from performance.

5.9. Breach and Remedies

Non-performance of any obligations embodied in a contract constitutes a breach. If performance of the breached obligation is deemed by the court to be essential to the agreement, the party not at fault is entitled to request specific performance or termination of the agreement. The parties may determine contractually which provisions or obligations are to be considered of the essence.

5.10. Termination

In general, termination of a contract (for breach of an essential provision, impossibility to perform) must be declared by a court upon request of the injured party. Under certain conditions, however (and apart from the case of termination by mutual agreement of the parties), a contract may be terminated on the initiative of one party without the need for a court decision. Legal proceedings are only necessary if the other party raises objections to the termination or if damages have been requested.

5.11. Damages

The main principle is that the party not at fault should be restored to the economic position which would have prevailed had the breach not occurred. Damages may be recovered either upon termination of the agreement or in addition to specific performance and normally include both costs incurred and profits lost as a direct result of the breach. If the breach is not wilful, liability is limited to foreseeable damages.

5.12. Penalty Clauses

The parties may establish pre-determined penalties for non-performance or delayed performance of the contract. The court has the faculty to review a penalty clause and reduce the amount of liquidated damages if there has been partial performance or if the penalty is evidently excessive.

5.13. Specific Performance

The party which is not at fault may also request specific performance in lieu of termination. If an action for specific performance has been initiated, the plaintiff retains the faculty to modify his pleadings and request the court to declare the termination of the agreement. If, however, the plaintiff initially requests termination, he may not thereafter change his pleadings and request specific performance.

5.14. Refusal to Perform

Under Article 1460 of the Italian Civil Code, a party is allowed to refuse to perform contractual obligations if the contract requires mutual performance and the other party does not perform or offer to perform its obligations. Furthermore, under Article 1461, a party may delay performance if it has knowledge that the other party's economic situation is such as to endanger its ability to perform. In this case, however, the other party can offer satisfactory guarantees of its performance and, thereafter, require the other party to fulfil its obligations.

5.15. Usual Contract Terms

Under Italian law, where no specific provisions are included in the text of the contract the corresponding provisions of the Italian Civil Code or of the relevant applicable statutes are automatically applicable. For instance, while it is certainly advisable to include a *force majeure* clause in a contract, should it not be included *force majeure* causing impossibility of performance will nevertheless be applicable (Sections 1218, 1256, 1463).

Even when a contract can be concluded verbally it is highly advisable that the agreement be made in writing, including at least the following provisions:

- full identification of the parties;
- premises and/or recitals (where applicable);
- clauses relative to the object of the contract;
- precise and exhaustive details of the obligations of the parties;
- territory (where applicable);
- exclusivity (where applicable);
- duration or time of performance;
- details and terms of payments;
- auditing (where payments are envisaged totally or partially under the form of royalties);
- *force majeure* (enlarging on specific events which should be included under this heading);
- no joint venture or partnership clause;
- causes for termination;
- post-termination arrangements (survivals);
- penalty clauses (if applicable);
- applicable law;
- choice of forum, or arbitration (and language of arbitration).

The above list is not exhaustive and is intended only as an initial guide to the main issues to be dealt with.

6. Standard Contract Terms

The principal types of contract utilised in this sector are the following:

(1) sponsorship agreements;
(2) merchandising agreements;
(3) endorsement agreements;
(4) commissioning agreements (e.g. commemorative medals, coins and stamps);

(5) franchise agreements;
(6) films and videos;
(7) public appearances;
(8) supplierships.

In practice, agreements between the sponsored party and the sponsor frequently include elements characteristic to more than one of the above-mentioned contracts.

Generally speaking, the agreements between the parties are not subject to particular restrictions with the exception of those mentioned below. The contracts listed above are of relatively recent origin and are similar in their basic elements to those of the majority of countries in which they are used.

The following are the most common forms of sponsoring:

(a) Sponsoring of companies or sports associations or teams. In this case, the contract governs the relations between a non-sports subject, which pays a contribution or consideration, and a company or association or team which undertakes to perform certain actions which are advantageous to the former (e.g. by affixing the sponsor's logo on sports equipment, using the sponsor's trademark on banners, posters, medals, trophies, and at stadiums, and, in general, carrying out any activity which is suitable for promotional purposes).
(b) The sponsoring or patronage of a sports event, where the object of the contract is the diffusion of an advertising message through a single event (e.g. where the event carries the name of the sponsor, or wherein the winner of the event receives a trophy which carries the name of the sponsor);
(c) The sponsoring of an individual athlete, where the advertising vehicle is the athlete himself (who will then be required to wear sportswear distinguished by the sponsor's logo or trademark, or use equipment, e.g. a bicycle or motorboat carrying the sponsor's logo or trademark).

The following comments are pertinent to sponsoring:

(1) There are restrictions as to persons and entities who may sponsor events and also as to products which may be sponsored. Such restrictions and limitations will be discussed in further detail in the section 'Advertising and Promotion'.
(2) There are no limitations on investments in this sector.
(3) When selecting an event or individual to sponsor, it is important to ascertain whether the name, trademark and activity are, or have been linked to other products or former sponsors which may damage or have a negative impact on the new sponsor. Co-sponsors should also be carefully investigated to ensure that the new sponsor's product does not become associated with other products which may dilute or damage the image of either product or sponsor.

(4) In the case of long-term contracts, expiry dates should be carefully checked to ensure that termination does not fall prior to an important sports event (National or World Championships, Olympic Games), thus significantly reducing the value of the contract to the sponsor.

(5) Prior to concluding a contract, it is also advisable to make sure that the individual or association to be sponsored is the best vehicle to reach the desired objectives, and that he/they are in fact capable of achieving the required results. Nothing generates adverse publicity so effectively as litigation with a popular sports personality or association. To avoid this pitfall, it is wise to include in the contract clauses of an economic nature which aim at discouraging non-performance (e.g. penalties and reductions).

(6) Often the general and contractual freedom of athletes, sports associations and clubs is restricted by contract, or by the bye-laws of the association or club, or by the fact that the club or association is a member of another higher level association. Football clubs can be taken as an example of this, as they must respect the rules laid down by the national association, the FIGC (National Italian Football Federation), as are players whose freedom of action may well be limited by the contract which binds them to their clubs.

(7) It is worthy of note that it is common practice in Italy to establish a sponsor 'pool', e.g. the America's Cup or the FISI (Italian Federation of Winter Sports). It may well be worthwhile to investigate the possibility of organising a number of sponsors interested in forming an organisation of this type.

(8) It is also common practice when sponsoring certain sports, in particular, basketball and volleyball, to change the name of the sports association to reflect the name of the sponsor, either by adding the sponsor's name to the existing name, or adopting it outright (e.g. Simmenthal, Scavolini, Nivea Fuchs).

(9) Where possible, it is sound practice to scale the amount of the sponsoring in proportion to the results obtained.

(10) Finally it must be kept in mind that, in certain sports, sponsoring contracts may be fully or partially subject to the approval of the security commissions of the sports sector involved.

7. The Rights

The principal rights available to potential sponsors, suppliers, merchandisers and licensees, and detailed comments relative to options, pre-emption, exclusivity, copyright, licence, trademark licence, territory, media, merceological classes, duration, post-termination and accreditation, have already been illustrated in the chapters dealing with other countries (*cf.* in particular the UK).

In general, the same comments and principles apply to Italy.

Trademark licences constitute the only peculiarity worthy of note in this context. Licences must be exclusive for territory and product. Italian law states that there can be only one trademark user for the same product and over the same territory (except in special cases established by law such as 'quality trademarks').

In the case of trademark assignment or licence, it is obligatory to cede the branch of business relative to the trademark together with the trademark itself. In order to overcome the grave difficulties created by this limitation, the Italian courts have established that this requisite can be considered fulfilled if the assignment of the trademark is accompanied by the formulas or know-how connected to the product or service it distinguishes.

Current Italian trademark law, which dates back to 1942, no longer reflects commercial requirements and it is expected that a new law, in line with the EEC Directive on trademarks, will soon be brought into force.

8. Financial Terms

8.1. General Comments

The comments of a general nature regarding this topic contained in the chapter on the UK are also applicable to Italy.

With particular reference to Financial Terms, it should be noted that, under the Italian Civil Code, as a general rule, 'set off' is allowed (Sections 1241–1252 of the Civil Code). Also in case of 'set off', however, it is necessary to comply with the applicable tax provisions (e.g. withholdings at source, VAT). Interest for late payment is established at the rate of 10% (Section 1284 of the Civil Code) where no other interest rate has been agreed by the parties in writing.

8.2. Insurance

As to insurance, it would be necessary – whenever applicable – to obtain public liability insurance coverage as well as product liability insurance, the latter whenever a liability may derive from the use of trademarks on products or merchandise distributed at the event. In this regard it is worth mentioning that Italy has enacted the Decree of the President of the Republic No. 224 dated 24 May 1988, on Product Liability, in compliance with the EEC Directive 85/374, dated 25 July 1985 on the same subject.

9. The Venue

As to the venue, it will be necessary to check compliance with the applicable health and safety rules, and to obtain the necessary permits from the local authorities.

Furthermore, the airspace above the place of the event can be used for advertising purposes, subject to obtaining permits from the competent authorities.

Although the theory of trespass would probably not be applicable in Italy against third parties intruding in the airspace above the venue, they could certainly be liable, either for unfair competition, or under the general action for 'unjust enrichment' (Section 2041 of the Civil Code).

It will also be necessary to ensure that the venue is free from competitive products and advertising so that display rights, supply rights, pouring rights, and so on can be delivered to the official sponsor(s).

Accreditation passes and access to the venue, as well as providing an appropriate service of public order at the event, are all matters that need to be carefully and timely checked and documented.

10. Advertising and Promotion: Limitations

Advertising activities in Italy are regulated by both legal and private rules, the former being comprised in a system of laws and regulations, certain of which are national implementations of EEC Directives, while the latter are contained in the 'Codice di Autodisciplina Pubblicitaria' (Code of Self-Discipline in Advertising) which is a private agreement binding the great majority of the members of advertising associations, the Italian Federation of Press Editors (FIEG) and State and private television networks. The Code of Self-Discipline does not have power *erga omnes*; it can only bind those who have expressed, explicitly or tacitly (through their trade association), their adhesion to its norms. This limitation is however purely formal, as, from a practical point of view, all those who wish to operate in the field of advertising are bound by the Code, even if they have not expressed their adhesion directly. In fact, it is not possible to operate in this field without entering into working relationships with at least one entity bound by the Code, and the ensuing contract necessarily binds the 'independent' operator also.

In general, the Italian legal system subjects advertising for particular merceological categories to bans and limitations designed to eliminate or reduce the diffusion of products which are considered to be either actually or potentially harmful to health.

Two distinct groups of regulations pursue the above aim:

(1) the first applies a total or partial ban on direct and, in certain circumstances which will be expounded upon later, indirect advertising for particular product categories which are specifically cited;
(2) the second prohibits the sponsoring of television and radio programmes by specific parties.

The bans on advertising referred to in point (1) are formulated in two laws. The first law prohibits advertising for any tobacco product, whether produced abroad or by the domestic market, while the second forbids any form of advertising for medicines for the purchase of which a doctor's prescription is required, permitting only the technical information necessary to medical personnel. The relatively recent Law 223 issued in 1990 confirms these bans with specific reference to radio and television advertising.

These regulations which prohibit advertising for particular product categories are flanked by others, as mentioned previously, which forbid certain parties from sponsoring radio and television programmes. This second group of regulations is contained in Law 223 of 1990 and in the subsequent Vizzini decree, both implementations of EEC Directive No. 89/552. In particular, programmes cannot be sponsored by 'individuals or juridical persons whose principal activity consists in the production or retail of cigarettes or other tobacco products, the production or retail of spirits, the production or retail of medicines or in providing medical remedies available only on presentation of a doctor's prescription.'

Programmes are considered to be sponsored when containing or connected to forms of promotional communication, which cannot be considered as standard advertising, against payment of a specific contribution by the 'sponsor' or the party operating on its behalf.

As stated previously, the law has also placed restrictions on advertising for other product categories.

Specific limitations are applicable to alimentary products; without going into detail, the law penalises acts aiming at creating confusion and illicit appropriation of positive qualities. It is interesting to note that, in the case of food products, the law considers the appropriation of therapeutic qualities to be illicit, even when those qualities effectively exist.

As already mentioned, particular limitations are imposed on television advertising for alcoholic beverages with a regulation aimed at implementing the EEC Directive.

The limitations imposed on advertising can be divided into those which aim at avoiding messages which may cause offence to the public and those which aim at avoiding infringement of specific interests of individual parties.

10.1. Protection of the Public

The regulations which protect the public can be divided into two groups:

(a) those which aim at safeguarding the public from misrepresentation in advertising;
(b) those which protect public morals and values.

With regard to the first sub-group, Italian law has not yet formulated specific regulations against 'misrepresentation in advertising'. To date, the consumer is only protected by general regulations against illicit conduct and practices by dealers, entrepreneurs and, in general, by all individuals and juridical persons operating in the market. However, implementation of the EEC Directive No. 84/450 which deals with this issue is imminent.

The second sub-group, i.e. regulations protecting the values and morals of the public, covers a wide range of situations. As in all other countries, Italy has many laws of various types to safeguard a range of individual and public values, from decency to social and religious convictions, safety and so on.

10.2. Protection of Individual Parties

The second category, which covers limitations aiming at protecting specific interests of individual parties, can be divided into three sub-categories:

(a) regulations which safeguard personal rights;
(b) regulations which safeguard manufacturers other than the advertisers: this group of norms includes those of a more general nature protecting commercial names and distinctive signs belonging to third parties and those against defamation through advertising;
(c) regulations which safeguard the proprietors of the rights to a particular advertising message.

Comparative advertising and the relative positions of the laws of the State and the Code of Self-Discipline are of particular interest. There are three main types of comparative advertising:

(a) Direct comparison: in this case the second product is expressly named. In Italy this is forbidden at present.
(b) Indirect comparison: comparison made with unidentified and unidentifiable parties. State law admits this form of comparison, as long as the truth is respected and the message is limited to supplying information.
(c) Use of the relative superlative: State law does not, in general, consider that use of the relative superlative constitutes infringement of point 2 of article 2598 of the Civil Code.

10.3. Protection of Rights Holders

Proprietors of rights to advertising messages are protected through several laws:

- copyright law;
- trademark law (there have been cases in which a court sentence has accepted that a slogan has mutated into a trademark);
- laws regulating competition: point 1 of Article 2598 of the Italian Civil Code represses the counterfeiting of competitors' products and, therefore in consequence the counterfeiting of advertising messages (considered in this instance

as a product, the property of whoever created the message or purchased the proprietary rights thereto).

The same article condemns any conduct which may lead to confusion with competitors' products or activities. As above, this regulation is obviously to be applied to the advertising message considered as a product.

11. Tax Deductibility: Nature of Activity

Under Italian law, for fiscal purposes a different treatment is awarded to expenses incurred for advertising and publicity and to those incurred for *spese di rappresentanza*, i.e. expenses for public relations and related activities met to exploit a representative function and to improve the image and decorum of the subject. Under Section 74 of the Unified Code of Direct Taxes (Law 917/86, as amended), advertising and publicity expenses shall be deductible in the first fiscal year in which they are incurred or in equal instalments in said year and the two subsequent years. On the contrary, only one third of the amount of the expenses incurred for representative functions shall be deductible in equal instalments in the year in which they are incurred and the two subsequent years, i.e. the amount deductible is equal to one third of the total and it is to be deducted in three equal instalments over a period of three years.

With regard to sponsorships, it is often difficult to define when they qualify to be included in the category of advertising expenses (*latu sensu*) and when they should be considered as *spese di rappresentanza*.

A precise definition of this latter term is not available. This is, in fact, the object of a long-standing dispute between the fiscal authorities, authors of legal works, lawyers and tax experts. In principle, it may be maintained that for the purpose of making the above distinction, taxwise, expenses qualify as advertising whenever they are aimed at improving the sales of the products or services of the sponsor as opposed to those met or incurred only to improve the image of the sponsor. Whenever the prospective sponsor is a resident tax subject a preliminary evaluation of this issue is highly advisable.

12. Dispute Resolution

12.1. Choice of Forum

According to the Italian Code of Civil Procedure the parties to a contract may avoid the jurisdiction of the Italian courts and submit a contractual dispute to a foreign jurisdiction of their choice only if they are non-Italians, or, in the case of one of the parties being Italian, if this party is neither a resident of Italy, nor domiciled therein. However, the application of this very restrictive provision is limited by the Brussels Convention on Jurisdiction and the Enforcement of Judgments, dated 27 September 1968, which has been ratified by all EEC countries.

According to Article 17 of this Convention, the parties to a transaction may select another signatory country as the competent forum, provided that at least one of the parties is domiciled in a signatory country and that the agreement is not in conflict with the exclusive jurisdiction provisions established by the Convention. These provisions state that the exclusive forum for disputes regarding real property, status of corporate bodies, public records, trademarks, copyright and patent, and enforcement of judgments is the place where the object of the controversy is located.

12.2. Ordinary Courts

An action can be filed with the appropriate court, usually the 'Pretore' or 'Tribunale', depending on the subject matter of the dispute. Depending on the complexity of the case, the proceedings may be extremely lengthy (the average is five years in first instance and three for appeals). Provisional remedies and temporary relief may be granted by the court where appropriate.

Legal costs are at the discretion of the courts. Generally, they are charged to the losing party, but in this case the winning party is usually only able to recover from 50% to 70% of the costs actually incurred.

Italian courts are not bound by juridical precedents, but lower courts usually adhere to the trends set by the higher courts or by the Supreme Court.

12.3. Arbitration

12.3.1. Formal arbitration

Italian law permits contracting parties to resolve conflicts through arbitral awards. Certain issues, including matters of public interest (e.g. trademarks, patents, personal status), may not be subject to arbitration. Italy is also a signatory to several treaties regulating international arbitration with respect to commercial matters (Protocol of Geneva of 1923, Geneva Convention of 1961), and on the recognition and enforcement of foreign arbitral awards (Geneva Convention of 1927 and New York Convention of 1958).

According to Italian law an arbitration agreement or clause must name the arbitrators or provide for a specific number thereof and the manner in which they will be selected. The parties may also determine the rules of procedure by which the arbitrators are to proceed. If these rules are not provided, the arbitrators themselves are empowered to regulate the manner in which the proceedings will be conducted, provided the procedure does not constitute a violation of the basic principles of due process.

Arbitrators do not have the faculty to grant provisional remedies; however, the parties may apply to the competent court.

An award must incorporate the reasoning followed by the arbitrators in arriving at their decision.

The award may be submitted to the competent court which, if the award has the necessary requisites, will declare it enforceable (as if it were a court decision).

Arbitral awards are not subject to appeal, but they may be annulled or revoked by ordinary courts under special circumstances as listed in Section 829 of the Code of Civil Procedure.

12.3.2. Informal arbitration

The parties may sign a blank sheet of paper, which is then delivered to the 'arbitrators' who determine the merits of the controversy, complete the paper with contractual provisions designed to settle the dispute in accordance with their determination.

The contract resulting from this procedure is not enforceable in the same way as a formal arbitration award, but only as a contract. In the same manner, it can only be contested on general contract principles and not under the provisions governing the validity of arbitration awards.

SPORTS
MARKETING

Luxembourg

by Guy Harles

1. Sports Marketing – A Business

The sports industry does not represent a large part of the Luxembourg trade. Importations represented 176 millions of Luxembourg francs in 1991 and exportation 19 millions.

One person has participated in the 1992 Winter Olympics in the skiing section and the number of participants in the 1992 Summer Olympics has increased to fifteen.

The Luxembourg TV Channel of 'Compagnie Luxembourgeoise de Telediffusion' broadcasts a programme relating to sport every week, during one hour.

In 1990, there were 618 clubs relating to non-Olympic sports, representing 16,069 persons, and 629 relating to Olympic sports, representing 69,815 persons. The most popular sports are football, which has 126 clubs with 21,752 members and tennis with 51 clubs with 10,534 members.

Luxembourg has a national football team, but nobody is a professional player.

2. The National Legal System

The Luxembourg legal system follows a codified legal system which contains three principal branches of law:

- public law;
- private law; and
- social and economic law.

The court system in Luxembourg is divided into three degrees of jurisdiction except in administrative matters. The ordinary courts of first instance are the Justice de Paix and the Tribunal d'Arrondissement. Appeals from the judgments of these courts are made to the Cour Supérieure de Justice. Writs of error against appeal judgments are filed with the Cour de Cassation.

The sources of the national law are of three kinds: international legislation including EEC regulations; national legislation composed of statutes, regulations and orders; Luxembourg and foreign case law.

3. Applicable Laws

There is no special law and no case law relating to sports marketing in Luxembourg. Some general laws are applicable in this matter and the relationship between the parties is governed by contract. The contract must respect public policy and the rules of the Civil Code relating to the formation of contracts.

4. Intellectual Property Rights

Among the three Benelux countries (The Netherlands, Belgium and Luxembourg) the rules relating to trademarks and industrial designs and models are uniform. Luxembourg is also a party to the Berne Convention, to the Convention of Paris and a member of the World Intellectual Property Organisation (Madrid Convention).

4.1. Trademarks

Trademarks are governed by the Benelux Convention of March 1962. The Uniform Benelux Law recognises the Nice international classification of trademarks.

Trademarks which are protected by the Benelux Uniform law are defined in the first article as any symbol which distinguishes the products or the services of a company.

To register a trademark, a file must be deposited with the Service de la Propriété Intellectuelle of the Ministry of Economics in Luxembourg which transmits the file to the Bureau Benelux des Marques in The Hague.

The Bureau Benelux des Marques controls the form requirements of the file and sends the applicant an examination of priority rights of other trademarks, whereupon the applicant decides if he maintains his registration or not. The Bureau Benelux des Marques does not control whether a similar trademark has been registered. However, the first registration gives a right of priority to the applicant for the use of the trademark.

Trademarks are protected during a period of ten years after registration. This protection can be extended for further terms of ten years indefinitely.

The owner of the trademark can license his right to use the trademark. The contract of license must be in writing.

The trademark becomes void if it has not been made use of within three years following registration or during a continuous period of five years.

4.2. Copyright

The Law of 29 March 1972 protects copyright. Article 1 of this law employs the definition given by the Berne Convention and provides that the author of a literary or artistic work has an exclusive property right on this work. The words 'literary and artistic work' are defined as 'every production in the literary, scientific and artistic domain whatever may be the mode or the form of its expression . . .'.

Copyright exists automatically. The author needs no registration of his work.

The protection is given during the author's life and for 50 years after his death. Photographic works are protected for only fifty years from the making of such works.

Copyright covers works in literary, musical, dramatic and artistic works, sound recordings and films.

Under Luxembourg law, the author of a work protected by copyright can transfer the right of exploitation but keep the moral rights on his work.

Under the terms of the Law of 29 March 1962, the author has a moral right on his work. The moral right is attached to the author. After his death, this right continues to exist until the end of the right of exploitation and during this period it can be exercised by the heirs of the author or by a third person if the author gives it this right by a clause of his will.

4.3. Industrial Designs and Models

On 1 January 1975, Luxembourg acceded to the Benelux Convention on Designs and Models and to the Uniform Law for the protection of designs and models.

It is necessary to apply for registration to obtain protection under the Uniform Law.

Article 1 of the Uniform Law provides that the novelty of a product having a useful purpose can be protected as design or model. The novelty is not taken into consideration if, during the past 50 years, another product has had a similar appearance in the Benelux territory.

The owner of a design or model has the exclusive right to exploit it commercially or industrially in the Benelux territory or to license it.

Protection is granted for five years from the date of registration and may be extended for two periods of five years each.

4.4. Unfair Competition

When the elements of identification are not protected, the solution consists in bringing an action on the basis of the Unfair Competition Act and to claim damages on the basis of Article 1382 of the Civil Code.

Unfair competition is sanctioned in Luxembourg by the law of 27 November 1986 which regulates certain commercial practices and prohibits unfair competition.

Article 16 of this law provides that the seller, the manufacturer or the craftsman who, by an act against either the fair practices in the commercial sector or a contractual agreement, removes or tries to remove from his competitors or from one of them part of their customers or affects or tries to affect their capacity of competition, commits an act of unfair competition.

5. The Contract Generally and Preliminary Agreements

Sports marketing is essentially governed by the law of contract.

5.1. Preliminary Agreements

The usual practice before the preparation of the contract is to discuss it with all the parties to the contract.

After the preliminary discussions, the parties draw up a document specifying the principal obligations of the parties.

5.2. Intention to Create Legal Relations

Article 1134 of the Civil Code gives to the contract the force of law. It provides that contracts legally concluded serve as law to the parties to these contracts.

To be legal, the contract is subject to four conditions: the consent of the parties; their legal capacity to contract; a certain object which is the subject matter of the contractual commitment; and a fair 'cause' in the obligation.

5.3. Offer and Acceptance

Consent is generally analysed as an offer followed by an acceptance. An offer is a unilateral action whereby a person makes known its intention to contract and the conditions of the contract. The contract is formed once an offer made by a party is accepted, without conditions, by the other party.

If the consent of a party to the contract has been obtained by violence or fraud or if it has been given by error, the contract may be voidable by the party concerned.

5.4. *Consideration*

A contract is void in the absence of a valid cause. The cause will be invalid if it is contrary to public policy or *contra bonos mores*.

5.5. *Form and Execution*

The contract needs to be in writing (for the purpose of evidence) except in commercial matters between two traders.

The written contract must be signed by all the parties to the contract and the number of originals of the contract must be equal to the number of the parties having a conflicting interest.

5.6. *Void and Illegal Contracts*

A contract must not be against public policy or *contra bonos mores*. Such contracts are void. Luxembourg law does not distinguish between void and illegal contracts. Parties to a void contract are entitled to restitution, except in certain cases, for example, in cases of 'moral turpitude' (*nemo auditur propriam turpitudinen allegas*).

5.7. *Privity*

Under Luxembourg law (Article 1165 of the Civil Code), contracts have effects only between the parties and are not effective against third parties.

5.8. *Interpretation*

Articles 1156 to 1164 of the Civil Code describe the rules governing the interpretation of the contracts.

The basic rule applied, when interpreting a contract, is to look for the common intention of the parties. The other rules concern the interpretation of certain clauses.

If there is a doubt on the interpretation, the contract is interpreted against the creditor or, in the case of an 'adhesion contract' (standard form agreement), the party who prepared the contract.

5.9. Frustration and Force Majeure

Article 1148 of the Civil Code provides that no damages are due if a circumstance of *force majeure* or a fortuitous event prevents one party from performing its obligations.

Sometimes, the parties to a contract include a provision relating to circumstances of *force majeure*. Generally, in this clause, the parties add some events which are not considered as *force majeure* by Luxembourg general law, for instance, strikes.

5.10. Breach of Contract

If a party fails to meet its obligations, the contract will be breached. Under the terms of Article 1142 of the Civil Code, all breaches of contracts give rise to damages except in the case of *force majeure* (see previous paragraph on frustration).

6. Standard Contract Terms

Most contracts, which deal specifically with sports marketing, contain similar clauses. These clauses are in particular:

- the name and the address of the parties or, in the case of a company, the registered office and the name of the person who represents the company;
- the terms of the contract;
- the conditions for termination: with prior notice or not;
- intellectual property rights;
- liability clauses;
- penalties for non performance or late performance of the obligations; and
- the applicable law and the competent courts.

7. Different Types of Business Arrangements

7.1. Sponsorship Agreement

Sponsorship is governed by contract and there are no special rules concerning this matter.

The purpose of the contract is for the sponsor to give money, sometimes goods, against some rights, which concern generally the possibility to make publicity.

There are no legal restrictions to these sponsorship contracts except the fact that certain types of publicity are forbidden (see on these restrictions p. 218).

7.2. *Merchandising*

This matter is governed by contract. Intellectual property rights are the central element of this type of contract.

7.3. *Commissioning Agreement*

Again, a commissioning agreement is governed by contract. The most important clauses of these contracts concern intellectual property rights. The party which orders the manufacturing of commemorative medals, coins or stamps does not have the copyright in these works.

It is important to provide in the contract that the right of economic exploitation will be transferred, but that the author will keep his moral rights on his work.

The use of the arms or emblems of the Grand-Duchy of Luxembourg is sanctioned by the Penal Code which provides that there is a non-authorised use particularly when this use is made for a fraudulent purpose or a business, industrial, professional or publicity purpose.

7.4. *Films and Videos*

Films or videos intended for sale are a matter of the law of contracts. But, except in certain cases, such as the 'Tour de France', no contracts (either orally or in writing) are really concluded and films or videos are made without control of the organiser. No royalties are then paid.

7.5. *Suppliership*

The organiser of a sports event can grant to a supplier the right to be the supplier of a certain product or services during the event. The supplier will usually wish to be the sole supplier of this product or services and obtain a right of exclusivity, i.e. no competing supplier has the same right.

8. The Rights

8.1. *Options*

To grant an option is an act by which the organiser of a sports event offers to a supplier, merchandiser or sponsor the right to make publicity during the demonstration. The sponsor or supplier must decide within a certain period of time whether or not to take up the option. During the same period of time, the organiser cannot revoke the option.

8.2. Pre-emption

The right of pre-emption is different from the right of option. Pre-emption gives somebody the right to obtain something by priority. The right of pre-emption does not permit the organiser to offer something without proposing it first to the beneficiary of the pre-emption right.

8.3. Exclusivity

The organiser can chose to give to a supplier, merchandiser or sponsor an exclusive right, who will be the sole person entitled to exercise the right.

8.4. Copyright Licence

Article 3 of the Law of 25 March 1972 on Copyright provides that the right of exploitation can be transferred, totally or partially, according to the rules of the Civil Code. Moral rights cannot be the subject of a transfer according to Article 9 of the Law on Copyright.

8.5. Trademark Licence

Under the Benelux Uniform law, a trademark licence must be expressed in writing, under penalty of nullity. These contracts will be opposable to third parties after their registration with the Bureau Benelux des Marques.

8.6. Territory

The contract can expressly provide for a special territory in which the party may perform its obligations. This clause is required in case of a licence.

8.7. Duration

The term of the contract must be expressly specified in a special clause. The contract also must indicate under which special conditions the contract can be terminated by anticipation, for instance, if a party fails to perform its obligations.

8.8. Post Termination Arrangements/Restrictions

Generally, the contract defines the restrictions or the arrangements after the termination of the contract, for instance, to stop using a trademark or a logo or to return goods.

9. Financial Terms

9.1. Royalties

The contract provides for the payment of royalties and the conditions of such payment: the amount and currency; period of payment; number of the bank account; the interest in case of late payment; termination in case of non payment and sometimes the amount of damages.

9.2. Payment

There are two possibilities: payment in cash, and payment in kind, for instance, the obligation for the sponsor to supply specific goods, such as sports clothing or sports material, which generally bear the logo of the sponsor.

10. Insurance Aspects

In the field of sports, insurance essentially covers public liability. The organiser takes out an insurance to cover the risk of claims of spectators and sportsmen. Sportsmen also have insurance to cover their public liability. Generally, this insurance is subscribed by the sports association for the benefit of its members.

11. Advertising and Promotion

There is no legal system of supervision of advertising in Luxembourg. Every publicity agency controls the advertising itself.

Two years ago, a 'Fédération des professionnels de la Communication' was created by advertising agencies in Luxembourg. This association has elaborated a Code of Advertising Practice and has created a private organism of control of publicity.

Television advertising is organised by the publicity agency 'IP' (Information Publicité) which has developed an internal system of control of advertising campaigns which are broadcast.

Luxembourg law regulates or forbids certain publicity of certain items, such as, tobacco, pharmaceutical products, illicit drugs, financial products and foodstuffs.

Luxembourg has introduced in 1989 a law relating to restrictions on tobacco advertising. Article 6 of this law strictly fobids tobacco advertising during a sports event.

Under the terms of the Code of Advertising Practice, producers and traders undertake to make no advertising on alcohol in schools or social or health institutions. The Code also regulates the contents of advertising relating to alcohol.

12. The Venue

12.1. Control

The event organiser must control the access to the place of the sports event during the time it is held. He must also ensure that the stadia are free from competitive advertising if it is provided by the contract with sponsors. If this control is not exercised, a sponsor can claim damages. This action is brought in the Civil Division of the Tribunal d'Arrondissement.

12.2. Public Liability

The liability of the event organiser or of the owner of the stadium is not organised by special regulations. It is subject to general rules of civil or penal liability.

The owner of the venue of the sports event can be considered liable. The owner has an obligation of prudence and care: the stadium or the swimming pool or any other place must not present any risks for the sportsmen.

The event organiser must take all necessary measures to insure the good progress of the sports event. The event organiser must obtain all necessary administrative authorisations and respect rules relating to fires or public safety.

Generally, the organiser will not attempt to limit his liability by a mention on the admission ticket. Under case law, this clause is not binding on the spectator and has no value. The same clause in a contract between the organiser and a sportsman has been judged invalid.

12.3. Access and Accreditation

Access to the place of the sports event (stadium, swimming pool, circuit, and so on) is generally subject to payment.

The guests, sponsors, reporters and other persons who do not pay to attend the sports event are considered as normal spectators as far as the liability of the event organiser is concerned (see previous paragraph, on Public Liability).

13. Dispute Resolution

When a dispute concerning the interpretation or the execution of an agreement arises between the parties, two solutions have to be considered:

(1) the contract provides for an arbitration clause; or
(2) the contract prescribes that the normal court is competent.

If the matter in dispute concerns rights of intellectual property, arbitration may be admitted in matters of licence. In matters relating to the cancellation of a trademark, the sole remedy is recourse to the courts.

13.1. Court Procedure

The competent court is generally that of the place where the defendant is domiciled or has its registered office (or if it is different its actual seat, *siège réel*).

Additionally, in the field of contracts the claim must be brought before the court of the right level (if the dispute concerns a sum of less than 100,000 LUF, the competent court is the Justice de Paix, at more than 100,000 LUF, the Tribunal d'Arrondissement becomes competent).

13.2. Remedies Including Damages and Equitable Relief

When a party to a contract does not respect its obligations, the other party can claim damages.

A formal notice must be sent by registered mail to the party who does not comply with its obligations.

In personam relief is available, unless the obligation is considered as being of a strictly personal nature, so that an order for specific performance would unduly restrict the personal liberty of the defendant. In that case, damages are the only remedy.

13.3. Arbitration

Luxembourg law (Articles 1003 to 1028 of the Code of Civil Procedure) provides for arbitration as a means of settling disputes.

Arbitration is conditioned upon an arbitration agreement by the parties to arbitrate any dispute that can arise.

The parties can also decide to submit a dispute to an arbitration when the dispute has arisen.

An arbitral award may be contested before the Tribunal d'Arrondissement only by way of an action for annulment. Annulment may be declared only in the cases described in Article 1023 of the Code of Civil Procedure.

13.4. Enforcement of Foreign Judgments and Arbitral Awards

13.4.1. Foreign judgments

The procedure for the enforcement of foreign judgments depends upon whether the country where the judgment has been rendered is a Contracting Party to the Convention on Jurisdiction and the Enforcement of Judgments in Civil and Commercial Matters signed in Brussels in 1968. Under the provisions of this Convention, to obtain the enforcement of a judgment, the party must introduce a *requête d'exequatur* before the President of the Tribunal d'Arrondissement.

When the country of origin of the judgment is not a party to the Convention, it is necessary to proceed in an ordinary action. The full court will examine several conditions and will authorise the enforcement of the judgment if these conditions are met.

13.4.2. Luxembourg arbitral awards

The winning party must register the award with the clerk of the court which would normally have been competent to hear the case. This party obtains a writ of execution from the President of this court and the award becomes enforceable.

13.4.3. Foreign arbitral awards

Luxembourg is a party to Geneva Convention and to the New York Convention on the Recognition and Enforcement of Foreign Arbitral Awards.

In order to enforce a foreign award against a Luxembourg defendant the winning party has to follow the same procedure as that for obtaining a writ of execution.

SPORTS
MARKETING

The Netherlands

by Sven A. Klos

1. Sports Marketing – A Business

Sport in the Netherlands relies for an important part of its funding on sponsoring. In 1988 sporting clubs had 4 million members out of 14.5 million inhabitants in the Netherlands. They and everybody else who goes in for sport spent Dfls. 250 million on it. That year Dfls. 270 million was spent on sports sponsoring, while the total amount of sponsoring came to Dfls. 300 million. In 1984 only Dfls. 160 million was spent on sports sponsoring, while in 1991 the sum came close to Dfls. 500 million. This last amount is Dfls. 100 million more than was expected in 1989. Sports marketing is, therefore, a booming business.

2. The Legal System in the Netherlands

The Dutch legal system is mainly based on codified law. The most important part of this legislation consists of formal law, which is enacted by the Government (ministers and the Queen) following parliamentary approbation. Legislation, deriving from this formal law, is issued in the form of a Royal Decree by the Queen and Government alone, without the consultation of Parliament. These Royal Administrative Orders (*Algemene Maatregelen van Bestuur*, AMvB) have the same force as statutes. An important difference between AMvB's and formal law is that these AMvB's cannot impose penal sanctions; these have to be based on formal law. Ministers alone may exercise delegated legislative power by way of decrees. Lower public authorities also have regulatory power: provinces, municipalities and statutory boards for trade, industry and some professions.

All these laws and regulations come under the competence of the national courts. There are two separate types of jurisdiction: the ordinary courts handle all civil and criminal cases; and in administrative judicial proceedings judges decide on disputes between administrative bodies and private persons or companies on matters of administrative law and regulations. These judicial decisions are important for the interpretation of statutory law, but the doctrine of precedent does not exist. No court is bound by previous decisions, even if they are pronounced by higher courts. In practice, however, the decisions of the Supreme Court (*Hoge Raad*) are mostly followed.

The general judicial hierarchy consists of four different types of court, which deal with three instances. Proceedings at first instance are divided between the cantonal courts (*Kantongerecht*) and the district courts (*Arrondissementsrechtbank*). Second instance consists of appeals on points of fact and law. Appeals from cantonal court judgments are decided by district courts, and judgments of district courts by courts of appeal (*Gerechtshof*). Final appeals are before the Supreme Court (*Hoge Raad*), which reviews points of law and ensures compliance with essential formalities.

In the Dutch system no laymen participate in the proceedings. The number of judges varies from one (cantonal court and preliminary proceedings) to five (Supreme Court).

In urgent civil cases, this rather cumbersome and time-consuming procedure can be avoided by using a quick, informal action, known as preliminary proceedings (*kort geding*). In very urgent cases, it is even possible to obtain a judgment within one day. Such cases are handled by the President of a District Court, who pronounces a 'provisional decision'. This judgment cannot prejudice any rights in later proceedings, which, in practice, hardly ever follow. Appeals against such a decision are to a court of appeal or the Supreme Court.

Certain areas of law are regulated by self-imposed regulations. Private commissions ensure that such regulations are observed. An important example of this is the Dutch advertising industry with its own Advertising Code and a board of judges in two instances (see p. 237).

3. Applicable Laws

There is no one specific body of law that deals with the phenomenon of sports marketing as such. Instead the different aspects of sports marketing either fall under the scope of the general civil law (embodied in the entirely new Civil Code ('CC') in force since 1 January 1992) or under the scope of specific laws, such as the different intellectual property laws. Aside from these formal laws, self-imposed regulations in the field of advertising also touch upon various aspects of sports marketing.

4. Intellectual Property Rights

4.1. Trademarks

The Netherlands is a signatory to the Paris, the Vienna, the Nice and the Madrid Conventions. The Dutch regulation on trademarks – the Uniform

Benelux Trademark Act ('BTA') – is also a product of international co-operation with the other Benelux countries, Belgium and Luxembourg. This law is part of the national legislation. After registration the trademark is valid in any of the Benelux countries.

Any symbol that is suitable to distinguish a company's goods or services can serve as a trademark. This symbol can be a word or a picture, but also a single character or figure, a colour combination or a single colour, a slogan and even the shape of a product or a form of packaging. Shapes which are determined by the very nature of goods, produce a technical effect or influence the essential value of the product are excepted (Art. 1 BTA). Although all these types of trademark are possible, they cannot all be given equal protection. One has to distinguish between 'strong' trademarks which have broad scope of protection and 'weak' trademarks which have a more narrow scope of protection.

The trademark has to be registered to acquire any trademark rights. The Benelux Trademark Office cannot refuse the registration of a trademark on grounds other than failure to meet the requirements of form (Art. 6A BTA). Only in a later lawsuit can the registration be declared null and void. The most important grounds to do so are (Art. 14 *jo.* 4 BTA):

- the symbol does not meet the requirements to be a trademark, especially in the case of lack of distinctiveness;
- the filing has been effected in bad faith;
- the trademark is filed for goods for which the use of the trademark might mislead the public.

After registration the trademark has to be used normally within three years from registration and once it has been used it must not be left unused for a period longer than five years, otherwise the right to the trademark ceases to exist (Art. 5 BTA).[1] A registration is valid for ten years (Art. 10 BTA). The licensing of a right is valid without registration, but one can only invoke the licence against a third person if it has been registered in the trademark register (Art. 11 BTA).

The owner of a registered trademark can institute proceedings against the user of a trademark which is identical or similar to his own trademark and which is used for the same or a similar product.[2] He can also oppose any other commercial use of a similar symbol made without a valid reason and likely to cause damage (Art. 13A.2 BTA).[3]

1. Interpretation of 'normal use': Benelux Court, 27 January 1981, NJ 1981, 333, *Winston*.
2. Resembling trademarks: Benelux Court, 20 May 1983, NJ 1984, 72, *Union*.
3. Types of damage: Benelux Court, 1 March 1975, NJ 1975, 472, *Claeryn/Klarein*; valid reason: Benelux Court, 27 January 1981, NJ 1981, 333, *Winston*.

4.2. Copyright

The Netherlands is a signatory to the Berne Convention on Copyright, the Geneva Universal Copyright Convention, the Rome Convention for the protection of record producers and the International Geneva Convention for the protection of performers, record producers and broadcasting organisations. The national situation is governed by the Copyright Act of 1912 ('CA').

For protection, according to the Copyright Act, no notice, registration or any other formality is required. The only requirements are that the work may be perceived through any of the senses and that it has an original and distinctive character and bears the personal imprint of the author.[4] The work, in short, has to be original.

The duration of the copyright is generally the lifetime of the author plus 50 years from the date of the author's death. In the case of anonymous, corporate or posthumous works, the 50 year term starts from the date of first publication (Arts. 37–42 CA).

The author is the person who created the work of Art. However, when a person creates such a work of art under the supervision of another person, or in the course of his employment, his supervisor or employer will own the copyright (Arts. 4–9 CA).

Copyright consists of two exclusive property rights: the right to publish the work and the right to reproduce the work (Art. 1 CA). There are some exceptions to this rule. The most important of which are private use (Art. 16b CA); non-profit educational and scientific use (Arts. 12.3 and 16 CA); use for news reporting (Arts. 15 and 16a CA); a right to make limited quotations (Art. 15a CA) and to impose an injunction on the author of a work in which persons are portrayed to reproduce this portrait without permission of the persons portrayed (Arts. 19 and 20 CA).

Apart from these rights, the Copyright Act recognises the author's moral rights (Art. 25 CA). The author retains those rights, even after he has transferred his copyright. Those moral rights consist of the right to oppose publication of his work without his name being mentioned; modification of the work, the title or his designation as author; and the right against any other distortion or mutilation which could be prejudicial to his honour or reputation.

4.3. Registered Designs

The Uniform Benelux Act on Designs and Models ('Act') provides protection for the new form of a utility product, except when the form is necessary for a technical effect (Arts. 1 and 2 Act). In order to gain protection, the model or design has to be registered in the Benelux Design Register (Art. 3 Act). A model is only considered new if, 50 years prior to registration, no identical model or a model with only minor differences has been known in the relevant

4. Supreme Court, 4 January 1991, NJ 1991, 608, *Van Dale/Romme*.

circles of trade and industry (Art. 4 Act). The protection lasts for a maximum of fifteen years (Art. 12 Act).

If a model meets the requirements of the Benelux Act as well as the Copyright Act, it can be protected by both. Copyright protection after the fifteen years of model protection have passed is only possible if a notice to that effect is filed with the Benelux Design Register (Art. 21.3 Act).

4.4. Unfair Competition

Unfair competition in the Netherlands is legally defined as tort (Art. 6:162 CC).[5] Unfair competition consists of numerous unwanted, unfair activities, aimed at an increase in a company's profits, which are inadmissible in normal commercial intercourse. Examples are:

- to be a parasite on the commercial activities, results or goodwill of another company, or on the reputation of a famous person;
- to make damaging statements about the competitor or his products;
- to swindle the competitor out of company secrets, employees or orders;
- to give misleading information about goods or services which one offers.

Only this last example of unfair competition is separately laid down in the Civil Code in the section under tort (Art. 6:194–196 CC).

5. The Contract Generally and Preliminary Agreements

Preliminary agreements as such are not common in the Netherlands. Mutuality of consideration is not required either.

5.1. Intention to Create Legal Relations

Although the parties to the contract usually have the intention to create a legal relationship, this intention is not a legal requirement for the realisation of a contract. Contracts can be realised without communion of the wills, when, for example, an irrevocable offer is accepted at a time when the offering party no longer wished to tender an offer but could not withdraw (Art. 6:219 CC). Another example is a contract that is realised because of the fact that the absence of intention to contract by one party could not be invoked against the other, which other has interpreted a declaration or conduct on the part of the

5. Supreme Court, 31 January 1919, NJ 1919, p. 161, *Lindebaum/Cohen* and Supreme Court, 11 November 1937, p. 1096, *Kolynos*.

first party in conformity with the meaning which he could reasonably attribute to it in the circumstances (Art. 3:35 CC).

During the negotiations on the contract, the parties have to reckon with the justifiable interests of the other. This can mean that, at a certain moment, the negotiations can no longer be broken off, or, if they are, only when the breaking party pays the costs of the other party. Breaking off is not allowed when parties both may assume that any contract will be formed.[6]

5.2. Offer and Acceptance

A contract is formed by an offer and acceptance thereof (Art. 6:217). The offer has to include all the essential elements of the intended contract, otherwise it is only an invitation to the other party to make an offer.[7]

There are no formal requirements to offer and acceptance, as long as the intention to enter into legal relations has manifested itself by any declaration (Art. 33 *jo.* 37 CC). The meaning that one party could reasonably attribute to this declaration or conduct is of importance. When the circumstances justify the notion that the offer is accepted, the accepting party cannot invoke his absence of intention against the offeror (Art. 3:35 CC).

The contract comes into being at the moment of the acceptance, that is to say, the moment at which the offeror could reasonably be expected to take note of the acceptance.

5.3. Form and Execution

For the contract to be valid it need not be in writing, unless there are special requirements, such as an assignment of any intellectual property rights, which must be in writing. When written, only one signature at the end of the document will suffice. When a contracting party is a corporation, it has to be represented by an authorised person.

5.4. Void and Illegal Contracts

An agreement is null and void if its content or necessary implication is contrary to good morals, public order or an imperative statutory provision (Art. 3:40 CC). An agreement may be annulled if it was entered into as a result of threat, fraud, abuse of circumstances or error (Arts. 3:44 and 6:228 CC).

There are some other specific rules about illegal clauses in contracts, of which the one about general conditions is the most important. See below at 5.8.

---

6. Supreme Court, 18 June 1982, NJ 1983, 723, *Plas/Valburg*.
7. Supreme Court, 10 April 1981, NJ 1981, 532, *Hofland/Hennis*.

5.5. Privity

According to Dutch law, a third party stipulation in a contract is permitted (Art. 6:253 CC). The contracting parties must have intention to create a private right for the third party beneficiary, who has to accept it (no requirement as to form). After this acceptance, he becomes a party to the contract (Art. 6:254 CC).

5.6. Interpretation

The introductory considerations (recitals), which precede the clauses of a contract, can be of great importance in the interpretation of the contract in cases of disagreement. The aim of the contract and the eventual preceding stages of negotiations or agreements need to be clearly defined in such introductory considerations.

Most important of all nevertheless is that the whole contractual relationship is governed by reasonableness and equity. No rule that is binding on parties by virtue of law, usage or their own contract, applies to the extent that that would be unacceptable according to standards of reasonableness and equity, in view of the given circumstances (Art. 6:2 CC).

5.7. Failure in the Performance

In principle, every failure in the performance of an obligation obliges the debtor to compensate the creditor for its damages (Art. 6:74 CC), unless the failure cannot be imputed to him, i.e. it does not result from his fault or otherwise results from circumstances beyond his control (Art. 6:75 CC).

Any failure in the performance can also be a ground for termination of the contract in whole or in part, unless the failure does not justify this severe measure (Art. 6:265 CC).

The court can, at the request of one of the parties, modify the effects of a contract or set it aside, in whole or in part, on the basis of unforeseen circumstances, which are of such a nature that, according to standards of reasonableness and equity, it cannot be expected that the contract be maintained in an unmodified form (Art. 6:258 CC).

Termination of a contract while the obligation can still be performed, though it would be too late, or while the failure can be repaired, is only possible after the debtor is given a written notice of default, granting him a reasonable period to perform, and he fails to do so within this period (Art. 6:265 *jo.* 82 CC).

5.8. General Conditions

Written stipulations which have been drafted to be included in a number of contracts – so-called general conditions – are subject to strict rules (Arts. 6:231–247 CC). Most of them are intended to protect the consumer, but it is generally assumed that they can affect general conditions between (large) professional parties by way of the doctrine of reasonableness and equity. They, therefore, should be taken into account in any contract.

With respect to both consumers and professional parties, general conditions are binding upon the party who accepts them, regardless of whether the other party has any knowledge of their contents. The applicability is, therefore, easily assumed (Art. 6:232 CC). For consumer-parties there is a counterpart to this main rule, namely that any clause in general conditions is subnect to annulment if the clause, all circumstances considered, is unreasonably onerous towards the other party, or if the person who uses the general conditions has not offered the other party a reasonable opportunity to take note of the general conditions (Art. 6:233 CC). It is, therefore, very important to always send a copy of one's general conditions to a possible future contracting party.

To determine whether a clause is unreasonably onerous towards consumers – or to some extent towards other parties – two lists have been drafted: a so-called 'black' and a 'grey' list. The 'black' list contains clauses that are considered to be unfair in consumer contracts; the 'grey list' contains clauses that are presumed (subject to evidence to the contrary) to be unfair in consumer contracts (Arts. 6:236 and 237 CC). Examples of unfair clauses on the black list are clauses which:

- exclude or limit the right to set aside a contract;
- exclude or limit the right to suspend performance;
- oblige the other party to compensate a third party for damage for which the person employing the general conditions is liable.

Examples of provisions that are presumed to be unfair are clauses which:

- release the person employing the general conditions entirely or partially from its legal obligation to pay damages;
- give the person employing the conditions an unusually long or an insufficiently determined period for performance;
- impose on the other party a notice period for termination of the contract of more than three months, or longer than the notice period imposed on the person employing the conditions.

6. Standard Contract Terms

Most contracts related to sports marketing are licence agreements or have licence aspects. The following issues should be considered in drafting such contracts.

6.1. Recitals

Recitals may aid a correct understanding of the contract. This is particularly relevant where the interpretation of the scope of the rights granted to the licensee is concerned. It is, therefore, advisable to explain in clear language in the recitals what it is that the licensee will do in exercising the rights granted and what the licensor is willing to allow.

6.2. Legal Relationship

Since the licensee will, under a license contract, be allowed to use certain of the licensor's distinctive marks (trademarks, emblems, logos), it is wise to expressly stipulate in the agreement that the licensee will not be allowed to act in any way for or on behalf of the licensor, subject to a fine.

6.3. Quality Control

The licensee will, under most licence contracts, either produce or market products that the public will associate primarily with the licensor. In order to safeguard its reputation, the licensor must stipulate that he is given the possibility to inspect the products or even that he may veto the salc of a particular batch.

6.4. Termination

The grounds for termination should be carefully defined in the contract. Among these grounds a performance clause may be included, stating that the agreement may be terminated by the licensor if the volume of sales by the licensee falls below a certain level. See further at page 236.

6.5. Applicable Law

If the contract deals with an international situation, the parties have freedom to choose which law will apply. The contract should expressly state which law is applicable.

7. Different Types of Business Arrangements

7.1. Sponsorship Agreement

The sponsorship agreement is primarily governed by general contract law. There is no specific body of law relating to the sponsorship agreement.

The sponsorship agreement may be defined as a business arrangement whereby one party (the sponsored party) delivers communication possibilities and/or facilities to the other party (the sponsor) against payment by the latter.

A sponsorship agreement should first and foremost define the mutual rights and obligations of the sponsor and the sponsored party.

The sponsor's obligations may involve more than just payment of a certain sum. The sponsor may deliver services and/or goods such as time measurement equipment, catering, and so on. The legal construction under which goods or services are delivered (such as leasing and lending) deserves careful consideration.

If the sponsor's obligations merely exist in the payment of a certain sum, the terms of payment should be carefully considered. For instance, a sponsor may be well advised to stipulate that a substantial part of the amount will be paid only after the sports organisation or event has proven itself to be the desired communication possibility.

The rights that the sponsor are granted in return may vary from a single mention of its name on a leaflet relating to the event or organisation to a full scale exclusive relation whereby the event or organisation itself carries the sponsor's name or the brand name of its products.

An essential issue concerning the rights of the sponsor is exclusivity. The agreement should contain a provision barring the sponsored party from engaging other sponsors or similar sponsors (i.e. sponsors that market similar products or services).

Only after the primary mutual rights and obligations have been meticulously defined, a number of other more general matters should be considered in the contract:

- the contract should contain a mutual warranty and indemnity that all requirements under the applicable laws and regulations (such as advertising codes and local rules concerning permits) will be observed;
- the matter of liability for damages suffered by third parties as a consequence of the event (for instance, a rally car bearing the sponsor's name causes an accident in which spectators are involved) has to be settled; normally the sponsored party will have to indemnify the sponsor against claims of this nature;
- the contract should contain provisions concerning the right of the sponsored party to use the sponsor's brand name(s), and/or tradename; preferably the sponsored party should not be allowed to use the sponsor's trademark at all independently from the sponsor and/or without his consent; the provision

should also clearly limit the right of the sponsored party to use the trademark after termination of the sponsorship agreement.

In principle, there are no restrictions as to who may sponsor any given event. However, if the sponsored event is given coverage in the media and/or is advertised, several regulations apply, among which are the several advertising codes (discussed at p. 237 *et seq.*). In these codes, the tobacco and beverage industries have accepted various restrictions in the field of sponsoring.

7.2. Merchandising

The merchandising agreement is the agreement whereby one party grants the other party the right to use a certain symbol that has commercial value (i.e. a certain 'drawing power'), such as a trademark or the name or portrait of a celebrity, for commercial activities other than those for which the symbol was originally used.

Central to a merchandising agreement is, therefore, the granting of the right to use the symbol for which, if the symbol is protected by an intellectual property right, such as a trademark or copyright, a licence is granted. A merchandising agreement should, therefore, contain the provisions that are standard to a licence agreement.

Among these standard provisions are a warranty by the licensor that he is the owner of the intellectual property right and an undertaking by the licensor to indemnify the licensee in respect of any third party claims for any infringement.

The agreement should also deal with product liability aspects. Under the EC Product Liability Directive, that has been incorporated into the Dutch Civil Code, any mention of the trademarks of the licensor may be construed as manufacturership, which means that the licensor may be liable for any defects in the products marketed by the merchandiser that causes injury to a member of the public. A licensor may not exclude product liability in the merchandising contract as far as the claims of the consumers of the licensed product are concerned. However, it is possible to obtain a warranty from the merchandiser that he will indemnify the licensor in respect of these claims.

7.3. Endorsements

In promoting an event, organisation or product by means of endorsement by a sports personality, several areas of the law come into play.

The Copyright Act 1912 (Art. 21) provides for protection for the depicted person against unauthorised use of a picture or portrait. The depicted person may enjoin third parties from using a picture or portrait only if he or she has a 'reasonable interest' in doing so, although this does not, *expressis verbis*, follow from the Copyright Act. The Dutch Supreme Court has widened the scope of 'reasonable interest' to include a merely financial interest of the depicted person.

In using a picture or portrait for promotional ends, the commercial value (i.e. a financial interest for the depicted person) is acknowledged. Therefore, a licence should always be obtained if a picture or portrait is commercially used. However, under the current Supreme Court doctrine, a depicted person may only enjoin others from the use of a picture or portrait if his or her face is recognisable.

A contract concerning a licence for the use of a picture or portrait should, if the licence is granted exclusively, always contain a provision that the licensee is empowered to act on behalf and in name of the depicted person against infringement by third parties. A power of attorney should be attached to or incorporated in the agreement.

The name of a sports personality giving an endorsement should be registered as a trademark.

7.4. Commissioning Agreements

The contract for the design of a logo, emblem, design or advertisement, should entail an assignment of the designer's copyright to the commissioning party. Under Article 2 of the Copyright Act 1912, the copyright assignment must be in writing in order to be valid. Copyright assignments are interpreted restrictively, so that no more rights are deemed to be transferred than are mentioned explicitly or as follows from the context of the agreement. Preferably, the agreement should explicitly state that the complete copyright is transferred, all rights included. Even better is the incorporation of a complete catalogue of rights that are transferred.

The designer should waive his moral rights under Article 25 of the Copyright Act. Since under this Act not all moral rights can be waived, the provision concerning the moral rights should state that the moral rights are waived in so far as the Copyright Act allows.

7.5. Concessions/Franchises

There is no specific franchising law so that, again, franchising is a matter of contract.

7.6. Films and Videos

The contract for the commissioning of a film or video should contain an assignment of the copyright subsisting in the film or video. Article 45 of the Copyright Act deals with films and contains a presumption of ownership of copyright for the producer of the film. Nevertheless, since derogation by contract is allowed, the commissioning party should ensure his position by obtaining a warranty from the producer of the film that he is the owner of the copyright and that he will indemnify the commissioning party against copyright related claims from any person involved in the production of the film (such as actors and writers).

It should be noted that sportsmen and women do not have copyright claims in relation to the films or other representations made of their actions during sporting events.

In a recent case, the Dutch Supreme Court decided that the basis for the payments that have to be made by the Dutch National Broadcasting Corporation to the National Soccer Association for the right to broadcast soccer matches, is neither copyright nor protection against unfair competition, but the simple fact that the soccer associations owns the stadia where matches take place and may, therefore, refuse camera teams admission.

7.7. Public Appearances

The contract governing a sports personality's obligation to make a personal appearance within the framework of a promotional activity, should clearly define the place and the time of such appearance, the duration, and so on. Failure to show will, notwithstanding a possible case of *force majeure*, be a breach of contract, enabling the other party (even if this is not expressly stated) to terminate the contract and claim damages.

7.8. Suppliership

A company may advertise itself as the 'official supplier' of a certain sports event or sports organisation, when granted the right to do so.

Potential 'official suppliers' of individual athletes should be aware of possible restrictions on the freedom of the athlete to grant rights to suppliers imposed on them by their clubs or the national federation of their sport (in the Netherlands this is very common). Individual athletes should give warranties in this respect.

Sports organisations may enjoin third parties from presenting themselves as 'official suppliers' when not authorised, either by invoking their trademark rights or by an action based on unfair competition.

8. The Rights

The rights that may be granted to potential sponsors, suppliers, merchandisers and licensees by sports organisations or individual athletes, are manifold and, in principle, of an unlimited variety. Some of these rights and types of rights are discussed below.

8.1. Options

The organiser of a sports event or sports organisation may grant options on the several marketing and commercial rights. An option is an irrevocable offer to which the grantor of the option is bound during a certain agreed period of time.

The option gives the party that is granted the option the right to conclude a contract by a unilateral declaration within the option term.

An option contract should preferably contain all the provisions that the contract formed by the exercise of the option should contain. If the option is exercised, it should be clear what the contract formed entails. An option can also be granted on the basis of a mutual obligation to negotiate the terms of the contract in good faith upon the exercise of the option.

8.2. Pre-emption

A pre-emption right amounts to an offer of first refusal, that is, if a rights holder is considering granting or licensing a right or entering into a certain arrangement, a first opportunity of acquiring that right will be offered to the pre-emptive right holder.

The grant of the right of pre-emption is not a positive offer in the same way as an option; the duty is negative in that the grantor may not contract with any third party unless he has first offered to do so with the grantee. In certain circumstances, the grantor is prevented from refusing the grantee's offer at one price then accepting a third party offer at a higher price.

In addition, the parties may enter into a 'matching' agreement whereby the party granted the right of first refusal, may, in the event that his offer is not accepted by the rights holder, be given the right to match the offer of a third party.

As with options, the terms of the grant and the conditions of exercise of pre-emptions, including timing, should be carefully defined in the agreement.

8.3. Exclusivity

If rights are granted exclusively, the grantee will require warranties from the grantor that he will not himself exercise these rights and that he will refrain from granting them to third parties.

8.4. Copyright Licence

Under the Copyright Act the two main rights of the copyright owner are the right to publish and reproduce the work. These two rights cover all different forms of publishing or reproduction.

A copyright licence can concern any one of the different publishing or reproduction forms or a combination of them (for instance, the right to publish a film in translation or video cassette).

A copyright licence may also be limited geographically (the right to publish the work in a certain country only). Within the EC however, territorial division of copyright is not very effective, since a licensee cannot enjoin the importation of products lawfully licensed in another member country into its territory.

8.5. Trademark Licence

Under the Benelux Trademark Act, a trademark licence must be registered with the Benelux Trademark Office in order to have effects against third parties.

Under EC competition law, any undertaking not to challenge the validity of the licensor's trademark(s) is contrary to Article 85(1) of the Rome Treaty.

The licensee will most likely insist on warranties from the licensor that he owns the trademark and will indemnify the licensee in respect of any third party claims.

A trademark licence agreement will most likely contain provisions on quality checks by the licensor and detailed instructions on the use of the trademark, in order to protect the validity and reputation of the trademark.

8.6. Territory

The different rights may be granted for specific geographical regions. Geographical division of rights may conflict however with Article 85 of the Rome Treaty. The agreement in which a territorial division is made may require *notification* under this Article of the Treaty.

8.7. Media

Intellectual property rights may be divided according to media. In essence, a division according to media is nothing more than the granting of limited licences valid only for a certain form of publication or reproduction of the work. It all comes down to the all-important definition of the licensee's rights.

8.8. Product Classes

A sponsor of a major sports event will usually require exclusivity as to certain product and/or service classes. The class of products/services that the sponsor will either supply for the event and/or will market under the event's name or logo must be carefully defined.

8.9. Post Termination

The agreement should provide for detailed provisions dealing with the obligations of the licensee upon termination of the agreement.

The licensee may be required to deliver up the remaining stock of the licensed product. Alternatively, the licensee may be granted the right to sell off such stock during a certain period after termination of the contract.

8.10. Accreditation

The event organiser should also consider accreditation rights. These are the rights of entry to different sections of the stadium or arena, under the control of the event organiser, for example, for the purposes of corporate hospitality. The rights that are being granted should be specified and accreditation passes issued accordingly.

9. Financial Terms

The financial terms should be given careful consideration in the contract. Typically in the contracts discussed here the financial terms will concern royalty payments. The following points should be considered in formulating provisions dealing with royalties:

- Structure of the royalty payment. Royalty payments may be structured in any number of ways. A choice should be made between payment of a lump sum licence fee, a mere royalty or a combination of both. The lump sum may also be construed as an advance on royalties so that the royalties may be deducted from the advance. Deductibility may be limited to a certain period. The advance may also be made non-refundable.
- The basis of calculation of the royalty. The royalty may, for instance, be calculated on the net retail price of the licensed products. This means that the licensor should have some control over the price of the licensed products. The possibility of discounts by the licensee should also be taken into account.
- Usually the agreements contain a minimum amount of royalty owed by the licensee regardless of the actual sales made by the licensee in the licensed product. The agreement may also contain a minimum turnover to be achieved by the licensee (yearly) in default of which the agreement may be terminated. Such minimum royalty and minimum turnover may be calculated on a yearly or monthly basis.
- Currency. The currency of obligation and payment, as well as the exchange rate, will have to be fixed in the agreement.

- Interest. Interest and contractual fines may be incorporated in the agreement. If interest is not mentioned in the agreement, the interest articles of the Civil Code will apply.
- The licensor should have the right to inspect the accounting records of the licensee and have them audited. The licensee should undertake to give its full cooperation to these inspections and audits.

10. Insurance Aspects

It is advisable to try and obtain insurance coverage for a number of liabilities. Among these are:

- liability for damages suffered by the public at the venue as a result of defective premises;
- product liability for damages caused by defective goods;
- liability for damages suffered as a consequence of cancellation of an event.

11. Advertising and Promotion

11.1. Netherlands Code of Advertising

The Netherlands Code of Advertising ('NCA') lays down rules of conduct for all types of advertising. It is a private initiative of the media, advertising agencies and consumer organisations, which means that the rules are not legally binding: compliance with these rules is based on voluntary agreements. Any person, who feels an advertisement is contrary to the NCA, may file a complaint with the Advertising Code Commission, and, if the complaint is considered to be well-founded, the Commission can issue a public or private recommendation that the advertising should no longer be used. Such a recommendation is usually respected by advertising agencies and the media. The Commission cannot order rectification.

The competence of the Commission concerns every public recommendation of goods, services or ideas. This means that posters, leaflets, brochures, packaging of products and so on also have to meet the requirements of the NCA.

Article 2 of the NCA states: 'Any advertisement must be in compliance with the law, truth and the requirements of good taste and decency'. As a general rule, advertisements which draw attention in a too realistic way to unaesthetic or intimate situations should be considered contrary to good taste and decency.

The Advertising Code Commission does not permit mentioning well-known persons or bodies without their consent, nor using their photographs. Neither may a product be recommended by a person who enjoys a certain authority or trust with a certain sector of the public.

The Commission is also responsible for the enforcement of certain special codes. At the moment there are five of these, the most important rules of which are mentioned below under 11.2 to 11.4.

11.2. The Code on Tobacco

Radio or television commercials for tobacco products are absolutely prohibited; other advertisements must include a warning of the impact of smoking on one's health. The Code contains a list of more than 40 sports to which there may be no connection with smoking either in advertisements or in sponsoring. Also attached is an annex containing a list of (sports) magazines in which no tobacco advertisements may be placed. A sportsperson, who is widely known as such, may not advertise tobacco products.

11.3. The Code on Alcoholic Beverages

In commercials for alcoholic beverages on television or in cinemas a statement must be added which advises on the restriction of consumption. No relation may be made between alcohol on the one hand and on the other hand safety in traffic, minors, situations connected to the pursuance of one's profession, or active sports practice which requires physical exertion. It is, however, permitted to link the tradename of an alcoholic beverage to a sporting event when sponsoring such an event. The producer of alcoholic beverages is not allowed to sponsor individual sportsmen or teams, nor to put his tradename on cars and motors entering a competition.

11.4. The Advertising Code on the Environment

These days it is very trendy to put an environmental claim in an advertisement. The Advertising Code on the Environment tries to steer such trend in the right direction. Such a claim may not be misleading as to the environmental aspects of the recommended products. Any exaggeration on this point is forbidden. Should a complaint be filed, the advertiser is under a duty to prove that his claim is correct.

11.5. Media Advertising

The Media Act ('Act') forbids advertising on radio and television unless it is expressly permitted (Art. 52 Act). This principle holds for national as well as regional and local media. The Ether Advertisement Foundation ('STER') decides on the admissibility of radio and television commercials. A refusal can be referred to the Advertising Code Commission.

11.6. Programme Sponsorship

The situation as to programme sponsoring is currently very unclear. The Dutch Government should have implemented the EC Television Directive into its legislation in October 1992, but, to date, has not done so. Pending this implementation both the Steering Committee Advertising (a private organisation and spokesman for all advertising in the Netherlands) and the Commission for the Media (a governing body, see Art. 9 Media Act) are waiting with their own directives which elaborate the legal rules. The only way of sponsoring programmes on television is by means of placing an advertisement in between the programmes (billboarding). Any type of advertising or product placement within a programme is forbidden.

11.7. Advertising in the Official Programme

An event organiser or sports federation may commission an official programme, book, film or year book and may sell advertising space in such merchandise. In addition, a sponsor may sponsor the book or film itself. Such rights should be defined and documented.

With respect to matches themselves, the Dutch Sport Federation has laid down a Regulation Non-dominating Advertising by Sporting Events, which is based on Art. 30 of the Media Act.

The organisation for professional football has made a sponsoring regulation for professional football.

11.8. Comparative Advertising

Generally speaking, a company is allowed to compare its own products with similar competitive products, unless the information is misleading (Art. 6:196 CC).[8] According to the Netherlands Code of Advertising, comparative advertising is permitted if the products are comparable, the comparison deals with all the relevant aspects, and is not misleading or unreasonably denigratory (Art. 14 NCA).

The biggest problem for comparative advertising, however, is the Benelux Trademark Act, which prohibits the use of a trademark without a valid reason causing damage to the trademark owner. In case law it has been decided[9] that individual comparative advertising is not a valid reason for using a competitor's trademark, because there are other methods of advertising. According to the draft EEC Directive with regard to Comparative and Misleading Advertisements[10] in the future it might be possible to use a trademark in comparative

8. See Supreme Court, 29 March 1985, NJ 1985, 591, *Pokon/Substral*.
9. E.g. Court of Appeal Arnhem, 5 September 1989, BIE 1991, 41, comparative lists.
10. OJ EEC 1991, No. C 180/14.

advertisements, subject to strict conditions, but the discussion on this subject has not yet been concluded.

11.9. Defamation

The advertiser should also ensure that the advertisement is neither defamatory nor libellous. Two laws and the Netherlands Advertising Code provide relief for a person, whose personal or business reputation has been damaged, in the eyes of the public, by the statements of another. Under the Criminal Code (Art. 261 *et seq.*) a fine or imprisonment can be imposed; under civil law it can be considered as a tort (Art. 6:162), on which ground damages and rectification (Art. 6:167) can be requested.

11.10. Airspace

Advertising in the airspace is strictly ruled by the authorities and by a self-imposed regulation. The governmental rules mainly concern safety with respect to the materials used and the minimum height for flying. Four airspace advertising companies have made their own Code for Airspace Advertising, in order to avoid unnecessary irritation by uncoordinated use of airspace advertising.

12. The Venue

12.1. Public liability

The event organiser will need to ensure compliance with the health and safety and local authority rules relating to the construction of the stadia, fire regulations, public safety and so on. Failure to do so will result in fines being imposed by the local authorities.

The organiser will be liable to participants and to members of the public, under the law of tort, if he has not secured the safety, as far as is reasonable, taking into account the risks of the sport in question. If a contractual relationship exists between the organiser on the one hand and the participants or the public on the other hand, the liability is a result of fault. The organiser has a responsibility to provide for the safety of the event, which responsibility increases as to risk as the event becomes more professional and more specifically a spectator-event.

The organiser may try to limit his liability by placing an exclusion clause on the admission tickets or on a notice board. The Civil Code presumes this limitation to be unfair to consumers (Art. 6:237f CC). The exclusion of liability for fraudulent intent or gross negligence is not permitted. The doctrine of reasonableness and equity can also prevent the exclusion of liability. Under certain conditions, the organiser is also liable for damage caused by employers and subcontractors (Arts. 6:170 and 171 CC).

12.2. Control

To what extent the organiser is free to do with the stadia he hires whatever he wants totally depends on the contract of hire and on the permit the lessor has obtained from the municipality. The organiser must carefully consider the extent of his liability.

The event organiser himself will need a permit from the local authorities, if the event takes place in a public place, like a public highway. The Act on Drink and Catering (*Drank- en Horecawet*) imposes restrictions on the sale and admission of alcohol at any location. The local government can also forbid the supply of alcohol.

12.3. Sponsor Access and Protection

If a sponsor wishes to be the only representative of his branch of industry present at the event, this must be stipulated in his sponsoring contract. In case of default, the organiser of the event is liable. Only persons who have permission – that is a contract – from the organiser to present themselves at the event (by way of advertising or any other promotional activity whatsoever) are allowed to have access to the venue. Uninvited visitors, who display promotional activities can be removed, if necessary by the police. This also holds for uninvited film crews.

13. Dispute Resolution

13.1. Court Action

Most actions are brought before a District Court, both parties being represented by an attorney. Some specific lawsuits are initiated by a petition filed with the court, but most suits are initiated by a writ of summons, in which the defendant is called to appear in court and in which all essential facts upon which the demand for relief or injunction is based and the claims are contained (Arts. 1 *et seq.* and 126 *et seq.* Code of Civil Procedure ('CCP')). The progress of the proceedings can be severely delayed by a number of actions. In a standard procedure, the exchange of written conclusions can take some months. Oral and written pleadings are rather comprehensive, in which the parties argue both the law and the facts of their case, the latter being supported through documentary evidence and – after permission of the court – possibly witness hearings (Art. 135 *et seq.* CCP). The rules of procedure and proof are very strict. The judge plays an active role by allocating the burden of proof and deciding on admissibility of non-documentary evidence (Art. 176 *et seq.* CCP). Examination in chief, cross-examination and reexamination of the parties by attorneys is not permitted.

The suit is completed by the judgment. This may contain an injunction to either do (e.g. perform the act the parties agreed in the contract) or refrain from doing something (e.g. in the case of infringement of an intellectual property right), or to pay damages. Judgment can bring about a new legal situation, e.g. by dissolving the contract, and it may contain a declaratory judgment, giving a statement in case of dissenting opinions regarding the legal relationship between two (or more) parties.

An attachment can be made before (conservatory or provisional attachment, Art. 700 *et seq.* CCP) and after (seizure under a writ of attachment, Art. 439 *et seq.* CCP) having an enforceable title or judgment. Before obtaining an enforceable title or judgment, the plaintiff can attach the defendant's assets, in order to ensure that the goods which the plaintiff wants, or which he wants as security for his claim, will not disappear after the suit.

In general, both parties' costs are paid by the losing party (Art. 56 *et seq.* CCP).

13.2. Arbitration

Arbitration is available as an alternative to court action, with the exception of matters that are not at the parties' free disposition and matters under exclusive court jurisdictions. In the Netherlands, arbitration is highly developed and popular; in various branches of industry specialised standing arbitration committees exist. Arbitration law is incorporated in the Code of Civil Procedure (Art. 1020 *et seq.*).

Parties can agree to arbitration by inserting a clause in their contract, which stipulates that disputes arising from the contract will be submitted to arbitration, or by a deed of compromise after a certain dispute has arisen. It is common practice to declare specific existing arbitration rules (like the rules of the International Chamber of Commerce, or of the Netherlands Arbitration Institute) to be applicable. If they have not done so and they fail to agree on the choice of arbitrators, the District Court, upon application, can appoint a panel. Any natural person having legal capacity may be appointed; he does not need to be a Dutch citizen. If the arbitration has been validly agreed, the court will declare itself incompetent, if one of the parties so requests.

The award has to be filed on record with the registrar of the District Court, but only in order to end the appointment of the arbitrator(s). For execution of an arbitral award the permission of the President of a District Court is requested. The grounds for refusal are very limited.

Appeal against an award is only possible if the parties have so previously agreed in either the arbitration clause or the deed of compromise. Arbitration awards can be annulled on limited grounds by a District Court. Preliminary proceedings procedure also applies to arbitration.

The Netherlands is a signatory to the 1958 New York Convention on the Recognition and Enforcement of Arbitral Awards.

13.3. Binding Advice

Differences arising between parties on points of law and fact can also be settled by resort to the custom of 'binding advice': a kind of '*expert determination*'. Both parties have to agree thereto. Contrary to arbitration, binding advice does not provide a title to enforcement, nor any other relief which can be equated with a judicial decision. The party, in whose favour the advice was granted, can only ask the court to order compliance with the binding advice, with a penalty against the other party for failure to comply with such order. There are no specific legal provisions dealing with binding advice, but the unanimous view of Dutch legal authors and the courts is that in binding advice proceedings the rules of procedure for arbitration proceedings should be observed wherever possible.

Norway

by Hans E. Skirstad

1. Sports Marketing – A Business

The Norwegians are very keen on sports, especially winter sports, not least because of the climate!

Sports events are partly related to elite sports, but also to exercise sport.

World-wide, the yearly Holmenkollen Ski Festival is well known. In 1993, Oslo will arrange the world championship in cycling and, in 1994, the Winter Olympic Games will be held in Lillehammer.

Due to this very great interest in sports, there is a great potential for the sports marketing business through television, newspapers and other forms of advertising channels and, of course, sponsorship.

One other aspect of the Norwegians' involvement in sports is that each year about one fifth of all personal accidents are related to sports activities.

2. The Norwegian Legal System

The Norwegian legal system has a tradition which goes back to the end of the first century. Through the years of considerable development, it has found great inspiration in particularly Roman law and the continental schools of jurisprudence in the Middle Ages. Foreign influence and domestic development have resulted in a system of civil law. In contrast to British and American case law, the written statutes are the basic source of law. However, the court's interpretation of statutes is indispensable in the process of achieving a correct and precise understanding of the law. In complex legal questions, where statutes and decisions by courts do not give a satisfying answer to the question, a Norwegian lawyer must look into legal literature and administrative decisions, and, finally, consider what would be a fair decision in the particular matter.

The Norwegian Constitution is based upon the French philosopher Montesquieu's theory of separation of powers. The purpose of this system is to avoid abuse of power by the State upon the individual. Briefly, Norwegian courts interpret the statutes enacted by Parliament after having been prepared by the Government. The legal basis is the Constitution of 17 May 1814. Statutes of today must not interfere with the rights given to individuals by the Constitution. The Supreme Court of Norway has the power to declare statutes unconstitutional. In this way, the Supreme Court, the Parliament and the Government are all important parts of the legal system, and through their work they control each other's exercise of power.

3. Applicable Laws

There is no particular law specifically related to sports marketing, and freedom of contract is the main rule.

However, in the field of sports marketing one must observe the different national and international rules and regulations from the sports and media associations.

4. Intellectual Property Rights

Also in Norway intellectual property rights will form a very important part of any contract or legal basis related to sports marketing.

The most relevant intellectual property rights are trademarks and protection against unfair competition, followed by copyright and designs according to the particular circumstances.

4.1. Trademarks

Norway and the other Nordic countries (Sweden, Denmark and later Finland) have coordinated their trademark legislation which took effect in 1961.

The Norwegian Trademark Act is dated 3 March 1961. Norway is also a signatory to the Paris Convention.

According to Norwegian law, a trademark can be a figure, word or collection of words – also slogans, letters and numbers – or it can be the product itself, if the product has distinguishing features.

Trademarks can be applied to goods and services.

A trademark can be registered in the official trademark register (*Patentstyrets varemerkeregister*) or rights to a trademark can be obtained when it is well known and distinguished from other trademarks.

The registration is valid for 10 years and can be renewed for further periods of 10 years indefinitely.

From 1 January 1993, if a registered trademark is not used for 5 years, its registration can be cancelled.

4.2. Unfair Competition

Unfair Competition is regulated by the Marketing Control Act of 16 June 1972. The main purpose of this Act is to counteract the use of improper and unfair marketing methods.

Section 1 of the Marketing Control Act (the general provision) provides, as a general principle, that no act may be performed in the course of business which is either contrary to good business practice between business enterprises or is unreasonable in relation to consumers. The question whether an act is in breach of Section 1 will often be a matter of discretion.

The general provision may be applied together with or instead of the special provisions of the Act.

The most used special provisions are in short: Section 2 (misleading business methods); Section 3 (insufficient information); Section 4 (premiums); Section 5 ('lotteries'); and Section 9 (imitation of another's product).

Public control has been introduced through the Consumer Ombudsman ('FO') and the Market Council (*Markedsrådet*).

The authority of the Consumer Ombudsman and the Market Council is limited to cases where the interests of consumers are concerned.

When a business enterprise considers its rights infringed it may submit the case to the Unfair Competition Committee (*Konkurranseutvalget*). The Committee's opinions are not legally binding, but, in most cases, the parties submit to the opinions issued.

The 'case law' established by the Committee is of major relevance to the question of what is to be considered unfair competition or contrary to good business practice.

4.3. Copyright

Copyright is governed by the Copyright Act of 12 May 1961 and applies to writings of all kinds, oral exposition, music, drawings and paintings, films, architecture, buildings, applied art, advertising material and EDP programmes. Norway is a signatory to the Berne Convention.

To be entitled to copyright protection, a 'work' must have been initiated by man and have a certain degree of originality and aesthetic creation.

Copyright lasts generally for the lifetime of the 'author' and for 50 years from his death. For example, catalogues enjoy copyright protection for 10 years after first publication.

There are no special formalities required for the assignment of copyright.

Moral rights of 'authors' are recognised and protected in Norway under the Copyright Act and include the right to be identified as the 'author' and the right to object to derogatory treatment of the 'work'.

4.4. Designs

Designs are governed by the Design Act of 29 May 1970. Section 1.1 of this Act states that a design is the pattern of the appearance of a product or an ornament.

A design can be registered and will be protected for 5 years. Such registration can be renewed for two further periods of 5 years each.

Registration of designs is not very common in Norway, since the Marketing Act contains rules on unfair competition related to the copying of products.

5. The Contract Generally and Preliminary Agreements

5.1. Preliminary Agreements

Preliminary Agreements as Heads of Agreement, Letter of Understanding, or Letter of Goodwill are known in Norway but must be interpreted in the particular context in which they are written and the wording used, in order to determine whether such preliminary agreements can be sued upon.

5.2. The Agreement, Offer and Acceptance

The Norwegian legal system is based upon the so-called principle of the importance of the promise, which means that a declaration, whose substance serves to establish a claim against the person making it, is binding from the moment it comes to the knowledge of the addressee. An acceptance or a written contract is not necessary to establish a right for the addressee.

The acceptance of the principle of the binding force of the promise ties in with the fact that normally no special forms are required by Norwegian law. A purely oral promise is normally binding, regardless even of the magnitude of the obligation and of whether any consideration or similar compensation is contemplated. Norwegian property law prescribes fewer forms to be used for contracts than most other legal systems.

On the whole, Norwegian law takes an informal approach. The strict and legalistic approach, which sacrifices equity in the individual instance in favour of a lucid and easily applicable rule, does not have much following. There is a distinct tendency to prefer a solution which is in keeping with realities to a result which would emanate from a logical analysis.

5.3. Consideration

According to Norwegian law, it is not necessary to have a 'consideration' and benefit between the parties in order for a contract to be valid.

The term 'consideration' is not known in Norwegian legal terminology.

5.4. Form and Execution

As mentioned under 5.2 above, no formal requirements are needed in order to make a contract legally binding. However, due to terms of interpretation and proof it is advisable to make a written contract.

Any contracts involving companies should be signed by either one or more members of the board, who have the right to sign on behalf of the company, or the managing director.

Such contracts could also be signed by designated employees who formally have the right to sign for the company.

5.5. Void and Illegal Contracts

Terms in a contract that are contrary to mandatory law will be null and void, in part or in whole.

For example, a contract with a foreign coach engaged by a Norwegian football team must be regulated by the Working Environment Act of 4 February 1977. The provisions of the Act cannot be departed from by agreement, except where the Act expressly stipulates it.

In the Agreements Act of 31 May 1918, Section 36 states that a clause in an agreement may be set aside, wholly or in part, in so far as the application of any term would be unreasonable or in conflict with good business practice.

Also, in the Norwegian Price Act of 26 June 1953, Section 18 states that: 'Charging, demanding or contracting unreasonable prices shall be prohibited. It shall likewise be prohibited to demand, contract, or maintain business terms which unreasonably affect the other party or which are obviously contrary to public interest'.

Unless an explicit exception has been made, this provision applies to any kind of business undertaken against valuable consideration.

5.6. Interpretation

The contracting parties should be mutually loyal. This is emphasised in theory and has also had a distinct impact upon the legislation and legal practice. With this as a starting point interpretation of a contract will take place.

The court will seek help first of all in the terms of the contract, the parties involved and in other relevant circumstances.

5.7. Frustration and Force Majeure

A clause in a contract related to *force majeure* is well known in the Norwegian legal system.

For example, a seller may claim that he has no liability under the Sale of Goods Act because *force majeure* occurrences have prevented him from delivering the product in compliance with the contract. Pursuant to the Act, there is no liability due to *force majeure* if the seller demonstrates that the defect is due to occurrences beyond his control which he could not reasonably have taken into account at the time the agreement was concluded or later have avoided or overcome the effects thereof.

5.8. Breach of Contract

Breach of contract, consisting of the breaking of an obligation imposed by the contract, confers on the injured party a right of action for damages. It also entitles him to treat the contract as discharged if the other party renounces the contract or makes its performance impossible, or totally or substantially fails to perform his promises.

In cases of breach, the payment of damages to the injured party is the usual remedy.

6. Standard Contract Terms

6.1. Applicable Law

Any contract involving parties from different countries should state which law is to be applicable and where (in what country) any dispute should be settled. In the absence of choice and, from a Norwegian point of view, most contracts, but not all, will be governed by the law of the country to which the contract is most related.

6.2. Definitions

Unless there are specific grounds for it, definitions are not used in contracts based on the legal system in Norway.

6.3. Recitals

Recitals and introductions can be used to state the object(s) of the contract.

6.4. Parties

The parties to the contract should be explicitly named at the beginning of the contract.

6.5. Implied Terms

As long as a contract is not in violation of 'mandatory' law, the interpretation of the contract will be based on the terms and the wording of the contract. Examples of 'mandatory law' are the Instalment Sales Act of 21 June 1985, the Sales Act of 13 May 1988 and the Commercial Agency Act of 19 June 1992 (particularly in relation to termination).

Of course, the court may imply terms from different acts if the contract does not include such terms.

6.6. Legal Relationship

From a legal point of view the legal relationship between the parties involved in a contract will be based on facts. However, it is always preferable to state such relationship especially in agency and dealers agreements.

6.7. Force Majeure

In most cases, it is advisable to include a *force majeure* clause in a contract.

6.8. Address for Service

If it is of any practical use, such clause should be included in the contract.

6.9. Reputation

From a legal point of view, it should not be necessary to include a specific clause about reputation, unless the contract is subject to any special rules, for example, the IOC Charter.

6.10. 'Social Conventions'

Clauses in a contract related both to 'reputation' and 'social conventions' will first of all have moral aspects. From a legal point of view, conduct of one of the parties involved which is contrary to 'good behaviour' could give the other party the right to terminate the contract and claim compensation based on general rules for damages.

6.11. Royalties and Accounting

In a contract providing for the payment of royalties, an accounting clause is of the utmost importance.

6.12. Books Open to Inspection

Such clauses are well known in Norway, especially when royalties are to be paid.

6.13. Termination

The contract should have a termination clause unless it is agreed that the contract shall only last for a special event or for a certain time.

The party shall state a valid reason when terminating the contract.

Termination of agency agreements will give the agent the right to compensation according to 'mandatory' rules in the Commercial Agency Act of 19 June 1992.

7. Different Types of Business Arrangements

7.1. Sponsorship Agreement

There is no special body of law governing the sponsorship relationship. Also, in general, there are no specific restrictions as to who may sponsor an event.

Any advertising related to alcohol and tobacco are banned in Norway. Sponsors within that area will, therefore, as a rule not be found in Norway.

Furthermore, the Norwegian Broadcasting System (Radio and Television) does not allow any advertising. There are, however, several private radio and television stations using advertising as their main source of income.

7.2. Merchandising

The subject is covered by contract and is most common in relation to trademark, copyright and design licence agreements.

Both trademarks and designs should be registered in Norway for the sake of legal protection.

7.3. Endorsements

Any misleading advertising would be in violation of the Marketing Control Act and could also be punished.

Use of misleading trademarks would be in violation of the Trademark Act.

Individuals have the right to privacy and endorsements by individuals should only be used in advertising with their consent.

7.4. Commissioning Agreements

It is advisable to define the product (logo, emblem, design) very clearly in the contract. If possible, it should be registered as a trademark or, if appropriate, as a design.

Copyright cannot be registered, but should be assigned by the commissioned party to the commissioning party.

The best practical protection would probably in most cases be through the Marketing Act (Section 9 – imitation of another's product).

7.5. Concessions/Franchises

Concessions and franchises, for example, appointment as an exclusive supplier of certain goods or services to a particular sports event, are a matter of contract.

The precise terms and conditions should be defined in the agreement. Exclusive arrangements may raise unfair competition matters for the Market Court Unfair Competition Committee.

7.6. Films and Videos

The terms and condition for the production and exploitation of films and videos are a matter of contract.

Most film and video companies have their own standard agreements.

There are restrictions on sex and violence when using film, television and video as a media. Advertising directed towards children is also very restrictive when these media are used.

7.7. Public Appearance

Failure to show by the individual would most probably constitute breach of contract and should, consequently, give the other party reasons for termination, and a claim for damages.

7.8. Suppliership

This is well known in Norway, especially in relation to the commercial arrangements for the staging of the Lillehammer Winter Olympics in 1994. Many such arrangements are related to the exclusive use of the Olympic Rings and often take the form of a trademark licence.

8. The Rights

8.1. Options and Pre-Emptions

Options and pre-emption rights are well known in the Norwegian legal system. With the basic contractual freedom such rights can be defined as the parties involved wish.

8.2. Exclusivity

Unless a clause of exclusivity is contrary to the Norwegian Price Act of 1953 about competition and refusal of business dealings, such clauses are very common, especially in agency and dealer agreements.

8.3. Copyright Licence

Could be based on standard agreements.

8.4. Trademark Licence

Could be based on standard agreements.

8.5. Territory

The rights can be divided according to geographical territory, but, again, one must be aware of the regulations in the Price Act of 1953 regarding restrictive business arrangements and dominant enterprises.

8.6. Media

In an agreement intellectual property rights can be split according to media and product/service category.

8.7. Duration

All contracts should have a termination clause, unless the contract is related to one or more specific arrangement(s) or event(s).

Serious breach of contract from one party will always give the other party the right to terminate immediately.

8.8. Post Termination

Provision is often made in a merchandising agreement for a licensee to be allowed a certain period of time (e.g. 6 months) in which to dispose of unsold stocks of the licensed products. Other post-termination restrictions may raise issues for the Market Court Unfair Competition Committee.

8.9. Accreditation

Should be used with discretion by the event organiser.

9. Financial Terms

Unless the parties to an agreement have made other provisions, interest for late payment amongst merchants is payable at the rate of 18% per annum. Interest claims for late payment against consumers may not exceed 15% per annum.

10. Insurance Aspects

General insurance covers economic losses stemming from loss of or reduction in value of property or rights belonging to the insured person or to other persons. The compensation is connected to the extent of the economic loss. There may be various types of loss, such as costs involved in replacement or repair, loss of income or liability that may arise. Consequently, there are three main forms of general insurance: property insurance; loss of profit insurance; and liability insurance. Property insurance provides the insured with coverage of damage caused to his own property. Loss of profit insurance covers losses in income due to discontinuation of the insured's own activities. Liability insurance covers liability to pay compensation incurred by the insured in relation to another person.

Insurance with regard to cancellation is very well known in Norway due to the weather conditions, especially in wintertime, e.g. mild weather with speed-skating, and wind or fog with ski-jumping.

In the event of product liability, the injured person may have his loss covered through an insurance taken out by himself. In case of personal injury this will be a personal insurance, otherwise it may be a property insurance or a loss of profit insurance. Should the insurance not provide adequate cover, the injured person may claim from the party at fault the difference between the loss and the insurance amount paid. Premiums for public and product liability insurance cover in Norway are not particularly high.

Product liability in Norway is strict, in line with the EC Product Liability Directive of 1985, which Norway has adopted in its legislation.

11. Advertising and Promotion

11.1. Advertising Controls

All kinds of advertising directed towards the consumer is watched (controlled) by the Consumer Ombudsman (*Forbrukerombudet*) and the Market Council (*Markedsrådet*) based on the Marketing Control Act of 1972. The main purpose of the Marketing Control Act is to counteract the use of improper and unfair marketing methods.

The ban on advertising for alcohol and tobacco are controlled by the Ministry of Health and Social Affairs (*Sosialdepartementet*) and the National Council on Smoking and Health (*Statens Tobakkskaderåd*).

Certain regulations apply to advertising on radio and television. These regulations are set by the Norwegian Board of Film Censure (*Statens Filmkontroll*) and the Department of Justice (*Justisdepartementet*).

11.2. Tobacco Advertising

Such advertising is banned in Norway.

11.3. Programme Sponsorship

Programme sponsorship is known in Norway and practised in the private television channels.

The basic rules are laid down by the Government and are in line with those applicable in the UK.

11.4. Affinity Marketing

In Norway, there are also restrictions on using customer and client lists in connection with direct mail marketing and advertising. The Data Inspectorate (*Datatilsynet*) controls and is able to ban such activity.

11.5. Comparative Advertising

Comparative advertising must not be in violation of the Marketing Control Act of 1972. The comparison should be fair and loyal.

11.6. Defamation

Claims for compensation can be raised if a persons or a company's reputation has been lowered by use of comparisons and unauthorised endorsements in advertising.

11.7. 'Ambush Marketing'

The Marketing Control Act, the Trademark Act, the Design Act and the Copyright Act can be used as a basis for obtaining preliminary injunctions against 'ambush marketing'.

12. The Venue

12.1. Public Liability

In the case of product liability, the injured person may have his loss covered through an insurance taken out by himself. In the case of personal injury, this will be a personal insurance, otherwise it may be a property insurance, or a loss of profit insurance. Should the insurance not provide adequate cover, the injured person may claim from the party at fault the difference between the loss and the insurance amount paid.

The loss inflicted on the injured person as a result of a defective product may also be covered by a liability insurance taken out by the party at fault. The liability insurance covers the liability to which the party at fault may be subjected. Thus, it is not the injured person who is the insured, but the party at fault.

There is no general obligation to take out liability insurance. There are, however, some exceptions with regard to particularly dangerous products or activities.

Liability insurance is part of the general industrial insurance, and, therefore, this kind of insurance has become comparatively widespread. The Norwegian insurance companies use standardised insurance conditions which do not differ much from one company to another. Liability insurance for damage caused by defective products ('product liability insurance') is part of the general liability insurance and the liability insurance conditions contain specific provisions regulating the insurance cover in cases of product liability.

12.2. Control of Airspace

Basically, the airspace above an event venue is free for anybody to use for promotional and advertising purposes, the only restrictions being those of a military and commercial air-traffic control nature.

13. Dispute Resolution

13.1. Court Action

As regards civil cases, there are three ordinary court instances: the County or City Court, the High Court (the Court of Appeals); and the Supreme Court. The proceedings are initiated by the plaintiff submitting a writ of summons to the City or County Court. The writ contains a statement of the claim, the circumstances on which it is based, a preliminary list of the evidence to be brought by the plaintiff and a definite citation.

In most cases, the action must be brought before the court in the judicial district where the defendant has his residence or, if it is a company, its registered office. Suits regarding damages due to a tortious act or an accident may be instituted in the judicial district where the act or the accident took place. A person who is not resident in Norway may, in cases regarding economic claims, be sued in every judicial district where he has an asset of economic value. Any relationships between the asset and the lawsuit is not required.

A party who is dissatisfied with a judgment delivered by the City or County Court may appeal the decision to the High Court. Evidence not presented at the first trial may be taken into account by the court, which will try the inferior court's decision in every respect, both with regard to the established facts and the application of the law.

Judgments delivered by the High Court may be appealed to the Supreme Court. The right to appeal is limited in several ways. The economic value of the claim in dispute must exceed NOK 100,000. Furthermore, the appeal may be rejected by an unanimous decision of the Appeals Selection Committee of the Supreme Court, if it is of the opinion that the appeal will not achieve its object, or if it considers that neither the decision's importance for the parties involved in or outside the case in question, nor any other grounds, make it reasonable for the appeal to be decided by the Supreme Court.

13.2. Specific Performance and Injunctions

Both specific performance and injunctions can be obtained through the courts.

In order to get an interlocutory injunction, the plaintiff must prove that he has a good arguable case and that he will suffer substantial loss or damage if the injunction is not granted.

13.3. Legal Costs

The legal costs of the parties may include fees to the court, fees to witnesses and experts, fees to the party's counsel, expenses relating to the procurement of evidence and production of documents, and other expenses in connection with the litigation.

The main rule is that if a party loses the case, he will be ordered by the court to indemnify the other party in respect of his legal costs. However, there are several exceptions to this rule. If a case is partially won and partially lost, each of the parties must usually pay their own costs. The court may further decide that each of the parties shall defray their own costs if the case was so doubtful that there was justifiable reason for the losing party to allow it to come before the court, or if it may be claimed that the winning party, in whole or in part, has unnecessarily brought the case to court.

13.4. Recognition and Enforcement of Foreign Judgments

Judgments delivered by Norwegian courts, which have become *res judicata*, may be enforced according to the provisions of the Enforcement of Claims Act of 13 August 1915.

The enforcement is, as a rule, restricted to the territory of Norway. In some cases, Norway has, however, entered into agreements with foreign States regarding mutual recognition and enforcement of judgments. This applies to the other Nordic countries (Sweden, Denmark, Finland and Iceland). Since 1936, the Nordic countries have had a mutual Convention regarding recognition and enforcement of judgments. Today, this Convention has been replaced by identical Acts in these countries (except for Iceland) regarding Nordic judgments. Furthermore, Norway has concluded agreements regarding recognition and enforcement of judgments with the United Kingdom of Great Britain and Northern Ireland (Convention of 12 June 1961) and with Germany (Convention of 17 June 1977). As a consequence of these agreements with foreign States, Norwegian judgments are to a large extent recognised and enforceable in those countries.

Judgments rendered by foreign courts are recognised and enforceable in Norway if the Norwegian party has expressly accepted the jurisdiction of the foreign court. Furthermore, foreign judgments are recognised and enforceable in Norway if the judgments are rendered by a court of one of the States with which Norway has concluded an agreement regarding mutual recognition and enforcement of judgments.

13.5. Arbitration

It frequently happens that parties to commercial disputes refer their cases to arbitration.

Under Norwegian law, an agreement referring a case to arbitration is only valid if it is made in writing. The agreement may concern a legal dispute which has arisen, or any future legal dispute arising from a specific legal relationship, for example, all future disputes between the buyer and the seller, including product liability claims, arising from the purchase of a product. However, disputes concerning the invalidity of trademarks or designs may not be submitted to arbitration, but must be resolved in the ordinary courts.

The Civil Procedure Act contains detailed provisions regarding the composition of the arbitration tribunal and the arbitration procedure. Unless otherwise agreed, the tribunal must consist of three arbitrators, each of the parties nominating one arbitrator, and these two arbitrators then nominating a third, as chairman. If anyone, having the right to nominate an arbitrator, neglects to do so, or, if the arbitrators cannot agree on the choice of chairman, the nomination must, unless otherwise agreed, be made by the City or County Court.

If the arbitration agreement lays down rules of procedure, the arbitration tribunal must abide by them, unless this is impracticable. Apart from this, the tribunal settles its own procedure within certain limits specified in the Act.

The arbitration award has the same legal effect and is enforceable in the same way as a final judgment, unless the parties in the arbitration agreement have provided for an appeal to another arbitration tribunal.

In some special cases, specified in the Act, the parties can obtain a court judgment setting the arbitration award aside. This applies if the arbitration tribunal has gone beyond its terms of reference, if legal or specially agreed rules of procedure have been neglected and it is likely that the error has affected the result, and if the award entails something contrary to law or decency.

In commercial matters where one of the parties is a foreigner, the case will often be referred to international arbitration, for example, arbitration according to the ICC rules in a foreign country. As Norway has ratified the New York Convention on the Recognition and Enforcement of Foreign Arbitral Awards of 10 June 1958, awards delivered by arbitration tribunals abroad will in most cases be enforceable in Norway.

13.6. Alternative Dispute Resolution

ADR is neither very well known nor developed in Norway.

Poland

by Dr. Andrzej Rogóyski
and Dr. Wlodzimierz Szoszuk

1. Sports Marketing – A Business

A sports industry exists in Poland, though it is in an embryonic state, since for years sports have been sponsored solely by the State. There is, however, great potential for growth in this arena as a market economy develops in Poland and the popularity of sport increases amongst the Polish people.

For almost 50 years, sport in Poland was financed either directly through the State budget or indirectly through State-owned industry. Under the Communist regime, professional sports did not exist – all sports were officially amateur. In the past several years, however, the transformation from State-sponsored amateur sports to market-driven professional sports has begun, and with it the business of sports marketing is developing.

2. The Polish Legal System

The Polish civil and commercial legal system is characterised by a certain similarity to the German, Swiss, Austrian, and French legal systems. The basic legislation regarding civil law is the Civil Code of 1964 (*Kodeks Cywilny*); regarding commercial and company law, the basic legislation is the Commercial Code of 1934 (*Kodeks Handlowy*). Upon Solidarity's triumph in 1989, deep structural changes were initiated to remove the laws of socialised trade from the Civil Code, as well as to reinstate the provisions of the Commercial Code which had been dormant for decades. In the course of transforming the socialised economy into a free market system, dozens of laws have been passed or amended and the legal system remains in a state of flux.

3. Applicable Laws

Sports activity in Poland is regulated by:

1. the Law of 23 July 1984 on Physical Training and Education;
2. the Ordinance of the Director of the Agency of Physical Education and Tourism, issued under the above-mentioned law;
3. other ordinances of the Agency of Physical Education and Tourism.

However, these legal acts still do not include any laws referring directly to sports marketing.

In this state of affairs one should say that entities involved in sports marketing may shape their relationship freely by concluding the appropriate civil contracts according to the principle of freedom of contract formulated in Article 353 of the Civil Code.

Such contracts and agreements cannot violate any provisions of 'peremptory character' included in the Polish Civil Code and the norms included in other laws and legal acts which regulate aspects of sports marketing. The norms of foreign exchange law, customs law, trademarks law, provisions of the Unfair Competition Act, and norms concerning advertising are particularly applicable.

4. Intellectual Property Rights

4.1. Trademarks

The law on trademarks in Poland is governed primarily by the 1985 Law on Trademarks. Poland is also a signatory to the Paris Convention.

The 1985 Law defines 'trademark' as 'any sign capable of distinguishing the goods or services of a given enterprise from similar goods or services of another enterprise'.

Such signs may include, but are not limited to, 'words, designs, ornaments, combinations of colours, plastic forms, melodies or other acoustic signals, and a combination of such elements'.

For a sign to constitute a trademark, it must be distinctive. It must be distinctive enough to enable the origin of the goods to be identified and to distinguish it in the public's eye from other goods, and it must maintain that distinctiveness, otherwise the right to protection will lapse.

The sign must not be identical or similar to a trademark already registered in the name of a third party, to a well-known but unregistered trademark, or to a trademark the registration of which has expired within the three previous years. When considering the similarity of trademarks, the similarity of the goods themselves is also examined.

Finally, the sign must not mislead the public as to the origin of the goods, contain any false statements, contradict Polish law or public policy, or infringe upon the personal or economic rights of a third party. Any person whose rights may be prejudiced by registration of a trademark may submit his objections to the Patent Office.

Though the law requires that a trademark be registered in order to be protected, special provisions are made for trademarks which are well-known but not yet registered in Poland. The owner of such a well-known trademark may request the annulment of a registered mark, which so closely resembles the well-known mark as to be misleading, or the prohibition of the use of such a misleading mark by third parties. However, the duration of this right is somewhat limited, so as to encourage registration.

Trademark protection is granted for 10 years from the date of filing. The owner may renew his registration any number of times, so long as the requirements for registration continue to be met. Furthermore, third parties will be prevented from registering a mark identical or similar to a previously registered trademark for three years following the expiration of that trademark. The rights accruing from a trademark may not be annulled after the passage of five years unless the owner registered the trademark in bad faith. If a trademark is not used for three consecutive years following registration, the right lapses.

In the event of infringement of trademark rights, the registered owner may seek an injunction, either to prevent future infringement or stop current unlawful actions; seek damages to compensate for either lost earnings from the sale of goods or royalties, which would have been earned had the owner concluded a licensing contract; sue for the surrender of unlawful profits, under the theory of 'unjust enrichment'; or oblige the infringing party to publish an explanatory statement. There is a three year statute of limitations for proceedings based on a trademark infringement. Trademark infringement also carries the threat of penal sanctions: anyone placing on the market goods or services which he has labelled with a registered trademark which he is not entitled to use is subject to a fine or up to one year's imprisonment.

4.2. Copyright

Poland is a signatory of the Berne Convention and the national situation is governed by the Copyright Act of 1952, as amended in 1975.

Polish copyright is a part of the civil law dealing with intangible property that arises from the creative activity of the human brain, including literary, artistic, musical and scientific creation. The 1952 Act of 1952 stipulates that copyright can protect creations which are the immaterial products of intellectual activity or imagination. Under Polish law the works which may by protected are not expressly listed. The duration of a copyright is generally during the life of and up to 25 years after the author's death.

Personal rights in Poland, also called moral rights, enable an author to protect his good name, dignity and emotional feelings relating to his work. Such rights are enforceable against everyone, are permanently tied to the author, and therefore are non-transferable and cannot be waived. They expire on the death of the author.

4.3. Registered Designs

According to Article 73 of the Polish Inventory Law: 'A registered design being a subject of protection is a new and useful solution of technical character concerning shape, structure or combination of an object having durable shape.'

Registered designs are protected in Poland for a period of five years, which can be extended once for a further period of five years.

4.4. Unfair Competition

The provisions of the Polish Unfair Competition Act can be applied to sports activity. The first three articles of that Act are of general character and can be related to the situations when one is gaining an unfair advantage of another's good reputation. Article 1 stipulates that an enterprise shall have the right to demand another enterprise (competitor) not to attract customers to whom it offers its products, goods or services in such a misleading manner as to pass them off as coming from the former enterprise. The enterprise, whose the rights have been infringed, may demand that such practice be discontinued and the source of the customers' misunderstanding be removed. Where the enterprise has lost a number of its customers, the wrongdoer shall deliver the unjustified benefits obtained during the three years immediately preceding the date when the claim was lodged at court. When customers were intentionally or negligently misled, the wrongdoer shall be obliged to redress the injury and give him satisfaction for any personal harms, by announcing the sentence or by an appropriate public declaration, and, in case of malice, by paying punitive damages, if no satisfaction has been provided by the penal sentence.

The Act also stipulates that the designation of the enterprise must not mislead the customers in such a way as to make them confuse its identity with that of another competitive enterprise. Where this provision of the Unfair Competition Act is infringed the injured party may make the same claims as in the case of infringement of the provisions of Article 1.

Where trademarks are unregistered, the provisions of the Unfair Competition Act could be an appropriate means of protecting rights and reputation in any international or local sports events.

5. The Contract Generally and Preliminary Agreements

5.1. Preliminary Agreement

Article 389 of the Civil Code defines 'preliminary agreement' as 'a contract by which parties bind themselves to conclude a specific contract and in which they define the essential provisions of the promised contract and the date on which it is to be concluded.' Such an agreement is legally binding, and if one party fails to fulfil its obligations under it the other party may claim for any damages incurred in reliance upon the contract. As long as a preliminary agreement is concluded in the correct form, a party to it may demand specific performance (i.e. the conclusion of the promised contract).

5.2. *Intention to Create Legal Relations*

For a contract to be valid, both parties must express their intention to enter into an agreement. A contract is voidable where consent was obtained by threat, or where a party lacks the mental capacity to consent (as in the case of mental disease or mental deficiency, even if temporary).

5.3. *Offer and Acceptance*

According to the Polish Civil Code, an offer must contain a declaration of the will of the parties to make an agreement and the term within which acceptance must be made, although, in practice, offers are made during negotiations in which the parties jointly settle the provisions of the contract. The offeror is bound by the offer until such time has lapsed. Acceptance is made by means of a declaration.

5.4. *Consideration*

The Polish legal system uses the notion of '*causa*', meaning the basis of the legal transaction. The idea of *causa* is broader than that of 'consideration'.

5.5. *Form and Execution*

According to Polish law, most agreements may be concluded in any form, including orally. However, in some cases the law requires an agreement to be made in a particular form, such as a notarial deed, for an agreement to be valid. An agreement concluded improperly is invalid where such penalty is provided by law. Contracts are often required to be in writing for evidentiary purposes.

5.6. *Void and Illegal Contracts*

Agreements made in a proper form and with a valid '*causa*' will still be invalid if provisions therein are contrary to law or the rules of social cooperation. An agreement prepared so as to make performance impossible is also invalid, and so also is one made by a person who is acting as a plenipotentiary without a proxy, or in excess of it, and the person in whose name an agreement was made did not accept its validity.

5.7. Privity

According to Polish law, an agreement is binding only with respect to the parties to the agreement. If an agreement provides that a third party shall incur an obligation or fulfil the performance, the person who made such a promise is obligated with regard to the other party for the damage caused by non-fulfilment of this reservation. The third party who incurred such an obligation may release himself from liability by fulfilment of the promised performance.

5.8. Interpretation

According to Polish law, a declaration of will should be interpreted in accordance with the circumstances in which the declaration was made, the rules of social cooperation, and custom. In particular, in case of making agreements, the unanimous intention of the parties and the purpose of the agreement should be sought rather than the literal purport of its terms.

5.9. Frustration and Force Majeure

According to Polish law, an obligation is terminated if its performance becomes impossible as a result of circumstances beyond the obligated party's control. Such situations may arise as a result of the activity of third parties or of *force majeure*. *Force majeure* is defined as an extraordinary, external event which is impossible to avoid, such as war, flood or other catastrophe, as well as acts of State authorities, which alter the legal status of the parties.

5.10. Breach of Contract

A contract can be breached if the conditions of the contract are infringed. The consequences of a breach depend on the terms of the breached contract. The breaching party is obliged to pay damages to the party which bears such loss. An obligated party who fails to fulfil his obligations in a timely manner is in default, unless such default is caused by circumstances beyond his responsibility.

6. Standard Contract Terms

One of the main principles of the Polish legal system is the principle of freedom of contract. This generally means that parties are:

1. free to enter into any agreements not forbidden by the law;
2. free to chose contracting parties; and
3. free to decide about the conditions of their contract.

This freedom may only be limited by the existing provisions of positive law. This means that what is not forbidden or ordered by law is up to the decision of the contracting parties.

The basic rules of contract are provided by the Civil Code of 1964, as amended. This Code governs obligations (i.e. contracts) in general and also provides for such typical contracts as: sales agreements, contracts to perform a specified task or work, lease and tenancy agreements, and agency agreements. The Civil Code provides definitions, forms, terms and other matters related to specific types of contracts.

Generally speaking the following issues are of importance:

6.1. Form of contract

Contracts should be concluded in writing. When contracts are prepared in Polish and other languages it is necessary to decide which version shall prevail in case of dispute.

6.2. Parties

Parties to a contract should be defined very precisely and a contract should be signed by duly appointed representatives of both parties.

6.3. Implied terms

If a certain provision is necessary for the successful completion of a contract, but it is not expressly stated therein, such provision shall be inferred to have been inserted. Likewise, if a provision of a contract is in contradiction to the law, such provision will be invalid and substituted with the legal provision which it violated.

6.4. Definitions

The scope of a contract should be described precisely. Parties are entitled to define both the scope of the contract and certain provisions according to their will.

6.5. Applicable Law

Parties are free to choose which law shall govern a contract within the limits of Article 25, section 1 of the Polish Private International Law of 1965: 'The parties are allowed to subject their contractual relations to the law of their choice if such law is connected with their obligation'.

However, if the contract relates to a property, the contractual relations will be subject to the law of the property's location (*loc. situs*).

6.6. Execution of Foreign Judgments

According to the provisions of the Polish Code of Civil Procedure of 1964, the judgment of a foreign court in Poland may be executed only where there exists an international agreement between Poland and the country in question. Because only a few such agreements have been concluded, mainly with ex-communist States, it is generally advisable to stipulate that any disputes arising in relation to a contract shall be settled in the Polish courts.

7. Different Types of Business Arrangements

7.1. Sponsorship Agreement

There is no special body of law governing the sponsorship relationship, this being regulated solely by the contract between the parties. No restrictions have been imposed with regard to who may sponsor an event.

7.2. Merchandising

Merchandising is regulated by contract and not by any branch of the Civil Code. When trademarks are being licensed, the licence should be registered to ensure that the licensee has the right to the licence.

7.3. Endorsement

Under Polish law, an author has the right to sue anyone who appropriates his work in accordance with the Criminal Code.

7.4. Commissioning Agreements

Commissioning agreements are widely used in Poland. Different types of business arrangements are regulated by commissioning agreements, including suppliership, film and video. According to Polish law, it is possible to grant a company the right to be the 'official' product or service supplier of various items for a particular event. There are no special regulations regarding this task. Under Polish law this agreement between suppliers and the organiser is known as a 'commissioning'.

7.5. Franchises

Franchising agreements, whereby a franchisee may acquire an express licence to use various trademarks and copyrights, has only recently been introduced into the Polish legal system.

8. The Rights

A variety of marketing and commercial rights are available in relation to sports activity, including organising, management and sponsorship of sports events.

8.1. Options

Option rights are not regulated by a separate branch of Polish law. The organiser of an event may grant an option to the sponsor and such an offer cannot be revoked without the grantor being in breach of the contract.

8.2. Pre-emptions

Reservation may be made in an agreement, if a rights holder is considering licensing a right, whereby the first opportunity to acquire the right will be offered to the pre-emptive right holder, although there is no obligation under Polish law to include such a clause in the agreement.

8.3. Exclusivity

According to Polish law, it is forbidden to run a business in such a way as to divide a market according to the territory, products or other subjective criteria. This anti-monopoly rule does not infringe the exclusivity laws which result from the regulations concerning registered designs, trademarks, copyrights and other provisions connected with the laws of intellectual property.

8.4. Copyright Licence

The Copyright Act does not regulate licence agreements, except that the Council of Ministers may allow for a compulsory licence without the consent of an author or his successors so as to:

– disseminate the work in a definite, limited manner;
– revise or adjust the work as necessary for theatrical, film or radio purposes.

Licence agreements are regulated by the general provisions of the Civil Law. Such an agreement should provide for the rights to revert back to the licensor following termination of the contract, and may also provide for sub-licensing.

8.5. Trademark Licence

According to the Polish Law on Trademarks, the owner of the right derived from the registration of a trademark may authorise another enterprise to use the mark for goods covered by the registration under the licence contract.

Where not otherwise stipulated by the licence contract, the licensee may use the trademark in the same way as the registered owner of the trademark. If stipulated by the contract, the licensee may be authorised to use a trademark within a less extensive scope than the owner. In practice, this means that the licensee has only limited authorisation to use the trademark, or that its use may be limited to one of the areas specifically provided by the Law on Trademarks as follows:

1. affixing the mark to goods of the type registered or to their packaging;
2. marketing goods marked in this way;
3. affixing the mark on documents relating to the marketing of such goods;
4. advertising in the Polish mass media.

The licence contract may also restrict the use of the right deriving from registration to only certain of the goods included in the registration.

Sub-licensing is not allowed without the licensor's permission.

The licence contract should specify the rights to be granted, territory, duration, and post termination arrangements; in the absence of such provisions the general rules of the Civil Code relating to contracts will be applied.

8.6. Media

The intellectual property rights in Poland can be split in Poland according to the media and product category. Equally a trademark might be licensed separately.

8.7. Product Classes

A sponsor may be the exclusive sponsor for a particular product category. Such products must be carefully defined.

8.8. Duration

The duration of a contract is one of the most important aspects of the agreement and should therefore be expressly defined (e.g. early termination in specified circumstances).

8.9. Post Termination Arrangements

A licensor is free to provide in the licence agreement that his rights shall revert back to him upon termination of the agreement.

Post termination arrangements may fall under the Act of 24 February 1990 on Counteracting Monopolistic Practices (Dz. Vst. [1990] No. 14, poz. 403). Article 4.1.1. of this Act includes a broadly formulated prohibition against agreements which include 'onerous contract terms which yield the economic subject, forcing them, undue benefits' to the enterprise that imposes them. Non-competition clauses might be considered to be 'onerous contract terms' and, therefore, prohibited under this provision. It should be mentioned that Article 4.1.1. itself provides for conditions under which such practices would be allowed. The Act also provides for a kind of 'rule of reason' in Article 6, which states that monopolistic practices are prohibited 'unless they are necessary to conduct an economic activity and do not induce a substantial limitation of competition'. Because of the lack of practice to date in this area, it is difficult to assess how these provisions will be interpreted in concrete situations.

9. Financial Terms

From the point of view of business, the financial terms of the intended transaction are of fundamental importance. Apart from the normal terms of a deal, such as the amount of payment and the duration of the contract, the following risks must be carefully considered when dealing with the Polish market:

1. currency exchange rate (inflation) – especially in case of foreign creditors;
2. lack of payment and insolvency of the debtor;
3. the potentially poor quality of things to be delivered.

The first of the above-mentioned exposures is closely connected with the currency specified in the contract. If the contract concerns 'the turnover of goods and services with foreign countries', payment must be provided for and made by the parties in foreign currency (Article 12 of Polish Foreign Exchange Law of 1989). Exceptions are possible after obtaining a foreign currency permit from the National Bank of Poland. In the case of domestic turnover, the contract must provide for payment in zlotys (the domestic currency). In such case, however, parties usually include a 'valorisation' clause based upon foreign hard currency (e.g. US dollars) in order to reduce the inflation exposure.

Parties may also, on the basis of Article 359 of Polish Civil Code, provide for interest. The parties are free to set the rate of interest as they wish; if no such provision is made then interest shall be paid at the statutory rate, as provided by the Ordinance of the Council of Ministers. The current rate is 60% per annum.

Independently of any interest due, the creditor may claim from the debtor compensation for the delay in performance of his obligation, if such a delay is the result of the fault of the debtor.

Stipulations for contractual penalties is an another way of securing the creditor's interest when an obligation is not performed or is performed improperly (including late performance). Unlike in the case of interest, a legal effect of stipulation for contractual penalties is that a creditor cannot demand indemnity in an amount higher than the value of the contractual penalty, unless the parties have mutually so agreed. As far as the risk of non-payment is concerned, one should consider (if the contract proceeds for postponed dues) whether to stipulate for security in the form of, for example, a bank guarantee, guarantee or guaranteed promissory note.

Where the total amount of a cash performance is to be determined in relation to some amount/standard of value (for example, with regard to income or the licensee's profit), an agreement should define the minimal amount due to the licensor, irrespective of profit or income gained by the licensee.

Where an agreement is for the delivery of goods (for example, sports or technical equipment) instead of payment, a contractual securing of the proper quality of goods to be delivered is very significant. It is necessary to include provisions in an agreement concerning the quality of goods and the precise description of the creditor's rights and claims in the event that the equipment turned out to be of improper quality or imperfect.

10. Insurance Aspects

The range of insurance cover available on the Polish market is limited. It is impossible to insure against liabilities which are connected with intellectual property rights or with sports events, although, in general, many forms of public liability insurance exist.

In practice, some forms of insurance are the subject of agreements between Polish sports unions and insurance companies or Government instructions. These forms are not commonly used and concern only organised sports activity (e.g. members of the sports clubs).

The Act of 28 July 1990 on Insurance Business and the regulation of 18 December 1990 of the Finance Minister appear to provide for three exceptions from the rule that insurance agreements must be with an insurer authorised under the Act of Insurance Business. These exceptions arise when the insurance is for:

1. risks against which insurers operating under the above mentioned Act do not insure;
2. risks located outside Poland if insurance with a local insurer is required by the local law;
3. risks required to be insured with a particular foreign insurer by an international convention.

11. Advertising and Promotion

There are no exclusive regulations under Polish law with regard to the question of advertising in relation to sports marketing. Certain ministers have issued ordinances regulating specific issues, without intending to settle the whole of this area.

Current laws do not forbid the advertising of cigarettes and tobacco products at sports events. However, there is currently a draft Act to combat the health hazards of smoking, which has been prepared by the Ministry of Health. Article 8 of this draft Act stipulates that any advertisement of tobacco in the country is forbidden, in particular advertising through the sponsorship of sports events.

There is a total legal ban on the advertisement of alcoholic products (*Dziennik Ustaw* No. 35 of 1982, item 230 and amendments).

Apart from the laws of advertising, however, there are also the 'Rules of Advertising in Polish Radio and Television Programmes', approved by the Radio and Television Committee, which govern the advertising activities on Polish radio and television. The Rules adopted by this Committee are much more detailed than the general rules of advertising in Polish legislation.

Advertising must not violate the law. Therefore, for example, advertising must not promote behaviour which may be dangerous to one's health. The Rules deal with the matter of advertising in a much broader way than the legislation currently in force. Thus, the advertising of cigarettes and tobacco products is also considered to be prohibited, as well as that of alcohol and medicine.

Sponsorship is also subject to certain limitations under the Rules. For example, it is said that programmes especially connected with sport or cultural events must not be sponsored by persons whose basic activity is connected with products whose advertising is banned.

The Rules do not have the status of law. Rather, they are internal regulations of an informative and instructional character, and are employed only within the scope of the Committee mentioned above. Private broadcasts are not, therefore, bound by them.

12. The Venue

12.1. Public Liability

An event organiser as an 'economic subject' under Polish law is obliged to conform to the regulations concerning the running of business activity with regard to the protection of life, health, safety and the other conditions defined in contractual, sanitary, fire, and environmental regulations. Failure to do so will result in the imposition of restrictions on the organiser by such administrative authorities as: the State Sanitary Inspection, the State Trade Inspection, the local fire brigade and building inspectors. Apart from the above-mentioned restrictions, Article 434 of the Civil Code imposes general responsibility upon a person in independent possession of a building for its collapse, unless such collapse did not result from any failure to construct or maintain the building properly. Relevant articles in the Criminal Code also provide for penalties against a malfeasor in such an instance.

12.2. Control

The event organiser exercises full control during the sports event. The organiser has the exclusive right to grant special admission to VIPs or to limit access to certain sectors of the stadium. The organiser also grants accreditation and is responsible for the security of members of the public throughout the event. The event organiser has to define precisely the areas of the stadium which are especially prepared for the fans of the arriving club, the police, camera crews.

12.3. Sponsor Access and Protection

There is, as yet, little market in Poland for sponsors. It is between the organiser and the sponsor to settle the conditions of the sponsor's access to the venue and the protection of his rights.

12.4. Permits

Permits for organising sports events and competitions are issued by the Chairman of the Physical Education and Tourist Office, pursuant to the provisions of the Act on Permits for Articles, Entertainment and Sports Activity for 1968.

12.5. Airspace

The airspace above a venue (e.g. outside stadium) may be used for advertising and promotional purposes, subject to the control and supervision of the Polish Air Traffic Authorities, pursuant to Articles 44 and 46 of the Air Law.

13. Dispute Resolution

13.1. Court Jurisdiction

According to the Polish Code of Civil Procedure cases may be heard by the general courts and the Supreme Court. District Courts recognise all cases except those which fall within the jurisdiction of *Voivodship* Courts (i.e. regional courts of second instance after the District Courts). The following cases fall within the *Voivodship* Courts' jurisdiction: claims for non-pecuniary rights and the pecuniary claims which accompany them, claims in connection with press law; and pecuniary claims where the value of the subject of the dispute exceeds 20 million zlotys. Commercial cases (i.e. cases concerned with the civil relations between entities carrying out commercial activity), fall under the jurisdiction of the Commercial Courts, which are separate organisational entities from District and *Voivodship* Courts.

13.2. Court Procedure

In the event of a dispute, a party may lodge the claim with the court competent for the particular kind of claim. Cases are heard in a trial. Parties have the right to appeal from the decisions of first instance courts.

Principles regarding proceedings at civil and commercial courts are set out in the Code of Civil Procedure.

13.3. Remedies and Damages

The claimant may demand the execution of an agreement concluded between the parties as well as the reparation of any damage resulting from the non-performance or improper performance of an obligation. The party defines such damage by bringing an action before the court. If the debtor delays the performance of a pecuniary obligation, the creditor has the right to claim interest for the period of such a delay, even if no damage was incurred. The court hearing the case may issue an interim injunction in order to secure the claim, if such claim is justified and the creditor might be deprived of satisfaction should the claim not be secured.

The court may also issue an interim injunction when it is necessary for the securing of the decision. An interim injunction is issued by the court on request of a party or *ex officio.* The securing of a claim can consist of, *inter alia*, seizure of the debtor's movable property or establishing a mortgage on his real property. A decision regarding an interim injunction can be appealed.

13.4. Action for an Agreed Sum

An action for an agreed sum is a simple action and remarkably faster than an ordinary action. Such an action falls under the jurisdiction of the District Courts. The plaintiff may demand that the court force the defendant to pay the amount claimed by the plaintiff, or any third person to pay a sum arising from tender or cheque. The circumstances justifying the claim are normally evidenced in full by files attached to the writ. In an action for an agreed sum the court issues its decisions at a closed session without a hearing.

13.5. Costs

The court recognises a case only after the plaintiff has paid an 'initial fee'. In a civil case, this fee is equal to 8% of the value of the subject matter of the claim; in a commercial case it is between 5% and 12%, depending on the value of the subject matter. Therefore, bringing an action to court always results in the plaintiff incurring high fees at the beginning of the proceedings. The successful party may demand, however, that the losing party reimburse him for the costs of the trial, including the initial fee. Due to the high costs of legal proceedings parties often choose to submit disputes arising from an agreement to an arbitration court for settlement.

13.6. Arbitration

The parties may submit disputes regarding pecuniary rights to an arbitration court. When the parties have so agreed, they may not later demand that the case be heard by a regular court. Where at least one of the parties has its residence or seat in Poland at the moment the action is instituted, and where the dispute arises from a legal relationship regarding a company with foreign participation or from any other legal relationship regarding foreign business, the parties may submit their disputes for settlement by an arbitration court at the Polish Economic Chamber. Proceedings before such court are governed by the Rules of the Polish Economic Chamber.

The Polish Code of Civil Procedure allows disputes relating to intellectual property rights to be submitted to arbitration, Article 687 providing that any dispute related to pecuniary rights, except alimony and labour disputes, may be arbitrated. Disputes relating to an author's personal or moral rights, not being pecuniary in nature, cannot, however, be settled by arbitration.

13.7. Enforcement of Foreign Judgments and Arbitral Awards

The recognition and execution of foreign judgments in Poland is governed by the Code of Civil Procedure. Legal effect in Poland of non-coercive foreign judgments in civil cases is determined by recognition thereof by the Polish court. Foreign judgments (including awards of foreign arbitration courts) are granted execution in Poland if their enforceability is provided for by international convention. Thus, an agreement made before a foreign court is granted enforcement in Poland if it is enforceable in the State where it was made, if it is not contrary to the essential principles of the legal policy of the People's Republic of Poland, and if its enforceability in Poland is provided for by international convention. The above-mentioned provisions do not apply if Poland is a party to international treaties which stipulate otherwise.

Poland is a signatory to the New York Convention of 1958 on the Recognition and Enforcement of Foreign Arbitral Awards, to the Geneva European Convention on International Commercial Arbitration of 1961, and to the Geneva Protocol of 1923 concerning arbitration cases. Poland is also a party to the Moscow Convention on the Settlement by Arbitration of Civil Law Disputes arising out of the Relationship of Economic, Scientific and Technical Co-operation of 1972. The Moscow Arbitration Convention is still in force, although it has lost most of its significance and must soon be replaced by normal rules of international arbitration.

Portugal

*by Manuel P. Barrocas
and Henrique S. Pereira*

1. Sports Marketing – A Business

As far as State intervention in sport activities is concerned, including the grant of financial subsides, it is of importance to distinguish between professional sports activities and amateur sports activities. It is also useful to distinguish between the large sports clubs (some of which are organised as real enterprises) and small clubs existing mainly in the countryside. As far as the latter are concerned, State and municipality support is usually limited to financial and other supports.

Larger clubs are usually self-sufficient, although most have significant losses each year. They obtain funds through the members' contributions, revenues from the entries in competitions, a small percentage of the sports lottery and other sources. In addition, increasing revenues arise from the link between sports and advertising.

Every large or medium-sized sports stadium and other sports area are in the centre of the advertising agents' attention as important marketing vehicles and practically all first-rank teams are sponsored.

Finally, television is playing more and more an important role in financing some clubs as compensation for the transmission of sports competitions, particularly after October 1992 due to the appearance of private TV networks competing with public TV networks.

In conclusion, advertising through sport is a growth sector. There are no available annual figures that could give a clearer idea about the importance and evolution of the business.

2. The National Legal System

Portuguese law has been influenced by Roman law, later by the Napoleonic codification and recently by German concepts, mainly by the BGB. The national legal system is comprised of several codes and of separate statutes published in the *Official Gazette*.

In accordance with Articles 1 to 4 of the Civil Code ('CC'), the sources of national law are the statute, the so-called *assentos*, i.e. case law adjudicated by the Supreme Court in certain limited conditions, and customs and usage, provided that they are specifically admitted by law and not contrary to the principle of *bona fide*.[1] In very few cases, the settlement of court cases may also be based on equity.

Both civil and commercial cases are heard in the same courts, which we may call the civil courts. Their jurisdiction includes all matters relating to civil and commercial law. Courts of first instance (*Tribunais de Primeira Instância* – traditionally the name of the court of first instance is *Tribunal de Comarca*) are spread throughout the country's 120 districts. Generally speaking, these courts may hear cases worth up to Escudos 2 million.

Each court is part of a larger area having a court (*Tribunal de Círculo*) hearing cases whose value exceeds Escudos 2 million. The *Tribunal de Círculo* is a court of first instance on the same level as the *Tribunal de Comarca*.

All civil and commercial cases have a monetary value – the amount involved in the case – which establishes which court takes jurisdiction, the possibility of appeal and the basis for calculation of the legal fees. Both are lower courts.

Above them are the *Tribunal da Relação*, appeal courts, which are exclusively engaged in hearing appeals lodged in writing. The country is divided into four appeal courts districts, which are located in Lisbon, Oporto, Coimbra and Évora.

The highest court is the Supreme Court of Justice (*Supremo Tribunal de Justiça*) located in Lisbon.

3. Applicable Laws

There is no statute ruling specially advertising in sports. Therefore, the general advertising legislation is applicable which means that the most relevant statutes are the Civil Code, which concerns contract agreements in general, and a Bill comprising the Advertising Code (*Código da Publicidade*) enacted in October 1990 through the Decree-Law No. 330/90, which specifically concerns advertising activities.

1. *Bona fide* in this sense (as it will be used in other parts of this chapter) is the set of statutory rules implying a particular duty of diligence by both parties to advise, cooperate and protect the interests of the counter-party, when negotiating a contract, during its performance and even after the performance of the contract, taking into account the particular circumstances at all times.

4. Intellectual Property Rights

Portugal is a founding member of the International Union for the Protection of Patents and Trademarks established under the Convention of Paris dated 20 March 1883, and has also signed all subsequent revisions.

The main source of law regarding trademarks, registered designs and models, business names and emblems is the Decree No. 30679, dated 24 August 1940. The following protection is provided under Portuguese law:

- patents – 15 years;
- trademarks – renewable periods of 10 years;
- industrial drawings and models – renewable periods of 5 years;
- business names and emblems – 30 years.

Patents and trademarks registered or pending in any of the Union members have priority during 12 months and 6 months, respectively, in applying for registration in Portugal.

Portugal did sign and ratify the 1973 EC Munich Convention on Trademarks and Patents and will sign the 1975 EC Luxembourg Convention on EC patents. Industrial property registration is made with the *Instituto Nacional da Propriedade Industrial.*

The main legal source ruling copyright is the Decree-Law No. 63/85, enacted on 14 March 1985, the so-called *Código dos Direitos de Autor e dos Direitos Conexos*. Portugal is a member of the Berne Convention of 1886 since 1911 and is also a member of the Universal Copyright Convention, signed in Geneva on 6 September 1952.

Generally, the duration of protection is for the author's lifetime plus 50 years.

Copyright registration is made with the *Conservatória da Propriedade Literária, Artística e Científica* and protection is dealt with by the *Sociedade Portuguesa de Autores*, which is a private association.

In recent years, particularly after joining the EC, much effort has been made in Portugal to try and defend free competition. In 1983 a law was passed (Decree-Law No. 422/83, 3 December) which introduced a legal regime based on Community law. According to this law, fixing of minimum prices, refusal to sell goods or services and discriminatory sale conditions are considered as individual practices which restrict competition. The fixing of minimum prices is allowed in exceptional cases, as in the case of new products, special commitments of the producer concerning guarantees of high quality, and so on, but only if prior consent is given by the Government.

If companies agree to disturb free competition, this is considered a collective restrictive agreement. The law specifies cases wherein such practice is considered restrictive. The legal framework is based entirely upon Article 85 of the EEC Treaty.

Abuse of dominant position is also governed by the Competition Law, in a manner similar to that which is applied by other EC countries and according to Community law (Article 86 of the EEC Treaty).

A list of infringements and fines is provided by law, which are under the fiscalisation of the Ministry of Commerce. Usually, Governmental regulatory authorities meet with the enterprises concerned to discuss possible infringements and to correct the situation.

A body also polices the law. A Competition Board (*Conselho de Concorrência*) has been organised to judge cases where free competition is infringed. Appeal can be lodged with the courts. A Consultative Commission on Competition has also been organised comprising representatives of industry, commerce and agriculture, as well as of consumers and they meet together with a representative of governmental regulatory authorities.

5. The Contract Generally and Preliminary Agreements

5.1. General Legal Contracts

The general legal regime on contract agreements is laid down in the Civil Code.

Articles 405 to 456 establish a set of rules governing all contracts, whether those covered directly by law or those freely established by the parties within the legal limits. The general rule of contract agreements is based on four principles:

5.1.1. The principle of contractual freedom

Within the limits of the law the parties may freely establish the content of their contracts, enter into contracts other than those provided for in the Civil Code or include therein such clauses as they may wish (Art. 405). That is to say, (1) the parties may decide whether they will enter into the contract or not (sub-principle of freedom to enter into a contract); (2) they may choose the contract they wish to sign (sub-principle of freedom of selection of the type of contract); and finally (3) they may agree on the specific contents of the contract which they have elected (sub-principle of freedom of stipulation).

Contracts are classified as:

- Typical or specific, regulated under Articles 874 to 1250 of the Civil Code: these are contracts for which the law provides express provisions and regulates the same either mandatorily or through additional provisions which apply in the absence of any stipulation to the contrary by the parties.
- A-typical or non-specific which are those created by the parties (using the principle of contractual freedom) outside the sphere of typical contracts.
- Mixed, in which the parties may include the provisions of two or more typical contracts.

5.1.2. The principle of mutual agreement

The mere agreement of the parties is sufficient for the contract to be completed (Article 219). That is to say, the validity of the contract does not depend, in principle, on the fulfilment of any special form, except when so required by law. This principle is subject to those exceptions which exist in those cases where the law requires a specific form (usually, written documents which sometimes must be notarised but rarely registered).

5.1.3. The bona fide principle

The law subjects the following three stages of the creation of a contract to the principle of *bona fide*:

- its formation;
- its interpretation and completion;
- the exercise of the rights and fulfilment of the obligations deriving from the contract.

In the pre-contract stage, Article 227 Civil Code stipulates that any person negotiating with other parties for the conclusion of a contract must, both in the preliminary stages and in entering into the contract, proceed in accordance with the rules of *bona fide*, failing which he shall be liable for any damage which he may wilfully cause to the other party. This principle concerns wilful liability in the formation of the contract (*culpa in contrahendo*), i.e., pre-contractual liability.

The *bona fide* principle is a general principle which must be fulfilled case by case, that is, only in a specific case can it be concluded whether a specific behaviour, in the circumstances of the case, meets the *bona fide* principle.

5.1.4. The principle of mutual commitment

Once the contract has been signed this constitutes a legal commitment between the parties (Article 406). The contract must be performed 'exactly' and may only be amended or terminated by mutual consent of the contracting parties or in the instances permitted by law. This principle may be subdivided into the three following rules:

- rule of exactness: the contract must be performed point by point;
- rule of irrevocability: neither of the parties may revoke the contract unilaterally;
- rule of inviolability: the parties may not unilaterally amend the provisions of the contract.

5.2. Preliminary Agreements

A preliminary binding agreement (*contrato-promessa*) is often used in business in Portugal. It consists in a binding contract to enter into another contract as soon as all pending negotiation clauses are agreed and/or other conditions are met. The object of a preliminary agreement is not the economic or legal objective of the appropriate final contract, but the entering into the final agreement itself.

It is important to distinguish between the preliminary negotiations of a contract which, finally, is not signed and so does not create any contractual binding relationship, and the preliminary agreement. As a matter of fact, preliminary negotiations that are not materialised in a legal contract agreement (including the so-called 'letter of intent') have no legal effects, except in cases of pre-contractual liability affecting the *bona fide* principle.

By contrast, a preliminary agreement is a binding contract, like any other contract agreement, which the parties undertake to fulfil by entering into the promised definite and final contract (say the main contract) subject to specific performance and/or indemnity if it is not fulfilled by any party.

In compliance with Article 410 of the Civil Code, the preliminary agreement is subject to the same rules applicable to the promised contract agreement (the main contract), except where the contractual forms are concerned.

Usually, the preliminary agreement comprises a down payment where there exists the obligation of a payment in the main contract. Failure to accomplish the preliminary contract entitles the innocent party to apply for specific performance unless there is a clause agreed by the parties providing otherwise. It is understood by the law (except where the parties expressly have agreed otherwise) that the existence of a down payment or a liquidated damage clause prevents the parties from applying for specific performance.

Specific performance consists of applying to the court for a court judgment that declares the main contract (even though not signed and executed by the parties) as entered into, valid and effective between the parties.

5.3. Offer and Acceptance

The Civil Code rules in detail the question of offer and acceptance. They are essential parts of the contract agreement.

An offer consists of a statement towards the entering into a specific contract and aiming to obtain the effects of such a contract once accepted by the other party.

A contractual statement may be express or tacit. An express statement is made through words (orally or in writing). It is tacit when the statement is deduced from facts which all in all likeliness reveals its existence.

A silent behaviour is only valid as a legal statement where there exists a specific law or an agreement by the parties providing legal binding effects for such behaviour.

A statement is effective when it is received or is known by the addressee and, in such situation, it cannot be withdrawn by the offeror. The contract is entered into when the acceptance of the offer is received or known by the offeror.

However, the law establishes an important rule: the contract is not concluded and entered into while all clauses that the parties have thought necessary to accept in the contract are not fully agreed.

5.4. *Consideration*

Consideration is the inducement to a contract. It is the cause, the motive, price or compelling influence which induces a contracting party to enter into a contract.

This is treated by Portuguese law as the 'function-cause' (*causa-função*) of a contract and it has particular practical importance in two aspects. First, each contract is designed by law based on the typical elements that characterise a contract. For instance, in a sale and purchase agreement the price is an essential element of the contract. Without the definition of a price there is no contract of such a type, despite the possible existence of an intention to transfer the title to a good. Such intention without a price to pay means a donation, but not a sale and purchase contract. Secondly, the legal regime of mistake as a cause of voidability of a contract.

The consideration is of much importance in both aspects mentioned (i.e. essential elements of the contract and mistake), in addition to other important points, such as the definition of the contract contents and even its construction.

However, it is not usual in Portuguese drafting practice to separate the consideration from the stipulations of a contract.

5.5. *Form and Condition*

As said above, in principle, the law does not require a formal statement. However, in certain exceptional cases, the law requires that the contract must be expressed in a formal document to be valid. Sometimes, such a document must be notarised.

If the formal requisites are not fulfilled the contract is null and void.

This is not the case with sale and purchase contracts except where the object of the contract is real estate or other registrable movable assets (cars, aircrafts and ships). It is also not the case with an advertising agreement, even though in practice they require a written form due to the complexity of clauses involved in a contract of this kind and also for reasons of evidence.

If the parties have agreed to submit to a written form the entering into of a contract or some aspects of its performance (for instance, the sales orders processing), the law assumes that only where such form is observed by the parties have they accepted to enter into the contract (Article 223(1) Civil Code).

5.6. Void and Illegal Contracts

A contract is invalid where there exists a lack or irregularity of any essential elements as explained above in 5.4. That is, it cannot be said that a contract is agreed and entered into force if the parties have not agreed on the essential elements constituting the framework of such a contract (for instance, the price in a sale and purchase contract).

The invalidity of a contract may be of one of the following three kinds: (1) non-existence of a contract; (2) nullity; (3) voidability.

A contract is nonexistent when there is no apparent will of the parties or when such will is not relevant for the formation of the envisaged contract.

Nullity and voidability assume that the contract exists, but the required legal elements are not (in whole or in part) in existence or, if they exist, they are not in compliance with the law, i.e., in accordance with a mandatory provision of law establishing a specific element, the content of the contract or a certain form.

The distinction between nullity and voidability is:

- Nullity operates *ipso jure*, that is, it is not required for the innocent party to apply for its acknowledgment and declaration by a court. A contract is null irrespectively of its declaration as such by a court. It operates at any time. There is no time bar to apply for it in court if the innocent party decides to file an action in court to have a public or *inter partes* acknowledgment of the nullity. Finally, it may be invoked by any third interested party.
- The voidable contract is, in principle, valid and it becomes void only if one the parties of the contract or its successors apply for its acknowledgment and declaration by a court. Application must be made within a certain time limit (usually one year as from the date the party knew of the voidability of the contract). Finally, only the interested party of the contract may apply for the court declaration.

Cases of null contracts are, among others, those concerning the non-observation of the required legal form (in writing and, sometimes, notarised) and simulated contracts. Contracts against a mandatory provision of law may be null, entirely, if the nullity concerns the object of the contract (for instance, the sale and purchase of an illegal drug or other illegal goods), or, partly, if only a part of the contract (a specific clause, for instance) is illegal if such clause does not concern the essential elements of the contract.

Cases of voidability are, *inter alia*, contracts entered into by mistake by one party or both parties and others.

Both the declaration of nullity or voidness of a contract by a court operate retroactively as if the contract was not entered into, except in the case of continuing performance of the contract (the supply agreement for instance) as to the effects already produced.

5.7. Privity

In principle, a contract relates and is effective only between the respective parties and successors (Article 406 Civil Code). However, the following are exceptions:

- The parties may attribute *erga omnes* effectiveness to certain contracts (i.e. those contracts having as their object an asset of which ownership is subject to registration – real estate, cars, aircrafts and ships). This is the case, not only for the respective sale and purchase agreement or donation agreement, but also for preliminary contracts (*contratos-promessa*) or agreements establishing pre-emptive rights.
- A contract may be in favour of a third party, for example, a contract under which one party undertakes towards the other to give a benefit to a third party (certain insurance contracts are of this type).
- One party may be entitled to appoint another person to perform the contract.

5.8. Interpretation

The Civil Code follows the doctrine based on the impression that the statement produced in the addressee's mind.

The relevant provision of law establishing the interpretation rule is Article 236 which provides for the following regime.

The contractual statement is effective within the sense that a normal (ideal) addressee, if placed in the real addressee's position, should deduce from the declarant's behaviour, except if such interpretation cannot be reasonably ascribed to the declarant under the circumstances.

If there exists doubt about the interpretation to follow, the valid interpretation is the one which should lead to a more balanced conclusion. In formal contracts (i.e., written contracts) only such declarations are valid which have a minimal basis in the contract wording, even though it may be imperfectly expressed.

The filling of contractual gaps is made by the court based on the hypothetical will that the parties would have had if they had foreseen the gap when entering into the contract or, alternatively (in the discretion of the court), in accordance with *bona fide* principles if this solution is preferable.

5.9. Frustration and Force Majeure

There is unfulfilment of a contractual obligation whenever a duty of a party is not fulfilled in a suitable way.

An obligation may not be accomplished due to a fact attributable to any party or due to *force majeure*. A party obliged to accomplish an obligation is discharged from his liability if the accomplishment became impossible (not only delayed) due to a cause attributable to the other party or *force majeure*.

Force majeure is usually considered as an effective cause attributable to natural forces or to a third party which impedes the accomplishment of the contract.

5.10. Breach of Contract

The basic principle is that the party who undertakes to accomplish an obligation is liable for the consequences of the unfulfilment if he has acted in fault against the law or contract. The unfulfilment can be definitive (in fact or even if the interest of the other party to the contract cannot be satisfied any more) or transitional (a mere delay or a defective fulfilment).

An assumption of fault by the obliged party is established by law which means, in practical terms, that the burden of proof that there is no fault is on him.

He is liable: (1) if he acted with fault (*culpa*); (2) if the innocent party has suffered damages; (3) if a link is established between those damages and the action or omission of the obliged party.

The law allows penalty clauses or liquidated damage clauses within reasonable terms, which may be reduced by the court if too excessive charges are established in practice.

Definitive unfulfilment (the unfulfilment that is not a mere delay or a defective performance) entitles the innocent party to terminate the contract and to indemnity.

The termination of a contract implies the restitution of everything that has been delivered by one party to the other, except in case of continuing performance, as it is the case of the supply agreement, in relation to the effects already produced in full.

A mere delay or a defective performance does not entitle the innocent party to terminate the contract, but to claim for indemnity (that in case of money is only the respective interest, except where the parties have agreed otherwise) and to demand the performance of the contract in full. However, the innocent party may lose its interest in the contract as a result of the delay. In such a case he must fix a reasonable term for the other party to fulfil the obligation subject to termination if he continues in default.

Portuguese law provides the following main remedies in favour of a party who undertakes to accomplish an obligation towards the other party:

- exception of non-fulfilment of the contract when the other party does not accomplish at the same time (*exceptio non adimpleti contractus*) which is only invokable in case of mutual obligations to be accomplished by the parties at the same time;
- a lien which entitles a party obliged to deliver certain goods to refrain from such delivery until the other party accomplishes the respective obligation;

- finally, the exceptional termination or modification of the contract based on abnormal changes in the circumstances of the contract whenever its fulfilment is against the *bona fide* principle and it is not covered by the normal risk of such a contract.

6. Standard Contract Terms

Portuguese law regulates the standard contract terms or the so-called General Terms and Conditions of Contract.

First of all, it is necessary to distinguish between the contractual relations between a party acting professionally as a merchant and the other party as a non-merchant (or the consumer or end user), on the one hand, and between merchants, on the other hand.

The general principle is, however, in both cases this: the general terms and conditions against *bona fide* are null and void.

The following clauses, *inter alia* (as general clauses on terms and conditions), are in all cases null and void:

(1) Excluding or limiting liability: for damage to person; in tort; for unfulfilment, delay in fulfilment or defective fulfilment of contract where there exists fraud or gross negligence; for acts practised by employees or others hired by one party, where there exists fraud or gross negligence.
(2) Excluding or limiting the retaining right under the law.
(3) Excluding the right of any party (1) to refuse to fulfil his obligation whilst the other party does not also fulfil the contract whenever both obligations must be accomplished simultaneously or (2) to terminate the contract based on unfulfilment by the other party in accordance with the contract or the law; the statutory right to set-off.
(4) Clauses granting to the party who has proposed the General Terms and Conditions the right to assign the contract or only the debts to third parties and to subcontract without the prior agreement of the other party unless the identification of the third party is mentioned in the contract.

The following clauses, *inter alia*, are merely voidable:

(1) Establishing in favour of the party who has proposed the General Terms and Conditions: excessive terms for the acceptance or refusal of any proposal to contract; excessive terms for the fulfilment without delay of contractual obligations; excessive liquidated damages in proportion to suffered damages; assumptions of delivery or acceptance of goods based on insufficient facts.
(2) Electing: a court to settle disputes raising serious difficulties for the other party without justification of the interests involved; a law applicable to the contract causing serious inconvenience to the other party based on less important interests of the party.

As to the relations between merchants (producers, distributors) and end users or consumers in general the following general terms and conditions, *inter alia*, are null and void:

- clauses in favour of those who have proposed or prepared the general terms and conditions of contract;
- limiting or amending obligations previously established in a contract (for instance, in the sales contract);
- granting, directly or indirectly, the exclusive right of checking and establishing the quality of the goods or services supplied;
- allowing non-correspondence between the obligations to be performed and the indications, specifications or samples made or shown before entering into the contract;
- altering the legal provisions in respect of the burden of proof and of the risk of loss.

7. Different Types of Business Arrangements

7.1. Sponsorship Agreement

This agreement is not especially regulated by Portuguese law and for this reason the general contractual statutory provisions of contract laid down in the Civil Code are applied.

Thus, the law allows that the parties establish all clauses they wish to establish provided that they are not against any mandatory legal provision.

7.2. Merchandising

The same as under 7.1.

7.3. Endorsement

The endorsement agreement entered into with athletes within the limitations established by the sporting authorities and clubs is legally allowed.

Restrictions are practically non-existent when the athletes are not bound to a club.

Also, there are no specific statutory regulations for this kind of agreement.

7.4. Commissioning Agreement

The same as in 7.1 above.

7.5. *Franchises*

Although franchising has grown substantially in Portugal during the last few years, the law does also not contain any special rules relating to franchise agreements, which are, therefore, subject to the general contractual law. Every usual provision of a franchise agreement will be allowed provided that it is not against the law, i.e., the freedom of the parties to contract and to engage in a lawful business is respected.

Portuguese law allows the franchisor to terminate the contract for fair cause if the franchisee is bankrupt, and the franchisor is not bound to deal with the trustee in bankruptcy of the franchisee.

7.6. *Films and Videos*

Production of films or video records is not statutorily regulated. Such contracts generally contain the agreed budget, the terms of validity and the renouncing by the producer of any future interests and rights.

7.7. *Public Appearances*

Particularly relevant in this kind of business arrangements is the agreement of the parties on the causes of termination of the contract and liquidated damages clauses in certain situations, such as unjustified absence from public events provided for in the contract.

7.8. *Suppliership*

The same as in 7.1 above.

8. The Rights

Beyond the basic contractual terms and conditions usually laid down in a sports marketing contract, a party is free to grant specific rights to the other party, in accordance with the above-mentioned sub-principle of freedom of stipulation.

8.1. *Options*

The option allows the sponsor to extend the contract which is of great importance when, for example, the up-front investment is substantial.

The specific structure of this right must be carefully outlined by the parties and laid down in writing.

8.2. Pre-emption

Pre-emption is the agreement according to which a party is obliged to, in equal circumstances, choose someone (the other party or a third party) to enter into a contract, provided that the obliged party has decided to enter into that contract (Art. 414 CC).

The pre-emption is different from the option as the former foresees a new contract which is the object of the pre-emption, and in the latter the contractual statement of one party during the formation of the contract was already produced.

As with the option, the pre-emption must be laid down in writing.

Having decided to enter into the contract that is the object of the pre-emption, the grantor must communicate to the grantee the project of the contract, i.e., all the clauses of the contract. If the grantee decides to enter into the contract he has a term of 8 days to inform the grantor of his decision, unless a longer term was agreed by the parties.

8.3. Exclusivity

The exclusivity right, granted in various kinds of contracts, allows the grantee to exercise the right in a exclusive manner.

It is particularly relevant to define the geographical area in which the exclusive right will be exercised and, on the other hand, the period of time of this exclusiveness.

The only possible restrictions regarding the granting of exclusive rights are those related with infringements of free competition.

8.4. Copyright Licence

No specific rules apply to copyright licences regarding sports contracts.

8.5. Trademark Licence

No specific rules apply to trademark licences in a sports marketing agreement.

8.6. Territory

The rights deriving from a sports marketing contract usually are limited to a specific geographical area.

8.7. Media

It is legally possible to license the same intellectual property rights to different entities.

8.8. Product Classes

It is very important to define as accurately as possible the products that will be sponsored (e.g., clothes, drinks).

8.9. Duration

The term of the contract must be the object of the agreement of the parties as well as the cases that may imply the dissolution of the contract before the expiration of the term agreed (just cause).

8.10. Post Termination Arrangements/Restrictions

Any contractual obligations that will remain in force after the termination of the contract should be expressly provided in the agreement.

9. Financial Terms

As to the fulfilment of the clauses regarding the payment of the amounts involved in the contract, the parties should agree on the following points:

- payment terms (foregoing payments, payment in instalments, lump sum payment);
- payment method;
- payment dates;
- currency;
- rate of interest on late payment.

10. Insurance Aspects

It is advisable to cover the risks that may arise from the sports marketing contract, for example: public liability; product liability; cancellation of sports events.

11. Advertising and Promotion

The two principal statutes regarding advertising activities are the Decree-Law No. 330/90, dated 23 October 1990 (*Código da Publicidade*) and the Law No. 97/88, dated 17 August 1988 (which rules the affixing and inscription of advertisements).

In accordance with Article 6 of the Advertising Code, this activity is ruled by the following principles:

11.1. Principle of Lawfulness

Advertising whose form, object or purpose infringes the principles of the Portuguese Constitution is forbidden. Consequently, it is not legally possible (1) to produce any advertisement that does not consider the dignity of the human being and (2) to use, without the necessary authorisation, the image and/or speech of someone.

It is only allowed to use foreign languages when the advertisement is exclusively or principally directed to foreigners (this rule is frequently disregarded).

11.2. Principle of Identification

The advertisements must be unequivocally identified as such, whatever the form used. Occult or hidden advertising is consequently forbidden.

11.3. Principle of Truthfulness

The advertising must respect the truth and not corrupt the facts. All the statements have to be exact and, at any time, admit expert evidence. Deceitful advertising is forbidden.

11.4. Principle of Respect for the Consumer's Rights

The advertising must not violate the consumer's rights, for example, by stimulating harmful behaviour.

The law establishes the following restrictions as to the contents of the advertisement:

- advertisements directed to children must take into account their psychological vulnerability;
- advertisements employing testimonies must be trustful and provable.

11.5. Comparative Advertising

Comparative advertising is not allowed.

11.6. Alcohol, Tobacco, and Pharmaceuticals

The advertising of alcoholic beverages is subject to some limitations. The law does not allow the advertisement of alcoholic beverages directed to minor children and it is only possible to advertise these products on TV and radio between 9.30 p.m. and 7 a.m.

Advertisements for tobacco are forbidden.

The advertising of medicines, which are only available with a prescription, is forbidden.

11.7. Sponsoring Audiovisual Media

The Decree-Law No. 330/90 defines sponsorship as the activity performed by individuals or companies financing any audio-visual works, series, reports, independently of the vehicle used on its diffusion, aiming to promote its name or image.

The companies having as their main activity the manufacture or sale of tobacco or medicines are not allowed to be sponsors of TV programmes.

The contents and scheduling of a broadcast cannot be influenced by the sponsor in order to avoid any infringement of the editorial responsibility and independence.

The sponsored programmes must not incite the acquisition of the products or services of the sponsor or of a third party, e.g., by means of specific promotional references.

11.8. Affixing

The Decree-Law No. 97/88 rules the affixing and inscription of advertisements. In accordance with this statute, advertisements must obey the rules of the *Código da Publicidade* and depend on previous licensing by the town hall of the area concerned.

12. The Venue

12.1. Control

The stadia are usually the property of the State (town halls) or owned by the clubs. Ownership of the stadia allows the owner their unlimited use and enjoyment.

The stadia are subject to the same rules applicable to all urban edifications, not only in relation to their construction but also to their necessary and continuous maintenance. Consequently, the State may prohibit some edifications and impose the accomplishment of maintenance works. In the latter case, failing the performance of such works, the authorities may decide to close the stadium (this happened during the Summer of 1992 with the stadium of a leading club of Lisbon).

12.2. Access and Accreditation

The access to the stadium is controlled by the organiser of the event, usually the owner. This control is sometimes defective (e.g., normally it is not possible to know the exact number of spectators and, worst of all, it is common, with the major sports events, to sell more tickets than the site permits).

The media have free access, although with the limitations defined by the organiser, on a case by case basis.

12.3. Public Liability

The liability of the organisers of sports events is subject to the general rules of civil liability laid down in the Civil Code.

12.4. Concessions

The sponsors of sports events – exclusive or not – usually have the right to display their products at the site and, if intending to do so, offer free samples.

It is not common in Portugal to have only one sponsor of a sports event. Usually there are several sponsors in relation to different classes of products.

13. Dispute Resolution

13.1. Court Procedure

As said above at p. 280, the jurisdiction of the civil courts includes all matters relating to civil and commercial law. All civil and commercial cases have a monetary value – the amount involved in the case – which establishes:

- which court takes jurisdiction within the first instance courts (*Tribunal de Comarca* or *Tribunal de Círculo*);
- the possibility of appeal;
- the basis of calculation of the court's legal fees.

The lawsuit is commenced by the initial pleading which is filed in a *Tribunal de Comarca* or in a *Tribunal de Círculo*. Once the writ of summons is served the defendant has a specific time period to produce the statement of defence. In some particular cases, the plaintiff is entitled to present a reply to the statement of defence.

Third parties are allowed to intervene in a specific pending lawsuit either on their own initiative or if called on to do so by the original litigants.

Every pleading should be in writing and contain a detailed recital of the facts and a brief conclusion on the relevant and applicable rules of law. The lawyer should prepare the pleadings and conduct every step requiring the intervention of his client.

13.2. Injunctions

A set of injunctions are provided for in Portuguese law which are in general very simple and quick. Some of them do not admit the preliminary intervention of the defendant and are adjudicated by the court without the prior notification of the defendant in order to avoid the injunction becoming useless. Types of injunction include the seizure of assets (*arresto*) which is used whenever there exists a real threat of the debtor's assets disappearing before the claimant can obtain enforcement of a judgment within the jurisdiction of the Portuguese courts.

13.3. Action for an Agreed Sum

The legal actions aiming to recover outstanding amounts do not follow any specific type of proceedings and general law is applicable. Nevertheless, generally the defendant fails to produce any statement of defence and this fact will imply faster proceedings as all the facts alleged by the plaintiff in the initial pleading will be considered proved.

13.4. Costs

The court fee is a fixed amount calculated by reference to the monetary value of the action, usually the amount claimed.

In general, each party pays 25 per cent of the fee on issuing and answering a claim. The other 25 per cent each is usually paid before the trial.

The losing party is liable for the payment of the legal costs. A winning party will only pay such costs as are deemed not reasonably incurred.

The advance payments for legal costs made by the winning party are refunded by the court automatically. Other expenses of the party (claimant or defendant) directly connected with the lawsuit (excluding the lawyer's fees) have to be claimed.

13.5. Arbitration

The parties may normally refer disputes to arbitration in substitution for trial (except in certain family law cases). The parties may apply for arbitration even where a lawsuit is pending.

The arbitrator is selected by mutual agreement of the parties. If no agreement is reached, each party will appoint one or more arbitrators and these will choose the trial arbitrator to complete the constitution of the arbitration panel. The panel always consist of an odd number of arbitrators.

The decision of an arbitrator or panel is binding on all parties to the arbitration.

If the parties have decided not to renounce their right to appeal against the decision of the arbitrators, the decision of the arbitrators' panel is deemed equivalent to a judgment adjudication by a first instance court and the rules relating to appeals are the same.

13.6. Alternative Dispute Resolution

Beyond court procedures and arbitration there is no other kind of dispute resolution provided for in the Portuguese law.

13.7. Enforcement of Judgments and Arbitral Awards

The enforcement of judgments is possible, in general terms, when the judgment has become *res judicata*. It includes every form of execution needed to accomplish the judicial order, including the attachment of assets and other compulsory measures. Enforcement is also possible where an appeal has not been accepted by the court as suspensive of the enforcement.

However, the executory proceedings will stop as soon as the attachment of assets is completed in cases where an appeal is lodged against the judgment.

Foreign judgments, i.e., those issued by a foreign court, may be enforced in Portugal after obtaining an '*exequatur*' from a *Tribunal da Relação* (court of appeal). Irrespective of the multilateral conventions or some of the bilateral treaties on this matter, Portuguese civil procedure accepts every foreign judgment previously recognised by a *Tribunal da Relação*.

The same rule applies to the enforcement of arbitration awards. Every award may be accepted provided that an '*exequatur*' has been granted.

The Russian Federation

by Dr. Robert Starr

1. Sports Marketing – A Developing Business

With the dissolution of the USSR in December 1991 and the emergence of non-communist independent States in its wake, every area of society has been affected. New systems are slowly emerging, and the future political, economic and social structures of the States of the former USSR are difficult to predict at this time, when so much is in flux. This is particularly true in the Russian Federation ('RF').

The demise of communism, and the move towards a market economy in the RF, has had profound implications for the sports industry in that country. Although reliable statistics are not available, it may be expected that, if present trends continue, the sports industry in the RF will evolve in a radically different way than under the administrative-command economic system of the past.

Sports marketing in the USSR traditionally involved the following areas: (i) organisation of sports events, including negotiation and execution of contracts between the organiser and the venue, the organiser and sports figures, and in some cases the organiser and other entities holding exclusive rights to sports figures, (ii) arranging for billboard advertising of events (iii) sales by organisers of 'neighbouring rights' to television and radio stations, and (iv) production and sale of merchandise relating to events and athletes.

Typically, organisers would give a percentage of the ticket proceeds to the venue in exchange for lease of the venue. The percentage would depend, among other factors, upon whether the provider of the venue received a percentage of the takings from food and beverage concessions.

In the past, the use of television and radio rights was very undeveloped. In part this was because the USSR would typically exchange (rather than sell) rights with other countries, usually in Eastern Europe. The television system was subsidised by the State, and, to a large extent, this still seems to be the case today. It was uncommon for organisations to buy rights to broadcast sports events. More typically, these would be exchanged for advertisements on television, or would be passed back in the form of a sharing of advertising revenues. This area was unregulated and was governed by complex contractual arrangements.

Practices in these areas are in flux, as market mechanisms take root. New legislation in such areas as trademark and copyright (discussed below) will have a major impact on the evolution of sports marketing as a business in the RF.

2. Overview of the Legal System and Applicable Law

The RF Constitution that is presently in force was originally enacted in 1978 and amended subsequently. A new Constitution is currently under active consideration, but, in view of the current political situation, it is difficult to predict when it might be adopted. It is important to note that the RF is a federation: it encompasses a number of republics and other levels of administration, including krais, oblasts, autonomous oblasts and autonomous regions.

The RF and the other States of the former Soviet Union have had to decide how to deal with the question of the validity of legislation of the former USSR. The RF has taken the view that such legislation will continue to be considered in force to the extent that it is not contrary to the Constitution of the RF or RF legislation adopted after 12 June 1991 (the date of a 'Declaration of Sovereignty' by the RF).

Likewise, the RF has indicated that it will respect and consider as continuing in force in the RF the multilateral treaties to which the USSR was a party, as well as those bilateral treaties to which the USSR was a party that would be of interest to most foreign companies, such as tax and trade and investment protection treaties.

A new legal system to support the introduction of a market economy is fast emerging. It is radically different from that which existed in the communist era. In July 1992, the Supreme Soviet of the RF decided that, pending the adoption of a new RF Civil Code, the 1991 Fundamental Principles of Civil Legislation of the USSR and Republics (which had not yet entered into force in the USSR) would be accepted and adopted into the legal system of the RF to the extent that the Fundamental Principles were not contrary to the RF Constitution and RF legislation enacted after 12 June 1991.

These Fundamental Principles reflect a modern, market-orientated approach to civil law, in keeping with the approach followed in other countries that have adopted a 'codified' (as opposed to a common law) system.

The Civil Code of 1964, which some observers believe was a servile tool of socialist planning, remains in effect to the extent that it is not contrary to RF legislation adopted after 12 June 1991, and other legally binding rules in effect in the RF.

In contrast to certain other formerly communist countries such as Poland and Czechoslovakia, the RF has not sought to adopt a separate commercial code to regulate relations in the commercial sphere.

Numerous laws have been adopted over the last several years governing such matters as company law, property, taxation, banking and currency, import-export, insurance, anti-monopoly and other areas.

As in most other countries, there is no one particular body of law in the RF specifically applicable to sports marketing. However, a number of enactments (including laws, decrees, presidential edicts, ministerial decisions, instructions and other so-called 'normative acts'), would apply to different aspects of sports marketing.

Broadly speaking, the relationships between the parties to business arrangements involving sports, whether sponsorship agreements, supplier arrangements or the sale or licensing of different rights, are generally governed by the relevant provisions of the applicable civil law, which allows considerable freedom of contract. Particular aspects of sports marketing will, in addition, be subject to special legislation in such areas as trademarks and copyright.

3. Intellectual Property Rights

The intellectual property rights that are perhaps most relevant to sports marketing in the RF are trademarks and copyright. These are discussed in some detail below. Protection of trade secrets is also noted.

As part of the sweeping legal reforms enacted in the last year of the USSR's existence, a comprehensive series of laws were enacted on intellectual property matters, including a law on inventions, a law on trademarks and service marks, and a law on industrial models (in addition to the provisions on intellectual property contained in the Fundamental Principles). Only one of these laws came into force before the demise of the USSR, the law on inventions.

After much discussion, four important new laws on intellectual property came into force in the RF in October 1992: a new patent law; a new law on trademarks, service marks and origin names of goods; a law on legal protection of computer programmes and databases; and a law on legal protection of topographies of integrated micro-circuits. A new law on copyright is still under preparation.

On the international level, the RF has acceded to all the international conventions and agreements to which the Soviet Union had been a party in this field, including the Paris Convention for the Protection of Industrial Property and the Universal Copyright Convention. It is understood that the RF will adhere to the Berne Convention for the Protection of Literary and Artistic Works when the status of the Russian copyright legislation is resolved.

3.1. Trademarks and Service marks

Under the law on trademarks and service marks, there is to be legal protection for marks that are registered and certified for inclusion in a State trademark registry. There is also provision for protection of so-called 'collective trademarks' and 'product place of origin', concepts not recognised under former Soviet law.

Registration is with the RF patent authority, in a procedure similar to that provided for registration for patents.

Once registered, a trademark is protected for ten years, with registration renewable every ten years. Applications for renewal must be submitted during the final year of validity.

Priority can be established by various means: filing a complete application with the patent authority; filing an original application in a country that is a member of the Paris Convention (provided that the Russian application is submitted to the RF patent authority within six months of that date); conditions set in international agreements; and other means.

The law permits the involuntary termination of a registration if a mark is not used continuously for five years from date of registration or five years preceding the submission of a claim.

The law deals with sanctions for infringement, and contemplates further legislation in this regard. It is premature to judge whether the law in its present form offers prompt and effective relief from infringements. It allows for removal and destruction of infringing trademarks, for example, but the right to destroy and seize counterfeit goods remains untested.

In 1992, a Russian Agency for International Property (RAIIS) was created, and the USSR State Agency for Copyright and Related Rights (VAAP) was transformed into an agency of the RF.

Although the new RAIIS will not enjoy monopoly rights (authors will be free to conclude whatever commercial arrangements they choose with publishers and producers), the RAIIS is likely to play an important role in administering authors' and related rights, and in other areas.

3.2. Copyright

As noted above, the RF presently has no separate law on copyright. For the time being, questions of copyright are regulated by Section IV of the Fundamental Principles.

The Fundamental Principles increase the level of copyright protection to Berne Convention level, but not to the level of the more recent draft US-USSR trade agreement. Computer software was protected under the Fundamental Principles, but only to the extent published after 1991. This protection has been supplemented by the recently adopted laws on protection of computer programmes and databases, and on protection of micro-circuitry, mentioned above.

In order for a work to enjoy copyright protection in the RF, no registration or compliance with other formalities is required at present. A work's copyright is separate from the right of ownership of the actual object in which the work is expressed.

The author of a work, who is recognised as the owner of the corresponding copyright, is 'the citizen by whose creative work it was created'. Copyright operates for the entire life of the author and fifty years after death. Protection of authorship, the name of an author and the inviolability of a work extends in perpetuity. The author of a work enjoys exclusive rights to the work. The author may transfer such rights, within or outside Russia, to any natural or legal person (including foreigners).

One feature of the provisions of the Fundamental Principles on copyright is that, unlike earlier legislation, there are special provisions regarding public performance and protection of cinema, television and video rights. The list of items subject to copyright specifically includes 'all dramatic and musical works with or without text, musical dramas and theatrical works, audio-visual works (cinema, television, or video works) and radio works'.

The Fundamental Principles specifically state that the author's exclusive right to use a work includes, in particular, 'the right to effectuate or authorise its reproduction by any means – in the press, by way of public performance, broadcast, video and sound recording, cable television, with the assistance of satellites or other technical means; . . .reworking of a work; dissemination of copies of the reproduced work; . . . and the like'.

The Fundamental Principles resolved the question of whether rights to cinema, television and video films should belong to producers or authors, by giving such rights to authors.

For the first time, rules are included which provide for protection of contiguous rights (of performers, producers and others). The main features of these rules include:

- The rights to the name, to protect staging and performance against distortion, to effect and authorise a staging or performance, and to remuneration, belong to performing artists, producers, and directors. Recordings of a performance, broadcasts of a performance by radio or television, broadcasts of the recording of a performance, and other use may be made only with the consent of the performer.
- The rights to effect and/or authorise reproduction belong to the creator of the sound or video recording. The use of a sound or video recording is permitted only by authorisation of that person or his successor. The rights to a sound or video recording include the rights of reproduction by any means, public distribution, including transfer abroad, protection against importation and dissemination of examples of the recording without the authorisation of the holder of the right.
- The rights of a creator of a sound or video recording and any broadcasting organisation are governed by their agreement with the author or performer. Performers' rights are subject to the rights of the authors of the works being performed by them.

The contiguous rights provided for by the Fundamental Principles operate for 50 years, calculated from the date of first performance or staging, first publication of the sound or video recording, or first broadcast. The legal successors of the performer or person who created the sound or video recording acquire the rights to authorise the staging, performance and recordings.

Where performers, creators of sound and video recordings, and foreign broadcasting organisations have effected the first staging, performance, recording, or broadcast outside the RF, their rights within the RF are governed by the relevant international treaty to which the RF is a party. This presumably means that foreign owners of neighbouring rights will not be granted national treatment until the RF accedes to the Rome Convention.

The principle is recognised that authors, performers, creators of a sound or video recording, broadcasting organisations, and their legal successors, have the right to seek injunctive relief as well as other remedies, including damages.

3.3. Trade Secrets

Protection granted to trade secrets in the RF marks another step in the RF's move towards a market economy. Historically, know-how and other confidential information could be protected by contract in the USSR, but under the administrative-command system, Soviet enterprises could be obliged to share technology with other entities, and contractual restrictions on the flow of information were difficult to enforce.

A 1990 Law on Enterprises and Entrepreneurial Activity guaranteed enterprises the right to withhold information containing 'commercial secrets' from data which must be delivered to RF authorities for official purposes (e.g. verification of taxes and compilation and processing of economic data).

The Fundamental Principles provide grounds for relief against infringement of trade secrets by third persons. For example, the holder of 'technical organisational or commercial information which comprises a secret of production (or know-how)' has the right to protection against illegal use of the information by third persons, provided that three conditions are met: (i) the information has actual or potential commercial value by virtue of its being unknown to third persons; (ii) there is no free access on legal grounds to the information and (iii) the holder of the information takes appropriate measures to protect its confidentiality. The period of protection extends indefinitely, provided that such conditions continue. The holder has the right to compensation for losses from unlawful use except from those who have acquired the information independently and in good faith. For the present, however, companies should not rely on trade secret protection except in the context of a written contract. Also, it is not clear whether the protection noted above will apply only to 'secrets of production' and, if so, whether commercial information that is not directly related to production (e.g. accounts, management systems, customer lists) will fall within that category.

4. The Contract Generally and Preliminary Agreements

As in many other countries, it is common practice in the RF to enter into a preliminary understanding that is not usually intended to create legally binding obligations on parties.

Such pre-contractual arrangements are typically known as 'protocols' in Russian practice. If the parties do not intend to create legally binding obligations, it is important that this be clearly expressed in any writing. If, on the other hand, certain provisions of a protocol are intended to create legally binding obligations (e.g. regarding exclusive dealing or confidentiality) it is important to clarify the parties' intentions in regard to such matters.

A curious new principle has been included in the Fundamental Principles regarding so-called 'preliminary contracts'. If a written document fulfils the requirements of a preliminary contract, and one of the parties to the preliminary contract fails to conclude the contract provided for therein, the other party might have legal redress.

The civil law rules reflected in the Fundamental Principles as regards contracts are part of the general provisions on obligations.

The rules with respect to such issues as offer and acceptance, form and execution, void and illegal contracts, interpretation of contracts, breach of contract, and other matters are – broadly speaking – in keeping with modern practices in other civil law jurisdictions. Some features of Russian law in this regard are worthy of note. For example, in contrast to certain common law jurisdictions, penalty provisions that go beyond mere 'liquidated damages' are not uncommon and are likely to be enforceable.

The form of an agreement generally is subject to the law of the place in which the agreement was concluded. However, an agreement concluded outside the RF might not be deemed void simply because it fails to comply with a foreign jurisdiction's requirements as to form, if the requirements of Russian law as to form are complied with. In foreign economic transactions concluded by Russian natural or legal persons, irrespective of the place in which the contract was concluded, the requirements as to form are governed by Russian law.

Under Russian law, the rights and duties of the parties with respect to a transaction are determined by the law of the place where it was concluded, unless the parties have otherwise agreed; the place of concluding a transaction is determined according to Russian law.

In foreign economic transactions, the parties are free to select a governing law, and in the absence of such agreement, the applicable law under Russian civil law principles would depend on the type of transaction: in the case of a purchase-sale contract, it would be the law of the seller; in a licensing agreement, it would typically be the law of the country of the licensor; in a contract of agency, it would be the law of the country of the agent.

Where unjust enrichment has occurred, the law of the country where this has occurred is to apply to obligations as a consequence of unjust enrichment.

Many non-Russian companies have participated in the creation of so-called 'joint enterprises' in Russia (whether in the form of stock companies or otherwise). It is questionable whether the parties to a contract concerning the creation of such a joint enterprise can exclude the application of Russian law.

Special legislation may also limit the freedom of the parties to stipulate governing law in other matters, such as land use rights.

5. Negotiating Sports Marketing Agreements

In preparing a contract relating to sports marketing it would be important to know whether the contract will be governed by the rules applicable to foreign economic transactions, and the identities of the parties to the proposed transaction. These issues have particular relevance in connection with decisions regarding applicable law and dispute settlement.

With few exceptions, the USSR was not a party to any bilateral or multilateral treaty concerning the recognition or enforcement of foreign court judgments, and it was common practice in agreements between Soviet and foreign parties to provide for arbitration as a means of settling disputes. The Soviet Union was a party to the 1958 New York Convention on the Recognition and Enforcement of Foreign Arbitral Awards as well as the 1961 European Convention on International Commercial Arbitration, and it appears that the RF considers itself bound by these treaties as well.

In the absence of a bilateral or multilateral intergovernmental agreement regarding enforcement of foreign court judgments, it may be expected that attempts to enforce a foreign court judgment in the RF could give rise to serious legal and practical problems.

For these reasons, contracts with RF partners typically provide for arbitration as a means of settling disputes. This may be either institutional or *ad hoc*. Western companies generally prefer to avoid arbitration in Russia, and Russian parties will usually readily agree to arbitration in a Western country (e.g. Stockholm and Vienna).

If a proposed contract involves rights claimed by a Russian organisation, the foreign party would be well advised to exercise as much 'due diligence' as is reasonably possible under the circumstances. There have been numerous cases where foreigners have 'acquired' rights from Russian organisations, only to learn later, to their dismay, that the same 'rights' had also been 'sold' to other parties. The foreign party should also make appropriate enquiries to determine whether authorisations or permissions may be required. This issue may be particularly troublesome if State property is involved.

In some sports marketing arrangements there may be a need to refer to accounting principles. Russian accounting principles are evolving rapidly from those in force previously, under the old administrative-command economic system. Nonetheless, considerable differences remain between current Russian accounting principles and generally recognised accounting principles in the West. Any business arrangements that may be dependent on determinations such as 'net profit' and the like should be careful to clarify the basis upon which such concepts are to be construed.

Numerous contract issues arise, depending on the type of arrangements under consideration.

Price, payment and other financial terms are nearly always central issues in any negotiation. Western companies should be wary of establishing a contract price before all details are fully agreed.

The Russian ruble enjoys only limited convertibility and the use of foreign currency, as well as settlement of obligations in foreign currency in the RF, is subject to special legislation, including rules established by the Central Bank of Russia.

The parties are also well advised to investigate the possible applicability of import/export licensing requirements, quotas, tariffs, and taxes such as VAT. Any arrangements involving escrow or other accounts to be established outside the RF might involve requirements for obtaining Russian Central Bank permission. The same would apply to grants of credits to RF companies (trade-related credits of 180 days or less are excluded from this requirement) under current regulations. There are significant legal constraints affecting barter and other types of transactions, and these should be investigated at an early stage if such transactions are contemplated.

Force majeure clauses are common in Russian contracts. In the past, two types of events were often a subject of difficulty: industrial disputes, and acts of government authorities (e.g. granting any required export or import licenses).

As Russian contract partners move away from the standard type contracts that were typical in Soviet foreign trade, it may be expected that there will be increasing scope for negotiating contract provisions tailored to the business realities, and reflecting international practices. Foreign companies should be aware, however, that doing business in Russia presents special challenges. They face a uniquely untested and particularly fluid legal and regulatory environment, with a constant stream of new laws, often inconsistent with existing legislation and sometimes given retroactive effect.

There are also gaps in the legal rules that make planning and financial assumptions difficult indeed. These are particularly problematical issues if an investment in Russia is contemplated. Certain areas of law are as yet highly undeveloped or untested, e.g. antitrust, anti-monopoly, consumer protection, environment regulation, securities regulation, intellectual property protection, and secured lending. If a business deal is contemplated in Russia involving a State-owned partner or State assets the foreign company will also have to consider the impact of privatisation legislation.

A new series of State agencies are now charged with managing State property and developing rules for the privatisation of enterprises in the RF on a scale never before experienced. State enterprises are now required to be self-sufficient. It is far from clear how quickly or smoothly this process will proceed, particularly in the face of political changes.

If a foreign company is considering a joint venture with a State-owned entity, it will want to identify and approve its future partners, and clarify future rights to assets previously under the control of the State entity (e.g., property rights). The need to address such concerns marks a fundamental departure from the *perestroika* period.

The government has opted for a mass privatisation programme, involving the creation and distribution of vouchers. However, the emphasis thus far has been on '*corporatisation*' of State-owned entities (i.e., their transformation into stock companies), and the future of the current privatisation programme is far from clear.

Foreign companies involved in a privatisation project will want to consider carefully any potential environmental liabilities and all existing rights and obligations of the local enterprise, particularly if the enterprise continues to be bound under the old system of 'State orders'. The fiduciary role of the relevant State property agencies and funds, the rights of workers and collectives, and the probable introduction of investment funds all pose substantial legal and management issues requiring careful attention. Particularly if certain shareholdings are reserved for future voucher holders, investment funds, or the State itself, foreign investors may need to identify and approve their future partners and rights to key assets of the enterprise.

In acquisitions of shares in a State-owned enterprise, balance sheet restructuring is usually a required exercise. Uncollectable or unwanted assets may need to be written down, obligations to works quantified, and the maintenance costs of non revenue-producing assets of a social infrastructural nature carefully examined. There may be limitations on the ability to dispose of unwanted or unprofitable assets. Profit and loss projections should reflect the uncertain market conditions, including the effects of inflation, currency restrictions, shortages of supply or transport, or other factors that could materially have an impact on profitability.

6. Tax Aspects

Many arrangements related to sports marketing are likely to be affected by applicable tax rules. In some cases, the tax considerations could be paramount. For example, under current RF law, certain gaming revenues may be subject to a 70% tax on revenues (not profits). Profits from so-called 'mass spectacles' in public squares, stadia, sports palaces and other venues with capacity in excess of 2,000 places are subject to a 50% tax.

Broadly speaking, RF law provides for taxation at three levels: federation taxes; taxes of the republics, krais, oblasts, autonomous oblasts and autonomous regions; and local taxes. Federation taxes include: VAT; excise taxes; tariffs; payments for the use of natural resources; income and profit taxes from enterprises; income taxes from citizens; various types of fees; and taxes on property.

Regional taxes (republics, oblasts, and so on) include a tax on the property of enterprises and payments for use of resources. Local taxes include taxes on property of natural persons, land taxes, registration fees and resort fees, among others.

Taxpayers who conceal taxable income or otherwise violate tax laws are subject to fines. The authorities also have the right in certain cases to prohibit activities of taxpayers guilty of violations and seek the liquidation of enterprises violating tax laws.

There is a general enterprise (or corporate) profits tax rate of 32%, with a 45% tax on profits from 'middleman' operations. These rules generally apply to branches of foreign companies as well as to Russian enterprises. The representative office of a foreign company in the RF, if it engages in commercial activity, will be taxed as a branch. Dividends, interests and revenues from share participation in enterprises with foreign investment are subject to a 15% withholding tax. Other forms of revenue (e.g., royalties, leasing income) are generally subject to a 20% withholding tax, which may be significantly reduced or completely eliminated under applicable tax treaties.

As currently applied, there is a top marginal tax individual rate of 40% on a very broad tax base (income over 600,000 rubles).

Foreign citizens present in the RF for fewer than 183 days in any calendar year are considered to be non-resident and will not be taxable in the RF on their employment-related income within or without the RF (if paid from non-Russian sources). Investment income from non-Russian sources is also exempt. Conversely, subject to applicable tax treaties, presence in the RF for 183 days or more in any calendar year constitutes permanent residency for tax purposes and triggers taxation on world-wide income.

Foreign citizens expecting to become tax residents must register with the tax authorities within 30 days after their arrival and must file a declaration with the same authorities more than 30 days prior to departure. Resident foreigners are also required to report their world-wide income to the RF authorities during the period of their residence.

In view of the significance of RF taxation for foreign citizens working in the RF, tax planning to mitigate the impact of RF taxes is an important consideration.

A number of other taxes may have a significant impact on business operations in Russia. The principal taxes of general interest include VAT and import and export tariffs.

Effective January 1993, VAT applies to sales of most goods and services at a 20% rate. Special rates apply to some items (e.g. foodstuffs) and certain items are exempt from VAT.

A complex array of import and/or export tariffs may affect sports marketing operations. Under recent import tariff rules adopted by Presidential edicts, import tariffs comprise a percentage of the customs valuation of imported goods. The new tariffs, in force from July 1992, initially ranged from 10–25% of value for a variety of specified products (including alcoholic beverages, video and audio equipment, automobiles) and 5% for all other non-specified products. However, these were subsequently increased to a 20–50% range for specified products, with a general rate for non-specified items of 15%, effective 1 September 1992. Products not originating from a country enjoying most favoured nation (MFN) treatment in the RF are subject to double the stated tariff rates. Products originating in developing countries listed in the tariff rates are duty free or subject to half the MFN duty. Products originating in other States of the Commonwealth of Independent States (CIS) are not exempt.

USSR Customs rules continue in force except to the extent that they may be contrary to RF rules.

Individuals entering the RF may bring in duty-free items whose aggregate value is less than US$10,000.

Under a 1991 law on foreign investment, items imported as capital contributions of foreign investors in Russian enterprises, items designated for material production of such enterprises, and items imported for personal use by foreign employees of enterprises with foreign investment are entitled to certain exemptions from customs duties.

Export tariffs apply to a number of goods, and there is a 50% surcharge imposed on exports in barter transactions.

In addition, excise, property, land and other types of taxes and charges may be imposed by different governmental authorities.

It is worth noting that the various regional and local governments may not grant tax privileges on an individual basis and may not impose taxes in addition to or in excess of those of the RF.

There were a number of tax treaties between the USSR and other nations, including Austria, Canada, Cyprus, Denmark, Finland, France, Germany, Italy, Japan, Malaysia, the Netherlands, Norway, South Korea, Spain, Sweden, Switzerland, the United Kingdom and the United States. The RF government has generally recognised the continuing validity of tax and other USSR treaties in the RF, as noted above. Several tax treaties have been negotiated by the RF since the demise of the USSR, including a treaty with the US (which was not yet in force as this chapter was written). The USSR tax treaties typically did not contain anti-treaty shopping provisions. Variations in these treaties should be taken into account by a foreign party in determining where to base its participation in a Russian project and to which country or countries profits will be remitted. A foreign company may also need to consider this aspect of tax planning if its involvement with a Russian project gives rise to other types of income (e.g., interest payments, profits on sales of goods and services to Russia, etc.). The foreign party will normally want to ensure that it obtains the permanent establishment protection offered under most treaties.

The treaty between the USSR and the UK specifically exempted dividends from withholding tax, as did the treaties with Austria, Cyprus and Finland. The USSR tax treaties with other countries, by contrast, permitted a reduced withholding tax on dividends, typically 15%. The US and Swiss treaties did not reduce the otherwise applicable 20% withholding tax on dividends and 15% withholding on distributions from enterprises set up in the USSR.

Most USSR tax treaties exempted royalties from withholding tax. Exceptions include Canada (10%) and Spain (15%). Interest payments by a USSR entity to a foreign entity were also exempt from USSR withholding tax under most treaties, but some treaties only reduced the rate (e.g., Canada (15%), Germany (5%), France (10%)), and special rules apply in other treaties (Italy, USA).

Most USSR tax treaties permitted one country to tax the commercial activities of a resident of the other when that resident had a permanent representation in the country. In connection with foreign sales of Russian-produced products, it should be noted that some jurisdictions impose an additional branch level tax to substitute for the dividend withholding tax which would have been applicable had the business been operated as a subsidiary corporation, and some treaties between those countries and other treaty partners preserve the right of the country to ignore this branch tax. Thus, if the Russian venture conducts sales in a foreign country through a branch office it may be liable to one or two levels of tax in that country. In order to avoid a situation where its income from sales in a foreign country is subject to domestic tax (although a foreign tax credit against Russian tax for foreign taxes paid is generally available), the Russian entity may need to consider establishing a local subsidiary to perform those activities which require a branch operation.

So far the Russian authorities have evidenced some flexibility with respect to tax matters, and the scope for tax planning is becoming clearer. Foreign companies should consider what structure would be most beneficial under the tax regime of their home country. The applicable tax rules may dictate whether to participate directly or through an entity based either in a tax haven or in a country that had a favourable tax treaty with the USSR or, in time, has one with Russia. These tax rules will also affect how to structure contributions to any venture in the RF, and how to take profits.

7. Other Aspects

Product and public liability, insurance and advertising and promotion are considerably underdeveloped in Russia, and Russian law, accordingly, is very much in a state of flux.

8. Dispute Resolution

As to the settlement of disputes, see p. 308.

SPORTS
MARKETING

Spain

by Sonia Cortés
and Rosa Mariá Muñoz

1. Sports Marketing – A Business

The question we are dealing with must be looked at from two distinct points of view:

(a) from the point of view of the companies producing or distributing products which use sporting competitions organised by third parties for promotional purposes, and
(b) from the point of view of the companies which, although having other objects, regularly organise sporting competitions or tournaments for publicity (trials, marathons)

The question posed is not new in Spain, although sport, having always been a public attraction, is ideal for the marketing of companies, in either of the ways set out above.

The most striking development, from this point of view, is the concern of the public authorities for sporting activities, a concern which took concrete form at the constitutional level in the year 1978, the date of the passing of the 'Great Charter'. This gave rise, as will be seen later, to the approval of the recent Sports Act in 1990, replacing a previous Act of 1980 which, in turn, repealed one of 1964.

During 1992 the holding in Barcelona of the Olympic Games has centred attention on the subject we are dealing with. This sporting event, as well as promoting public works (and the resulting contracts for construction companies) for the preparation of the city, has given rise to the participation as sponsors of various important companies in the Olympic Games themselves and to additional sponsorship of parallel activities and programmes.

2. The National Legal System

The Spanish legal system is based on the existence of laws created by the Legislature ('laws' in the strict sense of the word) and rules of an inferior level issued by the Executive ('regulations'). The latter must be in accordance with the laws which they develop and usually have a more specialised content.

It is important to underline that, since 1978, when the Spanish Constitution was passed, the State has been made up of seventeen Autonomous Communities (on a regional scale). These Autonomous Communities are governed by their Statute of Autonomy, which lays down the jurisdictional scope of each of them, notwithstanding the fact that certain matters may, on account of their importance, only be legislated by the State.

Each Autonomous Community has its own legislative body which, on the basis of the laws issued by the State and concerning the matters within its competence, approves its own legislation for that particular regional area. Each Autonomous Community also has an executive which in turn issues regulations on the matters within the jurisdiction of that Community.

On the other hand, judicial power depends on the State and is made up of judges and magistrates, officers who assume their positions by virtue of examinations or public competitions. The main difference between judges and magistrates lies in the fact that, while the first is subject to a court as a unipersonal unit of the same, the magistrate forms part of a tribunal together with other magistrates and these take decisions in a collegiate manner.

The organisation of the courts in Spain is regulated by law in the following manner:

(a) In civil matters, in each court circuit[1] there are one or a number of courts 'of first instance'. Their decisions may be appealed against to the so-called 'Provincial Court' which is situated in the provincial capital for the court which issued the decision. The decisions of the Provincial Court may, in certain cases, be appealed against by way of a final appeal to be made before the Supreme Court (situated in Madrid) or before the Superior Court of Justice of the Autonomous Community involved (situated in the capital of the same) if the provision thought to have been infringed by the decision emanates solely from the Autonomous Community.

Equally it should be pointed out that, depending on the subject-matter of the claim, there are various procedures.

(b) In criminal matters (that is to say, where what is under consideration is a crime) the Courts of Instruction situated in each court circuit are those charged with the carrying out of investigations and the making of statements until the convening of the oral trial, which is carried out in the Criminal Courts (for very obvious crimes or where the public or private

---

1. Court circuits are made up of different towns or cities which are not provincial capitals and those surrounding them. Provincial capitals are always court circuits.

prosecutor's requested sentence does not exceed six years) or in the Provincial Court when other types of crime are being dealt with. The decisions of the Criminal Courts may be appealed against to the Provincial Courts and those of the Provincial Courts may be the subject of a final appeal to the Supreme Court situated in Madrid.

For certain crimes (drug trafficking, terrorism, currency crimes) the instruction or investigative stage up to the oral trial is carried out by the Central Court of Instruction in Madrid, and the oral trial, properly speaking, takes place in the National Court, also situated in Madrid.

What has been said up until now is important in the sense that, as we will see later, industrial property, for example, is also protected by the criminal law.

(c) In contentious-administrative cases (this refers to those cases arising against a public administration, where the latter is acting as such and is therefore invested with special powers with regard to the position of the citizen) at the moment the courts competent to judge these matters are the Superior Courts of Justice of the Autonomous Communities at first instance; the National Court, at first instance, and the Supreme Court at first instance or on appeal.

(d) In 'social' matters, there are the social courts in each court circuit, the Superior Court of Justice of each Autonomous Community, the Central Labour Court and the Supreme Court. 'Social' matters include those related to labour law, conflicts among workers and certain aspects of social security.

As regards sport properly speaking, we find legislation emanating from the State, which sets down the bases and guidelines for all of Spain, and legislation coming from each one of the Autonomous Communities which has assumed the jurisdiction to legislate on sport.

On the other hand, the legislation on the different contracts to be used in marketing techniques, as well as those concerning publicity and industrial property, are not different from one Autonomous Community to another, as the legislation regulating those contracts comes from the State and is the same for all of Spain.

In situations of conflict (as will be set out in more detail in section 13 below) it is necessary to approach, according to the circumstances, the civil courts (in matters concerning contracts) or the contentious-administrative courts (if it concerns the activities of the public administration concerning sport or the registration of trademarks).

3. Applicable Laws

In the area of sport and the organisation of sporting competitions, Act No. 10 of 15 October 1990, of State-wide application, sets down guidelines on this matter. This Act regulates the control of sport by the public administration, establishing the different types of association in sporting matters.

This Act is to be developed by regulations, which have not yet been approved.

In the area of sports marketing and the contracts which producers and distributors of products may enter into with sporting associations or entities, the applicable law is the general law of contracting, regulated by the Spanish Civil Code and by the Commercial Code, protected by the principle of free determination of terms by the parties.

Equally to be underlined is the Advertising Act, No. 34 of 11 November 1988, issued by the State. This Act prohibits misleading advertising, unfair advertising and subliminal advertising.

Also important is the recent legislation on trademarks, approved by the Act 32/1988, 10 November 1988, which is based on the principle of obtaining the trademark by means of its being registered by the Industrial Property Registry, an administrative body the decisions of which may be appealed against by means of the contentious-administrative procedure.

The Patents Act 11/1986 of 20 March 1986 and the Intellectual Property Act 22/1987 of 11 November 1987 should also not be overlooked.

4. Intellectual Property Rights

The applicable law has already been described above: the Trademarks Act, the Patents Act and the Intellectual Property Act.

Spanish law protects intellectual property, both from the civil point of view (and thus in relationships between private individuals), and also from the criminal point of view, there being crimes related to the said matters. Thus Article 534 (and following) of the Criminal Code punishes those who intentionally infringe industrial property rights, with penalties which, in some cases, can reach six years imprisonment and fines of up to 1,000,000 pesetas.

4.1. Trademarks

The protection of trademarks, as has been pointed out above, is guaranteed by the fact that their being entered in the Industrial Property Register constitutes the owner's right over the same (Article 3 of the Trademarks Act). Within the concept of the trademark are included words or combinations of words; images, figures, symbols and graphics; letters, numbers and their combinations and three-dimensional forms, such as packaging and the presentation of the product.

Spanish law prohibits the registration (Article 11 of the Trademarks Act) of trademarks the content of which is too generic or may induce error on the part of the public, or which are similar to trademarks which are already registered, each of these cases being detailed in the legal text.

As regards registration, the Registrar himself is responsible for verifying, before allowing registration, that the trademark does not infringe any of the above-mentioned prohibitions, without prejudice to the right of interested persons to challenge the registration of a trademark if they consider this appropriate. There is thus a double guarantee of legality: that deriving from the checks of the registrar himself and that deriving from the proceedings which may be brought by persons who are affected by the registration of a trademark.

Registration of a trademark is granted for the period of ten years. The taxes payable to the Industrial Property Registry are paid every five years. The payment of the appropriate taxes is a necessary requirement for obtaining the registration of a trademark. Trademarks may be renewed indefinitely for additional periods of ten years by requesting such renewal together with a document authorised by a notary public in which the registered owner declares that he is using the trademark for the particular products.

Holders of notorious or well-known trademarks in Spain, even if not registered in this country, may within a term of five years after registration abroad (or without term if registration of the other party was made in bad faith), request the courts to revoke the registration of a trademark registered after such notoriety for similar products if this may create confusion (Art. 3 Trademark Act).

Registration of a trademark may be declared void if a party with an interest in such a trademark proves that it has not been effectively used in Spain for a period of five years for the particular products or services, except for a justification thereof (Art. 4.1.).

The use or the ownership of a trademark may be transferred, as the subject matter of a licence (which may be exclusive or not) for all or part of the products or services for which it is registered and for all or part of the Spanish territory. This transfer must be entered in the register of trademarks for it to affect third parties.

4.2. Copyright

Within this concept and for the purposes of the subject being dealt with, we find: musical compositions and arrangements; audiovisual works; sculptures, paintings, drawings, recordings, lithographs; projections, plans, models and designs of architectural works. The title of the work is protected as a part of the same.

The Act refers to and protects not only Spanish copyright holders but also foreigners habitually residing in Spain and those who, not habitually residing in Spain, published that particular work for the first time in Spain.

The Act does not lay down, unlike the situation for trademarks, compulsory registration of copyright. The creator of the work is deemed to be the copyright holder, without the same having to be recorded in any register. Notwithstanding this, the Act does provide for the existence – for the *optional* registration of copyright – of an Intellectual Property Registry under the Ministry of Culture for the whole of the national territory.

The right to exploit the work (reproduction, public display and development) belongs to the copyright holder and lasts for the whole of his life and for sixty years after his death. This right of exploitation of a copyright may be licensed. Transfers must be carried out in writing. If the assignment is meant to be exclusive, this has to be expressly provided.

It is important to emphasise, for practical purposes, that if no period of duration is laid down in the contract transferring exploitation rights, this must be deemed to be five years. Exploitation rights over future works cannot be transferred, nor may the copyright holder bind himself not to create any works in the future from the time of the exploitation right being transferred.

Again for practical purposes it should be underlined that if the transfer of exploitation rights is made for valuable consideration, the payment to the creator of a proportional share of the income from the exploitation or, in certain cases, a lump sum may be agreed on.

There are regulations on the rights of artists, actors and performers, who have the exclusive right to authorise the reproduction and public display of their works and performances, which must be made in writing.

The Intellectual Property Act governs certain types of contract in particular, such as those for publishing and theatrical and musical performances.

The legal protection of the above-mentioned rights is guaranteed in civil proceedings in which can be sought, apart from the appropriate compensation for damage and loss, the cessation of the illegal activity which gave rise to the claim.

5. The Contract Generally and Preliminary Agreements

In contractual matters those terms and conditions may be agreed on which are thought appropriate, provided they are not contrary to the law, morality or the public interest.

Contracts only bind the contracting parties and the heirs to their estates, except where the rights and obligations produced are not transferrable.

It is equally important to emphasise that in contractual matters, and especially in the performance of the contract, the governing principle is that of the good faith of the parties, Spanish legislation provides expressly that the Act does not protect the abuse of rights or the anti-social exercise of the same and ordering of the courts to adopt the appropriate corrective measures to prevent the persistence of the abuse.

In Spanish law three requirements must be satisfied for a contract to exist:

(a) The consent of the parties. This consent is indicated by the concurrence of offer and acceptance concerning the subject-matter and 'cause' of the contract. The law declares void the consent given by reason of a substantial error, violence, intimidation or serious deception by one of the parties, and that given by persons lacking capacity.

(b) A definite object which is the subject-matter of the contract. All things which are not outside the scope of commerce may be the subject-matter of a contract, including future goods.

(c) The 'cause' of the obligation which is established.

The contract is perfected from the time when these three requirements exist.

If the contract lays down a condition precedent, it will not be effective (and therefore not enforceable) while the condition has not been complied with. The event which is laid down as a condition may not depend on the person who benefits from the clause.

Spanish law does not require any special form for the existence of the contract, although it is usually drawn up in a written document. In this respect we should underline that the Spanish legal system makes a distinction between private and public documents. A public document is one authorised by a notary or public official, the original of which remains in his power, copies of that document then being issued.

The importance of the public document lies mainly in the fact that it bears witness to the date of its execution. A private document, on the other hand, signed by two individuals, does not bear witness to the date recorded in it, and it becomes necessary to hold investigative proceedings to establish at what time the rights or obligations contained in it begin or end.

Any written contract, public or private, begins with the date and an outline of the personal details of the contracting parties.

If one of the parties is a corporation, or is represented by another person in the drawing up of the written contract, the power by virtue of which he acts must be referred to in the contract with particular reference to the date when the power was issued.

The contract then contains a part setting out the reasons bringing the parties to the contract, and then the terms and conditions. In these it is important to clarify as much as possible the content of each one of the rights and obligations, as well as what is strictly speaking the object, the period for performance of the contract (on what date it begins, on what date it finishes), the applicable law and the causes of termination of the same.

The contract must be performed according to its own terms, and any amendment of the same must be consented to by both parties. The law does not allow the performance of contracts to be left to the will of one of the parties.

The law provides that no-one is liable for events which give rise to breach of contract and could not have been foreseen or, having been foreseen were also inevitable. Notwithstanding this, so-called *force majeure* is interpreted very strictly by our courts.

The interpretation of a contract follows the principle of efficacy, that is to say: if a contract can be interpreted in different ways, it must be construed in the way most suited to produce effects, always according to the context and in favour of the greatest possible reciprocity of interests, if the contract is for valuable consideration. If the parties do not agree on the interpretation of the contract, an arbitration clause may be inserted, so that the interpretation is made by a third party appointed by both parties by mutual consent.

Apart from cases of termination on expiry of the contractual period, by performance of the obligations, by the occurrence of an event which has been specified as a termination condition or where a thing owed has been lost (in which case, if there is intention or negligence, there arises an obligation to compensate for damage and loss), the contract may be terminated at the instance of both parties by mutual agreement, or where termination is sought before the courts. The latter occurs basically in cases of breach by one of the parties. For these cases, the law lays down that the party prejudiced by the breach may choose between requiring performance, plus damages for loss caused, from the party in breach, or he may apply for the termination of the contract, again with compensation for the damage and loss.

6. Standard Contract Terms

As has already been pointed out, it is important to state in any contract entered into by a corporation the power by virtue of which the person who is representing the corporation acts.

If the contract is with the public administration, it is necessary to check that the person signing the contract is competent to do this, as certain contracts may not be signed without the previous agreement of a particular body.

Equally important are the recitals where the 'cause' bringing the parties to make the contract is specified and the subject-matter which the contract concerns is established very clearly, both in as much detail as possible.

In contracts relating to sports marketing operations, and considering the complexity of the contents of the same, we advise laying down in the terms a list of definitions, so as to be able to determine what is understood by each one of the concepts.

The consideration agreed by the parties must be ascertained or ascertainable, and it is equally advisable to fix the consideration excluding VAT. If there is delay in payment it is necessary to specify the rate of interest which such delay brings with it, taking into account that it must be made clear in the appropriate clause that the delay is deemed to exist from a particular date. We say this because, in Spanish law, if this is not agreed on, the period of delay does not begin to run if payment is not required from the debtor, unless the situation is one of reciprocal obligations in which one party has complied with his obligations and the other has not.

The duration of the contract also has to be clear and specific, running either from a particular date or a specific event.

Special mention must be made concerning rights of use relating to trademarks or intellectual property of whether these are being transferred on an exclusive basis or not and, as regards any improper use, it is a good idea to establish from the outset the type of compensation this will give rise to.

Mention should be made of the law applicable to the contract being signed.

As regards the provisions concerning which are to be the courts which, in the event of any dispute, are to settle that dispute, it must be remembered that, while the parties may submit to the courts in a particular area, they may not make express submission to a particular court. Where one of the parties is the public administration, the courts of the area where the latter is situated will always have jurisdiction.

It is possible to include within the contract an arbitration clause so that, in the event of any dispute arising, a third party or institution is appointed to settle it. This clause, which does not require any particular form, should record which person or institution is to be entrusted with the arbitration.

7. Different Types of Business Arrangements

The contracts we refer to below are contracts frequently used in the field of sports marketing. They are mostly non-standard contracts in the sense that they are not specifically regulated by Spanish law. They are essentially based on case law.

7.1. Sponsorship Agreement

This has been defined in Article 24 of the General Act on Publicity of 11 November 1988 as 'that by which those being sponsored, in exchange for economic aid for the improvement of their sporting activity, undertake to cooperate with the publicity of the sponsor'. It adds that the provisions governing publicity distribution agreements (Articles 19–21 of the Act) are likewise applicable to such contracts.

As there are many methods of sponsorship in the sporting world, it is true to say that the regulation of sponsorship contracts depends basically on the free will of the parties to the contract, as limited by the law, morality and the public interest (Article 1255 of the Civil Code).

Sponsorship involves the putting into play of a copyright over a creation, a trademark, a tradename or even the right to use the industrial aspects of creations or productions – mascots, music, sporting garments, anagrams or logos. In these cases the entire system of protection for intellectual and industrial creations will be applicable, in accordance with what was said above in section 4.

Curiously, and regarding this type of contract, it must be pointed out that at the 1992 Olympic Games held in Barcelona, the national sponsorship programme was structured by setting out a closed list of categories of product by means of which it was possible to obtain sponsorship. Tobacco and alcoholic drinks, with the exception of beer and Spanish champagne, were excluded.

In each product category in turn there was only one participating company from each country, regardless of the type of participation arranged with that company.

7.2. Merchandising

This contract, the name of which derives from the commercialisation of a product or service or its being put on the market, a type of collateral licensing or marketing, consists of the transfer of 'selling power' or selling points, which well-known trademarks have over consumers through another type of product which it is sought to commercialise, creations of famous authors, rights concerning the personality of individuals, or famous persons. The essential point of the contract consists of the holder of the right authorising another person to exploit the suggestive value of the right.

With these contracts it is important to bear in mind the provisions of Article 13 of the Trademarks Act, according to which 'signs or media which involve the improper use of the reputation of other registered signs or media' may not be registered as such. In the same way Article 13 b) of the Trademarks Act provides that 'the civil name or image which identifies a person other than the applicant for the trade mark' may not be registered as trademarks 'unless there is the proper authorisation'. Article 13 d) has similar provisions regarding 'signs or media which reproduce or imitate creations which are protected by intellectual or industrial property rights, unless there is the appropriate authorisation from the holder of the right'.

In relation to the merchandising of copyright, the protection of copyright extends, as has been said under the heading 'Intellectual Property Rights' (section 4.2 above), for a period of sixty years, without any registration being necessary for the enjoyment of this protection. Drawings and photographs are protected by the Intellectual Property Act, but aspects of a work of art, such as the names of the characters in a work or its title, are not protected. For this reason it is advisable to apply for a trademark concerning these goods so that the lack of protection under the Intellectual Property Act is compensated for by the protection given by the Trademarks Act.

The merchandising of aspects of the personality is very closely linked to the rights of honour, personal and family privacy and self-image. For this reason Article 7(6) of the Act of 5 May 1982 is applicable, which provides that the unauthorised use 'of names, voices or images for advertising, commercial or other analogous purposes' is an injury to honour.

The Act 3/1991 of 10 January 1991 on Unfair Competition partially repealed the Trademarks Act. Thus 'all acts of competition which are contrary to the codes of conduct and good business practice' represent unfair competition, thus widening the protection offered to any goods which are the subject of marketing and which are not protected by the provisions mentioned above. Recourse to the Unfair Competition Act is possible even where the attack on the goods being merchandised takes place outside the framework of a competitive relationship between the owner of the goods being merchandised and the person making improper use of them (Article 19 of the Unfair Competition Act).

7.3. Endorsements

Contracts the object of which is the recommending of a product or service by a well-known personality from the world of sport are subject to the provisions of the Act of 10 January 1991 on Unfair Competition, according to which misleading actions consisting of disseminating false or inaccurate information which may cause misapprehensions concerning the nature, characteristics, fitness for use, quality, and so on of a product are to be considered unfair as contrary to the requirements of good faith (Art. 7).

Equally, the appearance of a well-known personality recommending a product will only be legal if the consent of that person has previously been obtained, in accordance with the provisions protecting the right to honour, personal privacy and self-image.

In contracts such as this the importance of an exclusivity clause for the time for which the advertising promotion is to last is clear.

7.4. Commissioning Agreements

Those entrusted with the production and sale of articles which are accessory to a sporting event – commemorative medals, coins, stamps – are considered by Spanish law under the heading of commercial commissioning agreements, governed by Articles 244–280 of the Commercial Code.

This is a cooperation agreement between traders, by which the agent or commissionaire binds himself to take part in an action or commercial contract on behalf of the principal. The commissionaire may act on his own behalf, in which case he is bound directly to the third parties he contracts with, as if the transaction were his own (Art. 246 of the Commercial Code), or on behalf of the principal, in which case legal effects are produced between the latter and the third party who contracts with the commissionaire (Art. 247 of the Commercial Code).

The commissionaire must follow the instructions of the principal and consult him in unforeseen matters, being obliged to pay compensation for damage and loss if he contravenes an express instruction of the principal (Art. 256 of the Commercial Code). For this reason, in the field of sports marketing, the use of any of the principal's intellectual or industrial property rights by the commissionaire is subject to the general rule that the consent of the principal is necessary. Thus, any infringement of these rights by the commissionaire gives rise to the obligation to compensate the principal, without prejudice to the use by the latter, against the commissionaire or against third parties, of the means of defending his intellectual and industrial property rights provided for by the Trademarks Act, the Intellectual Property Act and the Unfair Competition Act.

The commissionaire is equally bound to keep the principal informed of the contracts he enters into (Art. 260 of the Commercial Code) and the charges he makes, and he must provide accounts to the principal (Art. 263 of the Commercial Code).

For his part, the principal must pay the commission and compensate the commissionaire for any losses caused to him by it (Art. 278 of the Commercial Code). In order to obtain both amounts the commissionaire has a lien over the goods which are the subject-matter of the commission (Art. 276 of the Commercial Code).

As regards the copyright on the designs created by the commissioning party or the advertising agency, the law provides that, unless otherwise agreed by the parties, the exploitation rights on the designs or advertising creations are presumed to be exclusively assigned to the commissioning party for the purposes provided in the contract.[2]

7.5. *Franchises*

In Spanish law the franchise contract is another non-standard contract. For this reason the regulating principle of the free-will of the contracting parties applies.

Franchising, whether it be of production, distribution or of services, must carry with it the granting of a licence over the industrial rights and copyrights affected.

Franchise contracts should follow the EC block exemption for these agreements[3] in order to be exempted from the competition prohibitions set forth in the Treaty of Rome, which is also applicable in Spain for those agreements affecting the national market.

On the basis of this regulation, exclusive rights may be granted to suppliers, e.g. the exclusive right to supply soft drinks at a stadium of a sports event. The efficiency of this right may require two contracts if the franchisee is not the event organiser himself, i.e. a clause in the contract with the franchisee providing the obligation of exclusivity of the franchisee[4] and a clause in the contract with the event organiser, to avoid his granting other supply or sponsor agreements with competing brands.

Practical enforcement of these rights will require the cooperation of the event organiser's personnel during the event and eventually of the police to prevent 'ambush marketing' and other illegal activities at the venue.

---

2. Advertising Act 34/1988 of 11 November 1988, Section 23.
3. EC Regulation 4087/88 of 30 November 1988.
4. Section 2.c. Regulation 4087/88 of 30 November 1988.

7.6. Films and Videos

This is, like the majority of the contracts we have been examining, a non-standard contract in Spanish law, and is, therefore, also subject to the provisions concerning free will in the formation of a contract which have already been cited.

Nevertheless, a contract of this type presents important parallels with a business commission in which the charge to be carried out by the commissionaire consists essentially of filming a sporting event. It is thus essential that the commissionaire carries out this charge following closely the instructions he receives from the principal. The use which can be made of the film on the part of the commissionaire after the termination of the contract also depends on the instructions received.

The use by the commissionaire of any intellectual or industrial property rights which may belong to the commissioning party should be authorised beforehand by the latter, either in the form of a licence or that of mere consent, depending on the type of right in question.

The commissioning party may protect its copyright; however, if the contract is for advertising purposes, the exploitation of the film or video is presumed to be assigned to the commissioning party, unless otherwise provided. It is advisable to agree in writing beforehand that all the rights for the exploitation of the film or video, including broadcasting and diffusion, shall be granted to the commissioning party; a wide description of the purposes of such exploitation, together with the territory and the term thereof should be provided.

7.7. Public Appearances

Product-placement sponsoring is another non-standard contract the regulation of which depends essentially on commercial uses.

This type of contract essentially consists of identifying the virtues of a particular product with a particular sportsman. For this reason it is difficult for the intellectual and industrial property rights of the advertiser to be threatened, the insertion of a clause permitting the termination of the contract in the event of the sportsman appearing in public using a different product being enough for their protection.

The consent of the sportsman is also necessary here, on the basis of what was said above concerning the right to honour, personal and family privacy and self-image.

7.8. Suppliership

This contract can be basically reduced to the presentation of a company producing products or providing services as the official supplier of the product in question to the sports event. This contract is also based on freedom of the parties since the law does not expressly regulate the contract. Therefore, the parties may agree on the covenants they deem convenient as long as they are not contrary to the law, morals or public order.[5]

However, the rights and obligations agreed between the parties should not infringe competition law. To this extent, the EC Regulation on block exemption for exclusive distribution[6] or for exclusive purchase agreements[7] should be carefully followed. These regulations are applicable in Spain as regards restrictions to competition that may affect the national market.[8] Both regulations enable the supplier to impose on the distributor or purchaser the obligation not to sell competing products. On this basis, the supplier of products for a sports event may demand that the event organiser refrains from selling any competing product at the venue.

8. The Rights

Contracts regarding sports events may vary substantially according to the particular case. However, the possibility to include certain rights may be considered in most of the contracts.

8.1. Options

The event organiser may grant several options to sponsors and suppliers involved in the sports event. This may include an advertising show between sets or games in the event (e.g. in a rugby match), advertising spots to be shown up on the stadium screen (e.g. in soccer matches); booths to be used by suppliers on an exclusive or non-exclusive basis (e.g. in the Olympic Games).

The contract should consider these rights in detail in order to avoid misunderstandings or difficulties in reaching the agreement, particularly as regards the distance between advertising areas (distance between booths) or moments (spots in the screen). Also, it is worthwhile to expressly provide the terms of the agreement (prices and terms of payment) and whether these options involve further payments by the sponsor or supplier and to clarify who shall be paying any costs involved. In important sports events, the organiser usually wishes to control the image of the area and may even want to provide the booths himself, which may entail an additional cost that the sponsor or supplier may have expected to be included in the consideration he paid to take part in the event.

The option may be construed either as an option of the sponsor or supplier to exercise a right, thus being an obligation of the event organiser if such right is exercised, for example, an option to take one of the booths; or the contrary,

---

5. Section 1255 of the Civil Code.
6. EC Regulation 83/83 of 22 June 1983.
7. EC Regulation 84/83 of 22 June 1983.
8. Royal Decree 157/92 of 21 February 1992, Sections 1.a and 1.b.

i.e. the right of the event organiser to exercise the right, thus being a right of the sponsor or supplier, for example, an option to acquire the fridges that were provided by the supplier in the stadium bars. These options should be clearly defined.

8.2. Pre-emption

Given the relationship of cooperation and trust between the parties, pre-emptive rights are also quite often agreed on in this kind of agreement. This means the right to be offered first the opportunity to agree on a particular term, for example, the event organiser may grant the supplier the pre-emptive right to acquire some of the equipment used in the event or the sportsman could be given a pre-emption on the equipment used in a particular event (acquire a prototype motorcycle used in such event and discarded for further competition). An interesting pre-emptive right is that granted to a sponsor by a team to sponsor it again the following year, for example, if the team is to continue playing in the same category.

Although it is not so important to fix the terms of the agreement, given the fact that the party to which the right is offered is not bound to exercise the right (as with the option described above), it is useful to provide in the contract the maximum terms of such a pre-emptive right, for example, the price that may not be exceeded or a percentage.

8.3. Exclusivity

Agreements whereby a company sponsors a sports event often provide exclusive clauses whereby the sponsor has the exclusive right to sell a kind of product in the stadium, thus preventing competitors from selling there. The sponsoring contracts for the Olympic Games of Barcelona 1992 provided this kind of clause and thus only one brand of beer, cola beverage, chocolate bars, photograph films, and so on were provided. This clause is also essential in suppliership agreements. Enforcement of this right requires an effective police network to prevent 'ambush marketing'.

This kind of clause usually covers the surroundings of the stadium in order to avoid competitors placing their advertising booths in the accesses thereto.

8.4. Copyright Licence

According to the Act on Intellectual Property (Act 22 of 11 November 1987), it is the author who has all rights on the copyright, unless he has licensed the exploitation right to a third party, which shall always be done in writing. These may include the right to broadcast the event on TV or in advertising spots, the right to use a particular computer programme for the organisation of the event.

However, there are certain rights that the author may not waive, for example, the right to decide whether the 'work' is to be disclosed and how; decide whether this has to be under his own name or under an alias; demand that he is acknowledged as the author; demand that his work is not changed; the right to change the work himself; the right to remove the work from trade.

Exploitation rights on the copyright are protected during the life of the author and sixty years therefrom, unless the work is disclosed after the author's death, in which case, such rights are protected for sixty years after the date of disclosure (which may not take place after sixty years after the author's death).

The contract should clearly provide that the licensor has sufficient right to license the copyright, thus having obtained the necessary authorisation from the creator of the work. If no consent has been obtained from the author or from the holder of the rights, the licensor shall be jointly liable with the licensee for any obligations or liability stemming therefrom.

Also, it may be advisable to insert in the contract the obligation of the licensee to inform the licensor of any infringements of the copyright and to cooperate as feasible in the defence thereof. Copyrights may include confidential information that the licensor may want to be kept confidential, thus a particular provision in this sense should be included in the contract. It should be highlighted that this kind of obligation may survive the termination of the contract and, therefore, it is interesting to expressly provide this survival in the contract.

The duration and territory of the licence should be provided in the contract, since the law provides that if no express duration or territory is agreed upon, it shall be understood that licences are granted for the relevant country and for a period of five years.

In certain cases, the broadcasting of the image of a sportsman requires his consent, as provided in the Act on the Image, Honour and Privacy.

8.5. Trademark Licence

Sponsor contracts for sports events usually include trademark provisions. These cover various forms of trademark licence, for example, the holder of the right of the league or of the team licenses the sponsor the use of its trademark in its advertising, for example, the holder of the rights in a rugby team licenses a manufacturer of sportswear the right to use the team's trademark in its T-shirts.

The licence should provide the duration, consideration and other terms for the licence. It is essential to include a list and description of the trademarks involved in order to obtain the licensee's cooperation for third party infringements and to ensure that he shall use the trademarks in a similar format. The trademark holder may be asked to warrant that he is the trademark's registered owner or has sufficient rights to license the right to use the trademark and to free the licensee of liability from any claims.

8.6. Territory

As regards the territory, EC competition aspects should be carefully considered, as well as EC provisions on the free movement of goods (parallel imports). In general terms, it should be mentioned that the definition of the territory where the rights are to be used is very important and should not only cover the stadium, but also accesses thereto, assuming they are controlled by the event organiser.

8.7. Media

Images on sports events may be broadcast in different media, including video, film, TV and radio, each having some particularities. In the case of broadcasting of TV images of sports events, it should be taken into account that new technologies ensure broadcasting in more than one country. This may entail that advertising regulations of the different countries, where the image is to be broadcast should be considered; for example, as described in section 11 below and in other chapters, some Spanish regions and probably other countries as well do not allow that alcoholic beverages or tobacco are related to sports.

8.8. Product Classes

As stated above, sponsoring of sports events usually includes exclusive rights for product classes. Therefore, it is important to clearly define the products included in a particular class.

8.9. Duration and Termination

The duration of the contract should be clearly provided. It should be taken into account, though, that the sports event may eventually be postponed (e.g. because of rain). It should be carefully studied whether this is to be considered *force majeure*, thus relieving the parties from their obligations, or an extension of the duration of the contract. The duration may be defined by providing a defined period, a championship, a sports event, and so on. It may be wise to provide a defined period but with additional one-year terms unless prior written notice by either party is sent before a specified number of days. The falling in a lower category of the sponsored team (e.g. basketball team), the sale of the trademark by the sponsor and other events may be inserted as causes of termination of the agreement.

8.10. Post Termination Arrangements/Restrictions

Most copyright and trademark provisions in licence agreements should continue in force after expiration or termination of the agreement. Some licence contracts (that may go together with a sponsor agreement) provide for the obligation of the licensee to destroy the products to which the name or logo of the sports team has been affixed if they have not be sold after termination of the contract. Restrictions on a party as to sponsoring similar business in a competing field after the contract expires may unjustifiably restrict free competition and could eventually be challenged. Although there is no specific legislation on this matter (except for non-competition in labour agreements), Spanish courts have considered this type of agreement null and void if they are abusive or if no consideration has been given therefor.

9. Financial Terms

9.1. Financial Aspects

As regards the consideration to be paid by the sponsoring entity to the organiser of the sports event or to the sportsman, it is advisable to clearly fix the type of consideration that will be paid. This concerns, in particular, the following possibilities:

(a) *The payment in money*. This must clearly establish, in particular, if the amount agreed will be net or gross, the timing of the payments and in case of cross-border payments, it should be stated in which currency such payments must be made and the effects for the parties of variations in the exchange rate.
(b) *The payment in kind*. In relation to this matter, it must be agreed what type of consideration in kind will be paid by the sponsor company (clothes, sports tools), its quality, its frequency, the replacement of these goods by others of the same quality, and so on.

Although this depends on the parties to the contract, it is not uncommon in Spain that the sponsoring agreement and the payments stemming from this type of contract are not made directly to the sportsman but to companies set up by them. The relation in this case is the following:

- the sponsoring agreement is signed between the sponsoring entity and the company owned by the sportsman;
- the payments are performed by the sponsoring entity and the company;
- the relation between the company and the sportsman is, usually, a professional agreement.

The incomes received by the sportsman are usually:

- those derived from a services agreement between the company and the sportsman;
- those derived from an 'image agreement' between the company and the sportsman, under which the company may use and exploit the image of the sportsman;
- indirectly, the dividends distributed by the company, as the case may be.

This will be further developed in the following section on tax aspects.

9.2. Tax Aspects

9.2.1. Tax aspects for the sponsoring body or for the sponsoring company

The amounts paid by the sponsoring entity under the sponsoring agreement or without such agreement existing may have different fiscal treatment. The alternatives are the following:

(a) Payments in favour of a 'sports federation' (*Federación deportiva*). Provided they take part in national official sports competitions, the sports federations, either depending on the national authorities or depending on the regional authorities, are deemed to be 'entities of public utility'. Therefore, the gifts made by the sponsoring company to these federations are a deductible expense under the corporate tax with the limit of 10% of the taxable amount of the company. It is important to note that in these cases no sponsoring contracts are required. These types of contributions are unilateral gifts.

(b) Payments derived from the provisions of a sponsoring agreement. The amounts paid by the sponsoring company either to the sportsman or to its company are a deductible expense under the corporate tax. No limit is applicable on these expenses.

(c) No other payments than those mentioned in the two above paragraphs will be tax deductible. They will be considered a gift with no other tax effects.

9.2.2. Tax aspects for the recipient

In the case where the payments are made directly from the sponsoring company to the sportsman, these amounts are considered a professional income for the sportsman and will be subject to individual income tax.

In the case where the sponsoring contract is performed between the sponsoring company and the company owned by the sportsman, this payment will be income of such company and subject to ordinary corporate tax.

However, Act 18 of 8 June 1991 provided that the companies complying with the conditions referred to below are subject to tax transparency. The conditions to be transparent are the following:

- more than 50% of their income has to derive from sporting (and artistic) activities carried on by individuals or from any other activity related to sports (or artistic) activity (e.g. the publicity and promotional activities developed by sportsmen); and
- the sportsman and the members of his family up to the fourth degree (second cousins and great-great grandparents) are entitled to participate up to 25% of the incomes of the company.

The consequences of the tax transparency regime are the following:

- The positive incomes obtained by the company are not subject to corporate tax. The taxable amount is attributed to the shareholders of the company in proportion to their participations in the share capital of the company.
- The negative taxable amounts (losses) are not attributed to the shareholders. These losses may be set off during the 5 years following the one when they were obtained.

9.2.3. Value added tax (VAT)

Payments derived from sponsoring agreements are subject to VAT, at the ordinary rate of 15%.

Either the company or the sportsman, who is the recipient of the funds, must comply with the following obligations:

- The issuance of an invoice in favour of the sponsoring company including the amount of the consideration and the amount resulting from the application of VAT (15%) on this amount.
- VAT paid will be charged VAT and may be compensated with borne VAT.

VAT will be applicable to the considerations derived from sponsoring agreements but not to the gifts given to sports federations, disregarding whether they are tax deductible or not.

9.2.4. Specific tax benefits

For the particular event of the Barcelona Olympics of 1992, three specific tax benefits were granted and which have been applicable until the fiscal year of 1992.

(1) Gifts granted by companies in favour of the 'Comité Organizador Olímpico Barcelona 1992' were tax deductible up to 30% of the taxable amount of the grantor company. This deduction was compatible with other gifts granted by the same company but in that case the limit of the total amount of the gifts could not exceed 50% of the taxable amount.
(2) If the gifts were granted by individuals, these individuals could deduct from the amount to pay as individual income tax 10% of the amount granted within a limit of 30% of the taxable amount.

(3) Companies that invested in assets, recovery (*recuperación*) of buildings, edition of books and production of films, could deduct 15% of the amount invested from the corporate tax.

10. Insurance Aspects

The sponsoring of a sports event entails high risks, not only because of the high sums that are often involved, but because of the number of persons and companies involved in the event (media, sportsmen, advertising agency, press, organisers).

Bearing in mind that there used to be no specific regulation for this kind of contract, quite often clauses whereby liability was excluded were inserted. This often placed the weaker party in a very insecure situation. The Advertising Act changed this situation by providing two main rules:

(a) a ban to insert any clauses whereby liability is attributed, excluded or excluded vis-à-vis third parties as a consequence of advertising activities;
(b) clauses whereby the economic profits, commercial results of the advertising or the liability for failure to achieve them is directly or indirectly undertaken shall be ineffective.

Besides these rules, the need to insure the risks of the contracts in question is becoming bigger and new insurance policies are being created. These insurances cover various risks, including the risk where a soccer match is cancelled due to transport delays of the sportsmen, an athletics competition is cancelled because of rain and a soccer match may not be broadcast as scheduled due to a strike in the TV company. All these risks not only entail the loss of the advertising opportunity for the sponsor and the organisers (among others), but also very high financial losses due to the costs incurred, for example, advertising agency, payment to the organiser, contracted personnel, facilities, equipment, cameramen. Therefore, although the premiums for these kinds of insurances are considerably high, it is advisable to insure the risks in order to avoid the losses that could stem therefrom.

As regards the liability stemming from the product, Spanish law has not yet implemented EC Directive 85/374 of 25 July 1985 although the term provided for implementation has long lapsed. This matter is thus still regulated in Spain (the direct effect of the Directive is very doubtful) by the Spanish Consumer Act of 1984 (Act 26 of 19 July 1984). Although this Act provides for a fault liability, except when certain products (foodstuffs, cosmetics, drugs) are involved, the Spanish case law often lays the burden of proof on the defendant and thus creates a system which is close to objective liability (liability without fault). The amount of damages declared by the courts has been increasing considerably in the last years. In view of this situation, the number of insurance policies covering product liability has also increased lately.

Insurance is also essential in order to cover public liability. All contracts regarding a sports event should contain the obligation of the parties to insure their own risks. This will avoid parties linked but not directly involved with the damage having to pay the negligence of the other less solvent party. Indeed, on the basis of the general principle of liability for negligence,[9] Spanish courts have sometimes distributed liability among the parties involved due to the serious damage caused to a consumer and thus the high compensation to be paid. Insurance for each party's liability shall cover any risks, for example, a stand collapses and kills and/or injures spectators at a sports event or a sponsor's perimeter advertising board collapses and injures spectators.

11. Advertising and Promotion

11.1. Advertising Controls

The Spanish legislation on advertising is mainly regulated by the Advertising Act, No. 34 of 11 November 1988 (see section 3 above). However, given the fact that most autonomous communities have competence to regulate on matters affecting advertising and promotion of sports events (health, home market, etc.), there are several regional provisions that should also be mentioned.

The Advertising Act prohibits several forms of advertising, namely:

(a) *misleading advertising:* that which induces error in its recipients or prejudices a competitor, as well as that which omits fundamental information concerning the product advertised, if this omission induces error on the part of the recipients;
(b) *unfair advertising:* that which devalues a person, a company or its products, that which causes confusion with other competitors and comparable advertising;
(c) *subliminal advertising:* that which through methods producing stimuli of an intensity on the edge of the range of the senses or similar methods, may act on the recipient public without being consciously perceived.

The advertising of drugs, cosmetics and cars is subject to specific regulations and restrictions. Advertising of alcoholic beverages and tobacco has several particularities that require specific mention.

9. Section 1902 of the Civil Code.

11.2. Alcoholic beverages

The national legislation does not ban the advertising of alcoholic beverages at sports events. However, two autonomous communities do have legislation that affects this matter, namely Catalonia and the Basque Country.

- *Catalonia.* The Catalan Act (Act No. 20 of 25 July 1985 as amended by Act No. 10 of 10 May 1991) bans advertising of alcoholic beverages in sports stadiums, except for static advertising and for the advertising made by a sponsor. Besides, advertising of alcoholic beverages over 23% of alcohol content is banned in beaches, water parks, theme parks, pools, zoos, streets, roads, cinemas, theatres, and so on. No alcoholic beverages shall be sold in sport centres that depend of the regional government.
- *Basque Country.* Act No. 15 of 11 November 1988 bans advertising of all alcoholic beverages in sports centres, as well as at their entrances and in open spaces ('external advertising'). This provision specifically bans advertising of these products on the basis of the sponsoring of sporting, cultural or social activities, except if it is due to the connexion with national channels. In general, advertising of alcoholic beverages may not be related to sport.

As regards advertising on TV, for example, broadcasting of sporting events on TV, advertising of alcoholic beverages exceeding 20% of alcohol content is banned; if the beverage has a lower alcohol content, it should comply with certain criteria (not to be addressed to minors, not to promote indiscriminate consumption, and so on).

11.3. Tobacco

The national legislation does not ban the advertising of tobacco at sports events, though it does ban advertising of tobacco on TV. Catalonia's and the Basque Country's legislation also restrict this advertising.

- *Catalonia.* The Catalan Act described above bans advertising of tobacco in sports stadiums, except for static advertising and for the advertising made by a sponsor. Besides, advertising of tobacco is banned in beaches, water parks, theme parks, pools, zoos, streets, roads, cinemas, theatres, and so on. No advertising of tobacco shall be made through media depending on the Regional Government except for sponsoring activities. No alcoholic beverages shall be sold in sports centres.
- *Basque Country.* Act No. 15 of 11 November 1988 bans advertising of tobacco in sports centres, as well as at their entrances and in open spaces ('external advertising'). Advertising of these products on the basis of the sponsoring of sporting, cultural or social activities is banned, except if it is

due to the connexion with national channels. In general, advertising of tobacco may not be related to sport.

11.4. Sponsoring of the TV Broadcast of Sports Events

As regards the contract of sponsoring in general, the Advertising Act expressly provides that if the media fail to honour their obligations with no justification by changing an essential element of the advertising or providing an incorrect version, the media will be obliged to repeat the advertising. If this is not possible, the sponsor shall be entitled to a reduction of the price and to compensation for the damages caused.

If the media fail to make the advertising at all, the sponsor may either demand that the advertising is made or dissolve the contract, both getting the money back and receiving compensation for damages.

As regards sponsoring of sports events on TV, Spain has two public channels and three private ones. Although no specific regulation has been approved as regards sponsoring or advertising through private channels, the provisions applicable to the public network are applicable to the former so long as no specific provision is approved for private channels.

The Resolution of 17 April 1990 for the public network (and thus applicable too to the private channels) implements in Spain the EC Directive of 3 October 1989 on Television Broadcasting. According to this resolution, any television programme may be sponsored unless it is a news or current affairs programme. Sponsored programmes should be clearly identified as such. The sponsor is not permitted to influence either the content or scheduling of the programme. The sponsor may not be the programme's presenter.

11.5. Advertising Agencies

Specific provisions apply to the contract between the organiser or sponsor of the sports event and the advertising agency. The agency must refrain from using for other purposes the information or advertising material provided by the organiser or rights holder in the advertisements. Should the agency fail to honour its undertakings without justification, the Advertising Act expressly provides that the organiser may dissolve the contract, get back the money it paid and get compensation for the damages caused.

11.6. Comparative Advertising

Although comparative advertising used to be banned in the past and is still unusual today, the Spanish legislation (Advertising Act No. 34 of 11 November 1988, Art. 6.c. and the Act on Unfair Competition No. 3 of 10 January 1991,

Art. 10) allows such an advertising as long as certain requirements are complied with, namely:

1. it should be based on essential characteristics of the products;
2. statements should be susceptible of being objectively evidenced;
3. characteristics being compared should be similar;
4. the compared products should be similar, known and not have a limited market share;
5. competitors or competitors' products should not be undervalued or disrespected.

12. The Venue

12.1. Public Liability and Control

The venue should comply with all regulations regarding safety, fire exits, electricity and elevator security, and so on. Measures should be taken as regards the capacity of the stadium, the temperature thereof, etc. A strict control and safety network should be organised in order to ensure a safe access to and exit from the stadium.

The Spanish Consumer Act (Act No. 26 of 19 July 1984) provides for the liability of those who provide services to consumers for any damages caused by their use, unless the former prove that they have complied with all applicable regulations and that they have taken all safety measures required and acted with sufficient diligence. Besides, a general and old rule provided in the Civil Code (Art. 1902) provides for the obligation of a party that causes damage to another party to compensate the former for any damages caused negligently or on purpose. The Spanish courts apply these provisions very strictly in the sense that the event organiser or any person who may have taken part in the event may be found liable for the injury caused to a spectator or sportsman. Therefore, it is essential that all measures are taken to avoid any damage and to minimise all risks.

Violence in sport has become an issue in the last two years, due to the polemic discussion on violence in sport. At the time that a Bill on sports was being discussed in Parliament, a Commission in the Senate, organised particularly to study violence in sport, approved in March 1990 a complete report on the matter, that pushed the Senate to expressly insert in the Bill on sports the ban on the sale of alcoholic beverages in stadia during sports events.

The Act on Sports No. 10/1990 was approved on 15 October 1990. The relevant clubs and stadia are responsible for ensuring compliance with safety provisions and may be found liable for any damages caused during the event (Arts. 63 and 69). Besides, administrative sanctions may be imposed if the provisions of the Act are not complied with. Sanctions may vary from 10,000 ptas. to 100,000,000 ptas.

Among other safety measures, the Act on Sports bans the sale and consumption of alcoholic beverages in sports stadia (Art. 67), the obligation of organisers to inform the municipality of the event, their obligation to ensure systems to separate supporters of opposing teams, access control and an organised system to sell tickets (Art. 64). This Act does not ban advertising of alcoholic beverages in stadia nor the sponsoring of sports by alcoholic beverage brands.

Other provisions that may be taken into account regarding safety during sports events and particularly regarding the ban on the sale of alcoholic beverages during sports events and not the promotion and advertising thereof, are:

- Council of Europe Convention on Prevention of Violence in Sports Events, Strasbourg, 19 August 1984, recommending the ban on sale of alcoholic beverages in stadia and even in the stadia's surroundings; this Convention was ratified by Spain on 1987;
- Report on Sports in the EC and Europe for citizens prepared by the EC Parliament on December 1988 and Resolution by the European Parliament on Sport Vandalism and Violence, 1988;
- Resolutions of international sports federations: UEFA 23 July 1985; FIFA 16 July 1989.
- Order (*Instrucción*) of the Security Secretary of State of 25 September 1987 and Order (*Circular*) of the Directorate General for Police of 20 November 1987.

In the Winter of 1991 a 12 year old child was killed in a soccer stadium in Barcelona due to a signal flare or bengal light that was negligently shot by a person sitting on the opposite side of the stadium. This caused very serious concern. The trial is still to take place, but since then measures to control security measures in Spanish stadia are stricter.

The police are further taking part in security programmes regarding sports events with a large audience. Persons entering the stadium may be carefully searched to ensure that they are not carrying any damaging objects or alcohol. However, the event organiser should provide all required measures to ensure the safety programme, including car parking facilities.

Should individuals infringe safety regulations or advertising arrangements, police cooperation should be sought to take the necessary measures. The procedure to be followed against these infringements shall depend upon whether the offence is a civil or a criminal one. Administrative sanctions such as fines (infringement of safety provisions), criminal penalties (causing personal injury to third parties) or compensation for damages ('ambush marketing') may eventually be imposed.

Lastly, the venue should also provide hygienic measures, such as sufficient toilet facilities.

12.2. Sponsor Access and Protection

Special arrangements may be granted to sponsors, including allocation of particular seats and lounges and the granting of free admission tickets. Measures have to be taken to ensure these rights and thus prevent other spectators from using these facilities or rights. Accreditations should thus be given to sponsors and the required instructions should be given to security personnel so that they are aware of these privileges.

Besides, sponsors should be given the time and help to arrange the display of their products and advertising, including taking measures of the space, having the drawings of the stadium and organisation beforehand, being able to have their personnel inside to display the boards, and so on.

13. Dispute Resolution

If the parties do not reach agreement on the manner of settling any disputes which may arise between them, there are two solutions: either go to court to obtain compensation for the rights presumably violated by the other party; or go to private arbitration.

13.1. Courts

Disputes between private individuals over the wording of a contract are the province of the civil courts, the decisions of which may be appealed against with, if appropriate, a final appeal to the Supreme Court.

The law requires the presence of a lawyer and a court agent for appearances before the courts. The court agent has a representative function on behalf of the litigant in the proceedings, being charged with receiving notifications and sending them to the lawyer. It is necessary for the court agent in civil matters to be selected before a notary, the appropriate power of attorney being executed, which must be attached to the first document presented to the court. It is not necessary for the name of the lawyer to appear in the document, which refers only to the court agent.

In civil matters, legal proceedings start with the presentation of the appropriate statement of claim, a document in which is set out what type of procedure is being followed, against whom, for what amount, and the facts giving rise to the proceedings. At the same time there exists in the statement of claim a part called 'legal bases' or 'bases of law' where there are references to the provisions cited in defence of the interests of the person signing the claim. The statement of claim is sent to the defendant who answers in the same terms and with the same requirements. There may be a time period for presenting evidence, if the parties request and the judge grants this, and subsequently judgment is given. There is the possibility of appealing against the judgment to the Provincial Court.

As far as costs are concerned, the law provides that they will be awarded against a party whose claim has been completely rejected, there also being the possibility of costs being awarded against a party who has instituted proceedings recklessly or in manifest bad faith.

The enforcement of the judgment can be carried out voluntarily by the loser or it may be necessary to institute enforcement proceedings of an obligatory nature which are carried out by the court itself.

During civil proceedings, it is possible to request from the court and obtain interlocutory remedies, with a view to ensuring that the judgment, were it to be favourable to the interests of the party bringing the proceedings, is complied with. For example, it is possible to bring proceedings for a preventative freeze on goods or to obtain a preventative registration of a claim. The latter consists of an entry in the Land Registry, attached to the folio which contains the description of a particular piece of land, of the fact that the same is the subject of litigation. Thus any person interested in acquiring the land in question during the proceedings will not be able to allege lack of knowledge. Interlocutory remedies are usually subject to the depositing of a financial security of a certain amount on the part of the person seeking them, to guarantee the damage and loss which may be caused to the owner of the land in question in the event of his not being found liable in the judgment.

Execution of foreign judgments depends on whether Spain has an international treaty with the relevant country. Spain has bilateral treaties with a considerable number of countries, has also ratified the Convention of Lugano of 16 September 1988 and is a party to the Convention of Brussels of 27 September 1968 (as amended in San Sebastian, Spain on 26 May 1989).

If there is no international treaty, the principle of reciprocity shall be taken into consideration. In this case, execution of the foreign judgment should be requested from the Supreme Court ('exequatur') and will only be granted if the following is sufficiently evidenced (Art. 994 Procedural Act):

(a) the judgment was issued after a personal action;
(b) the judgment was not given in the absence of the defendant;
(c) the obligation to be fulfilled is legal in Spain;
(d) the document containing the judgment is an original document in the relevant country and in Spain.

13.2. Arbitration

In private law and in matters the parties are freely able to dispose of, there is the possibility of submitting disputes between the parties to arbitration. This possibility is governed by the Arbitration Act of 5 December 1988.

The Act requires that, prior to the conflict arising, the parties have submitted themselves to arbitration in writing, indicating which person or institution is to carry out this activity. Apart from the requirement that it must be provided for in writing, there are no other formalities or special formulae for setting up arbitration, it also being possible to infer the will of the parties to submit themselves to arbitration from a simple exchange of letters in which such will is set out.

Reference to arbitration prevents the courts from entering into the matter which is the subject of the dispute, although the parties are free to waive such arbitration.

Once the arbitrator(s) have been designated (there must always be an odd number) the law requires their acceptance if the procedure is to be continued with.

As regards the procedure in a strict sense, the Act only lays down principles on which it must be based: thus, it must respect the principles of the right to a hearing, reply and equality of the parties, it being possible in other matters to arrange by mutual agreement the periods for formulating and answering allegations, as well as proposing and presenting evidence. The arbitration procedure does not necessarily require the intervention of a lawyer.

When the arbitral award has been made, it has the effect of a legally determined matter, it not being possible for conflicts to arise again concerning that which has been determined by the arbitrator.

For the compulsory enforcement of an arbitral award the same procedure is followed as for the compulsory enforcement of court judgments.

As regards the arbitrator's fees, the parties are free to agree on how these are to be met, the same criteria as for court matters usually being followed.

Sweden

by Jan Lundberg
and Jan Holmberg

1. Sports Marketing – A Business

At the time of writing, October 1992, sponsoring is, due to the recession, on the downgrade. The annual spending in 1990 was approximately SEK 850 million. For 1991 the figure was approximately SEK 650 million and for 1992 it is estimated to be less than SEK 600 million.

2. The National Legal System

Swedish law is primarily codified. In fields not covered by statutory law, guidance is to be sought in general principles of law, of which the main sources are precedents, customary law and legal doctrine.

Sweden is a party to the European Economic Area (EEA) Convention, due to come into effect as of 1 January 1993, and is under the obligation to implement all secondary legislation which was adopted by the EC Member States up to 31 July 1991. Sweden has applied for membership of the EC. When membership is granted, EC law will prevail in case of conflict with domestic law.

The court system of Sweden is divided between general and special courts. General courts have a three instance system – courts of first instance (District Courts), intermediate courts (Courts of Appeal) and the Supreme Court. The right to appeal to the Supreme court is strictly limited.

A special court of interest is the Swedish Market Court, a court of first and last instance, which has jurisdiction over unfair marketing practices and antitrust cases.

3. Applicable Laws

There is no law particularly applicable to sports marketing. Such a contract is governed by the general law of contracts of which the Contracts Act is the cornerstone. In addition, a number of general laws may, directly or by analogy, be applicable.

4. Intellectual Property Rights

4.1. Trademarks

Sweden is a signatory to the Paris Convention on Trademarks and the Protocol to the Madrid Agreement but not the Vienna Treaty or the Madrid Agreement. The Trademarks Act (1960) stipulates that trademarks may gain protection both by registration and use. Protection means that the proprietor has the exclusive right to exploit commercially the mark in his business. Registration (in *Patent- och Registreringsverket*, Stockholm) may be made in one or more specific products or services classes for a period of 10 years with the unlimited right to renew the registration. Registration is, in principle, granted if the mark is apt to distinguish goods or services of the proprietor from other goods or services. If the registered owner does not use the mark at all for a period of five years he risks that the mark will be struck off. This very liberal requirement of use will, according to a proposed Bill, be stricter as from 1 January 1993.

If the mark has been registered in several product classes but not been used under five years for products in all of those classes, the proprietor risks that the mark will be struck off from one or more classes of the products for which the mark has not been used. Protection by use is achieved when the mark has acquired a reputation, which means that it is known within the target group for which protection is claimed. A further criterion is that the mark should originally or by use be distinctive and not merely a generic term.

4.2. Copyright

Sweden is a signatory to the Berne Convention and the Universal Copyright Convention. The Copyright Act (1960) states that a person who has created a literary or artistic work shall have copyright therein. Examples of such work are fictional or descriptive representations, computer programmes, fine arts, architecture and applied arts. Copyright presupposes novelty and individuality.

There is no requirement of quality. Moreover it is the presentation that is protected – not the subject or the idea. No formalities are necessary for protection which is awarded to the creator for lifetime and fifty years thereafter.

Copyright includes both economic and moral rights. The proprietor is exclusively entitled, with a number of exceptions stated in the Copyright Act, to produce copies of the work or to make it available to the public, be it in the original or changed form, in translation or adaptation.

A copyright assignment could be oral, but a written contract is recommended.

Moral rights focuses the creator. When a mark is made available to the public the name or a pseudonym must be set out to an extent required by generally accepted principles in respect of intellectual property rights. The work must not be modified or made available to the public in an offending way. Moral rights cannot be assigned or transferred. Further, a general waiver of the moral rights is void. The creator could though waive his moral rights to a limited extent, e.g. when a story is adapted for the screen.

4.3. Registered Designs

Design protection under the Registered Designs Act (1970) can be granted regardless of whether the appearance of the product is conditioned by ornamental or technical functions. The design has to differ essentially from what has become known before the filing date of the application, i.e. the design has to be objectively new. The term 'design' in the Act refers to two-dimensional as well as three-dimensional forms. The protection is limited to the appearance of the product as represented when the design was submitted for registration and does not extend to the underlying technical concept.

The period of protection is five years with an opportunity to renew the registration twice. The proprietor has the exclusive right to manufacture, import, offer for sale, transfer and set out the design in the course of business.

4.4. Unfair Competition

Unfair competition as to marketing could be governed by the Marketing Practices Act (1975) which in Section 2 prohibits marketing practices which adversely affect consumers or businessmen. The purpose of the Act is not to protect products or trademarks. One purpose is, however, to prohibit marketing practices which, by use of imitations of distinctive marks and so on, are intended to deceive the public about the commercial origin. Prohibition, normally under penalty of a fine, is imposed by the Market Court.

5. The Contract Generally and Preliminary Agreements

5.1. Preliminary Agreements

Whether an agreement, headed as preliminary or as a letter of intent, is enforceable or not, and, if so, to what extent, is a delicate matter under Swedish law. The main principle is that such an agreement is not binding. However, the more detailed the contract is, the greater is the risk (or chance) that the parties are in certain respects bound by it. The heading of the contract is only an element amongst others to consider. Another important factor is how the parties have been acting towards each other. The legal consequences could thus be enforceability or, secondarily, liability to compensate the other party for direct costs incurred.

5.2. Intention to Create Legal Relations

Both parties must intend to create a legal relation. An offer made under duress is not legally binding.

5.3. Offer and Acceptance

Swedish law is based on the 'mirror image' principle, i.e. the offer and acceptance must correspond exactly. Often the acceptance does not comply with the offer; in such case, it is understood to be a refusal combined with a new offer. If, however, the party who receives the 'new offer' ought to realise that the other party believes he has agreed in whole, he must notify the other party and if he fails to do so, a contract is constituted on the terms contained in 'the acceptance'.[1]

A contract can be negotiated for a long period of time and may sometimes be considered as entered into by gradual stages. The parties solve important issues first and details thereafter. However, the main principle is that a party is free to discontinue to negotiate even if the negotiations are in an advanced stage, provided that he has acted in good faith and no preliminary agreement has been reached.

5.4. Consideration

There is no requirement for consideration under Swedish law.

5.5. Form and Execution

There is no requirement of written form, whether or not a transfer of intangible rights is included.

However, the execution of a contract in writing is strongly recommended as evidence of the existence as well as the scope of agreements pertaining to intellectual property and/or sponsoring.

1. Section 6 Contracts Act (1915).

5.6. Void and Illegal Contracts

A contract could be invalid, in whole or in part, if it contravenes the Contracts Act or principles of the general law of contract. Notable is Section 36 of the Contracts Act, which states that a contract term may be set aside or modified if it is found to be unfair having regard to the contents of the contract, the circumstances of the making of the contract, later events or other circumstances. If the term is of such importance for the contract that it cannot reasonably be required that the rest of it shall be valid with unchanged contents, the contract may be modified in other respects or set aside as a whole.

5.7. Privity

The contract is at the parties' exclusive disposal and is binding for them only. Therefore, if the sponsored is a club and if one of the covenants is that players should attend at the sponsor's sales promotion activities, the club should warrant performance.

5.8. Interpretation

Basically, interpretation means defining the meaning of the wordings of a contract. The first criterion to consider is the parties' mutual intention. If the wordings are unclear or contradictory an individually drafted clause will prevail over a standard clause and a detailed clause over a general one. As to standard contracts, an unclear clause is often interpreted to the disadvantage of the party from whom the contract emanates. Furthermore, exemption clauses are often construed narrowly.

5.9. Frustration and Force Majeure

A contract can be frustrated if the parties are prevented from performing due to events out of their control, such as natural disasters. A *force majeure* clause is normally valid, though construed narrowly. Such a clause may comprise labour conflicts even though they may involve parties to the contract.

5.10. Breach of Contract

If a contract is breached, it depends in the first place on the contract as to what the legal consequences will be. Normally the breaching party will be liable to pay damages. The other party may also have a right to terminate the contract prematurely.

6. Standard Contract Terms

The following should be considered when drafting a contract regarding sports marketing.

Define the terms used and give a background in the recitals. This will facilitate the interpretation of the contract. Clearly identify the parties by setting out registration number and addresses. State very precise and detailed obligations of each party. If, for example, a trademark licence is granted, the parties ought to determine how to deal with future infringements and by whom the costs incurred should be borne. If royalties are payable, it should be clearly stated how to calculate the royalties, when they are payable and how to ensure control for the receiving party (normally books open to inspection). Duration together with procedure and possibilities to (prematurely) terminate the contract are important issues to consider. *Force majeure*, jurisdiction, governing law and dispute resolution should also be determined in the contract.

If the contract contains a licence of intellectual property rights, the licensee is, if not otherwise agreed, prevented from granting sub-licences. Further there are implied terms with regard to competition and loyalty. The licensor may not upset the conditions on which the licence is built (hinder the licensee from using the licence). Such actions might entitle the licensee to prematurely terminate the contract and claim damages.

7. Different Types of Business Arrangements

7.1. Sponsorship Agreement

The drafting of the covenants of the sponsored party should be detailed and precise. It is recommended that the contractual period is relatively short (may be combined with a prolongation clause). Premature termination of a long-term contract because of breach of contract may lead to a dispute. To be involved in a dispute with a sports club might cause bad will.

The contract should contain a provision that bans doping and entitles the sponsor to prematurely terminate the contract and to reclaim payments made. The contract should further oblige the sponsored party to take necessary precautionary measures for any sports event and to follow any security requirement. An accident might lead to the sponsor's name being exposed repeatedly on television in connection with the accident. This will cause the sponsor bad will.

7.2. Merchandising

In practice it is mostly trademarks that are merchandised. It is recommendable that a trademark, subject to licence, should be registered. Warranties of licensor's ownership and licensor's indemnification of any third party claim for infringement should be included. The trademark carries good will, thus quality control provisions of the licensee's goods should be included.

7.3. Endorsements

To falsely claim to be endorsed (the company or any of its products) by a club or a company may be considered a criminal offence.[2] To use an individual's name or picture without his or her consent is a criminal offence.[3] Both are prohibited under the Marketing Practices Act as unfair marketing practices.

7.4. Commissioning Agreement

The designer of a commemorative coin or stamp should transfer any intellectual property rights to the assignor. However, it should be noted that a general waiver of the designer's moral rights is void.

7.5. Concessions/Franchises

A concession is primarily a matter of contract and, whether exclusive or not, normally valid. If the organiser warrants, towards the party that receives the concession, that the venue is free from competing products, he must have full control of the stadium. This means that he must make sure that the owner of the stadium has not entered into agreements with third parties in conflict with the exclusive concession. The owner should give satisfying warranties and indemnifications in this respect. The dominant remedy is damages. Tying clauses must be considered individually and are also primarily a matter of contract. If they are used to abuse the position of the owner/organiser they risk to be considered in restraint of trade and be declared void.

7.6. Films and Videos

The copyright of a film or a video normally belongs to the producer. If the film/video is ordered by the sponsor he should ensure that any such right is assigned to him (a general transfer of the producer's moral right is void, though).

2. Chapter 9 Section 9 Penal Code (1962).
3. Sections 1 and 2 (SFS 1978:800).

7.7. *Public Appearances*

Any individual public appearance should be warranted by the sponsored party (e.g. the club) to ensure, in case of failure, the right of the sponsor to reclaim or withhold payments or to prematurely terminate the contract.

7.8. *Suppliership*

Ordinary sales terms should be contained in the contract. The supplier should aim for the club or the venue being free from competing products.

8. The Rights

8.1. *Options, Pre-emptions and Exclusivity*

An option is a binding and irrevocable offer, normally limited in time. A pre-emptive right is a right of first refusal. Both could be used in sports marketing to facilitate long-term relationships. Neither is valid as to sale and purchase of real estate. An exclusive licence for intellectual property is normally valid and the same goes for exclusive supplierships.[4]

8.2. *Copyright and Trademark Licences*

If the licence is exclusive it should be specified in the contract whether the licensor is entitled to exploit the work or mark himself. A licence should be limited in time. If the licensee shall have the right to grant sub-licences, this right should be set out in the contract. The licensor should warrant ownership and indemnify the licensee for any third party claims as to infringement.

It is lawful to sell or licence a trademark with or without the business it is connected with as long as such disposal is not misleading to the public.

A proposed Bill, with effect from 1 July 1993, suggests a new Competition Act which will replace the present Act, the new Act being substantially harmonised to EC competition law. It is thought not likely that the new Act will lead to any substantial changes with regard to licensing intellectual property.

8.3. *Territory, Media and Product Classes*

A licence may be divided in territory, medium or product categories.

---

4. MD 1972:7 (*Dubbman*).

It is of importance to the sponsor to ensure that there are no competitors at the same venue. Such a competition clause is usually enforceable.

8.4. Duration and Post Termination Arrangements/Restrictions

It should be clearly set out in the contract for how long the parties shall co-operate and any prolongation thereof. It should further be set out that the licence and any other rights (including any outstanding stock) should revert to the licensor following termination. A restrictive competition clause with reference to post termination could be considered to restrain trade and be declared void.

9. Financial Terms

It should be determined in the contract when and how payment shall be made. Late payment leads to an obligation to pay penalty interest according to Swedish non-compulsory law (currently 18 per cent per annum).[5] A right of set-off applies if such right has not been excluded in the contract.

10. Insurance Aspects

There are few aspects of sponsoring which require additional insurance cover for the sponsor. Where the sponsored is an individual, the sponsor could consider a policy covering death or injury of the individual. The sponsor may also consider cancellation insurance cover.

If the sponsor e.g. installs a perimeter board in a stadium which falls down, he risks claims for damages from the public. If the sponsorship includes a licence to use the sponsor's trademark with regard to certain products, the sponsor risks product liability. Both aspects are normally included in a general insurance cover of the company.

11. Advertising and Promotion

11.1. General Advertising Rules

It is a mandatory requirement that marketing is correct. Important facts must not be withheld. The presentation of the product or service may not be deceiving. The requirement for correctness is even stronger when the marketing concerns products which cannot be examined before the purchase, products for

5. Sections 3 and 6 Interest Act (1975).

children, pharmaceutical products or food. Comparisons between different products are, like any type of comparison, in principle allowed but comparisons which are difficult to check are subject to the same strong requirement for correctness. Incorrect marketing is unfair.

Discrediting, false endorsements, deceiving about the commercial or geographical origin and marketing of illegal products are all examples of marketing which is not correct. It should further be noted that marketing practices where discount tickets (trading stamps) are offered, which do not represent money, or where consumers are invited to purchase goods which do not go together by nature, are forbidden.

If any advertising is unfair the Market Court may impose a prohibition, normally under penalty of a fine, as to future advertising. If any important fact is withheld, the Market Court may impose, also normally under a penalty of a fine, an obligation to give that information in question in future advertising. Entitled to bring such action in the Court is the Consumer Ombudsman and, secondarily, an organisation of consumers or businessmen or employees. An action as to prohibition may also, secondarily, be brought by any businessman concerned. A businessman, who wilfully deceives the public in his advertising in order to increase the demand of his products, risks to be sentenced to pay a fine or to imprisonment for one year maximum. If a businessman violates a prohibition imposed by the Market Court he risks to be liable to pay damages to his competitors.

Advertising on television is governed by the Radio Act (1966) and must not be political (including the labour market) or religious. The advertising must not address children under 12 years of age or use people or characters who have a substantial role in TV programmes which address those children. It is possible to sponsor a TV coverage of a sports event. In such case it is lawful that the TV company informs the TV audience that the programme is sponsored and who the sponsor is (in which context the trademark or the tradename of the sponsor may be shown on the screen).

Marketing of certain products is especially restricted.

11.2. Alcohol

The marketing must not be addressed to minors. Advertising on television and radio is forbidden. The same goes for advertising in newspapers or other periodicals. Any other marketing is subject to considerable restrictions. In practice this means that marketing alcohol is forbidden. Any marketing in conflict with the above is unfair.[6]

6. SFS 1978:763; see further guidelines (1979) given by the National Board of Consumers.

11.3. Tobacco

Marketing must not be addressed to minors. Advertising on television and radio is forbidden. The same goes for advertising in the sporting sections of newspapers or in sporting periodicals. Any marketing must contain information about the dangers of smoking and also a declaration of contents. Any marketing in conflict with the above is unfair. A proposed Bill suggesting that any tobacco marketing should be prohibited is, at present, under consideration.[7]

11.4. Pharmaceutical Products and Food

Marketing of pharmaceutical products is considered to be powerful and persuasive towards sick people who are presupposed to be less critical than other people. Such marketing is restricted by a strong requirement for correctness.[8] The same goes for naturopathic products.[9] Food, being an important everyday commodity, must also be marketed under the same strong requirement (especially nutritional information).[10]

12. The Venue

12.1. Public Liability

Normally, the event organiser has hired or leased the stadium from the owner. Both the organiser and the owner may become responsible to members of the public for damage. Negligence is preconditional to responsibility. Necessary precautionary measures must be taken which include compliance with fire regulations and other rules of public safety. The owner may become responsible for deficiencies in permanent safety devices. The organiser may become jointly responsible if such deficiencies make it obvious that the event should not have taken place there. The organiser is in addition responsible for the precautionary measures necessary for the event in question that have been taken.

12.2. Control

The stadium is generally under the control of the organiser. The organiser may restrict access (e.g. the press generally or subject to a prohibition from filming, taking pictures or advertising) or grant accreditation. The air space above the

7. SFS 1978:764; see further guidelines (1986) given by the National Board of Consumers.
8. Section 15 (SFS 1962:701); see further the Code (1990) of Marketing Practice laid down by the Pharmaceutical Industries' Trade Associations LIF and RUFI.
9. See guidelines (1989) given by the National Board of Consumers.
10. See guidelines (1977:1 and 1981:1) given by the National Board of Consumers.

property is controlled by the organiser to a limited height, i.e. he cannot hinder the airborne traffic. An unauthorised entry, in the stadium or in the air, could amount to trespassing. The civil remedy is damages. If any prohibition is violated that may also entitle to damages.

13. Dispute Resolution

The court proceedings consist of preparatory proceedings (hearings and in writing) and the main hearing. The proceedings are normally time-consuming and costly. The recovery sought could be either an injunction, a court order (including damages) or declaratory relief. The cause of action could be combined with an application for an interlocutory judgment of a seizure or an injunction. Damages sought could include consequential damages but often such claims have been excluded in the contract. The legal costs of both parties will, in principle, be borne by the losing party. Swedish law offers a$possibility to obtain an injunction to pay a contract debt but the procedure differs from an action for an agreed sum.

Any dispute regarding a question in the nature of a civil matter which may be compromised by agreement may be referred to arbitration by the parties. This means that any action because of breach of contract or claims for damages because of infringement may be referred to arbitration, while matters as to unfair competition, unfair marketing, invalidation of an intellectual property right and questions of punishment, forfeiture and other consequences (except damages) of a finding of criminal guilt may not be referred to arbitration. The procedure is governed by the Arbitration Act (1929).

An arbitration is very expensive and both parties are jointly and severally liable for the costs of the arbitrators. The legal costs for both parties including the costs for the arbitrators will, however, finally be borne by the losing party solely. The award shall be given within six months and it is secret and final.

There are no alternative dispute solutions at hand in Sweden. In court proceedings the judge may, if the parties agree thereto, refer the dispute to a mediator.

Sweden is a signatory to the Lugano Convention. From 1993, a foreign judgment, given in a country which has ratified the Convention, is enforceable in Sweden in accordance with the regulations in the Convention. Other foreign judgments, except for those given in the Nordic countries, are not enforceable, but may be introduced as evidence in the subsequent Swedish proceeding. Foreign arbitral awards are normally enforceable upon presentation to and validation by the Court of Appeal in Stockholm.

SPORTS
MARKETING

Switzerland

by Thomas Klooz

1. Sports Marketing – A Business

In Switzerland, the State does not directly fund the organisation and staging of sports events. It is the responsibility of each organiser to finance its event. Today, the most important sources of revenue are, besides entrance fees, income derived from sponsorship and/or from the sale of the television broadcast rights. Association with sports events upgrades a company's image and promotes its products and services. Swiss companies invest approximately 200 million Swiss francs each year in marketing activities related to sport. This substantial figure does not even include the additional sums spent on the exploitation of the acquired sports marketing rights and commercial opportunities.

Athletes do not receive financial support from the State and, accordingly, have to bear the burden of financing their sports themselves. In many cases, the athletes obtain a certain amount of support from the respective sports federations and/or clubs, as well as from private organisations. The Swiss Sports Aid Foundation, for example, now raises more than 5 million Swiss francs per year for the purpose of supporting Swiss athletes (compared with 1.7 million in 1980).

Sports marketing is an important part of the advertising and promotions industry, both on the media side and in corporate strategies. It is generally recognised by the public that, without sports marketing activities, many sports events might not take place at all, especially in view of the steadily increasing costs involved in their organisation and staging.

2. The National Legal System[1]

The Federal Constitution grants the lawmaking power to the Cantons, with the exception of those fields which are expressly delegated to the federal authorities by the Federal Constitution. Federal law always takes precedence over Cantonal law. Furthermore, the Federal Constitution, international treaties to which Switzerland is a party and the federal statutes are the most important sources of legislation.

Two main fields of law can be distinguished:

- Public law, being that part of law dealing with the State and its organisations as well as the relationship between themselves and individuals (e.g. constitutional law, administrative law, tax law, civil procedure law).
- Private law, being basically that part of the law covering the relationship between individuals (persons and legal entities). The most important statutes in this respect are the Swiss Civil Code ('CC') referring to persons, family, inheritance and property, the Swiss Code of Obligations ('CO') referring to the principles of contracts,[2] specific types of contracts, corporations, and other business organisations, as well as the Federal Statute on Private International Law of 1987, effective since 1989, referring to such matters as conflict of jurisdiction, recognition and enforcement of foreign decisions and international arbitration.[3]

3. Applicable Laws[4]

There are no statutes which address specific issues directly related to sports marketing. A mixture of various statutes are relevant in this case. The most important legal source covering the contractual relationship is the CO. In addition, intellectual property laws are often important in connection with sports marketing.

4. Intellectual Property Rights

The most relevant sources of law on intellectual property are the following:

---

1. See *Introduction to Swiss Law*, edited by F. Dessemontet and T. Ansay, Deventer/The Netherlands 1983; *Business Law Guide to Switzerland*, Pestalozzi Gmuer & Heiz, Wiesbaden/Germany 1991.
2. See *infra* p. 360 *et seq.*
3. See *infra* p. 364 *et seq.*.
4. A detailed overview with respect to the applicable laws described herein is given in the *Business Law Guide to Switzerland*, see *supra* note 1.

4.1. Trademarks

The currently applicable Federal Trade Mark Statute of 1890 will be replaced by a new trademark statute, due to come into force in the Spring of 1993.

The registration and protection of trademarks by owners not domiciled in Switzerland is governed by the provisions of the Paris Convention for the Protection of Industrial Property, the Madrid Convention for the Registration of Trade Marks and the Treaty of Nice on the International Classification of Goods and Services.

The new law, as opposed to the existing law, provides that the trademark right will be created by the registration of the trademarks (today the principle of first use applies). The new law will further allow the protection and registration of service marks. According to the new law, new marks will also be published for opposition, whereas today it is left to the owner of an existing trademark to raise any opposition. A trademark registration will be valid for ten (today twenty) years and may be renewed for similar periods indefinitely. Should the trademark not be used for five (today three) consecutive years, the cancellation of the trademark's registration may be ordered by the court following a petition for cancellation by an interested party.

4.2. Copyright

The main source of law is the Federal Copyright Statute of 1922. A new law has been passed by Parliament in October 1992 and is expected to become effective in the middle of 1993. Switzerland is also a member of the Universal Copyright Convention of 6 September 1952 and has ratified the Berne Convention for the Protection of Works of Literature and Art in its Stockholm version of 1967.

No copyright register exists in Switzerland. The requirement for the qualification as copyright is that the work is an original intellectual creation with individual features. A work is protected following its communication in any form (e.g. language, sound, picture, physical embodiment). Duration of protection is for the author's lifetime plus fifty years (in the new law seventy years).

The rights of exploitation of copyright may be licensed or assigned, but the moral rights (*droit moral*) remain vested in the author for his life. The moral rights are part of the personality rights pursuant to Arts. 28 and 29 of the CC. The author may waive, explicitly or implicitly, any right of exploitation of the work. As far as permitted by the rules for the protection of the personality, the author may also waive his personality rights with respect to the work.

4.3. Unfair Competition

The main legal source for protecting fairness in the market place is the Federal Unfair Competition Statute of 1986, in force since 1 March 1988. The aim of the Statute is to guarantee fair and correct competition in the interest of all participants. In addition, the rules protecting personality rights in the CC provide further protection against unfair competition but in a more restricted manner. The names of individuals and companies are also protected in the CC and CO respectively.

There are also private organisations that undertake to ensure compliance with the principles of fair competition. In particular, the Commission for Fairness in Advertising, established by a private foundation of the advertising industry, has developed an Advertising Code and decides upon advertising practices brought before the Commission.

At an international level, Switzerland is a member of the Paris Convention for the Protection of Industrial Property in its Stockholm version of 1967. Accordingly, Switzerland is obliged to provide effective protection against unfair competition to the nationals of other member countries.

4.4. Designs and Models

The main source of law is the Federal Statute on Industrial Designs and Models of 1900, as amended. Switzerland is also a member of the Hague Convention for the International Depositing of Industrial Designs and Models of 1960 and of the Locarno Convention for the International Classification of Industrial Designs of 1968.

Protection of a design or model (covering the aesthetic aspect of an object) is obtained through registration at the Federal Intellectual Property Office in Berne. Protection can be obtained for a maximum period of 15 years.

5. The Contract Generally and Preliminary Agreements

5.1. Preliminary Agreements

Contrary to the business practice in common law countries, there is usually only one agreement governing the relationship between the parties. Following the negotiations between the parties, arrangements are governed by the contract executed by the parties concerned.

Occasionally, the intent of the parties to enter into a business relationship is reflected in a letter of intent. It is, however, only binding for the parties and enforceable to the extent provided for therein.

5.2. *Freedom of Contract*

The contents of and the parties to a contract can be chosen freely. The parties are also free to enter into a type of contract which is not, or only in part, regulated by statute. As mentioned above, arrangements relating to sports marketing are governed by contracts which are not regulated in the statutes containing those elements the parties have agreed upon as being essential to the specific case. Finally, nobody can be forced to commit themselves to a contract.

On certain aspects, which, however, are not relevant to sports marketing arrangements, there may be specific limitations of the principle of freedom of contracts (e.g. in labour or environmental law).

Further, it should be noted that certain negative elements could make a contract null and void. Pursuant to the CO[5] a contract providing for an impossibility, having illegal contents or violating *bonae mores* is null and void. If such defect only affects particular parts of the contract, however, then only those parts will be null and void, unless it is to be presumed that the contract would not have been concluded without the defective parts.

5.3. *Offer and Acceptance*

A contract is concluded, when the parties have expressed their mutual consent. This can be either verbally stated or implied.[6] In practice, there is normally a negotiation process during which one party makes an offer and the other accepts it. The requirements and technicalities as to when and how a valid offer and acceptance is made are set forth in the CO.[7]

If the parties have reached an agreement on the essential terms of the arrangement, there is a legal presumption that a reservation of ancillary points does not affect the binding effect of the agreement.[8]

5.4. *Consideration*

Contrary to the common law system, the requirement of a 'bargained exchange' does not exist under Swiss law. A contractual obligation, which has been properly provided, is valid and enforceable, regardless of consideration. However, in most contracts relating to sports marketing a consideration is stipulated, either in the form of a payment or of the supply of goods or services.

---

5. Art. 20 CO.
6. Art. 1 CO.
7. Arts. 3–9 CO.
8. Art. 20 CO.

5.5. *Form and Execution*

Most contracts do not depend on the observation of formalities. Contracts can be validly entered into orally or even without any verbal expression of consent, for example, by actions implying an intention to enter into a contract. Certain contracts, however, are required by statute to be executed in writing (e.g. suretyship, assignment) and in specific cases even recorded in a public deed (e.g. mortgages, formation of a company). In the event of any formal requirement not being met, the contract is void.

A written contract needs to be signed in handwriting by the parties committed to it. If a company is a contractual party, the contract has to be signed by one or more authorised representatives, normally directors and/or officers of the company concerned. It is advisable for the signatories to initial all pages of the contract in order to prove its completeness.

5.6. *Void and Illegal Contracts*

As mentioned, a contract with an impossible, illegal or an immoral content is void.[9] Further, a contract that does not comply with the statutory legal requirements is void. Should a part of the contract be null and void, the remainder of the contract remains valid, unless it is to be presumed that the contract would not have been concluded without the defective part.[10]

If a party has been induced to enter into a contract by the wilful deception of the other party, the contract does not bind the deceived party even if the error so induced was not material.[11] Likewise, where a contracting party has been unlawfully forced to conclude a contract while under duress, the aggrieved party is entitled to void the contract.[12] The same applies to contracts that are concluded as a result of one of the parties exploiting the distress, inexperience or improvidence of the other party.[13]

5.7. *Privity*

The 'privity of contract' doctrine is not specifically known in Swiss law. However, it is recognised that only the parties to a contract can be committed through the obligations regulated in it. A third party can only be obligated, if it becomes a party to the contract. Alternatively, a contractual party could undertake to cause a third party to a certain performance or non-performance.

---

9. See *supra*, p. 361.
10. Art. 20 CO.
11. Art. 28 CO.
12. Arts. 29 and 30 CO.
13. Art. 21 CO.

5.8. Interpretation

The courts have developed certain rules which govern the interpretation of contracts. Primarily, based on the principle of confidence, the courts rely on the *bona fide* intent of the parties on conclusion of the contract. Words are interpreted in accordance with their general meaning. Unusual or technical terms have to be construed in such a manner that the other party can be expected to interpret the general meaning of such terms. Proponents of a provision cannot insist upon their own interpretation if the other party could reasonably understand it differently.

5.9. Frustration and Force Majeure

The frustration doctrine, as known in common law, is not recognised by the courts. Under Swiss Law, contractual obligations are discharged if the performance, which at the time of conclusion of the contract was possible, has become impossible.[14] The impossibility must be 'objective', meaning that the obligation cannot be performed by anyone. *Force majeure* events, such as an earthquake or other natural catastrophes, provide sufficient grounds for discharging obligations. To the contrary, 'subjective' impossibility, e.g. unforeseen lack of financial funds, is not sufficient. As long as the obligation could be performed by someone other than the party liable, there is no discharge of the obligation.

The common law principle of frustration comprises a broader concept than the rules regarding impossibility. Part of the frustration doctrine is governed by rules in the CO covering error as to the basis of the contract. Pursuant to these rules a contract is voidable, if a signing party relied in good faith on a basis which later proves to be non-existent.

Sports marketing contracts generally include a clause covering the issue of *force majeure* and its consequences to the contract.

5.10. Breach of Contract

The contract is breached if a party does not comply with its terms. Swiss Law distinguishes primarily the failure of performance and defective performance[15] as well as delay in performance.[16] The general contractual liability depends on the fault of the party liable.[17] The degree of fault is relevant for the determination of the amount of damage which the defaulting party has to pay. The

14. Art. 24 cl. 4 CO.
15. Arts. 97–101 CO.
16. Arts. 102–109 CO.
17. Art. 99 CO.

parties may restrict or exclude their contractual liability but not for intentional acts or gross negligence.[18]

Breach of contract does not automatically discharge the other party of its obligations. The CO foresees a mechanism which grants the injured party various options, including notice for subsequent performance, release from its own obligations and/or the award of damages.[19]

6. Standard Contract Terms

Although specific contractual terms vary from project to project, there are certain basic issues which should be covered in sports marketing contracts:

6.1. Parties

The contractual parties have to be identified at the beginning of the contract (full name and address of domicile).

6.2. Preamble

A preamble describes the authority and role of the contractual parties and addresses in the broadest terms the subject matter of the contract. The preamble can also help in the interpretation of the main provisions of the contract.

6.3. Definitions

Often many technical terms and abbreviations are used throughout the sports marketing contract. A list of definitions at the beginning of the contract facilities the reading and understanding of the document.

6.4. Governing Law

According to the Federal Private International Law Statute of 1987 ('PIL Statute'), the parties are free to choose the applicable law. However, the choice of law has to be explicit or clearly evident from the contract or from the circumstances.[20] In the absence of a choice of law, the PIL Statute provides that a contract is governed by the law of the country most closely connected with it. In this case it is presumed to be the country where the party making

18. Art. 100 CO.
19. Arts. 107–109 CO.
20. Art. 116 PIL Statute.

the characteristic performance has its habitual residence, or, if the contract is based on a business activity, has its business establishment.[21]

6.5. *Jurisdiction*

In the absence of an express choice of jurisdiction, the main rule is that a solvent debtor with a Swiss domicile must be sued, for personal debts, before the court of the debtor's Swiss domicile.[22]

Switzerland has ratified the Lugano Convention of 1988, effective since 1 January 1992, which parallels for the EC and EFTA countries the amended Brussels Convention of 1968 between EC countries on jurisdiction and enforcement of judgments in civil and commercial matters. The Lugano Convention applies to conflicts of jurisdiction between persons domiciled in EFTA countries as well as between persons domiciled in an EFTA country and in an EC country. However, the important Art. 5(1) of the Lugano Convention, which provides for the jurisdiction of the courts of the place of performance of the contractual obligation, will only become applicable in a claim against a solvent debtor domiciled in Switzerland as of 1 January 2000. The reason is that Switzerland, in its ratification of the Lugano Convention, has reserved the continued application of the above-mentioned main rule (solvent debtor to be sued at its Swiss domicile) set forth in the Federal Constitution.

The provisions of the PIL Statute remain applicable only against persons not domiciled in one of the Lugano Convention countries.

Pursuant to the Lugano Convention and the PIL Statute the parties are free to make a specific choice of jurisdiction or an arbitration agreement for an existing or future dispute arising from the contract.

6.6. *Financial Provisions*

The details of financial arrangements, in particular the monetary amount to be paid and the payment schedule, should be covered. It is advisable to include an interest clause in the event of delayed payments. The legal rate of interest is 5 per cent per annum unless a higher rate is agreed or the creditor can prove higher damages.[23]

21. Art. 117 PIL Statute.
22. Art. 59 Federal Constitution.
23. Art. 104 CO.

6.7. Term

The date of commencement and expiration of the contractual relationship should be stipulated. If the parties wish to deviate from the statutory termination provisions, the agreed terms must be specifically itemised in the contract.

6.8. Option

Many sports marketing arrangements, in particular sponsorship agreements, have a long-term perspective. An appropriate option provision may help to protect the investment for a continued involvement in the project concerned.

6.9. Force Majeure

Should the performance be impossible, for reasons beyond the control of the parties, the contract may be suspended. Such events considered by the parties to be impossible, as well as the consequences of such events, should be specified in the contract. The statutory provisions in this respect may prove to be not specific enough to cover the circumstances anticipated by the parties.

7. Different Types of Business Arrangements

7.1. Sponsorship Agreement[24]

The sponsorship agreement is a type of contract which is not regulated by statute, in particular not by the CO. Accordingly, the parties to such an arrangement are free to agree on its specific contents within the 'freedom to contract' principle. Thus, no formal requirements need to be observed. However, in view of the complexity of most sponsorship agreements, it is advisable to execute a contract in writing.

Contractual arrangements generally cover at least the following elements:

- Description of the sponsor, the party sponsored and the subject-matter of the sponsorship; these items are usually described in the recitals to the contract.
- The sponsor's obligations, in particular the payment of fees and/or the supply of goods, equipment and services and/or certain promotional obligations in connection with the sports event concerned.
- Grant of rights, in particular, the grant of marketing and other commercial rights in connection with the sports event concerned (e.g. advertising at the

24. See: Netzle Stephan, *Sponsoring von Sportverbänden*, Zurich 1988; Hauser Thomas, *Der Sponsoring-Vertrag im schweizerischen Recht*, Zürich 1991.

venue or licensing of event logos and designations), and obligations of the party sponsored relating thereto.
- Term of the agreement.
- Termination of the agreement.

Exclusivity is often a key element of a sponsorship relationship. This means that, within its designated and defined product category, a sponsor is granted an exclusive association with the event and/or the event organiser concerned.[25]

Based on statutory rules certain products may not be advertised or only to a limited extent. In particular, advertising for alcoholic beverages, tobacco and pharmaceutical products is substantially regulated. For example, the Federal Statute on Radio and Television of 1991, in force since 1 April 1992, expressly prohibits any advertising on radio and television for products within these categories.[26] Besides the previously mentioned statutory regulations, private organisations undertake to ensure compliance with advertising standards. The most significant body is the Commission for Fairness in Advertising, established by the Swiss advertising industry for deciding on disputed advertising practices submitted to it.[27]

7.2. Merchandising

Again, merchandising agreements are not regulated by statute. The specific contents of such an agreement depend on the nature of the intellectual property right(s) being licensed. Provisions accounted for in such licence agreements cover issues like ownership of the marks, protection of the marks, quality control, mark approval procedure, product liability, obligations in the event of unauthorised use of the marks and royalty provisions (royalty rate, amount of minimum royalty, advance payment, basis for the calculation of the royalty).

7.3. Endorsements

Depending on the regulations of the sports federation an athlete is a member of, an endorsement agreement can be concluded with the athlete. Some federations completely preclude arrangements with individual sponsors, others require the federation's prior approval and others limit opportunities for individual sponsorships.

Contractual arrangements are limited only by the personal freedom of an athlete which may not be unduly restricted. The danger of such restrictions is

25. As to the legal implications regarding exclusivity, see *infra* p. 369.
26. Art. 18 Statute on Radio and Television.
27. Details regarding the Commission for Fairness in Advertising and its procedure are set forth in the following publication: *Recht der Werbung in Europa*, Band 5, 'Schweiz' by R. Knaak and M. Ritscher, Bonn 1991.

latent in the event of endorsement agreements. For example, an agreement obliging the athlete, at its discretion, to be available at the sponsor's disposition may be in conflict with the statutory law protecting personality rights.[28] Based thereon, the use of designations expressing or implying a relationship or other association with an athlete or sports organisation demand the existence of a mutual understanding to this effect. Lacking of the necessary authorisation will constitute an infringement of personality rights protected by statute.

7.4. Commissioning Agreement

Beyond the issues relevant to a specific agreement, the assignment in the copyright should be expressly covered in the contract as far as possible under Swiss law. The copyright of a work always belongs originally to the individual author. As mentioned before[29] the rights of exploitation may be licensed or assigned, whereas the moral rights remain vested in the author. Although there is no particular form required for an assignment or licence of a copyright, it advisable to execute the respective agreement in writing.

8. The Rights

In addition to basic rights covered in a sports marketing contract there might be certain additional benefits to the parties.

8.1. Option

The success of a sponsorship depends, among other things, on the continuity of the sponsorship venture. The sponsor usually feels that a significant amount of its goodwill is being invested in an event or project besides the financial commitments. In order to protect the investment a sponsor should have some assurance of the opportunity for continued involvement. Such an assurance can be given in different forms, ranging from the right to first discuss and negotiate a new agreement, to the right of first refusal. The content of the specific option very much depends on the commercial arrangements agreed upon by the contractual parties. The provision itself needs to be carefully drawn up so as to avoid ambiguities or disappointment when the contract expires.

---

28. Arts. 27-29 CC.
29. See p. 359.

8.2. *Pre-emption*

There are no specific rules which would apply to the pre-emption right within the scope of the sports marketing agreement. However, a pre-emption right can be agreed between the parties, whereby the terms of such right need to be discussed between the parties. The result of such discussions should be provided for in the agreement.

8.3. *Exclusivity*

The scope of the exclusivity granted to a party always relates to a specific content. For example, in an event sponsorship rights package, the sponsor is granted exclusivity with respect to a defined product category, meaning that no third party may be granted such or similar rights with respect to the product category concerned. Exclusivity can also be defined on a territorial basis. No third parties within the defined territory may be granted the rights concerned.

Attention should be paid to the fact that exclusivity rights do not infringe upon the Federal Cartel Statute of 1986, in particular the rules defining unlawful restraints on competition. The Statute expressly declares all measures of a cartel or similar organisation to be illegal should such measures exclude, or significantly hinder, third parties from competing or hinder them in a significant way from taking up or exercising competition in a given particular market.[30] In the event of an arrangement having an effect in the common market countries, the EC fair competition rules may become relevant.[31] These rules would have become applicable to Switzerland, if it had ratified the Agreement for the European Economic Area ('EEA').[32]

8.4. *Copyright Licence*

No specific rules apply to the licence of a 'work', protected as a copyright, within the scope of a sports marketing related agreement. The provisions normally included in licence agreements are equally applicable.

8.5. *Trademark Licence*

Again, there are no characteristic rules which would primarily apply to the licence of a trademark in a sponsorship or other sports marketing agreement. Generally, trademark licences cannot be registered in Switzerland. Accordingly,

30. Art. 6 Cartel Statute.
31. See p. 404 *et seq.*
32. The referendum was held on 6 December 1992.

the trademark owner may require the licensee to manifest the licence relationship by indicating it on the product itself.

8.6. Territory

Usually, the rights granted under a sponsorship agreement are limited to a defined geographical area.

8.7. Media

One and the same intellectual property rights can be licensed to different parties, provided the rights relate to different media and different ways of exploitation (for example, with respect to a certain film and video material one party is granted the theatrical exploitation rights, another party the non-theatrical exploitation rights).

8.8. Product Classes

Most sponsorship programmes are based on a product exclusivity concept. This means that, within its designated product category a sponsor expects the privilege of exclusive relationship with the event organiser and the event itself throughout the entire period of its sponsorship.

8.9. Duration

The term of the contractual relationship should be covered in the agreement; generally, the agreement starts on the date of its execution and ends on a certain pre-agreed date.

8.10. Post Termination

Any undertakings which may be valid beyond the term must be specifically identified (for example, the undertaking not to create a logo similar to the federation logo or the undertaking to keep the financial terms confidential). Equally, any rights which may be exercised even after expiration of the agreement must be carefully defined (for example, if the sponsor may continue to sell off the existing inventory of products bearing the event logo).

9. Financial Terms

With respect to the payment of the agreed fees the following points need to be itemised in the contract:

- whether payment is to be in advance;
- whether payment is to be paid in instalments or in a lump sum;
- the payment dates, the payment method (for example, by cheque or swift transfer);
- in which currency payment has to be made;
- whether payment is dependent upon the fulfilment of certain conditions (for example, in an athlete endorsement agreement the payment might only be due upon qualification of the athlete for the Olympic Games).

In the event of default of payment, interest is due on the stipulated amount at the rate of five per cent, unless the parties have agreed on a different rate.[33]

The agreement may also stipulate that payment obligations have to be performed without a payer's right to invoke set-off, which is permitted under Swiss law if the applicable requirements have been met.[34]

Apart from payment the parties may agree on the provision of 'value in kind', meaning the supply of certain goods, equipment and/or services to the other party. For example, event organisers require the provision of technical products and services for the execution of their organisational duties (e.g. timing, measurement and computer equipment; television monitors; beverages; food; clothing for officials and the like). The nature and the value of the material and services to be supplied as well as times of delivery should be specified in the agreement in as much detail as possible.

Lately, an additional element has become important in sponsorship contracts. Certain event organisers (e.g. organising committees of the Olympic Games) require a sponsor's commitment to frequently use the event marks (in particular, the event logo), in order to contribute to the promotion of the marks and thereby increase their recognition and value.

10. Insurance Aspects

Various risks and related liabilities may be a result of transactions regarding sports marketing. For example:

- Third party liability for the organiser of a sports event: according to Swiss law the owner of the premises on which a sports event takes place (such as

33. Art. 104 CO.
34. Art. 120 CO.

a stadium) is strictly liable for damage caused in connection with the premises, as a result of faulty design, the construction or inadequate maintenance.
- Product liability: no specific statutory provision governs product liability, with the exception of an article in the PIL Statute governing the applicable law in international arrangements. However, the Federal Supreme Court has recently developed a case law which is similar to the manufacturer's liability under the EC Directive on Product Liability (which would have become effective for Switzerland in the event of ratification of the Agreement for the EEA). The 'producer' of a product is liable for damage caused by a defect in the product. The liability is strictly for the whole production process (i.e. the claimant has not to prove the 'producer's' fault) but not absolute, because the 'producer' has certain possibilities of defence. Nevertheless, the claimant still has to prove that the defect caused the damage.
- Cancellation: if an event has to be cancelled due to a *force majeure* event, such as bad weather conditions, then there is a risk of loss of revenues.

In order to be adequately covered against such risks, it is advisable to take out an appropriate insurance coverage.

11. Advertising and Promotion

11.1. Source of Law

From a constitutional point of view, advertising is an economic activity and accordingly is protected by the principle of freedom of trade and industry as guaranteed by the Federal Constitution.[35] Any restriction of such freedom requires a statutory basis, which has to be in the public interest and proportional. However, Switzerland does not have a uniform codified advertising law. A number of aspects are regulated in the private law, for example, the law covering the protection of personality rights, as well as in the public law, for example, in the field of food advertising. The most important source of law in connection with advertising is the Unfair Competition Statute. The purpose of the Statute is to guarantee fair and unhindered competition in the interest of all participants. For example, any deception with regard to quality, quantity, price, origin or sales conditions of one's own goods or services is prohibited by the Statute. The Statute on Radio and Television includes, *inter alia*, rules regarding advertising and sponsoring on television and radio, with further specification in an administrative regulation of the Federal Government.

Besides the statutory rules, private organisations undertake to ensure the compliance with the standard of fair competition. As mentioned above, the Commission for Fairness in Advertising is the most important organisation in this respect. The basis for the practice of the commission is its Codex of 1989,

35. Art. 31 Federal Constitution.

amended in 1990, which has been developed from principles of the International Code of Fair Practice in Advertising of the International Chamber of Commerce.

Finally, it should be mentioned that in 1991 Switzerland ratified the European Convention on Transfrontier Television adopted by the Council of Europe Committee of Ministers of 1989.

11.2. Restrictions

The Federal Food Statute of 1908, currently being substantially revised, aims to protect the consumer of food products from deception in connection with information provided about the products. Further, this Statute contains a number of restrictions concerning the advertising of alcoholic beverages. For example, liquors may not be advertised on radio and television, on means of public transport, on sports grounds, at sports events, and so on.

Regulations regarding the advertising of tobacco products are primarily set out in the above-mentioned Statute. Furthermore, the Association of Swiss Cigarette Manufacturers recently imposed voluntarily on its members restrictions relating to advertising of their products which go beyond the statutory law. For example, neither may athletes promote cigarettes nor may models under the age of 25. Compliance with these restrictions is controlled by the Commission for Fairness in Advertising.

Further, a concordat between all the Cantons regarding the control of pharmaceutical products contains limitations on the advertising of these products. For example, products which are only available on medical prescription may not be advertised at all.

As mentioned before, the Statute on Radio and Television generally prohibits any advertising for alcoholic beverages, tobacco and pharmaceutical products availablc on prescription on radio and television.

11.3. Comparative Advertising

In principle, pursuant to the Unfair Competition Statute of 1986 comparative advertising is allowed, provided the rules of fair competition are respected, i.e. the advertising is correct, neither misleading nor unnecessarily disparaging. There are a number of decisions of the Federal Supreme Court, which has examined comparative advertising practices under the aspect of disparagement. For example, it has been stated that a fair comparison in advertising or otherwise must be objectively true or that only comparable items may be compared.

12. The Venue

12.1. Control

The owner of a venue (e.g. a stadium), where a sports event takes place, is either the local community (e.g. the city concerned) or a private entity (e.g. a company or other private organisation). Ownership includes the right to use the venue and to exercise control over it, always, however, within the limitations imposed by law (such as, for example, construction, environmental and safety regulations). The owner may exercise control over the air space of the venue to the extent that the use of this area is of interest to the owner,[36] for example for promotional purposes. The terms of the use of a certain venue by an event organiser are the subject matter of an agreement with the event organiser.

12.2. Access and Accreditation

The event organiser needs to grant access to those parties, who have to perform specific functions at the event. For example, the host broadcasting organisation appointed to cover the event by television should have access to the venue, obtain suitable parking space for its vehicles, as well as space and facilities for production staff, crew and equipment. The issuance of accreditations to the authorised persons facilitates the control over access.

12.3. Public Liability

This issue has been addressed in the section on insurance, see pp. 371 and 372.

12.4. Concessions

Sponsors and suppliers of a sports event are normally exclusively entitled to display, sample and sell their products in the area of the venue controlled by the event organiser. This means that for the duration of the event no competitive products may be available at the venue. The organiser has also to ensure the availability of the utilities supply (power, light, water) and other facilities (e.g. storage space) required for exercising the above-mentioned rights on-site.

---

36. Art. 667 CC.

13. Dispute Resolution

13.1. Court Procedure

While the substantive law is mainly Federal, the law of civil procedure is basically Cantonal. Each of the 26 Cantons has its own Code of Civil Procedure as well as a Statute concerning the organisation of the Courts. The Federal Code of Civil Procedure deals with those few matters where the Federal Supreme Court has exclusive jurisdiction or where it has to decide appeals against Cantonal judgments.

Most trial courts consist of three or more judges. Cases of minor nature or which are the subject of a summary judgment are usually tried by a single judge. Besides the courts of general jurisdiction, some Cantons have specialised courts, such as, for example, labour courts and commercial courts. The Federal Supreme Court with its seat in Lausanne has primarily the function of deciding appeals on cantonal decisions.

13.2. Remedies Including Damages and Equitable Relief

The remedies available in a certain matter are usually provided for in the statute covering the substantive law. For example, in the field of unfair competition, persons affected or threatened by unfair competition may request under the Unfair Competition Statute:[37]

(a) an injunction against an imminent infringement, if the plaintiff establishes the existence of violation of the rules against unfair competition and resulting damage;
(b the removal of an effective infringement (a cease and desist order); or
(c) a declaratory judgment as to the illegality of the infringement if it continues to cause damaging effects.

In addition, the publication of the court order may be requested, allowing the plaintiff to remedy false, misleading or unnecessarily disparaging statements.

13.3. Costs

The costs of proceedings generally have to be borne by the losing party. If no party wins totally, the costs are allocated proportionally. Should, for example, a party cause unnecessary costs, the court may depart from this rule, under certain circumstances.

37. Art. 9 Unfair Competition Statute.

In principle, each party must compensate the other for costs and expenses, in proportion to the court costs it has itself been charged with. It must be stated, however, that usually compensation awarded by the courts does not fully cover all the costs and expenses incurred by the winning party.

13.4. Arbitration

In sports marketing agreements the parties often agree to have a dispute arising therefrom decided by an arbitration court. In comparison to ordinary court procedure the advantage of arbitration procedure is, for example, that the parties have the assurance that the case is decided on by judges having the necessary expertise on the matter concerned. Furthermore, the existence and the nature of the dispute can be kept confidential.

Domestic arbitration between parties registered or domiciled in Switzerland is primarily governed by the Swiss Intercantonal Concordat on Arbitration of 1969. Any right at the free disposal of the parties is arbitrable unless the case is subject to the exclusive jurisdiction of a State authority pursuant to a mandatory legal provision (e.g. claims concerning aspects of family law). The most important part of the Concordat concerns the organisation of domestic arbitration. The Concordat also covers some procedural rules but not in an exhaustive manner.

International arbitration in Switzerland is governed by the 'International Arbitration' chapter of the PIL Statute. 'International arbitration' is defined as arbitration conducted before an arbitral tribunal seated in Switzerland and involving at least one party that is not domiciled or resident in Switzerland at the time of consent to arbitration. Any dispute involving financial interests may be submitted to arbitration.[38] This includes, for example, disputes relating to copyright or trademarks.

There are two major features of the international arbitration law, namely the emphasis placed on party autonomy in the conduct of the arbitral process, and the restrictions placed upon challenges to the finality of arbitral awards. There are only five grounds for setting aside an award:[39]

(1) improper constitution of the tribunal;
(2) erroneous decision of the tribunal regarding its own jurisdiction;
(3) decision going beyond the claims submitted to the tribunal or failure to decide one of the claims;
(4) lack of due process;
(5) public policy.

Where none of the parties has its domicile in Switzerland, they may, by an express statement in the arbitration agreement or by subsequent agreement in

38. Art. 177 PIL Statute for international arbitration.
39. Art. 190 PIL Statute.

writing, exclude the action of annulment or they may limit it to one or several of the grounds listed above.[40]

Appeals against an award have to be submitted to the Federal Supreme Court.

13.5. Alternative Dispute Resolution

The parties to a contract may agree to submit the decision of a certain issue to an expert arbitrator, rather than to an ordinary court or arbitration panel. For example, in a sponsorship agreement, the supply of goods and services may have been agreed on up to a certain value and the parties may have agreed that the value of the goods and services actually supplied could be finally determined by an expert in the particular field, if the parties should disagree on each party's own evaluation. The decision of the expert arbitrator is not a judgment but a statement. According to procedural law, such a statement is binding upon the parties involved in subsequent court proceedings, if:

- it concerns a matter which is at the free disposal of the parties, and
- there was no reason for challenging the expert, and
- the expert's decision has been based on a normal procedure, and
- the decision is not evidently incorrect.

13.6. Enforcement of Foreign Judgments and Arbitral Awards

Foreign judgments rendered in a Lugano Convention country are recognised and enforced in Switzerland in accordance with the provisions of the Lugano Convention.[41] In general, such decisions are recognised in Switzerland without a specific procedure being required. A decision is enforceable, if this has been declared in the country of the decision. Judgments of non-Lugano Convention countries are recognised and enforceable in accordance with the bilateral treaties of which Switzerland is a party. If no bilateral treaty exists, the judgments are recognised and enforced in accordance with the PIL Statute. Pursuant to the statute, foreign decisions are recognised in Switzerland, if (a) the foreign court had jurisdiction to render a decision, (b) the decision has become final, and (c) the decision is not clearly incompatible with public policy.[42]

A foreign judgment recognisable under Swiss law is declared enforceable upon the petition by the party who desires to benefit from it.[43] The exequatur procedure is governed by Cantonal procedural law.

40. Art. 192 PIL Statute.
41. Arts. 25 *et seq.* Lugano Convention.
42. Art. 25 PIL Statute.
43. Art. 28 PIL Statute.

Final international arbitral awards made in Switzerland are, at the request of a party, declared enforceable by the state court at the seat of the arbitral tribunal.[44]

Pursuant to the PIL Statute[45] the recognition and enforcement of a foreign arbitral award is governed by the New York Convention of 10 June 1958 on the Recognition and Enforcement of Foreign Arbitral Awards.

44. Art. 193 PIL Statute.
45. Art. 194 PIL Statute.

Turkey

by Dr. Ahmet Tekeli

1. Sports Marketing – A Business

Turkey is a promising country for manufacturers of sports wear and equipment: with the strong economic growth during the last two decades an outburst in demand is bound to originate in the very near future. The reasons for increase in demand are:

- young population: 70 per cent of the population is below the age of 40;
- increasing size of population – 2.0–2.5 per cent per year – Turkey has an impressive growth of population, 58.3 million at the beginning of the 1990s and likely to reach around 67 million by the end of the decade;
- increasing emphasis on sports from government via issue of new regulations supporting sporting activities, tournaments, creation of sports federations;
- improving level of education: people are more aware of their health;
- increase in real income per capita: GNP growth over the last five years has averaged 5.2 per cent in real terms while population growth is 2.5 per cent; therefore growth in income per capita is 5.2 minus 2.5 = 2.7 per cent; as sports wear and equipment are relative luxuries, increase in the level of real income means higher demand for sports wear and equipment.

At the same time physical and institutional structures, such as inter-bank markets for local currency and foreign exchange, and legislative framework have been established and operating for the past 10 years.

Local manufacturers are using mainly obsolete or out of date equipment and machinery. They are, therefore, unable to compete with international standards. Local production is non-existent in materials and equipment for sports like tennis, sailing, surfing and skiing. Local manufacturers are in need of technological and equity capital support. However, local labour is considerably cheaper compared to Europe and America.

2. The Turkish Legal System

The Turkish Parliament is named 'the Turkish Grand National Assembly'. Legislative power is vested in the Turkish Grand National Assembly. This power cannot be delegated (Constitution, Article 7). Enacting, amending, or repealing laws, and approving the State budget are among prerogatives of the Turkish Grand National Assembly. The Constitution is the supreme law of country. No law can be contrary to its provisions (Constitution, Article 11).

The Turkish legal system is based on codification where laws are proposed by the ministers and members of Parliament and shaped by individuals or committees constituted by experts on the subject and finally voted and accepted by the Parliament, which has been elected by popular vote.

The Turkish legal system is part of the continental European legal system. The Turkish Civil Code and Code of Obligations are translations of the Swiss Civil Code and Code of Obligations.

The Commercial Code is based on German, Swiss and French laws. Central European legal publications, like text books, commentaries, law journals and court decisions, are common sources frequently used for interpretation and application of Turkish laws. Thus the Turkish legal system is not a strange or different one for those familiar with European continental laws.

However, modifications have been made to the adopted codes to take account of geographical, traditional, social and economic factors of the country, and new laws, regulations and decrees have been introduced in addition to the above; but the main themes of especially the Swiss Civil Code and German Commercial Code have been preserved.

3. Applicable Laws

A specific code applicable to sports marketing does not exist. The general codes of the Code of Obligations, the Civil Code and the Turkish Commercial Code can be applied to various aspects of sports marketing.

4. Intellectual Property Rights

The intellectual property rights of trademarks and copyrights are protected by the specific codes of the Trademark Code and the Code of Literary and Artistic Works.

4.1. Trademarks

Turkey is a signatory to the Paris Convention on Trademarks as amended in Stockholm in 1967. National law is governed by the Trademark Code, No. 551

established on 3 March 1965 as amended by Decrees with the Force of Law, Nos. 336 of 1988 and 3520 of 1989, and by instructions issued by the Ministry of Industry and Commerce (*Official Gazette* No. 12020 of 11 June 1965).

According to the Turkish Trademark Code, for the registration of a trademark in the Trademark Registry permission has to be had from the Ministry of Industry and Commerce in the first place and, following the approval of the Ministry, the trademark can be registered in the Trademark Registry. Finally the registration must be advertised in the *Trade Registry Gazette.* Any trademark which is not registered will be governed by general laws (Article 3).

The person who registers a trademark in the first place, is assumed to be the real owner of the trademark (Article 15). Upon determining the suitability of a mark as a trademark the impression of the trademark in general is taken into consideration rather than its elements (Article 7). The registration of the trademark must be renewed at the end of every 10 years (Articles 16 and 33).

Registration gives the proprietor an exclusive right to use the trademark during the above-stated time limit in relation to his goods and services. Any violation of this by using the same or a similar trademark that may be easily confused, other than by the proprietor, is an infringement. The proprietor has the right to sue any actions defined under the Trademark Code as infringement before the civil courts and claim indemnities for material and moral damages and interlocutory of permanent abrogation of infringement. Cases can also be sued before criminal courts with monetary charges, confinement and confiscation of equipment as sanctions. The proprietor has the right to sue in the above cases within 6 months of gaining knowledge of the situation and 3 years in all other cases (Articles 15, 47, 48, 49).

The mark can be removed from the register if it is not registered with a *bona fide* intention and the right to sue in this situation is not limited.

The mark has to be used for the goods and services for which it is registered, continuously and in the form it is originally registered. Any changes to be made to the mark are to be notified to the Registration Office. The use of a mark cannot be interrupted for more than 3 years without an acceptable reason (Article 18).

In case of the transfer of the mark and licensing the right to use the mark, the above provisions will come into effect against third parties from their date of registration at the Official Registry of Trademarks. Transfers of trademarks and licence agreements have to be notarised (Article 34).

4.2. Copyright

Turkey is a signatory to the Berne Convention on Copyright (has accepted the Brussels text of 1948), and the local regulation on copyright is governed by the Code of Literary and Artistic Works.

Copyright exists automatically in technical, literary, dramatic, musical, artistic works like sound recordings, films, plays, published editions, photographs, paintings, and so on.

The copyright continues to be valid throughout the lifetime of the owner and 50 years from the date of owner's death for his heirs (Article 27). The definition of owner varies according to the type of work. The owner is the one who brings it into existence. Works created by a person in the course of his employment will be owned by the employer. With films the owner is defined as the one who has the film produced by providing financing (Article 8).

Civil and criminal cases may be brought against infringement of copyright through copying, publishing, adapting, broadcasting, cable-casting, or performing in public without the written consent of the owner (Articles 66–75).

Foreigners in Turkey who have filed copies of their works are equally protected by the law. However, works published in a foreign language may freely be translated into Turkish after expiration of 10 years (Article 28).

4.3. Unfair Competition

The situation is governed by the Turkish Commercial Code, Articles 56–65, and the Code of Obligation, Articles 48 and 49. Unfair competition is the abuse of commercial competition with deceptive actions (Turkish Commercial Code, Article 56). Some examples of such actions are: to give false declarations about competitors, to give false information about productions, to use titles and marks of others.

The individual or the entity whose commercial status and interest has been damaged has the right to claim indemnification for existing or expected infringements. Both civil and criminal law suits may be initiated with material and moral indemnification claims within 1 year from the date of becoming aware of the infringement and 3 years in all other cases.

5. The Contract Generally and Preliminary Agreements

5.1. Preliminary Agreements

According to the Code of Obligations, Article 22/I, preliminary agreements which are entered into for intended future principal agreements are valid. But in most cases these agreements are not necessary. This does not restrict special situations stated by law which are viewed as preliminary agreements. An example of this would be the 'undertaking to sell a real estate'. Letters of intent can be viewed in this light.

5.2. Intention to Create Legal Relations

A contract requires: (a) mutual agreement, express or implied; (b) a '*causa*' only in certain cases, such as transfer of personal or real property; and (c) capacity of parties to contract.

Without an intention to create the agreement, the agreement will always be void, as in the case of fault, fraud, and duress.

5.3. *Offer and Acceptance*

Under Turkish law a contract is formed with the notification of the offer to the other party and the notification of acceptance from the other party to the offering party.

If the offer is made with a time limit, the offeror is bound to his offer until the end of this limit. If no acceptance is expressed within the time prescribed the offer ceases to be binding (Code of Obligations, Article 3). An offer with no time limit, made in the presence of the other party or by phone ceases to be binding if it is not accepted immediately (Code of Obligations, Article 4). When an offer without fixing a time limit has been made to a person not present, the offeror is bound until the moment when he can expect a reply dispatched in due course and time (Code of Obligations, Article 5). Where by reason of the special nature of the transaction or circumstances, an express acceptance is not to be expected the contract is presumed to have been concluded unless the offer is rejected within a reasonable time (Code of Obligations, Article 6).

5.4. *Consideration*

Under Turkish law, the consideration or benefit flowing between the parties is generally made up of an economic value, but this is not necessary. Consideration can be defined as any interest or benefit qualified to be protected by law. Therefore, it may include a deed which does not have an economic value. This consideration, benefit or deed may be an action to do or not to do, or to give.

5.5. *Form and Execution*

According to a general principle, the parties can express their intentions in whatever way they want, either verbally or in writing or by notarisation or by certain actions or even by keeping silent, unless there are special requirements stated in the law.

Although there are no particular execution requirements, as a matter of course the document has to be initialled on each page and signed on the last page by the parties.

5.6. *Void and Illegal Contracts*

Agreements which are in violation of the law and public policy will not be recognised under any law of the Republic of Turkey. These include for example a contract to commit a crime or an immoral deed (Code of Obligations, Article 20/I).

Any legal transaction entered into by a party who suffers from mental incapacity will be void (Civil Code, Article 15).

Any contract restricting the possession of rights, the freedom to enter into obligations according to these rights, and the moral and physical unity of a person is void (Civil Code, Articles 23 and 24; Code of Obligations, Articles 19 and 20).

Any contract with a subject matter which is impossible to accomplish legally, physically or naturally is void (Code of Obligations, Article 20/I).

Any contract which is entered into fictitiously in order to cover another secret agreement is void (Code of Obligations, Articles 18 and 20/II).

All contracts signed in Turkey must be drawn up in the Turkish language. A contract drawn up in a foreign language between a Turkish individual or legal entity and a foreign individual or legal entity is acceptable in a Turkish court provided the contract is signed outside Turkey; however, evidence must be produced that the act of signing has taken place outside Turkey.

5.7. Privity

According to the Turkish doctrine, a contract may be in force only between the parties who signed it. As a result of this only the parties to the contract may acquire rights and incur obligations, may sue and be sued.

According to the Turkish legal system, third parties may also be liable, but in their capacity as representative or guarantor.

5.8. Interpretation

The governing principle in the Swiss-Turkish legal system and the German legal system is the 'trust principle'. This principle is based on the 'principle of honesty' and governs the meaning which the other party is likely to give to the statement with good will (Code of Obligations, Article 1).

5.9. Frustration

A contract will be deemed to be frustrated on the occurrence of an extreme event, which could not have been foreseen by the parties, and which prevents the contract from being executed. These events are those out of the control of the either party to the contract, such as accidents, e.g. a fire, and *force majeure*, e.g. earthquakes or floods. As the parties are not deemed responsible for these events, the debt and/or obligation ceases automatically (Code of Obligations, Article 117).

5.10. Breach of Contract

Non-compliance with the terms by either party will constitute a breach of contract. The party at fault is held responsible to pay an indemnity in the case where he is not able to prove that his non-compliance does not constitute a breach (Code of Obligations, Article 96).

In case of default of the debtor, the creditor has the right to ask for compliance and for indemnity for damages caused by the delay, or the creditor may cancel the agreement and ask for indemnity due to non-compliance.

In case of default of the creditor the debtor may execute his part of the contract by committing the money or the goods involved to the custody of the court or by safekeeping in a warehouse determined by the court (Code of Obligations, Articles 90 and 91).

6. Standard Contract Terms

The following issues should be included in, or considered when preparing, any contract related to sports marketing in Turkey:

6.1. Applicable Law

Formal validity of contract is determined by the law of the place of contracting (*locus regit actum*). Under reservation of public policy, the parties to a contract are free to determine and to choose the applicable law. If such determination is not made, as a rule, the law of the place of performance will apply.

The debt obligations arising from the contract are governed by the law expressly opted for by the parties. In the case that no law is expressly opted for, the applicable law is determined as follows:

- the law of the place/country where the debt obligation is to be executed;
- where there is more than one place of execution, the law of the place where the major part of the debt obligation is to be executed;
- if it is not possible to determine the above places, the law of the place with which the contract has the closest connection (International Private Procedural Law, Article 24).

6.2. Definitions

It is general practice that specific terms in the contract be defined in a separate clause; either written in capital letters or abbreviated throughout the contract after this statement. The definitions introduced by the word ‘means’ exclude other meanings of that word.

6.3. Parties

The full names and addresses of the parties, and if the party is a company its full title, registered office and address, should be included in the contract.

6.4. Force Majeure

The consequences of delay of performance should be defined in the contract. It is common practice that in such a case either party may terminate the contract or suspend it for a certain period of time.

6.5. Address for Service

The addresses and instructions for serving notices and other deeds can be stated in the contract, if no other means of contact have been made available.

6.6. Royalties and Accounting

Specific details need to be included in the contract relating to royalties and payments related thereto, since the payment has to be approved by the Government as explained in 7.2 below.

6.7. Books Open to inspection

According to the Turkish Commercial Code, Section 5, Articles 66–87, any company formed under this Code is obliged to keep certain books which should be open to inspection both by tax inspectors and the auditors of the company.

Including a clause in the contract relating to the inspection and audit of these books and relevant commercial/financial data of a licensee by the licensor is strictly necessary, as parties and partners cannot inspect the books of one another's books freely according to the law.

6.8. Termination

The grounds for termination should be defined, stating remediable and non-remediable breaches, termination with or without notice, and the indemnities to be paid under different circumstances and how they are to be paid. The above-stated situations should be clearly defined and explained to prevent complications and misunderstandings.

In the case of trademark licences, it is recommended that the contract includes a clause to the effect that any abuse of the trademark by the licensee should entitle the licensor to terminate the contract immediately.

7. Different Types of Business Arrangements

7.1. Sponsorship Agreement

There is no specific code in the Turkish legal system governing the sponsorship relationship. Instead it is governed by the Code of Obligations (contract law).

7.2. Merchandising

This subject is also governed by the Code of Obligations (contract law).

Licence and know-how agreements may be entered into in relation to the sale and/or the manufacture of goods like sports equipment and sports wear. The Laws of Trademarks and Copyright should be taken into consideration when drawing up the agreements related to trademarks and copyright.

Proof of registration should be sought to ensure the right to licence of the licensor.

Patent matters essentially are governed under laws dating back to the Ottoman era. Patents are issued without any warranty as to accuracy or novelty and without discrimination between Turks and foreigners. As a matter of practice, pursuant to Law No. 6563 (21 May 1955), the Government may forward patent requests to the International Institute of Patents in the Hague, for study and verification of novelty. Patent requests must be filed with the Industrial Property Department, Ministry of Industry and Commerce.

A patent may be assigned by a notarial act. Licences may also be given under the patent, no particular form being needed to accomplish this transaction.

Turkey is a signatory to the London and Stockholm texts (with the exception of the first twelve articles) signed in 1934 and 1967 of the Paris Agreement of 1883 on Protection of Industrial Property.

Patent infringement could give rise to civil action, as well as criminal prosecution (seizure and, possibly, destruction of infringing goods, payment of damages, fines, and prison terms for repeated offences) (Code of Obligations, Article 48, Commercial Code, Article 56).

Where the trademark owner (licensor) allows a person to use his trademark on goods produced by a third party (licensee), the licence agreement should contain clauses relating to the amount of royalties, definition of billing, the terms and conditions for the use of trademarks, the control provisions on advertising, quality control, the time period of the agreement and dispute settlement. Especially the royalty amount, time period and dispute settlement clauses are of importance since licence agreements have to be approved by the Foreign Investment General Directorate of the Turkish Treasury.

7.3. Commissioning Agreement

This subject, which is also a matter of contract, is governed by the Code of Obligations.

7.4. Franchises

Again, this matter is governed by the Code of Obligations. The scope, terms and conditions of the agreement should be clearly defined.

8. The Rights

8.1. Options

An option is a privilege given to either party for compliance with the contract by different terms of obligation. The terms and conditions under which the option may be exercised, including time-limits, must be carefully defined.

8.2. Pre-emption

A condition of a pre-emption, the right of first refusal, may be inserted into the agreement to grant the opportunity of acquiring a certain right to the pre-emptive right holder according to the Turkish Law of Obligations (Civil Code, Article 658).

The terms and conditions of the pre-emption should be carefully defined.

8.3. Exclusivity

The rights that are granted may be exclusive. Words like 'sole' and 'exclusive' must be stated in the article to denote the desired result.

8.4. Copyright and Trademark Licence

The licence will usually include a provision that the licensee will use the trademark in a certain format. This is important for the protection of the trademark.

The licensor may need to include a provision that the licensee will execute a 'user agreement' and the agreement should contain a provision that, should the licensee challenge the marks, the licence will automatically come to an end.

8.5. Territory

The common practice is that copyright and trademark are separated according to territory and/or product in the agreement, and competition of another licensee within one territory is usually avoided; but this is not obligatory.

8.6. Duration

The term of the agreement should be clearly defined and there should also be an express provision for earlier termination in specified circumstances, such as failure to pay the sponsorship fee or royalties on time.

8.7. Post Termination

The licensor should expressly provide in the agreement that the rights should revert to him following termination and that any outstanding stock of the licensed product is also returned.

It is unlikely that the event organiser or licensor could prevent the other party from doing similar business in a competing field.

9. Financial Terms

The financial terms of the deal should be clearly defined in the contract.

Where royalties are payable, the following points are important: period of payment; on what the royalty will be calculated; will an amount be allowed for marketing and promotion expenses before the royalty percentage is calculated; what is the currency of payment and currency of obligation; how will the exchange rate be calculated; who will pay the costs of remittance of the money; will interest be payable on late payments; a right to inspect the accounting records and the right to have the accounts audited; the terms of payment of the auditor.

The payment may be expressed to be made net of all withholding taxes and other deductions.

All licence agreements with foreign licences have to be approved by the Foreign Investment General Directorate. There is a 21.25 per cent withholding tax from the royalties. However, if there is a bilateral tax treaty, the rate will be reduced under the terms of that treaty.

10. Insurance Aspects

Generally, it is not the practice to insure the public in our country, but it is possible.

11. Advertising and Promotion

11.1. Advertising Controls

Advertising in Turkey is governed by separate regulations of Government authorities like the TRT (Turkish Radio, Television) Code (Article 26), Municipality Code and Municipality Income Code etc.

The main theme of the Codes is that advertisements must not deceive the public, cause unfair competition, and discredit other products; in general advertisements must not oppose public policy.

11.2. Tobacco Advertising

The Council of Ministers Decree No. 91/1755 (Article 5c) restricts and prohibits the advertising of cigarettes and tobacco products through radio, television and other organs of the Government.

11.3. Programme Sponsorship

The new area of sponsorship may be relevant to sports marketing. The concept is governed by the Code of Obligations.

11.4. Agencies

The advertising agency handling the promotion of the event or the products will be bound by an agreement entered into between the parties.

12. Dispute Resolution

When a dispute arises between the parties it will most likely be in relation to the performance or non-performance of the agreement, or to an infringement of intellectual property rights. Remedies may be pursued either in the courts, which are time-consuming and costly, or through arbitration.

12.1. Court Procedure

Disputes arising from commercial matters are resolved in Commercial Courts. The first action to be taken is by applying to the court with a petition stating the event, its supporting legal sources, related articles of the Codes and evidence.

It is the rule that both sides to the dispute be represented by a lawyer registered with a Turkish Bar Association.

12.1.1. Injunction

An injunction is an order given by the court which stops someone from doing a specific act or forces a party to perform an act. An injunction is made in the interim stages of proceedings, but always before the matter is heard in court. The court may require an undertaking in respect of costs from the plaintiff.

12.1.2. Action for an agreed sum

The fast way of obtaining money due under contract which has not been paid, without the need to conduct a trial, is through the Execution Offices. In case of ordinary and commercial debts the creditor, before going to court, may serve a payment order on the debtor. If no objection is brought against this order within seven days (this term is five days for negotiable instruments) the claim is assumed to have been admitted and is executed.

The debtor is obliged to make a declaration and give a detailed account of his property to the extent sufficient to pay his debt.

Once the judgment has been obtained from the Office, the sum can be recovered by the help of Government authorities. Movable goods are seized and real estate is attached by registration on official record. All property must be sold by auction through the execution department. An order to put the company into liquidation may also occur.

12.1.3. General and consequential damages

In some agreements the parties include a clause to limit the measure of damages; this is a liquidated damages clause, and it either includes or excludes claims for consequential damages.

12.1.4. Legal costs

Generally the costs of both parties are paid by the losing party.

In commercial matters, parties are free to fix a rate of interest (Commercial Code, Article 8). If the contract stipulates for interest but is silent about the rate, or if interest is required by law, the rate is 30 per cent per annum for commercial matters. In civil matters parties are free to fix a rate not to exceed limits prescribed under the Law regarding Moneylending; when no rate is mentioned it is 30 per cent.

12.2. Arbitration

All disputes may be submitted to arbitration. Parties may enter into a separate agreement, or submission to arbitration may be provided for in the main contract (Code of Civil Procedure, Article 516). No particular form of submission is required except that it must be in writing (Code of Civil Procedure, Article 517). Unless otherwise provided by agreement, three arbitrators are appointed by the judge who is competent to try the case (Code of Civil Procedure, Article 520).

If there is an arbitration clause in the agreement or an arbitration agreement in existence between the parties, and despite this one of the parties pursues an action in the Turkish courts, an objection has to be made in court. For the court to dismiss the case the objection based on the arbitration clause or agreement has to be made at the initial stage of the trial as the first objection.

The articles on arbitration of the Turkish International Private Procedural Code are mostly based on the principles of the New York Convention on Arbitration of 1958.

The parties are free to choose the law applicable. If the applicable law is not stated the question of which law applies to the arbitration is dealt with in the interpretation of the agreement and the intention of the parties.

Arbitrators are obliged to give an award within six months after their first meeting. The decision of the majority is binding. After the award is certified by the court it can be executed.

Arbitration awards given in foreign countries and certified by a foreign court may be executed in Turkey under one of the following conditions:

(a) there must exist an agreement of reciprocity between the Republic of Turkey and country where the award is given; or
(b) there must exist in the country where the award is given, legal provisions whereby execution is possible of judgments awarded by Turkish arbitrators or courts; or
(c) in the absence of the legal provisions under (b) above, there must exist a precedent of such execution.

Foreign arbitration awards whose execution has been granted 'exequatur' by competent Turkish courts shall be executed as if awarded by Turkish courts (Law dated 20 May 1982, No. 2675).

Presently, Turkey has bilateral agreements with Tunisia, Rumania, Austria and Italy for the reciprocal enforcement of judgments and arbitration awards. Turkey has also ratified, on 5 May 1991, the New York Convention dated 10 June 1958, for the enforcement of foreign arbitral awards. There should be no problem for the enforcement of judgments and awards issued by the courts of one of the contracting States of these agreements; for the others, the legal reciprocity in (b) above or *de facto* reciprocity in (c) above must be sought.

International Sports Sponsorship and the EC

by Ian S. Blackshaw and Simon Topping

1. Introduction

Sport and sports sponsorship at both a national and international level is playing an increasingly important role in business promotion and marketing strategy. It forms a vital source of income for national and international sporting federations as they plan their events. Sport is big business and as such it has attracted the increasing interest of the European Community, both as politicians and as regulators.

The European Community has shown increasing interest in sport both as an industry and as a symbol. The aim of this chapter is to provide all those interested in sports sponsorship with an overview of the European Community, the importance it attaches to sport and the interplay between sport and sports sponsorship with, on the one hand, the Community's competition policy and, on the other, the programme of legal measures, designed to put in place the European Single Market by 1 January 1993.

However, in order to take up these new opportunities, it is vital that the sports industry from the event organisers to equipment manufacturers and sponsors have a thorough understanding of how the Community works, what its aims are and how it can influence the rules and regulatory structures being created. Equipped with such an overview, the sports industry, whether based inside or outside the Community, will be able to place national regulatory rules outlined in the preceding chapters in their proper context.

1.1. Sport as an Industry

In the 1980s sport came of age. As a social activity it benefitted from the shorter working hours in Western countries and greater health consciousness. As an industry it has grown to meeting the massive increase in consumer demand for sporting facilities, events and equipment.

The commercial success of international sports events has made them a prime outlet for sponsorship and advertising to the extent that a recent Communication from the European Commission estimated that 'sport and related activities account for 2.5% of world trade', and that the aggregate Community membership of national sporting federations and associations amounted to 60–80 million Community citizens, or between 20 and 25% of the population.[1]

These trends which started in the last decade are set to continue into the next century. In Europe they are likely to accelerate with the removal of trade barriers, flowing from the European Community's Single Market programme and the extension of the Community free trade rules to Scandinavia and Central and Eastern Europe.

1.2. Sport as a Symbol

The Community's interest in sport goes beyond simply supporting what it recognises as a significant element of the European economy. It sees sport as an important symbol, promoting a sense of Europe and creating a common cultural identity.

At the same time as it was launching the Single Market programme, the Community also emphasised the importance of sport as a means of fostering the popular perception of Europe. In the 1985 *Addonnino Report on a People's Europe*,[2] the Committee charged with promoting the Community as a reality in the life of ordinary citizens, placed particular emphasis on sport. The Commission took up this theme in its Communication on a People's Europe, highlighting: '*the very important* place which sport occupies in everyday life . . . [it] provides an excellent means of communicating with people and making them aware of the European idea'.[3]

This aspect of the Community's policy shows itself in its financial support for new sporting facilities, Community events such as the Constitution Yacht Race and by the promotion of the Community at the Winter and Summer Olympics. A recent unpublished report by the European Commission ('the Commission') reported the Albertville and Barcelona Games as '*an exceptional vector for the European idea*' because both events are being held inside the Community in the same year and because 1992 is the year of the Single Market. It provides an 'ideal opportunity for a major communication drive to make the general public aware of the European Idea and to celebrate 1992 as an historic year for the Community'.

---

1. Communication from the Commission to the Council and the European Parliament on the European Community and Sport, 31 July 1991, Section (91) 1438 final, p. 2.
2. Reports from the *ad hoc* Committee on a People's Europe (March 1985 and June 1985), *Bulletin of the European Communities*, Supplement 7/85.
3. Communication on a People's Europe, *Bulletin of the European Communities*, Supplement 2/88.

The 1992 Olympics provide a very clear example of how the Community, and in particular, the Commission has recognised the significance of major sporting events as a communications tool. In doing this it is simply acting as any commercial sponsor and its seems likely that the twelve gold stars and blue field of the Community flag will become an increasingly common sight at European sporting events.

1.3. Sport and the Single Market

The European Single Market presents the prospect of a frontier free trading area of 340 million citizens, where it will be as easy for a UK manufacturer of snooker tables to sell them in Manchester as in Milan, and where the sponsors of European Football Championships can see their products advertised and the football matches broadcast without restriction throughout the EC.

The development of the *European Economic Area*, encompassing the member countries of the European Free Trade Association[4] and the Community will, if successfully ratified, add a further 33 million consumers to the Single Market, with the possible extension of many of the Community rules to the Eastern and Central European Countries, through new trade agreements between them and the EC which are under negotiation, by the turn of the century.

As explained in more detail below, the sports industry is fully subject to the Community's rules on fair competition and the free movement of goods and services. It is affected by a whole range of measures creating the European Single Market, such as the rules liberalising cross-border satellite broadcastings[5] or the proposed uniform Community-wide ban on tobacco advertising.[6]

2. The Structure of the European Community

2.1. The Treaties

The European Community was founded by the 1957 Treaty of Rome ('the Treaty of Rome') establishing the European Economic Community between Belgium, France, Germany, Luxembourg, Italy and the Netherlands. The United Kingdom had been invited to participate in treaty negotiations but had decided to stay outside.

4. The EFTA States are Austria, Finland, Iceland, Liechtenstein, Norway, Sweden and Switzerland. On 11 April 1992 the EFTA and EC States signed the European Economic Area Treaty. This Treaty had not been successfully ratified at the time of writing.
5. Council Directive 89/552 of 3 October 1989 on the co-ordination of rules in the Member States concerning the pursuit of television broadcasting activities, OJ L298, 17.10.89.
6. Amended proposal for a Council Directive on advertising for tobacco products OJ C167, 27.6.91.

At the same time, those six Member States also created an Atomic Energy Community, which, together with the 1953 Coal and Steel Community, formed the three Communities, which today are collectively described as the European Community ('the Community' or 'the EC').

The Community was enlarged in 1973 with the entry of Denmark, Ireland and the United Kingdom. Norway had participated in the accession negotiations, but a referendum came out against Norwegian membership. The Nine became the Twelve after Greece became a member in 1980 and Spain and Portugal in 1986.

Applications for membership are currently on the table from, among others, Austria, Finland, Norway, Sweden, Switzerland and Turkey.

The Treaty of Rome has undergone one substantial revision. In 1985 the Single European Act, which overhauled the Community's institutional structure, provided an efficient legislative mechanism vital to the adoption of the 280 or so measures forming part of the Community's Single Market programme prior to the target date of 31 December 1992.

The Treaty of Rome may be revised by the 1992 Treaty on European Union ('the Maastricht Treaty'), which has been signed by the Member States but not yet ratified by all. If ratified, it will strengthen the Community's political dimension, increase the Commission's policy responsibilities, give a limited power of veto over Community legislation to the European Parliament and set the Community on course for a single European currency by the end of the decade.[7]

The Treaty of Rome has provided a highly flexible structure for the creation of a frontier-free Europe, unlike any grouping of nations which has gone before it.

2.2. *The Institutions*

The key institutions of the Community are:

2.2.1. *The European Commission*

The Commission, based in Brussels, is the Community's administrative civil service. It is divided into Directorate Generals ('DG's') in the same way as the national Governments are divided into ministries. DG III, for example, is responsible for the Single Market; DG IV for competition policy, and DG X for audio-visual policy, information, communications and culture.

The Commission is controlled at a political level by 17 Commissioners appointed by the Member States (two each by France, Germany, Italy, Spain and the United Kingdom, and one by each of the other Member States). The Commissioners are in overall charge of the policy of their DG's, but are

7. The ratification process was upset by the rejection of the Treaty in a Danish referendum in June 1992. At the time of writing it was not clear if and when the Maastricht Treaty would be adopted.

entirely independent of the Member States which appointed them. The Commission is headed by a President. In general it acts by consensus.

In the event of the Maastricht Treaty being ratified, the term of the Commission will be extended from 1995 from 4 to 5 years to coincide with the term of European Parliament.

The day to day operation of Community policy is carried out by around 35,000 Commission officials based primarily in Brussels and Luxembourg. The Commission is remarkably open and accessible to business in comparison to national civil services.

The Commission initiates, polices and enforces Community policy. It can propose Community legislation, though its final adoption generally rests with the Member States' representatives who comprise the Council of Ministers. The Commission has regulatory powers, for example, in relation to the operation of the Community's fair competition rules or national proposals for technical product standards,

The Commission can bring actions against the other Community institutions and against the Member States before the European Court of Justice for their failure to comply with Community law.

It administers Community funds for regional development, infrastructure improvements and for cultural and audio-visual initiatives.

2.2.2. The Council of Ministers ('the Council')

Within the Community structure, the voice of the Member States is heard through the Council, on which each Member State has one ministerial representative. When discussing sport these will be the ministers responsible for sport in each Member State and the relevant Council meeting, usually known as the Sports Council; when discussing trademark legislation, it will be the respective ministers for trade and industry. Political and foreign affairs issues are dealt with by the Ministers of Foreign Affairs meeting in the so-called 'General Affairs Council'. The Sports Council is a relatively recent development and meets only about once a year.

Each Member State presides over the Council for a six month term in alphabetical rotation. This allows them to push their own agenda during that period, so that the Dutch Presidency during the second half of 1991 concentrated on the Political Union and EMU Treaties, while the Portuguese Presidency, during the first half of 1992, emphasised the Community's social legislation and the reform of the Community's finances (from which it would benefit).

Once in each Member State Presidency, the Community Heads of State or Government meet in the *European Council*, which deals with major political decisions and international issues.

The Council can adopt Community legislation, though under the Maastricht Treaty this power would be shared with the European Parliament in respect of certain policy areas. The Council decides whether to accept or reject proposed amendments to the legislation made by either the Commission or the European Parliament.

The Council meets almost daily, either in Brussels or in the Presidency Member State. Non-controversial legislation will often be finalised at ambassador level or below in the Committee of Permanent Representatives ('COREPER').

Voting within the Council depends on the provisions of the Treaty of Rome on which a particular proposal is based. Legislation on VAT, for example, is subject to the unanimous agreement of all Member States. Other proposals, for example, harmonising national rules relating to firearms[8] or the movement of horses between Member States,[9] can be adopted according to a weighted or 'qualified majority' voting system. This gives the larger Member States a greater number of votes than the smaller States, and prevents any one Member State blocking the adoption of Community provisions. The extension of qualified majority voting under the Single European Act significantly speeded up this legislative process.

One of the consequences of the Maastricht Treaty would be a further extension of qualified majority voting.

Qualified majority voting leads to tactical coalitions to approve or block Commission proposals and often legislation may be adopted in the face of opposition from more than one Member State.

2.2.3. The European Parliament

The European Parliament, based in Strasbourg (full sessions), Brussels (committees) and having part of its administration in Luxembourg, consists of 518 MEPs. Within the Parliament they are grouped along political rather than national lines. The present Parliament, elected in 1988 for five years, has a socialist majority. Unlike a national Parliament, the European Parliament lacks the power to initiate and adopt legislation. It can and does, however, amend proposed Community legislation.

The European Parliament approves the appointment of and may sack the Commissioners as a whole, but not individual Commissioners, which turns a potentially powerful weapon into a blunt instrument. It also has a major say in the Community budget, alongside the Council.

2.2.4. The European Court of Justice ('the Court')

The Court (and the Court of First Instance of the European Communities) is based in Luxembourg. It is empowered to:

- rule on compliance by the Member States and the Community institutions with EC law;
- rule on the legality of Community action, for example, competition decisions imposing fines on private companies;

8. Council Directive on control of the acquisition and possession of weapons 91/477 of 18 June 1991, OJ L256 13.9.91.
9. Commission Decision 92/260 of 10 April 1992, OJ L130 and Council Directives 90/426 and 90/427 of 26 June 1990, OJ L224, 18.8.90.

– provide so-called 'preliminary rulings' to national courts on the application of EC law to legal problems raised before those national courts.

The First Instance Court was set up to relieve the case load of the Court, and deals primarily with competition law cases and internal staff cases. It cannot provide preliminary rulings to national courts, though other areas of its jurisdiction are likely to be expanded if the Maastricht Treaty is ratified.

The rulings of the Court are binding on the national courts of each Member State. In this way the general principle of primacy of Community law can be maintained, giving the Court a status in some ways similar to the Supreme Court in the United States. National courts can, and, in some circumstances, must refer matters of interpretation of the Treaty or the acts of the institutions of the Community to the Court of Justice.

2.2.5. Other Institutions

In addition to the four main institutions, a number of other consultative bodies and specialist agencies have been created to assist in the adoption and implementation of Community legislation. These range from the *Economic and Social Committee*, which is consulted by the Council on many Commission legislative proposals, to the Community's *Environmental Agency* and proposed *Trade Mark Office*.

2.2.6. The European Monetary Institute ('the EMI')

If the Maastricht Treaty is adopted, there will be a fifth institution in the Community, the European Monetary Institute.[10] The EMI aims to strengthen cooperation between the central banks of the Member States. Its responsibilities are to coordinate monetary policy, to monitor the EMS, to facilitate use of the ECU and to prepare for its replacement which will be the European System of Central Banks.

2.3. The Sources of Community Law

There are several different sources of Community law which can impose binding obligations on the sports industry in varying degrees.

2.3.1. The Treaty of Rome

The primary source of Community law is the Treaty of Rome itself. It provides a framework, establishing the basic principles and structure of the EC. The provisions of the Treaty take precedence over inconsistent national laws, for example, the provisions guaranteeing the free movement of services prevailed over conflicting Dutch rules, which required advertising material carried on

10. At the time of writing, it was not clear if and when the Maastricht Treaty would be adopted.

Dutch public channels to be sourced through a Dutch, rather than a foreign company.[11]

Many provisions of the Treaty create direct rights and obligations which bind individuals, businesses and even national governments. If they are breached complaints can be made to the Commission or through the national courts of the Member State concerned.

The Treaty of Rome was never intended to provide an answer to every question. Its general principles are filled out by a variety of secondary legislation. The Commission, in choosing which type of instrument to propose, is bound by the so-called principle of 'subsidiarity' which requires every Community policy to be implemented at the lowest appropriate level. This means, in theory, that binding Community rules will only be taken to resolve a problem where absolutely necessary because individual national regional or local measures by the Member States could not provide a solution. These various Community acts are:

2.3.2. Regulations

Regulations are binding law in every Member State from the moment of their adoption. They require no further national implementation. Regulations are used where precise uniformity is required throughout the Community, for example, in relation to uniform VAT procedures in a frontier free market[12] or the creation of a Community trademark.[13]

2.3.3. Directives

Directives set out general principles, which must be implemented into national law by a given date. The Member States enjoy a certain flexibility as to the means of transformation into national law, but not as to the content of the measure. Most of the Single Market legislation has been passed by means of Directives.

Where a Member State fails to implement, or implements incorrectly, by the specified date, companies and individuals can rely on the unimplemented provision to defeat contradictory national legislation against that Member State.

Under the 'Television without Frontiers' Directive, this could allow a third party non-national satellite broadcaster, for example, to protect itself from prosecution under the national law of a Member State, which had not yet implemented the EC-wide rules. In certain cases the third party might even be able to claim damages from the State for economic loss suffered as a result of the Member State's failure to implement on time.[14]

11. ECJ judgment of 25 July 1991, Case C-288/89, *Dutch Media Commission*.
12. Council Regulation 218/92 of 27 January 1992 on administrative co-operation in the field of indirect taxation (VAT), OJ L24/92, 1.2.92.
13. Amended Proposal for a Council Regulation creating a Community Trade Mark, OJ C230/84, 31.8.84.
14. See Cases C-6/90 and 9/90, *Francovich* v. *Italian Republic*. The Italian Government's failure to set up a compensation fund for workers losing their jobs because of their employer's

2.3.4. Decisions

Decisions may be made by the Commission or by the Council and can be directed towards Member States, individuals or companies. Decisions do not create general law, but are binding on the people to whom they are addressed. They are used by the Commission in areas such as enforcement of the EC's competition rules against individual companies or against Member States which have granted unfair subsidies contrary to the rules contained in the Treaty. In practice, although not creating general law, competition Decisions provide concrete guidance as to how the competition rules are applied by the Commission.

2.3.5. Recommendations and Opinions

These are non-binding acts which may be adopted by a number of the Community institutions, but are used primarily by the Commission. Often the Commission or the Council will recommend that Member States take certain action. This will be followed up after two or three years with formal legislative proposals if the Member States have not taken appropriate action. Opinions are simply statements of position, and are generally confined to the Court, the Economic and Social Committee and to the certain stages of the legal proceedings brought by the Commission or the other institutions.

2.4. How Community Law Is Made

In outline, the Community legislative process involves a proposal originating from the Commission; consideration and amendment of the proposal by the European Parliament and the opinion of the Economic and Social Committee; consideration of the Parliament's changes by the Commission and final adoption by the Council, with or without amendments made by the other institutions.

The precise procedure and the relative powers of the various bodies depends on the Treaty article on which a particular proposal is based. The Single European Act introduced a *cooperation procedure* with the European Parliament, introducing a second reading stage into the process outlined above, and allowing the Parliament more significant powers of amendment. The *cooperation* procedure has been used for most Single Market legislation.

A further extension of the Parliament's powers will result if the Maastricht Treaty is ratified. Legislation relating to, for example, the Single Market, education and training, culture, consumer protection and the environment, could only be adopted with the approval of the Parliament.

The legislative process involves an intricate balancing act within the institutions. Much turns on the Treaty article originally chosen by the Commission

---

insolvency, within the time limit provided in the Directive, allowed the employees to sue for damages.

as the proposal's legal basis which influences both the voting procedure within the Council and the ability of the European Parliament to introduce changes.

Under the old procedure, there is no guarantee that the European Parliament's amendments will be adopted, whereas under the *cooperation procedure*, its amendments, if agreed by the Commission, can only be rejected by the Council acting unanimously.

2.5. Influencing the Community decisions

The process of legislation and the development of Community policy is open at several stages to outside influence, which is often welcomed by the Commission as a means of ensuring that the rules coming out of Brussels meet the needs of those who will have to work within them.

Prior to adopting a proposal the Commission will consult widely with both the Member States and industry bodies. Additionally, it will often organise expert hearings to test out its draft proposals or consult with specialist committees, such as the Joint Committee set up between itself and the national Olympic committees, sports associations and federations in the Member States, or the new consultative body 'the European Sports Forum' proposed in the Commission's Communication on Sport.[15]

Once a proposal for legislation has been adopted by the Commission an attempt to shape its final form can be made to any of the three institutions: the Commission, the Council through the Member States and the Parliament. It is often within the Parliament that such lobbying activities can be most successful. In recent years one of the most effective campaigns has been that led by the tobacco, advertising and media industries against the proposal for an outright ban on tobacco advertising and sponsorship.

3. Community Rules Concerning Free Movement

Even before the advent of the single market legislation, the EC Treaty contained rules on the free movement of goods and workers and the free provision of services.

3.1. Free Movement Rules and Intellectual Property Rights

The Treaty of Rome guarantees the free movement of goods and services throughout the Community, subject to certain exceptions, including '. . . the protection of industrial and commercial property'.[16] Reliance on these excep-

15. See Note 1 above.
16. See Article 36 of the Treaty of Rome, which provides derogations from the general principle of free movement of goods set out in Article 30.

tions should not, however, constitute 'arbitrary discrimination' or 'a disguised restriction on trade'.

The role of Community law in this context has been to determine the limits imposed on patents, trademarks and copyright, which continue to be granted on a national basis. This has been done through a body of cases, which explain what type of acts constitute 'the specific subject matter' of the right in question. Providing the rights holder does not go beyond that limit, his use of his rights cannot be challenged before the Member States' courts.

Although intellectual property rights ('IPRs') are at the heart of successful sponsorship deals, sponsors should be aware that their freedom to rely on such nationally granted rights, for example, to keep out imports of products sold in another licensee's territory, is restricted by Community law.

Once a licensed product is 'marketed' (which may extend to promotional use, rather than straight sale) with the licensor's consent in one Member State, the use of copyright or trade marks to restrict its further sale anywhere in the Community is said to be 'exhausted' and such enforcement would breach the Treaty's free movement rules.

Rights to act against counterfeit and unauthorised goods are unaffected by these considerations.

The use of IPRs, particularly the refusal to grant licences, can, in certain circumstances, raise serious competition issues.[17]

3.2. The Free Movement of Workers and Services

Community rules on the free movement on workers and the free provision of services guarantee sports professionals the right to work anywhere in the Community, without discrimination based on nationality, or other restrictions.

Sports professionals are in many cases regarded as workers and are free to exercise their profession in any Member State. At present many European sports federations have rules which limit the number of foreign players. The Commission has recognised that a way will have to be found of reconciling the free movement of persons in the world of sport with national or regional sensitivities.

National league restrictions on the number of non-national players have been relaxed after Commission intervention because they conflict with the Treaty's rules on the free movement of workers under Article 48 of the Treaty of Rome throughout the EC.

Recently, a court in Liège in Belgium referred a question to the European Court as to whether the system of 'transfers' of professional footballers is contrary to the Treaty in so far as the system allows a club to require the payment of a sum of money before its players, who have come to the end of their contract, may be engaged by a new employer.[18]

17. See *Magill* Case referred to at note 24 below.
18. Reference for a preliminary ruling, OJ C187/12, 24.7.92.

4. EC Competition Rules

4.1. Agreements

Sports marketing is about agreements. These may take many forms and may relate to many different aspects of the event, for example:

- *broadcasting rights*, relating to both TV and radio, terrestrial, cable or satellite, live and delayed coverage, host country, regional or worldwide;
- *publishing agreements*, for the official event magazine or book;
- *franchise and display rights*, a concession allowing the sponsor to display and supply the product, from soft drinks to photocopiers and computers;
- *supply agreements*, whereby X is appointed supplier to the event in return for the designation 'official supplier';
- *premiums*, giving the right to supply promotional material, e.g. T-shirts or umbrellas, to the event. Sometimes this is with a linked obligation for all requests for premiums for sale through third parties to be sourced from the premium rights holder;
- *commemorative items*, from coins and stamps to the event video.

The Community competition rules set out in Articles 85 and 86 of the Treaty of Rome are designed to ensure that sponsorship agreements will not restrict, prevent or distort competition within the Community. At the same time, the rules will ensure that the terms on which such agreements are granted are fair, where the person (such as the event organiser or the host broadcaster) licensing the rights enjoys a particularly strong commercial position.

In outline, Article 85 outlaws anti-competitive agreements, whilst Article 86 controls the abusive use of market power.

In both cases an effect on trade between Member States must be shown, but where marketing or event broadcasts cover a number of Community Member States this will not normally be hard to establish.

Agreements which are only of minor importance (*de minimis*), because the size and market share of the companies involved means there is unlikely to be an appreciable effect on competition and inter-State trade are considered by the Commission to fall outside the scope of Article 85.[19] Additionally, agreements, which entail certain benefits for the consumer, can be cleared or exempted under the competition rules if notified to the Commission's competition services. There is no exemption procedure for conduct caught under Article 86.

The Commission is particularly wary of agreements which divide up markets on a national basis, even though this often makes sound commercial sense. The Commission also objects to agreements which charge excessive royalties or

19. The so called *de minimis* rule relating to agreements between parties, having an aggregate annual turnover of less than 200 million ECU and a market share of less than 5%.

apply other unfair terms and which restrict competition by closing off business opportunities for unconnected parties or which tie-in commercial partners.

At the same time, the Commission accepts the value, as a reward for investment and innovation, of intellectual property rights. Licensing and other arrangements will often, therefore, benefit from an exemption from the full rigour of competition rules.

4.2. What Are the Competition Issues?

4.2.1. Freedom to contract

In general the Commission recognises the freedom for commercial partners to agree whatever they want. The form and terms of contracts will be purely subject to national control, if they have no effect on trade between Member States and if they do not overstep the limits of permissible restrictions on competition, some of which are identified below, or if they fall within the *de minimis* exception outlined above.

No special rules are applied to sponsorship arrangements under Community law, although the Commission has started to make noises about legislating to ensure third party access to television coverage of certain types of sporting events.[20]

4.2.2. Sponsorship rights

The ability to be identified as the sole or one of a select number of sponsors of a major sports event is a very valuable marketing and advertising tool. However, the very exclusivity that makes the rights attractive to sponsors, or enables the event organisers to control the exploitation of those rights, may place that person in a dominant commercial position. Once in that position its behaviour is likely to be scrutinised more closely than that of its non-dominant competitors.

4.2.3. Exclusivity and territorial protection

The Commission often takes the view that the grant of exclusive rights to one company, precluding the grant of a licence to anyone else. This is a restriction of competition. Often licensing arrangements will attempt to seal off the territories of different licensees. Such partitioning falls squarely within Article 85(1), but may be exempted under Article 85(3).

In one case, the Commission intervened over the grant of exclusive rights by a Hollywood studio over its film library to the German television station, ARD, on the grounds that the number of films covered (1300) and the length of the licence (1984 to 1998) unreasonably restricted third party access to the films. The solution, agreed with the Commission, was to provide windows of between two and eight years for competing broadcasters in the German market

20. Speech by Jean Dondelinger, Commissioner in charge of Audio-Visual policy to the Financial Times Cable and Satellite Conference, London, February 1990.

to gain access to the films.[21] In practice, the commercial arrangement, as revised by the Commission, was brought to an end several years early by the parties.

Often, exclusivity is achieved on the back of nationally granted intellectual property rights, such as copyright. The Court has very clearly indicated that, where the holders of intellectual property rights use those rights to divide up national markets or to prevent the development of new markets by the refusal to grant a licence, this can constitute an abuse of a dominant position.

4.2.4. Broadcasting rights

The Commission has recognised that broadcasting rights are of key importance in the context of sports events. Twice during 1991, the Commission intervened in the field of sports broadcasting.

In one case, the Commission objected to the Eurosport joint venture, because of the harmful effects resulting from the joint venture's ability to corner the market for certain sports events. A restructured joint venture was subsequently given the 'green light'.[22] In a separate case, the Commission objected to the rules devised by the European Broadcasting Union, which links the main European broadcasters, concerning the acquisition of rights to sports coverage in Europe by all EBU members.[23] The Commission was concerned about the limited access granted to non-member broadcasters, and would only be prepared to exempt a revised agreement once these provisions had been relaxed.

It can be seen that a particular concern of the Commission is the possibility of rights holders restricting distribution, for example, by refusing to grant licences, or demanding excessive royalties before it will do so. Any such attempts may constitute breaches of Article 86. This is particularly so, where a broadcaster, or indeed, any supplier, refuses to supply an established customer, or fails to adequately meet market demand for the particular programming or product in question.[24]

4.2.5. Exclusive suppliers

The problem of exclusivity also lies behind the Commission's concern over exclusive supply or distribution arrangements. These could be for the supply of computers, soft drinks or promotional material, or for the distribution of commemorative memorabilia, supplied by a third party for the event. Such arrangements may need to receive specific clearance or exemption from the Commission.

In some cases, the agreements entered into by sponsors can escape the need for formal notification to the Commission, if they are drafted within the terms

21. ARD *Film purchases by German television stations*, OJ L284, 3.10.89.
22. Commission Press Release IP/91/1407, 7.5.91.
23. Article 19(3), *Notice EBU Eurovision System*.
24. See Case 6/73, *BBC* v. *Commission (Magill)*, [1974] ECR 223, and see also Case T-70/89, *Commercial Solvents* v. *Commission*, (1991) 4 CMLR 669.

of the so-called 'Block Exemptions' for certain categories of agreement.[25] These specify the precise limits on competition which might be included in the terms of supply and distribution arrangements. Restrictions going beyond this may require separate notification.

However, these Block Exemptions would not be suited to many sponsorship deals, as they relate purely to the supply of goods 'for resale' and they do not apply to the supply of services.

4.2.6. Official services and premiums

Problems also arise with a whole range of official services and premiums. On the one hand, the grant to one travel agency of official ticketing outlet status may exclude the grant of such status to others. On the other hand, the requirement for third parties to deal only with 'official' outlets or suppliers may constitute an unjustifiable tie, which again may be anti-competitive.

4.2.7. Tying arrangements

Generally, competition issues arise with any type of arrangement under which an individual is unjustifiably tied to taking a product, which is not necessary for the technically satisfactory exploitation of the main product or service. The problem might arise where X is appointed exclusive fax supplier to the event, subject to the requirement that all those using X's faxes, which are supplied cost free, have to purchase the fax paper to use with them from X. Many forms of promotion may risk being considered an unfair tie on the end customer. The Commission has even indicated that airlines' frequent flyer schemes could be unfair under Article 86.[26]

These are simply some examples of the common competition issues which may be raised in connection with sponsorship deals and the related documentation.

25. The following Group Exemption Regulations have been adopted by the Commission: Reg. 1983/83 on exclusive distribution; Reg. 1983/84 on exclusive purchasing; Reg. 2349/84 on patent licensing; Reg. 123/85 on motor vehicle distribution; Reg. 417/85 on specialisation agreements; Reg. 418/85 on research and development agreements; Reg. 4087/88 on franchise agreements; and Reg. 556/89 on know-how licensing. The Group Exemption Regulations essentially list both permissible and prohibited restrictions, serving as a skeleton upon which undertakings can hang their commercial arrangements. Providing they do not go beyond the restrictions provided for in the Group Exemption, the need for an individual notification is obviated. Certain other specialised Group Exemptions have been adopted in the transport sector.
26. Sir Leon Brittan, former Commissioner for Competition, Seminar on Competition Policy and Transport, Centre for European Policy Studies, Brussels, February 1992.

4.3. Practical consequences

4.3.1. The Commission's powers to intervene

One view is often 'why bother about the EC Competition rules?' – 'the Commission won't be interested or won't find out'. Unfortunately, sponsors, who rely on positive publicity from their involvement with the event, may not want to take this risk. In any case, such involvement with a prestigious international sports event may well attract the Commission's attention and with certain events, such as the Albertville and Barcelona Olympics, the Community's active involvement.

The Commission enjoys wide powers of investigation,[27] allowing it to demand information by letter or to turn up on your doorstep demanding to see your files. These powers will be used both in investigations carried out on its own initiative and those resulting from third party complaints.

4.3.2. Fines

Where agreements are found to infringe the competition rules or where behaviour is held to be an abuse of a monopoly power, the Commission can and does impose substantial fines of up to 10% of worldwide group turnover, even where the breach is committed by a small EC subsidiary. In 1991, Solvay was fined 54 million ECU for a market sharing agreement,[28] whilst Tetra Pak was fined 75 million ECU for abusing its dominant marketing position.[29] In 1992, Dunlop Slazenger was fined 5 million ECU for applying a general ban on exports.[30]

4.3.3. The validity of sponsorship agreements

A further consequence of the competition rules is that those aspects of sponsorship agreements which infringe those rules are automatically void and unenforceable, with the practical result that exclusivity may be removed and royalties may prove uncollectable.

Where such agreements infringe the competition rules, the risk of fines and uncertainty as to enforceability of an agreement can only be avoided by '*notification*' of the agreements for clearance or exemption by the Commission.

Furthermore, the validity of agreements is not only open to challenge by the Commission. A breach of the rules opens up the possibility of actions in the national courts by competitors or business partners for injunctive relief restraining the enforcement of the anti-competitive parts of the arrangements, or requiring absolution from abusive conduct under Article 86. A party to the

---

27. The Commission's investigative powers under the competition rules and its power to fine for breaches of those rules are set out in Council Regulation 17 of 1962.
28. Commission Press Notice IP/90/1057, 19.12.90.
29. Commission Decision of 24 July 1991, *Tetra Pak II*, OJ L72, 18.3.92.
30. Commission Decision 92/261 *Newitt/Dunlop Slazenger International and others*, OJ L131/32, 16.5.92.

arrangement or even a third party can claim for damages for any loss they can show.

4.4. Can the Commission Catch Events Outside the Community?

It is in the nature of sports sponsorship that it seeks a global, or at least, continental, audience. The rights to the Whitbread Round the World Yacht Race are sold worldwide. The English Football Association Cup Final attracts millions of television spectators from all over the world.

Sports events will almost inevitably have an impact within the Community, even if the event sponsored takes place halfway across the globe. Community rules are likely, therefore, to apply to any and all arrangements which have a commercial effect within the Community.

Even at the planning stage, the Community rules can apply to the grant of rights, and to licensing and marketing arrangements agreed and signed up outside the Community. Locating an international sports federation outside the Community does not necessarily give either the federation or those doing business with it protection from the Commission. Furthermore, the possible accession of Switzerland to the EC will place many international organisations and federations clearly within the Treaty of Rome rules.

5. Sponsorship and the Single Market

5.1. The Aim of the Single Market

The Treaty of Rome defines the Single Market as: 'an area without internal frontiers in which the free movement of goods, persons, services and capital is ensured' (Article 8A).

In adopting the Single Market programme outlined in its so-called 'White Paper' in 1985,[31] the Commission was simply accelerating the process of removing all trade barriers dating back to the inception of the Treaty of Rome. The programme has been perhaps an even greater success than the Commission might have hoped for, both in opening markets and moving the business horizon from national frontiers to the edges of the Community and beyond.

Whilst few, if any, of the 280 or so measures were directed primarily towards the sports industry, the impact of '1992' is felt as keenly there as in any other sector of the economy.

31. Completing the International Market: White Paper from the Commission, COM(85)310 final, 14.6.85.

5.2. The Main Principles of the Single Market

Certain basic principles can be identified within the Single Market programme as a whole.

5.2.1. Removing national barriers

The key aim is to ensure that barriers to the movement of goods, people, services and money are removed to open up the Community market. It follows from this that physical frontier posts will be removed, subject to the possibility of spot checks being carried out, together with immigration controls at the Community's external frontiers.

5.2.2. Harmonise or recognise

Throughout the Community, differences exist in national rules relating to product standards, or labelling requirements or restrictions on advertising. Whilst these may affect both domestic and imported goods and services in the same way, such regulations create barriers which prevent the sports industry from taking full advantage of the opportunities presented by a Single Market.

In some cases, the Community has adopted harmonising legislation designed to create *minimum standards* for products and services. Providing the products and services comply with these European standards, free circulation for them is guaranteed.

In most cases, however, Community law simply requires each Member State to recognise the validity of the equivalent rules imposed by the Member States from which the goods or services originate, rather than allowing them to require that their own standards are also being met.[32] The same approach is taken to qualifications, so that a British qualified ski instructor would not have to re-qualify in France in order to teach there.[33]

5.2.3. Creating a 'level playing field'

The final strand of Single Market policy is the desire to put everyone on an equal footing. The removal of State-imposed barriers goes hand in hand with the tighter enforcement of the Community's rules promoting fair competition and preventing any discrimination on the grounds of nationality.

Although the Commission does not have a specific power over sport, the role that sporting events have in everyday life and the economic strength of the sports industry means that there is a constant interplay with a wide range of Community policies.

---

32. The principle of mutual recognition of standards, allowing the free circulation of goods throughout the Community, if the product is lawfully marketed in one Member State, was established in the landmark *Cassis de Dijon* case (Case 120/78, [1979] ECR 1805).
33. For the mutual recognition of qualifications, see Directive 48/89 OJ L019, 24.1.89 (1st General System) and Directive [89/48] OJ L209, 24.7.92 (2nd General System).

5.3. The Single Market in Advertising and Broadcasting

The Television without Frontiers Directive, designed to promote harmonised national regulation of broadcasting, thereby enabling cross-border transmission, has placed some limits on what may be advertised. This will have a major impact on sponsorship by restricting the sort of sponsorship which may be exploited.

This clearly shows the weight attached by the Commission to broadcasting as a vehicle for means of advertising. In particular, the rules, which are implemented at a purely national level, prohibit, amongst others, the advertising of tobacco products and prescription medicines. On the other hand, the rules have made it easier for satellite services to operate throughout the Community, thereby increasing the potential audience for certain international sports events.

Other proposals on advertising will also have an important impact on sports marketing by drying up sponsorship sources. The proposal to ban all tobacco advertising is particularly significant, although there is no immediate prospect of this proposal getting through the EC Health Council of Ministers. However, in the medium term, it is likely to make it onto the European Statute Books.

The Commission has also recognised the potential barrier to broadcasting created by the existence of 12 different copyright laws covering the programme material and royalties due for the use of the copyright. In the context of satellite and cable broadcasts, which are aimed at a number of Community countries, a Directive harmonising those rules is now being discussed.[34] In principle, the copyright law applying will be that of the country where the decision about broadcasting and programme content is made (usually the country from which the signal is transmitted up to the satellite). The new rules will require Member States to create a specific cable transmission right, as well as harmonising the manner in which royalty arrangements with collecting societies are arranged.

6. Funding from Brussels

A further dimension to Community involvement in sport is the possibility of funding from Brussels in relation to sports events. This may take the form of direct event sponsorship, as a means of promoting the Community identity (such as the Olympics), or indirectly through the use of Community funds for regional development. In relation to the Albertville and Barcelona Olympics, the Commission prepared its 'Community marketing' in partnership with a major London advertising agency.

Similar Commission involvement in an attempt to 'Europeanise' a number of major sporting events can be seen in the European Community Swimming

34. Proposal for a Directive on the co-ordination of certain rules concerning copyright and neighbouring rights applicable to satellite broadcasting and cable re-transmission, OJ C255, 1.10.91.

Championships, the EC Tennis Championships and the Transatlantic Sail for Europe Race (in which the Commission sponsored a boat alongside private and commercial teams). As mentioned above, the Commission has established a Joint Committee with national sports authorities, as a forum for the discussion of sports issues. The Commission is also co-operating with national ministers of sport.

For organisers of sports events, indirect Community funding may be available through the Community's structural funds. Much depends on the region in which the event takes place, with economically backward or declining regions attracting the bulk of Community funding for infrastructural investment and/or job creation.

7. Conclusions

In view of the Commission's increasing involvement in the sports arena, organisers and sponsors of international sports events, whether staged within the Community or outside, need to take full account of its existing and developing rules, not only in the competition field but also in many other areas.

The Community is not only here to stay, but is also on the move, expanding its sphere of influence through the European Economic Area Agreement with the EFTA countries, as well as dealing with requests for additional membership by EFTA countries and, most probably others, including Eastern Europe, in due course. To ignore the European dimension to sport and sports sponsorship, therefore, would not only be possibly illegal but also sheer commercial folly.

Broadcasting

by Howard M. Stupp

1. Introduction

The purpose of this chapter is to provide background information regarding the broadcasting of sports events and to flag a number of issues which should be addressed when negotiating broadcasting agreements for such events. Due to the author's position at the International Olympic Committee ('IOC'), various references will be made, and examples will be given, in relation to the broadcast of the Olympic Games.

2. Important Role of Broadcasting

The entering into of agreements for the broadcast of sports events serves two important purposes. Firstly, it is important for sports events to obtain exposure to the general public. Television is clearly one of the major sources of achieving this goal. Without such exposure, it is difficult for an event to generate worldwide interest and popularity.

Secondly, broadcast agreements provide revenue to help finance the organisation of sports events. For example, the American television network NBC paid US$ 401 million for the exclusive right to broadcast the 1992 Barcelona Olympic Games in the United States. Approximately 73 per cent of this amount went to the Organising Committee for the Barcelona Games to help finance the staging of the Barcelona Games. The balance was shared, approximately one third each, by the IOC, the international sports federations which were on the programme of the Barcelona Games, and Olympic Solidarity (which distributes the money to the national Olympic Committees which attended the Games). Other rights fees paid by various networks and unions for the broadcast rights in the 1992 Albertville, 1992 Barcelona and 1994 Lillehammer Olympic Games are indicated in the table below. It is interesting to note that the European Broadcasting Union ('EBU') recently agreed to pay

US$ 250 million for the exclusive European broadcast rights to the 1996 Atlanta Olympic Games.

Of course, the amount of the broadcast rights fee is directly linked to the interest which the general public has in watching the event. However, it is the very broadcast of the event which helps generate such public interest.

List of some rights fees paid for current Olympic Games, in US$

	Albertville (Winter 1992)	Barcelona (Summer 1992)	Lillehammer (Winter 1994)
USA	243,000,000	401,000,000	295,000,000
Canada	10,000,000	16,500,000	12,000,000
Japan	9,000,000	62,500,000	12,700,000
European Broadcasting Union (EBU)	18,000,000	90,000,000	24,000,000
Organización de Televisión Ibero-americana (OTI-Latin America)	———	3,550,000	———
International Radio and TV Organization (OIRT-Eastern Europe)	2,175,000	4,000,000	———

3. Sale of Broadcast Rights on a Worldwide Basis

3.1. Exclusivity

For sporting events that are broadcast worldwide, the rights are generally sold, on an exclusive basis, continent-by-continent or country-by-country. For example, the rights could be sold to a broadcasting union for a continent (e.g. EBU for Europe, URTNA for Africa) and to a particular network in a particular country (e.g. NBC, CBS or ABC in the United States, CTV or CBC in Canada). Often networks are willing to pay a premium in order to obtain the right to broadcast an event on an exclusive basis. However, for sports events that involve a large number of matches or competitions, there is a problem in that a single network will not be able to cover all such matches or competitions. In such a case, the event organiser can allow the network, to whom it sells the exclusive rights, to sub-license such rights to third parties. Alternatively, the event organiser can sell the rights to more than one network.

In the case of the Olympic Games, the IOC allows certain networks or unions to sub-license their broadcast rights. This not only gives the original rights holder the opportunity to re-coup its investment, but it also ensures that more of the Olympic events can be seen by the general public.

3.2. Obtaining Wide Exposure

An important issue which event organisers are often faced with is the balance between obtaining a high rights fee and ensuring that their event receives the widest exposure possible. Often, private networks, which generally do not reach as many households as the public networks, are willing to pay more money than the public networks in order to obtain the broadcast rights to a popular sports event. An event organiser may be offered a larger rights fee by a pay-per-view channel but this positive aspect may be offset by the result that there would probably be a smaller viewing audience and that some viewers would become annoyed that they had to pay to watch the event.

Many sports event organisers choose to sell the broadcast rights at a lower price to a network (or a union of networks) that reaches essentially all the population, rather than sell to a different network at a higher price, if the latter network does not reach as large an audience. It should be noted, however, that the audience reach of the various private networks is generally increasing with time and this may affect the manner in which some of these negotiations take place in the future.

On a related note, it is important to sports event organisers that, once the rights to broadcast their sports event are sold to a third party, the third party actually broadcasts the event. It is not enough that the event organiser obtains the broadcast rights fee. It is essential that the event also be broadcast. In some cases, the event organiser does not receive a substantial sum of money for the rights fee. Rather, the event organiser may receive more money from his sponsors who pay for billboards appearing around the competition area, based on the assumption that such billboards will be widely seen during the broadcast of the event. In any event, sponsors aside, it is important for the popularity of an event that it actually be broadcast.

4. Role of Host Broadcaster

For major international sporting events, a host broadcaster is appointed to provide the basic television signals ('international signals') of the event to the various other broadcast rights holders. This eliminates the presence of a multitude of television cameras, from the various networks across the world, each filming the same action.

For example, at the 1992 Barcelona Olympic Games, the host broadcaster organisation, RTO'92, which was under the control of the Organising Committee for the Barcelona Olympic Games, had over 500 cameras covering the various sporting events. From these cameras, RTO'92 produced (an) international signal(s) for each event, which it made available to all the broadcast rights holders at the Games International Broadcast Centre ('IBC'). For some sports, where there was more than one activity taking place at the same time (e.g. athletics, gymnastics), there was more than one international signal being generated at the same time.

In addition to being able to source the international signals, certain major broadcasts rights holders brought their own cameras (known as 'unilateral cameras') to supplement the host broadcaster coverage. In the past, the major networks used their unilateral cameras to provide general supplementary coverage. However, as the coverage provided by the host broadcasters improves with each Olympic Games, the major networks now tend to rely more on the host broadcaster material and tend to use their unilateral coverage primarily when they wish to pay special attention to a particular athlete coming from their country. This increased reliance by the broadcasters on the coverage produced by the host broadcaster is a positive occurrence since it reduces the cost for the broadcast rights holders to produce their respective programming of the event.

Most of the major broadcast rights holders at the Olympic Games import substantive equipment into the host city of the Games, which they set up at their space within the IBC. Many of these networks set up their own studio at the IBC and create their programmes there, using the host broadcaster international signals, their own unilateral footage and their own studio commentary. The IBC contains a wide variety of services and facilities, which are made available to the various broadcast rights holders, at prices established by the host broadcaster and listed in a rate card, in order for the broadcasters to accomplish their various tasks. At all Olympic venues, commentary positions are available to the various broadcasters in order that they can provide live commentary during the various sporting events. In a number of cases, the broadcasters subsequently edit the material that they wish to use in their programmes and add a commentary at such later time.

5. Scheduling of the Event

If the sports event is one of worldwide interest, care must be exercised so that it occurs at a time that is beneficial to the various broadcasters. Sometimes, the interest of the broadcasters who are paying the largest sums of money are favoured over the other broadcasters; however, this must not go so far as to prejudice the athletes involved. In the case of the Olympic Games, the schedules of all sporting events are subject to the approval of the relevant international sports federations. In this way, the interests of the athletes are safeguarded.

Where possible, matches should be arranged so that they can be seen live in the part of the world that would be most interested in such matches. For example, if two European teams are playing in a competition in North America, it would be preferable if the match was scheduled in the afternoon in North America so that it could be seen live in Europe during prime time. Of course, matters would not be as simple if one of the teams was European and the other North American. In some cases, where the schedule is fixed in advance of when the event organiser knows which two teams will actually be playing in such match (e.g. the semi-finals or finals of a competition), this flexibility is more difficult to implement.

An interesting issue is the importance to the general public of seeing an event live. Generally speaking, the public would prefer to see matches, such as hockey or football, live (especially if they find out the final score before they are able to see the match on a delayed basis). On the other hand, the significance of the live element is less important with respect to sports where there is much emphasis on creativity and artistic impression – e.g. gymnastics, figure skating.

6. Coordination between Sale of Broadcast Rights and Sale of Advertising Airtime

6.1. Obtaining Preferential Treatment for Sponsors of the Event

It is very important that there be coordination between the sale of the broadcast rights and the sale of advertising airtime related thereto. It is strongly recommended that event organisers include provisions in their agreements with broadcasters providing preferential opportunities (e.g. a right of first negotiation) for the sponsors of their event to become sponsors of the broadcast of the event and to buy spot advertising. With respect to the broadcast of sports events, where there are sponsors of the event but where there are no billboards around the playing field, this coordination becomes even more important. For example, while there are sponsors of the IOC and the Olympic Games, there is no advertising around the playing field during the Olympic Games. The sponsors of the IOC and the Olympic Games pay large sums of money for the right to be such sponsors. If their competitors then become sponsors of the broadcast of the event or are able to buy spot advertising immediately before, during or immediately after the broadcast of the event, to the exclusion of the sponsors of the IOC and the Olympic Games, the sponsorship rights of the sponsors of the IOC and the Olympic Games will be undermined.

The broadcast agreements for the Olympic Games, therefore, provide for a right of first negotiation to be offered by the broadcaster to the Olympic sponsors to become sponsors of the broadcast of the Games and to purchase spot advertising. If the Olympic sponsors do not purchase such advertising airtime, it is possible for their competitors to do so for the same (or a higher) price as was offered to the Olympic sponsors.

In cases where the actual sponsors of the event do not buy advertising airtime, care must be taken in order to minimise confusion between who is a sponsor of the event and who is a sponsor of the broadcast of the event. Often, however, this distinction is still not satisfactory to the sponsor of the event if his competitor becomes a sponsor of the broadcast of the event. The ideal situation is that a sponsor of the event becomes a sponsor of the broadcast thereof. Another alternative is to try to ensure that, at least, the sponsors of the broadcast of the event are not competitors to the sponsors of the event. Also, it is desirable that the sponsors of the broadcast not be able to make express reference to the event, unless they are actually also sponsors of the event. For example, they should not be able to say 'the broadcast of the "event" is brought to you by . . .'. Rather, they should only be allowed to say something along the lines of 'this programme is brought to you by . . .'.

If the sponsors of the event are visible in the actual broadcast picture of the event – e.g. if there are banners or if there are billboards in or around the playing field – then the concerns addressed above, albeit still very important, are somewhat less serious. In fact, if there are banners or billboards in or around the playing field, this may prejudice the broadcaster in his ability to go out and find sponsors of the broadcast or spot advertisers, since competitors of the companies identified in such banners and billboards may be reluctant to buy advertising airtime during the broadcast of the event. As a result of this, the broadcasters may offer a lower rights fee when there are banners or billboards in or around the playing field. It is up to the event organiser to weigh the various pros and cons of how much any increase in revenues from billboard advertising may be offset by any decrease in broadcast rights fees.

On a related note, in some cases – for example, an international football match – an event organiser may arrange that each of the national networks from the two teams involved has its own complete set of television cameras on opposite sides of the field in order that each network captures its own specific set of sponsor billboards on the side of the field opposite them.

6.2. New Technological Developments Relating to Billboard Advertising

A new system has recently been developed pursuant to which a billboard appearing in the playing field can be read by a computer and changed to another name or design on the broadcast picture of the event. In other words, the system can locate a previously identifiable billboard and replace this billboard by a new billboard which will retain the same characteristics of the initial broadcast picture, such as focus, brightness, colour and movement. This can be done even if the original billboard is partially blocked by athletes running in front of it.

Apparently, this system has not yet been developed to the point that it can be done live. Rather, one needs a few hours delay in order that the appropriate conversions be put into effect. However, it is probable that this system will be perfected in the near future to the point that such conversions can be made during a live broadcast.

Such a system could have major implications with respect to coordinating the names of companies on the billboards around the field with the names of sponsors of the broadcast of the event. Of course, it is very possible that the event organiser does not want the names of the companies appearing on the billboards surrounding the event to be altered in any way. If such is the case, a clause should be included in the broadcast agreements accordingly. In order to protect against the alteration of billboards as described above, and to generally protect the integrity of the broadcast picture of the event (including helping to avoid over-commercialisation and conflicts with respect to companies who are sponsors of the event), the organisers of events may wish to add a clause to their broadcast agreements stating, more or less, that 'no advertising may be superimposed on, or appear on a split screen at the same time as, the broadcast of the event without the prior consent of the event organiser'.

7. Various Additional Issues to be Addressed in Broadcasting Agreements

7.1. Delivering Exclusivity; Broadcast by Satellite

As referred to earlier in this chapter, broadcasting rights are often granted on an exclusive basis in a given territory. It is essential that the event organisers take the necessary steps so that the exclusive rights of the broadcasters are protected. For example, event organisers should not grant a broadcaster the right to broadcast via satellite when the footprint of the satellite is such that it extends into the broadcast territory of another broadcaster to whom the event organiser has granted exclusive rights. In the alternative, the event organiser will have to adjust the grant of exclusivity accordingly.

7.2. News Access

Any grant of exclusive rights to broadcast a sports event should be subject to the exception that competitive networks may broadcast short excerpts of the event as part of news programmes. In some countries, this right to show excerpts of events as part of news programmes is provided by law.

For recent Olympic Games, the IOC stipulated in its broadcast agreements that the broadcaster to whom it granted exclusive rights could control the extent to which its competitors showed excerpts of the Games as part of news programmes. For the 1996 Atlanta Games and for subsequent Games, the IOC intends to impose minimum news access rules. This will mean that the networks to whom the IOC grants exclusive broadcast rights will have to accept that their competitors be allowed to broadcast short excerpts of footage of the

Games (e.g. maximum two minutes up to three times per day) in their regularly scheduled daily news programmes.

7.3. Granting Radio Rights

Up until now, although the term 'broadcasting' has been used throughout this chapter, the subject matter has been applicable mainly to broadcasting by television. Event organisers may, however, wish to grant the right to broadcast their event by radio. In such a case, event organisers should either not grant the radio broadcast rights on an exclusive basis or they should qualify their grant of exclusivity in the sense that they undertake not to grant radio rights to any third party. This is because it is not always possible for event organisers to prevent third party radio broadcasters from broadcasting the event over the radio. For example, such third party broadcasters can obtain the necessary information, to broadcast over the radio, while watching the event live on television.

7.4. Maintaining Ownership and/or Control over the Material Being Broadcast

The event organisers must include provisions in their agreements with broadcasters pursuant to which they maintain ownership and/or control over the material being broadcast. For example, when the event organiser grants exclusive rights to broadcast an event, such exclusivity should expire after a reasonable period of time. The event organiser may wish that (shortly) after network's broadcast of the event, all rights to broadcast the event revert back to the event organiser. The event organiser may, however, agree to allow the broadcaster to continue to have the right to show short extracts of the event, on a non-exclusive basis.

On a related note, the event organisers should include provisions in their broadcast agreements addressing the extent, if any, to which the broadcasters may use the broadcast material over and above the broadcasters' own actual broadcast of the event. For example, the extent, if any, to which broadcasters may assign or sub-license their rights should be addressed. Also, a clause should be included that restricts the broadcasters from authorising third parties to use any broadcast material to promote products or services, unless the prior consent of the event organiser is obtained. This will help protect the sponsors of the event from being 'ambushed' by their competitors.

In cases where the event organiser is providing the international signals to various different broadcasters (e.g. through a host broadcaster), the event organiser should take the necessary steps so that the copyright in the international signals is in the name of the event organiser.

7.5. Rights Ancillary to Television Broadcast of the Event, e.g. Video Rights

Organisers of certain popular sports events may wish to grant rights that are ancillary to the television broadcast of the event. For example, for major events or events which last over a number of days, the organiser may wish to make an official film of the event or may wish to subsequently market videocassettes of the event to the general public. If so, the event organiser should address this matter accordingly in its broadcast agreements. The event organiser may wish to include such rights as part of the broadcasting agreements or he may wish to enter into separate agreements to this effect with third parties.

7.6. Use of Emblem of the Event

Many major sporting events are associated with a distinctive mark or 'emblem'. The event organisers must address the issue of the extent to which the broadcaster may make use of such emblem. Clearly, the broadcasters should be allowed to use the emblem during their broadcasts of the event and in order to promote their coverage of the event.

On the other hand, event organisers must be careful to ensure that the broadcasters do not allow their television advertisers (e.g. broadcast sponsors and buyers of spot advertising) to use, or to link themselves with, the emblem of the event unless such advertisers are also sponsors of the event itself. Otherwise, the rights of the sponsors of the event will be prejudiced.

Although event organisers may allow the broadcaster to produce certain premium items containing the emblem of the event (e.g. T-shirts) to distribute free of charge to the broadcasters' employees and guests, the event organisers, as a general rule, will not grant to the broadcasters any other licensing rights with respect to the emblem of the event. Rather, the event organisers will enter into a separate agreement with someone normally in the business of marketing licensed merchandise.

7.7. Hospitality

An important element of many broadcasting agreements is the hospitality aspect. Not only do broadcasters need accommodation and accreditation for their employees covering the event, but often they wish to obtain additional accommodation and accreditation for the executives, other employees (who may be attending the event as a reward for previous work well done) and other guests such as the executives of the companies who buy advertising airtime from the broadcasters.

Sometimes the broadcasters will want access to a hospitality tent where they can entertain their guests (although this is probably a much more common requirement of the companies who are sponsoring the event).

Event organisers must anticipate these hospitality-type demands in advance in order to provide the appropriate accommodation, accreditation tickets and other appropriate services and facilities.

7.8. On-Screen Identification, e.g. Timing and Data Companies

Often agreements are entered into with the companies that provide timing and data services in relation to a sports event, pursuant to which such companies are granted the right to have identification superimposed upon the broadcast picture of the event.

When the event is of major international status, and there is a host broadcaster providing the international television signal(s), an agreement is often entered into directly between the event organiser and the timing and/or data companies. In this case, the event organisers should ensure in their broadcasting agreements that the broadcasters do not remove such identification.

Generally speaking, the broadcasters accept that there be some on-screen identification of timing and/or data companies provided that such companies are in fact furnishing a desired and/or necessary service in relation to the running of the sports event.

7.9. Contingencies Giving Rise to Termination or Abatement

Most broadcast agreements contain provisions which provide for termination of the agreement or a reduction of the rights fee should certain contingencies occur. For example, if the event does not take place, it is normal that the broadcaster can terminate the agreement and re-coup its rights fee. On the other hand, if the event takes place but there is a serious problem with the availability of the international signal furnished to the broadcaster by the event organiser and/or the host broadcaster, the broadcaster will generally be entitled to an abatement of its rights fee.

In some cases, abatements can also be foreseen where, after a broadcaster agrees to pay a particular rights fee based upon the assumption that a team representing the broadcaster's country will be participating in the event, such team does not, in fact, participate.

7.10. Insurance; Non-Occurrence of Event

In addition to the standard comprehensive general liability insurance policies that event organisers and broadcasters normally procure and maintain to protect themselves and to possibly indemnify each other, event organisers may also consider obtaining insurance to cover the contingency of the event not taking place.

With respect to the Olympic Games, due to the very high broadcast rights fees involved, the premiums for such insurance are extremely high. Consequently, recent Organising Committees for the Olympic Games have taken out such insurance to cover only a portion of their share of the rights fee. On the other hand, the IOC currently takes the position that, rather than take out such insurance, it will bear the risk with respect to its share of the broadcasting rights fee.

7.11. Assignment, Sub-licensing of Broadcast Rights

The event organisers must address the extent, if any, to which they wish to allow any broadcaster, to whom they grant rights to broadcast the event, to assign or sub-license such rights. As a general rule, event organisers should be cautious in this respect in order to be able to exercise control over who is ultimately broadcasting their event and how it is being broadcast.

If the event organiser allows assignment or sub-licensing, it should ensure that its agreement with the broadcaster provides that the sub-licensees will respect all the terms and conditions of the broadcaster's agreement with the event organiser. Similarly, if the event organiser allows the broadcaster to assign or sub-license any of its rights, the former should ensure that the latter remains fully liable for the performance by its assignees and sub-licensees of all obligations under the agreement between the event organiser and the broadcaster.

8. Effects of the Commission of the European Communities on Broadcasting

The Commission of the European Communities ('EC') is presently looking into the effects of EC law on sports, including effects that would occur with respect to broadcasting.

Currently, the EC Commission is questioning the extent to which EBU's manner of negotiating exclusive television agreements for sports events is in conformity with Article 85(1) of the EC Treaty, insofar as restraint of trade is concerned. As you are most probably aware, EBU is composed of a number of different networks from across Europe. Discussions are now taking place between the EC Commission and EBU regarding the manner and extent to which EBU can and should sub-license its exclusive rights. Examples of other areas where the EC Commission and EC law may come into play are with respect to news access rules, as well as the extent to which a broadcaster or group of broadcasters may acquire rights that are considered to be excessively exclusive.

This whole area of EC law and its effect on sports and the broadcasting of sports events should evolve further over the coming years.

Settling Sports-Related Disputes through the Court of Arbitration for Sport

by Dr. Gilbert Schwaar

1. Arbitration in General

The Swiss legal order does not give civil courts a monopoly on jurisdictional functions. Within certain limits, it allows parties to entrust, through a contract, the task of settling disputes in private law to non-State bodies, which the parties have set up for this purpose: arbitration courts. These intervene in place of the civil courts, and, within the limits of their competence, exclude recourse to ordinary courts. It necessarily follows that it is not possible to submit for settlement by an arbitration court a dispute which, by its nature, could not be the subject of a judgment pronounced by a state civil court.

A system of private justice has, therefore, developed alongside official justice. For its part, the State is well aware that it cannot keep the privilege of dispensing justice exclusively for its own courts. It, therefore, does not simply tolerate the existence of arbitral jurisdictions, but even goes so far as to lend its support, 'under certain conditions', in the enforcement of their awards, although the control it can exercise over them is extremely limited.

This private justice is attached to a system of civil jurisdiction, a legal order which determines the conditions of the existence and operation of the arbitration court and the effects of its awards.

Generally speaking, one can unequivocally regard civil justice as superior to private justice. However, while civil justice, with its elaborate organisation, can offer more security, it is also slower and less flexible. At the same time, as it has become elaborate, it has also become so complex, and its many regulations have lost so much of that simplicity which, it is said, befits laws, that we cannot ignore the popularity acquired by the expression 'the procedural jungle'. Thus, alongside this heavy justice, in our civilisation obsessed with feverish activity and speed, it is not surprising that there should arise another justice, less fair perhaps, somewhat partial, but simpler, faster, and less costly.

The absence of formality, and the saving of time and money, such are the generally acknowledged advantages of arbitration. In addition, arbitration allows for the discrete settlement of disputes, as these are heard *in camera* and the awards are only rarely published.

Finally, arbitration offers the possibility of choosing as judges people in the profession: colleagues or experts on the issues to be heard. Consequently, costs and procedural complications can be avoided in the majority of cases.

But arbitration also has its disadvantages. With certain reservations, it generally implies renouncing the guarantee of the double instance system which is standard practice in the official courts. Indeed, arbitration clauses almost always exclude the option of using the normal methods of appeal of the civil procedure. Furthermore, in spite of certain imperative legal prescriptions, the rejection of all legal formalities is likely to create the risk of arbitrariness in the hearing of the dispute.

Nevertheless, it is incontestable that arbitration jurisdictions have considerable practical advantages which are especially strengthened when they operate within the context of a previously constituted body. Depending on the circumstances, this body may have a simple administrative function or exercise jurisdictional power as a court of arbitration.

The institution of the private court can, therefore, be found in the most varied of fields. While its field of activity has become widespread and developed systematically in economic and commercial spheres, practitioners of sports activity in general, won over by the advantages of such an institution, have also not failed to equip themselves with their own system of arbitration.

A dispute can be validly submitted to arbitration only if two main conditions are met: first, the parties must have agreed to this; and second, the subject of the dispute must, by its nature, be able to be kept from official jurisdiction. To satisfy the demands of the State in terms of law, the procedure before the arbitration court must respect a whole series of fundamental principles: equality of the parties before the arbitrators; guarantee of the right to be heard and of the independence of the arbitrators; the possibility of attending or being represented at hearings; having the file at one's disposal; and so on. It is under these conditions that an award rendered by an arbitration court will be enforceable in the same way as a civil judgment pronounced by a State court.

The parties give their agreement to have recourse to this institution – and not to civil courts – by accepting an arbitration agreement. This agreement – which must be in writing – may be drawn up on the occasion of an existing dispute, or looking ahead to a dispute which might arise in the future. In the latter case, the arbitration clause is part of a more general agreement; it may appear among the statutes or regulations (I shall come back to this point when we look at the Court of Arbitration for Sport), in individual contracts or agreements, agreements in which the parties agree simply to submit to arbitration any dispute between them with regard to a given legal relationship.

2. Settling Sports-Related Disputes

By becoming a source of entertainment, a consumer product, advertising medium and provider of employment, sport is obviously influencing ever larger sections of our society. It is today an essential reality of social existence, and sport, at least organised sport, can no longer claim to be a stranger to the world of law. The scope for contentious issues within sport is enormous. The parties concerned by sports activities, particularly in view of the considerable financial interests involved, are increasingly demanding where law is concerned. The profound changes in the world of sport due to this evolution inevitably lead to an increase in differences and disputes connected with sports activities.

How are such pecuniary or doctrinal disputes to be resolved? Is it possible to reconcile sport and law when the boundary between what can be called 'sports rules' and legal norms is becoming increasingly difficult to define?

Apart from arbitration, the major principles which I have described and to which I shall return in the context of a study of the Court of Arbitration for Sport, the parties, clubs, teams, sports organisations and associations, athletes, patrons, sponsors, employers, employees involved in a dispute have only two options if they cannot or do not want to settle their differences amicably. They can:

(1) either turn to the bodies created by the competent national or international federations or other institutions governing the sport in question; or
(2) bring their dispute before the ordinary law courts in so far as these are competent to decide the issue.

In practice, parties submit their disputes to the institutions and bodies set up within federations. If one party is not satisfied with a decision concerning it, it brings the case before the ordinary law courts which sometimes act as a kind of court of appeal (second instance). But the ordinary law courts may also deal with a case when, at the request of one of the parties concerned, they find that they are immediately competent in an area related to sport.

Most national or international sports organisations obviously want the decisions that they make through the internal bodies which they have created to be definitive, binding and without possibility of appeal to the civil courts. It is clear, however, that since they do not meet the conditions of independence and impartiality – particularly because they are set up by the bodies of the association itself (general assembly, management committee, central committee), these institutions all too often do not meet the conditions, cited above, of independence and objectivity which the law requires. As a result, they do not exclude recourse by the dissatisfied party to the civil courts.

The confusion surrounding the legal status and competence of some of the arbitration institutions created by international sports organisations, therefore, gives rise to a number of problems, particularly concerning the authority of their decisions. One way of resolving these is to offer the world of sport an arbitration institution, which is independent, qualified and constituted in such a way that its decisions are definitive and binding: the Court of Arbitration for Sport.

3. The Court of Arbitration for Sport ('CAS')

It was in order to compensate for the above-mentioned drawbacks and to avoid parties having to call upon ordinary jurisdictions in the first or second instance (appeal against the decision by an association tribunal) that the idea of creating a specific arbitration institution was born. This institution would be devoted to settling disputes in the context of the practice of sport, and would hear disputes directly or indirectly connected with sport.

This idea was mooted in 1983 by the International Olympic Committee (IOC) President. The task of preparing a draft set of statutes and regulations with a view to the creation of an arbitration institution called the Court of Arbitration for Sport was entrusted to Kéba Mbaye, IOC member and Judge at the International Court in The Hague. The basic principles to be followed from the outset were as follows:

(1) a permanent institution independent of the IOC was required;
(2) the jurisdiction of this institution had to be optional;
(3) the principle of autonomy and will had to be guaranteed to this institution;
(4) the possibility of a solution by conciliation had to be built in;
(5) it was accepted that the IOC would be called upon to bear the costs and expenses occasioned by the operation of the court, including the payment of staff, secretarial costs, fees and travel expenses of the arbitrators.

The statutes and regulations of the CAS were rapidly drawn up and adopted by the IOC, and in the autumn of 1985 the CAS became operational. Its administrative headquarters are in Lausanne, Switzerland.

The CAS is composed of a panel of sixty lawyers who are familiar with issues relating to sport. They are proposed for a period of four years, with the option of subsequent re-election, by the international federations, national Olympic committees, the IOC and its President. The functions of the CAS President are performed by one of the lawyers on the panel who must also be a member of the IOC. The current President is Kéba MBaye, IOC Vice-President and former Vice-President of the International Court of Justice in The Hague.

The CAS sits in panels composed of three arbitrators. Each party appoints one arbitrator. Save for any agreement to the contrary, the third, who will be the President, is chosen by mutual agreement of the two parties. But the parties may decide that it is for the two designated arbitrators – and not the parties themselves – to choose the third arbitrator (President). Failing such agreement within forty-five days, the CAS President will ask the President of the Federal Tribunal of the Swiss Confederation to nominate the third arbitrator. The parties may also agree to call upon only one arbitrator whom they choose by mutual agreement. If the parties fail to designate a single arbitrator within forty-five days of the case being registered, a panel of three arbitrators will operate.

The arbitrators in such a panel must be chosen from those on the general panel of the sixty CAS members. While the administrative headquarters are in Lausanne, another location may, by agreement between the parties, be chosen as the seat of the panel called upon to hear a dispute. The official languages of the CAS are French and English, but the parties may agree to use another language. The CAS applies Swiss law, save for any express agreement to the contrary. If the parties agree, the CAS may apply the law *ex aequo et bono*. Finally, the parties may be represented or be assisted at hearings by a counsel of their choice.

In the same way as for commercial or economic arbitration, the CAS intervenes as the result of an arbitration agreement concluded in writing before or after the start of a dispute. In order to have valid recourse to arbitration – and in doing so waive any recourse to legal action before the ordinary courts - the parties must be bound by an arbitration agreement. Such agreement may be drawn up on the occasion of an existing dispute or looking ahead to a possible dispute in the future. In the latter case, the arbitration clause will appear in a contract or a particular agreement, but it may also be stipulated, under certain conditions, in statutes and regulations, subject to the formal acceptance thereof, or included in a licence.

The CAS is competent to hear any dispute arising from the practice or development of sport or, in a general way, any activity pertaining to the practice of sport, and for the resolution of which there is no provision in the Olympic Charter (Article 4 of the CAS Statute). Such disputes may involve questions of principle relating to sport or material interests such as commercial disputes connected with sport (sponsorship or management contracts); contracts between organisers of sports events and partners of firms specialising in communication regarding the granting of advertising rights; disputes of a civil nature connected with the organisation or broadcasting of sports events; disputes involving a member of a national or international federation, or between members thereof as a result of decisions taken by internal bodies; employment contracts of athletes, coaches.

The CAS may be approached by the IOC, international sports federations, national Olympic committees, associations recognised or not by the IOC, organising committees of events, national federations, sports associations and their members and, in a general way, any natural person or corporate body having the power to compromise.

During recent years, a number of national and international federations have introduced into their statutes a clause recognising the CAS as the sole legal authority competent to hear an appeal against decisions taken by their internal bodies (appeals jury, commission of appeal, federation tribunal). Thus any dispute arising from the application of statutes and regulations of any kind of the federations and the disputes, which federations may have between each other, or with their members which they cannot settle amicably, may be submitted, in the final instance, to the CAS, after the federations' own appeals procedures have been exhausted. In introducing these new statutory provisions for appeal to the CAS, the parties concerned refrain from having recourse to any kind of ordinary civil court.

The Statute of the CAS and its Regulations were modified in 1991 on the basis of experience acquired. It is noteworthy that the CAS is innovative in that it provides for, in addition to the normal procedure of arbitration, a summary conciliation procedure, which the parties may adopt, and which the arbitrators may apply as a matter of course if the parties concerned have no objection. This conciliation is particularly desirable in sports-related issues, and it has been possible to settle many disputes in this way.

While the primary objective of the CAS is to settle litigation connected with sports activities, it may also give an advisory opinion on numerous other problems of a legal nature with which different international organisations are faced. Any natural person or corporate body interested in obtaining such an opinion may approach the CAS President through the CAS Secretary General. A consultative panel of between three and five members will then be called upon to give the opinion requested, free of charge.

Although the CAS was set up by the IOC, which bears its operating costs, the institution is totally independent of the IOC, as are the CAS members when carrying out their functions.

In this way, therefore, by means of an arbitration agreement (arbitration agreement or clause as part of a contract or included in the statutes), athletes can avoid disputes being referred to the civil jurisdiction. The extreme simplification of the procedure means that the CAS is a valuable instrument for resolving quickly and cheaply a dispute arising from the practice of sport and the economic or financial activities to which sport gives rise. The CAS procedure is inexpensive, or even free of charge, as the operating costs of the institution are borne by the IOC. Only in cases of a pecuniary nature are the parties asked to contribute, and even then only towards the costs occasioned by the settlement of the dispute concerning them.

4. Activities of the CAS

Thanks to the CAS, many disputes have been settled satisfactorily and discretely without recourse to the ordinary jurisdiction. Approached on the basis of arbitration agreements and clauses integrated into contracts, the Panels of the CAS have had to resolve several demands for damages following the breaking or non-execution of contracts (e.g. the contract between an international federation and a TV company or between a coach or a player and his club or federation, or a failure to respect a sponsorship or advertising contract).

Numerous appeals have been lodged on the basis of statutory provisions naming the CAS as the sole legal authority of appeal (appeals by a national federation against the decision by the management committee of the international federation concerned, appeals against punishments imposed on members or clubs). Recently, several appeals against punishments imposed for doping have been heard by CAS panels.

The recent case of *Navet* v. *FEI* may serve as a useful example.

On 24 April 1992, the Judicial Committee of the International Equestrian Federation ('FEI'), meeting in London, decided that the horse Waiti Quito de Baussy and its rider, Eric Navet, should be disqualified from all the competitions of the European Championship held from 17 to 21 July 1991 in La Baule; furthermore, the rider was suspended for a period of four months. According to the Committee, the analyses performed on the samples taken allowed the presence of cortisol in extremely high and unusual quantities to be detected in the urine of the horse. The Committee regarded it as an established fact that a prohibited substance had been administered, entailing the punishments provided for by the Regulations in force.

At its appeal hearing, the Panel of the Court of Arbitration for Sport (CAS), composed of Professor D. Lévy, Paris, Mr. H.U. Sutter, lawyer in Geneva and chaired by Professor P. Lalive, Geneva, meeting in Lausanne on 13 July 1992, after hearing the parties and eight experts, quashed the decision taken, for reasons which may be briefly summarised.

Taking into account the presumption of innocence, the cardinal principle recognised by the Judicial Committee of the FEI itself; the endogenous nature of cortisol; the absence – with regard to the technical and scientific analysis – of a sufficiently broad and strong consensus among the experts on the subject; and the lack, in Annex IV of the Veterinary Regulations, of a specification of any level of tolerance, the CAS, while aware of the need to fight against doping, and despite the presence in the urine of excessive quantities of cortisol such as to arouse the suspicion of the experts, considered that it was not possible for it to exclude the existence of endogenous causes.

As a result, the sanctions imposed upon Mr. Navet were lifted.

The arbitrators have noticed that, in some cases, the suspension decisions had unfortunately been taken without regard to the fundamental legal principle of the right of the party concerned to be heard.

Finally, several requests for advisory opinions have been made in the most varied of fields, particularly concerning the interpretation of statutory provisions and the responsibility of internal bodies of federations.

5. Conclusions

Following the well-known formula, arbitration means: competent judges, minimum costs, rapidity and confidentiality of awards.

Sport is exposed to a growing number of disputes from outside. The ordinary courts are not really the bodies best suited to resolving private disputes connected with sports activity. Arbitration is better adapted to settling sports-related disputes. In particular, it allows the parties to choose their judges, so as to ensure that they have the required experience and knowledge of the world of sport. Such a choice does not exist in the ordinary law courts.

The institution created by the IOC, the Court of Arbitration for Sport, came about in order to enable sports organisations to settle their differences without recourse to the ordinary courts. The vocation of the CAS is to serve the interests and the world of sport. The CAS has proved to be a valuable instrument for resolving rapidly disputes connected with the practice of sport. This new arbitration institution corresponds to a real need of the family of world sport and its partners, which thus have at their disposal a jurisdiction which is adapted to their needs, being quick and inexpensive.

Taxation Aspects

by Larry Chrisfield

Space does not permit an exhaustive description of the fiscal situation in all European jurisdictions. However, a number of particular items of interest are summarised under the relevant country heading. The treatment of each territory varies since some countries inevitably have more detailed and sophisticated rules on the subject than others.

TAXATION
ASPECTS

The United Kingdom

1. Introduction

1.1. General

The UK tax system raises revenue for the UK Government via both direct and indirect taxation. The administration of the UK tax system is divided between that relating to the direct taxation of income and gains and that relating to indirect taxes such as Value Added Tax (VAT) and Customs and Excise duties. The different business arrangements and types of property involved in sports marketing agreements may be subject to both direct and indirect taxation. Accordingly, this introduction provides a brief description of the operation of the UK's direct and indirect taxes as well as an explanation of some words and concepts which are frequently used and have important tax connotations. It should be noted that this chapter does not deal with incidence of customs duties which may apply to the importation of goods.

The taxation treatment of the various transactions in the field of sports marketing is wide ranging. So far as the payer of any consideration is concerned this chapter essentially focuses on the position from a corporate perspective. This, it should be noted, will differ in some respects from the tax position of an individual. On the other hand the chapter covers the taxability of receipts to both a corporation and an individual. The taxation aspects outlined are in accordance with domestic legislation and are subject, therefore, to any tax relief provided by a Double Tax Treaty.

1.2. Direct Tax

The administration of the UK's direct taxes on the income and gains of individuals, corporations and other entities is undertaken by the Commissioners of Inland Revenue, collectively known as The Board of Inland Revenue. The Commissioners of Inland Revenue appoint Inspectors of Taxes who are responsible for determining the amount of a taxpayer's tax liability and Collectors of Taxes who are responsible for collecting the liability. The UK legislation dealing with the taxation of income and gains is predominantly contained in the Income and Corporation Taxes Act 1988 and the Taxation of Chargeable Gains Act 1992 respectively.

The UK does not yet operate a self assessment system for the taxation of income and gains (although a new Pay and File system will bring in self assessment for companies whose accounting periods begin on or after 1 October 1992). For the self-employed a self-assessment system is intended to be introduced for the tax year 1996/97 onwards. Accordingly tax is either assessed directly by an Inspector or withheld at source. Under the current system, a company or an individual who receives an assessment which they believe is incorrect may appeal, within the time limit allowed, against the assessment. An appeal may be heard by either General or Special Commissioners (referred to as Commissioners), officials who are distinct from the Commissioners of Inland Revenue. In broad terms the Special Commissioners hear more complex appeals which involve specialised knowledge of the UK direct tax system, the General Commissioners hearing the remainder of appeals. A decision by either body of Commissioners on a point of fact is final; however, on a point of law, further appeals may be made by way of case stated to the High Court, then to the Court of Appeal and finally by leave to the House of Lords.

Residency is an important concept in the UK tax system as individuals and companies resident in the UK are generally liable to UK tax on their worldwide income. By contrast non-residents are only liable to tax on UK source income. For individuals, residency for tax purposes is not statutorily defined but usually requires an individual to be physically present in the UK. However, residency for companies is to some extent statutorily defined[1] in that those companies incorporated in the UK on or after 15 March 1988 are automatically treated as UK resident. Companies incorporated outside of the UK may also be treated as UK resident if they are held to be managed and controlled in the UK.

Double Tax Treaties have been concluded between the UK and a large number of other countries. The intention of the treaties is to avoid double taxation. Treaties will generally, provided an advance clearance is received from the Inland Revenue, allow for a rate of withholding tax lower than the domestic rate of tax to be applied to sports marketing payments such as royalties.

1.3. VAT

The Commissioners of Customs and Excise are responsible for administering the UK's indirect tax system of VAT and Customs and Excise duties.

VAT was introduced in the UK with effect from 1 April 1973 following the admission of the UK to the European Community (EC) on 1 January 1973. The UK VAT legislation is derived in the main from the EC Sixth Directive and is predominantly contained in the Value Added Tax Act ('VATA') 1983 as primary legislation and the detailed rules are to be found in Statutory Instruments.

1. Section 66 FA 1988.

VAT is charged on the supply of goods or services in the UK and on the importation of goods into the UK made by a taxable person in the course or furtherance of his business. A supply is anything done for consideration in the furtherance of the business of a taxable person.[2] All supplies are subject to VAT at the standard rate unless they are specifically zero rated or exempted from VAT.[3] Anything which is not a supply of goods and which is done for a consideration is a supply of services.[4] Whether a supply of services is subject to VAT will generally depend on where the supplier belongs. In broad terms a supplier will belong where his business establishment is located.[5] An important exception to this rule, however, is where there is a performance of sporting, artistic or entertainment services. From 1 January 1993 the place of supply of these specified services are where the activity is physically carried out. The concept of belonging still applies to the payment of other amounts connected with sports marketing agreements such as endorsement income. Accordingly, for VAT purposes, a sports marketing contract will need to distinguish between payments for undertaking sporting activities in the UK, which generally will be subject to VAT, and other payments such as endorsement income which may be subject to VAT if the supplier belongs in the UK.

As with direct taxes, there is a system for appealing against VAT assessments which a taxpayer believes to be incorrect. Provided all the disputed VAT has been paid an appeal would be heard by a VAT Tribunal. As with the General and Special Commissioners' findings, the VAT Tribunal's findings on a matter of fact is final and cannot be subject of any subsequent appeal to the High Court or a higher authority. From a VAT tribunal an appeal may be made to the High Court, then the Court of Appeal and ultimately with leave to the House of Lords on a point of law.

2. The Taxation Treatment of Intellectual Property Rights

The taxation treatment of intellectual property rights varies significantly according to the type of rights involved. The transactions underlying any agreement should, therefore, be precisely analysed so as to focus on the nature of the rights concerned.

The intellectual property rights usually involved in sports marketing transactions are copyright, design rights and trademarks. Whereas the taxation of copyright and rights in designs is set out in statutory provisions, the taxation of trademarks is determined by general tax principles.

Firstly, a transaction will need to be examined to ascertain whether it displays the characteristics of either a revenue or a capital transaction. The distinction can be difficult to draw in practice and there is a large body of case

2. Section 2 VATA 1983.
3. Section 9 VATA 1983.
4. Section 3 VATA 1983.
5. Section 8 VATA 1983.

law relating to the distinction between revenue and capital.[6] Whether the receipt is actually income or capital is basically a question of fact for the Commissioners to decide. However, the fact that the consideration is paid in a lump sum does not make the payment automatically capital. Equally, a capital sum may still be paid in instalments and yet remain a capital sum. When a trader or professional receives a lump sum connected with his business it is likely to be held to be of an income nature whereas the consideration for an outright disposal of an intellectual property right is likely to be of a capital nature.

It is common to pay or receive advances in connection with intellectual property rights. These advances may be recoupable but non-refundable or both recoupable and refundable. The tax treatment of such advances is unclear. The Inland Revenue contend that non-refundable advances should be taxed when paid and may be seen, if paid for on signature, to be a reward for a completed act. However, in practice, the recipient will often be required to perform various obligations which supports the view that the advance should be taxed only when everything necessary to earn the advance has been completed. On the other hand, the Revenue will generally seek to defer relief to the payer and deny any deduction on a paid basis but instead expect the advance to be matched on an accruals basis against the relevant income stream.

2.1. Trademarks

Trademarks are commonly licensed by franchising where the proprietor of a trademark receives a royalty from franchisees who are using his name, business format and trademark.

The tax treatment of income received and royalties paid for the use of a trademark is not statutory and relies on the application of general tax principles to the specific transaction.

Where a transaction is of a revenue nature, the royalties paid will be relieved for the purposes of calculating business profits as a deductible trading expense on an accruals basis (provided they are incurred wholly and exclusively for the purposes of the trade). However, a royalty payable for the use of a trademark may exceptionally be treated as a so-called ‘annual payment’. This could arise if the trademark owner holds the mark as an investment and its income, therefore, is pure income profit, i.e. it does not incur expenditure in earning the income. Where a trademark royalty is treated as an annual payment the licensee will be obliged to withhold tax at the basic rate of income tax (currently 25%) on the payment and account for this tax to the Inland Revenue. This withholding may be relieved under the terms of a Double Tax Treaty. Where a royalty is treated as an annual payment the payer will only obtain tax relief for royalty payments on a paid basis.

6. *CIR* v. *British Salmson Aero Engines Ltd*, CA [1938] 22 TC 29 compared to *Desoutter Bros Ltd* v. *J E Hanger & Co Ltd and Artificial Limb Makers Ltd*, KB [1936] 1 All ER 535.

The taxation treatment of payments received by the licensor for the use of a trademark will depend on whether the transaction is treated as revenue or capital. Where the transaction is considered to be of a revenue nature, the receipt will be treated as income, either as a trading receipt or as investment income. Where the transaction is on capital account, the receipt may be subject to capital gains tax. A capital receipt should be received gross, i.e. not subject to withholding at source.

The tax treatment of the costs associated with the registration and renewal of trademarks is set out in statute.[7] This section allows as a trading expense the costs of preparing and filing a trademark application and the registration fee for successful applications. The renewal fees for previously registered trademarks are also allowed as trading expenses.

2.2. *Copyright*

Royalties received by an originator of a copyright work for the use of such work will be taxed as a trading receipt. Where an originator sells a copyright work outright or receives a lump sum for its assignment or for granting a licence, the consideration for such a disposal will also be assessed as a trading receipt. There is an option to have such an amount assessed over several tax years provided certain conditions are met.[8]

The tax treatment of royalties received by an assignee of a copyright will depend on whether the copyright is held by him as an investment, in which case the income will be assessed as investment income, or as a trading asset, in which case the income will be assessed as a trading receipt. The proceeds from the sale of a copyright by a subsequent holder will generally be assessed to capital gains tax. Where liability to capital gains tax depends on the *situs* of the asset (e.g. in the case of a non-resident trading in the UK) the location of the copyright or any right derived from the copyright is determined by whether such right(s) are exercisable in the UK.

A UK person who pays copyright royalties to a UK resident owner may make the payments gross.[9] However, basic rate tax generally has to be deducted from copyright royalties paid to non-UK resident copyright owners. There is an exception for payments in respect of film and video rights which may also be made gross. Payments may also be made by a UK licensee, either at a reduced or nil rate of withholding tax, provided there is a tax treaty between the UK and the country concerned and the necessary clearance is obtained. Although tax is required to be deducted from copyright royalties paid abroad, such payments are not deductible on a paid basis, but are deductible as a trading expense on an accruals basis, provided that the payer incurs the expense in the course of trade carried on by it.

---

7. Section 83 of the Income and Corporation Taxes Act ('ICTA') 1988.
8. Section 534 ICTA 1988.
9. Section 536(2) ICTA 1988.

2.3. Registered Designs

Since 1 August 1989, rights in designs have been treated for tax purposes like copyright. Royalties receivable by a designer under a licence granted for the use of the design will be a trading receipt. As with copyright, where a designer receives a lump sum for the assignment or licence of a design this will be assessed as trading income, but the amount may be spread over different tax periods, subject to similar conditions to those for copyright.

As with copyright, where the owner of the registered design is non-UK resident, the licensee will be obliged to withhold tax at the basic rate of income tax on all payments made under the licence, subject again to any relief available under the relevant double tax treaty, if any, between the UK and the country concerned.

2.4. Value Added Tax ('VAT')

For VAT purposes, a grant, assignment, or transfer of a trademark, copyright, or registered design is a supply of services. Therefore, the VAT treatment of any consideration received (whether it is a lump sum or in a form of regular payments, i.e. royalties) will be determined by the place where the supplier belongs. If the supplier belongs in the UK and the supply is made to a person who also belongs in the UK, that supply will be subject to VAT at the standard rate (currently 17.5%). Similarly, a grant, transfer or assignment of a trademark by a UK supplier to an individual in his private capacity, who belongs in another Member State of the EC, will be subject to UK VAT at the standard rate. However, such a grant by the UK supplier to a person in a business capacity who belongs in another Member State of the EC and who is registered for VAT there, or to a person in any capacity who belongs outside the EC, will be treated as made where the recipient belongs and therefore outside the scope of UK VAT.[10] Any VAT incurred on costs attributable to the making of these supplies will be recoverable in full by the UK supplier.

2.5. Stamp Duty

For the purposes of stamp duty no distinction is made between copyright, trademarks or design rights: all are classed as intellectual property.

The Finance Act 1991 included a provision to exempt intellectual property from the charge to stamp duty. The exemption is to apply from a date appointed by the Treasury and was to coincide with the introduction of paperless share trading via the TAURUS system. Introduction of this system has however been delayed for the foreseeable future and until a date is set a contract or agreement to transfer intellectual property is subject to stamp duty

10. The VAT (Place of Supply of Service Order) 1992 and Statutory Instrument 3121.

at the rate of 1% of the consideration paid for the intellectual property right. Where the consideration is other than a fixed sum the stamp duty treatment will depend on the degree of uncertainty involved. If the consideration is completely uncertain – if, for example, it depends on future sales – no stamp duty may be charged. However, if a contract includes a maximum consideration this will be the consideration on which stamp duty is assessed. Therefore, when drafting a contract the inclusion in the contract of a high maximum consideration should be avoided.

To be subject to UK stamp duty the document evidencing the transfer or licence of intellectual property must either be executed in the UK or the transaction involve something to be done within the UK. The outright transfer of intellectual property or the grant of an exclusive licence which comes within the above mentioned criteria will be subject to stamp duty. However, a limited licence agreement granted for the use of intellectual property will not represent a transfer subject to stamp duty.

A useful planning point to either defer or avoid completely the payment of stamp duty is for the document transferring the intellectual property to be signed and kept outside the UK. The document is not then stampable until it is brought into the UK. Alternatively, the document can simply be left unstamped. The lack of stamping does not affect the legal validity of the document. However, it may be necessary to stamp the document in the event it is required to be produced in evidence. If, as a result of that, the document is stamped late, there is a late stamping penalty equal to the amount of the duty involved.

3. The Taxation Treatment of the Different Types of Sports Marketing Business Arrangements

3.1. Sponsorship Agreements

3.1.1. General

A sponsorship agreement is a commercial transaction whereby a payment or series of payments are made to a sports body or sportsperson in consideration for the promotional opportunities the sponsor derives from the particular sporting activity. The sponsorship payment can be in the form of cash and/or a payment in kind, such as the provision of the sponsor's goods or services either for free or at less than cost. Provided the sponsorship payment is revenue in nature and is made wholly and exclusively for the purposes of the sponsor's trade it will be allowed for tax purposes as a trading expense.

In practice, there can be other transactions linked to a sponsorship payment, such as the provision by an event organiser of tickets and hospitality boxes to a sponsor. For UK tax purposes, all types of business entertainment are treated as disallowable expenditure in computing taxable profits. Accordingly, the sponsor should ensure that a separate payment is made to the event organiser to cover the provision of tickets and entertainment facilities, otherwise the

Inspector may seek to treat the whole of the sponsorship payment as disallowable. Employees of the sponsor company, who receive non-cash gifts, such as tickets from an event organiser, may be liable to tax on such benefits, although small gifts will not have income tax charged on them.[11]

A sponsorship payment may also be disallowed in computing the sponsor's business profits if it is a payment towards a capital project being undertaken by a sports body, for example, the construction of a new stand for spectators.

A number of sports organisations and event organisers may have charitable status. In such cases, a sponsorship payment may be made by means of a charitable deed of covenant or through the Gift Aid provisions provided the recipient is an eligible body. A payment under a charitable deed of covenant or Gift Aid will not be a deductible expense for the sponsor but instead will be a non-trading charge on income.[12] Relief for the payment will then be given in the tax period in which it is paid and not on an accruals basis. Should a sponsor make a loss in the period of payment, unrelieved non-trading charges cannot be carried forward for relief in subsequent tax years. Where a sponsorship payment is made by means of a charitable deed of covenant, the sponsor should not receive consideration from the event organiser, otherwise the payment may not be eligible for tax relief in the charity's hands. If the event organiser provides the sponsor with corporate entertainment facilities at the venue, then tax relief may be denied to the sponsor on the grounds that the payment is for business entertainment.

Where a sponsor of a sports event pays the contestants' fees and provides the prize money at an event, there will be withholding tax implications if any of the recipients are non-UK resident sportspersons. The Income Tax (Entertainers and Sportsmen) Regulations became operative on 1 May 1987. Under these Regulations, payments made on or after 1 May 1987, which can be attributed either directly or indirectly to a performance by a non-UK resident in his or her capacity as a sportsperson, should have UK withholding tax at the basic rate deducted from them. The Regulations are wide ranging and apply to payments made to third parties (i.e. service companies) and 'transfers of assets' such as benefits in kind provided to the entertainer. The obligation to withhold tax and account for it to the Inland Revenue rests with the sponsor or event organiser making the payment. Failure to withhold tax or late payment of the tax to the Revenue will make the payer liable to interest and penalties.

---

11. Extra-Statutory Concession A70. An extra-statutory concession is a concession granted by the Inland Revenue which allows for a more favourable taxation treatment of a transaction than the strict treatment as set out in the Taxes Acts. A concession will not be given in any case where an attempt is made to use the concession for the purposes of tax avoidance.
12. Relief as a charge on income for one-off donations is available to UK resident non-close companies (Section 339 ICTA 1988). If the donor is a close company there are a number of additional conditions to be satisfied in order to obtain relief. A company will generally be a non-close company provided it is neither controlled by any number of participators who are directors of the company, nor controlled by five or fewer participators. A participator is defined very widely and includes shareholders as well as loan stockholders.

3.1.2. VAT

The VAT treatment of the provision of promotional/advertising services will be determined in the same manner as the grant, assignment or transfer of copyright (see above at page 439), that is, by the place of belonging of the supplier (i.e. sports body or sportsperson). However, the VAT position becomes complicated where such a contract envisages the organiser providing additional supplies, for example an event organiser providing tickets and/or hospitality boxes to a sponsor or a sportsperson receiving, in addition to the sponsorship payment, non-cash gifts (such as items of merchandise and payment of entrance fee to an event).

For VAT purposes, the additional item supplied by the event organiser would be regarded as being supplied in return for the payment made by the sponsor and hence the sponsorship payment may need to be apportioned between the advertising/promotional services and the additional item. The VAT treatment of the additional item will depend on its nature. For example, if the additional item supplied is tickets to an event, that supply will be subject to VAT at standard rate; alternatively, if the additional item supplied is a book, then that would be zero rated under the current legislation.

Where a sponsorship contract envisages a sponsor providing a sportsperson non-cash gifts (such as merchandise in addition to the sponsorship payment), the non-cash gifts would be seen to be additional consideration for the promotional/advertising services provided by a sportsperson (i.e. a barter transaction for VAT purposes). The sponsor would then be required to charge VAT at the appropriate rate in respect of the additional items given and the sportsperson required to charge VAT on an amount equal to the value of the additional items on the grounds that these constitute additional consideration for his advertising/promotional services.

3.2. Merchandising

Merchandising usually involves the granting of a licence to use copyright material or a trademark on promotional goods for sale at a sports venue and/or elsewhere. The tax treatment of receipts and payments under licences to use copyright and trademarks has been discussed above at page 438. As indicated, for tax purposes, the most important issue is whether the payment for the merchandising rights is revenue or capital. Where a payment is revenue it should be allowed as a trading expense of the payer and conversely the recipient would usually be assessed on the payment as income. A capital payment may mean that the licensee will gain no relief for the payment in calculating business profits, albeit the licensor will still at least have made a disposal for capital gains tax purposes. In some cases, the distinction between capital or revenue may be difficult to determine. However, where an exclusive licence is granted for the majority of the economic life of the copyright or trademark, such a transaction will normally be treated as capital.

A distinction, for VAT purposes, should be drawn between a transfer, assignment or grant of a right to distribute goods and a right to be a sole representative in a particular territory. For example, if a sports goods manufacturer grants a UK distributor a right to distribute goods manufactured by him and he is responsible to deliver them either from stocks he holds in the UK or stocks subsequently imported into the UK, he will be treated as making supplies of goods in the UK. In such an event, the manufacturer will be required to register and charge VAT at the standard rate (unless the goods are specifically zero rated or exempt from VAT).

However, if the manufacturer merely grants a right to a UK distributor to be his sole UK representative and the representative is responsible as principal to purchase the goods from that manufacturer and then sell them in the UK, the manufacturer will be making a supply of services in respect of the grant of the distributorship right and not a supply of goods. Therefore, the VAT treatment of any income (for example, royalties) flowing from such a grant, assignment, or transfer will be determined in the same manner as the grant, assignment or transfer of copyright (see above at page 439), i.e. by the place of belonging of the manufacturer. Consequently, if he belongs outside the UK, his supplies will be outside the scope of UK VAT. Alternatively, if he belongs in the UK, his supplies will be standard rated, unless the supplies are to a person who, in his business capacity, belongs in an EC Member State or to a person who, in any capacity, belongs outside the EC.

Where a UK VAT registered person receives such services from outside the UK, he is required to account for VAT under the so called 'reverse charge' rules.

3.3. Endorsements

Product endorsement, that is, the commendation of a product by a sports personality, is allied to merchandising.

Endorsement payments made by sponsors to sportspersons usually have two elements: a 'pure' endorsement payment and a performance related payment.

Where a sportsperson assigns under contract the right to use his name and likeness, this is akin to granting a licence for the use of a trademark. Payment made to the sportsperson under this type of agreement is classified as a royalty and as such may be paid gross to the sportsperson.

Where performance is a factor in determining the compensation under a contract the UK Revenue may contend that part of any fee paid to a sportsperson for endorsing the sponsor's product is performance related. Unlike that part which is for the use of the individual's name and likeness, the performance related element will be subject to withholding tax where the individual is a non-UK resident (see above at page 441). Any performance related bonus paid under an endorsement agreement according to the sportsperson's performance in specific events and, for some sports, his place in the year end rankings, may fall within the withholding tax legislation.

For VAT purposes, such a grant is seen to be a supply of services and follows the VAT treatment outlined above for copyright, trademarks and registered designs (see above at page 439). Therefore, any fee received by a sportsperson, who belongs in the UK, will be subject to VAT at the standard rate, unless it can be treated as outside the scope of VAT as mentioned above at page 439.

3.4. Commissioning Agreements

Where an event organiser commissions the production of a logo or advertisement, copyright in the material will usually belong to that person. The payment for the commission will usually be a deductible expense for the purposes of computing that person's business profits for tax purposes. The costs incurred in applying for and registering a successful trademark application are also allowable revenue expenses.

The VAT treatment on the use of such copyright will depend on the nature of the agreement. Where the agreement grants, for example, a manufacturer the right to use the copyright material on products and sell them as principal in return for a royalty, the grant will be seen to be a supply of services. The VAT treatment outlined above at page 439 for copyright and trademarks will apply. On the other hand, where the agreement requires the manufacturer to produce a quantity of the products to the order of the event organiser, the manufacturer will be supplying the products in return for a consideration. For VAT purposes, the supply will, *prima facie*, be subject to VAT at the standard rate, assuming that the products are supplied in the UK, unless the goods are zero rated. If the products are exported outside the EC, such supplies should be zero rated. Following the implementation of the Single Market regulation in the UK on 1 January 1993, the UK manufacturer can only zero rate these supplies if the organiser is registered for VAT in a Member State of the EC other than the UK, that customer's VAT number is obtained and proof of export of the goods is retained.

3.5. Franchises and Concessions

An event organiser may grant a franchise or concession for a person to sell certain of its products at a sports venue. The direct tax treatment of the consideration received for the franchise/concession will be similar to the amounts received under official product supplier arrangements (see page 446). The event organiser will be assessed to tax on the payments received for the concession. The person paying for the concession will usually be able to claim the amount as a business expense, provided it was incurred wholly and exclusively for the purposes of their trade.

It is normal practice for a franchiser to grant a right to the franchisee to use the franchisor's name and goodwill in return for a management fee. This management fee will be standard rated. However, in addition, certain franchisors also arrange to take a lease for a premises and grant a lease thereto to the franchisee. For VAT purposes such a grant, being a short-term licence to use land, will be exempt from VAT, unless the landlord, that is the event organiser, has opted to charge VAT.

An event organiser may also enter into a contract with a person whereby that person supplies the event organiser with goods to be sold at the sports venue. Due to the promotional opportunities provided to the supplier the goods will often be sold to the event organiser at a discounted price. For direct tax purposes, the event organiser's profits derived from the sale of the stocks of goods will be assessed to tax. The VAT treatment of the supply of goods to an event organiser will depend on the type of goods being supplied. If the products are standard rated goods, the VAT will be accounted for on the actual consideration paid, that is, after taking account of the discount.

3.6. Films and Videos

Where a sponsor or event organiser commissions a production of a film or video, there will be similar tax considerations to those for a commissioning agreement for the production of a logo (see page 444).

The grant of a right to distribute a film, whether in cinematography or video form, is treated, for VAT purposes, as a supply of services and, therefore, follows the VAT treatment outlined above at page 439 for copyright.

However, the VAT treatment will be different if the owner is required to deliver copies of the film or videos to a distributor. In such circumstances, the grantor will be treated as supplying goods and the VAT treatment will be determined by the place where these copies are physically located when they are delivered to the distributor. Where the owner supplies them to a distributor in the same State, the supply will be standard rated; otherwise the supply should be zero rated, provided that the owner retains as evidence a proof of export and, in the case of a distributor located in another EC Member State, he has obtained the customer's VAT number as required by the Single Market Regulations, which came into force on 1 January 1993.

Apart from the above, it is possible that the organiser of a sports event may decide to show an event live by a satellite transmission direct to the members of the public. In such a case, the income received by a UK organiser would be subject to VAT at the standard rate, regardless of where the viewing takes place. This is because the transmission services are not services of a type which enjoy special treatment.[13] This could potentially lead to double taxation, if the viewing takes place in another Member State of the EC which treats the supply as taking place in that Member State. In such a case, it might be necessary to clear the VAT position with the VAT authorities of the relevant countries. It might transpire that the organiser is required to register in the

13. Schedule 3 VATA 1983.

other Member State in addition to the UK VAT registration. In such an event, the organiser should request UK Customs to treat the supply as made outside the UK and outside the scope of UK VAT.

3.7. Public Appearances

A sponsor may enter into an agreement whereby a sports personality/celebrity agrees to make public appearances at openings or parties. Payments made to a non-UK resident sportsperson after 1 May 1987 are subject to the withholding tax regulations discussed above at page 441. As noted in the section on sponsorship agreements (see page 440 *et seq.*), the legislation covers payments made to persons connected with the sportsperson as well as transfers of assets to the sportsperson such as cars and payment of the sportsperson's travel expenses.

The VAT treatment of such services are, following the implementation of the Single Market regulations on 1 January 1993, determined by the place where these are physically carried out and not determined by the place where the supplier of such services belongs. This means that a UK VAT registered supplier will be required to charge VAT at the standard rate if he makes a public appearance here and treat his services as outside the scope of VAT if he makes a public appearance outside the UK. He should consider, however, whether he is required to register and charge VAT in the country where he makes the public appearance.

3.8. Supplierships

An event organiser, who grants a right to a sponsor to be an official product supplier will be assessed to tax on the consideration received in return. The payment by the sponsor for this concession should be a deductible business expense, provided it is incurred wholly and exclusively for the purposes of the sponsor's trade.

3.9. Event Organiser with Charitable Status

A sports event organiser, who can establish charitable status by registering with the Charity Commissioners, may benefit from a favourable tax treatment. Certain income received by an event organiser with charitable status, for example, a charity's trading profits which are applied solely for charitable purposes, is exempt from tax.

As noted in the section on sponsorship agreements at page 440 *et seq.*, payments under a covenant to a charitable body qualify as charges on income in the payer's accounts. A charitable covenant must at the outset be capable of lasting for more than three years. Such a minimum period may not be attractive to potential sponsors/donors. Accordingly, a more attractive option to donors may be the ability to make a one-off donation under Gift Aid, although an event organiser would need to be an eligible recipient under this scheme. As with a deed of covenant, the donor would obtain relief for the one-off payment as a charge on income in the tax period in which it was paid. An alternative might be to loan the charity the full amount upfront. The charity would then repay part of the loan each year out of the annual covenanted amount.

3.10. General VAT Points

Sports marketing transactions may include a barter element where no cash passes between a sponsor and an event organiser. For VAT purposes such barter transactions represent two supplies and VAT will need to be accounted for on both. Failure to account for such VAT may lead to the supplier and the recipient being subject to substantial penalties and interest on late paid tax.

The liability to be VAT registered also needs to be examined. The organisation of a major sports event will usually involve a number of different sporting bodies at a national and international level. It is important to determine which body is to hold the tournament and, therefore, which body has the obligation to register if not already registered and account for the VAT on ticket sales. Failure to register for VAT (or even late registration) or account for the tax will render an organisation liable to interest and penalties.

A useful cash flow advantage may be obtained if a sponsor agrees to provide a sports event organiser with a loan and enters separately into a sponsorship agreement. This will provide the sports body with a loan which has not been subject to VAT. The loan repayments will also not be subject to VAT and may perhaps be used to fund the sponsorship payments under the separate agreement. The event organiser will generally be able to obtain tax relief on any interest payment on the loan either as a business expense or as a charge on income.

3.11. Tax Planning/Saving

As will be evident from the foregoing, sports marketing transactions frequently involve parties entering into a contract, the tax treatment of which is commonly complex, with a number of 'grey areas' open to interpretation and negotiation. This complexity and uncertainty presents the professionally advised company/individual with opportunities for tax planning and, consequently, tax savings. Professional advice should thus be sought at the beginning of a project or at least before any contract is entered into. Some specific opportunities are summarised below.

- A sponsorship contract entered into with a non UK resident sportsperson, which includes appearance, exhibition and endorsement requirements, should emphasise the element of the payments related to rights and minimise the element related to performance activities. This should reduce the amount of the payment which is subject to UK withholding taxes.
- For VAT purposes, it is necessary to state in any contract whether the consideration is VAT exclusive or inclusive. Where this is not stated, the consideration will be deemed to be VAT inclusive leading to a potential loss (of approximately 15 per cent at a current VAT rate) of the consideration.
- Organising an event in a tax efficient manner may provide an event organiser with a commercial advantage over its competitors. Sponsors are more likely to be attracted to sponsor an event if they can obtain tax relief for their sponsorship payments. A common tax problem with sponsorship agreements is the linkage of sponsorship payments to disallowable business entertainment which may call into question the allowability of the whole of the sponsorship payment. An event organiser is, therefore, advised to set up separate agreements for sponsorship and corporate entertainment facilities and in this way safeguard the sponsor's tax relief on the sponsorship payments.
- A business will only obtain relief in calculating trading profit for sponsorship payments which are incurred wholly and exclusively for the purposes of their trade. If the sponsor is to receive little publicity for his business, it may be appropriate to reflect the gratuitous nature of the payment by entering into a deed of covenant with the recipient or using the Gift Aid provisions as discussed above. Such action should generally also safeguard the tax deductibility of the sponsorship payment.
- For companies/individuals who own trademarks, copyright or registered designs, sports marketing transactions are likely to involve the receipt of royalties. A useful planning technique for an owner of intellectual property, resident in a country which has not entered into international tax treaties and who receives substantial royalties from a number of countries, may be to set up an intermediate royalty company, say, in the Netherlands. Provided the arrangement has commercial substance and is properly organised, a Dutch company can benefit from the favourable tax treaties concluded by the Netherlands on the royalties it receives and achieve a low level of direct tax on its income. Payments made by the Dutch company to the company/individual resident in the non-treaty country may, under Dutch domestic law, be paid without deduction of withholding tax. If the royalties had been received directly in the non-treaty country, it is likely they would have suffered higher withholding taxes.
- For VAT purposes, there are a number of tax planning/saving techniques applicable to sports marketing transactions. For example, it may be possible to be non-UK resident and thus avoid being subject to UK direct tax but nonetheless to have a business establishment in the UK for VAT purposes. An organisation in this position may be VAT registered and be able to reclaim VAT on business expenses incurred in the UK. Provided an organisation's outputs are not exempt or outside the scope of VAT without

the right to recover attributable input tax, the organisation should not be at a disadvantage in having to account for VAT on their outputs. This clearly requires careful handling.

- European countries have different rates of VAT and this may be used to the advantage of a sponsor or event organiser (refer to schedule at page 481). For example, an event organiser with charitable status should, where possible, locate in a country with a low rate of VAT in order to reduce the level of irrecoverable VAT suffered. Similar considerations apply to a sponsor who incurs expenditure on business entertainment, the VAT on which would be irrecoverable. Variations in the rates of direct taxes in Europe also provide scope for tax planning and saving.

TAXATION ASPECTS

Austria

1. Taxation of Intellectual Property Rights

1.1. Capital

Where the owner of intellectual property sells the asset outright the proceeds are fully taxable in the year of sale. Under certain circumstances there is a facility to postpone payment of the tax by deducting it from the cost of purchases of intellectual property made within the following three years.

The purchaser of intellectual property will, for tax purposes, treat the expenditure as capital. Tax relief on this expenditure can be obtained by amortising the payment over the contract period.

1.2. Revenue

Where the owner of intellectual property grants a licence for the use of the asset the income received will be taxable in the year to which it economically relates. Accordingly, a lump sum receipt will be apportioned over the contract period. Similarly, the licensee will obtain tax relief for the licence payments in the year to which the economic benefit of the payment relates. A lump sum payment will thus generally attract tax relief over the period of the contract.

2. VAT

For VAT purposes, a grant, assignment or transfer of a trademark, copyright or registered design is a supply of services. The VAT treatment of any consideration received is determined by the place where the intellectual property right is exercisable. Where a licence is exercised outside Austria it is not subject to Austrian VAT. If a licence is exercised in Austria it will generally be subject to Austrian VAT at the current standard rate of 20 per cent.

3. Property Tax

Intellectual property commercially exercised within Austria is subject to a property tax. Non-resident companies whose intellectual property is licensed and exercised in Austria are obliged to pay property tax on the intellectual property used in Austria. This provision may be overridden by the provisions of a relevant tax treaty. It is expected that from 1 January 1994 property tax will be abolished.

TAXATION ASPECTS

Belgium

1. Taxation of Intellectual Property Rights

Payments for the use of intellectual property such as copyright, design rights and trademarks are taxed as professional income.

2. Sponsorship

Sponsorship payments, including payments to cover the provision of corporate entertainment facilities, are tax deductible business expenses of the sponsor. Where sponsorship payments are made the sponsor is required to report to the relevant authorities the name and address of the recipient and the date of payment.

3. Endorsements

Endorsement payments made to sportspersons for the use of their names and likenesses are treated as deductible business expenses of the sponsor. For the purposes of Belgian tax there is no distinction drawn between the pure royalty and performance related part of such endorsement payments.

TAXATION
ASPECTS

Bulgaria

There are some specific tax regulations appertaining to sports marketing transactions:

- Sole traders can take, as a tax deduction, up to 20 per cent of their taxable income, for sponsoring sports organisations with non-profit making purposes.
- Companies can deduct up to 10 per cent of their employees' gross pay for providing their own sports facilities, as long as this is paid into a national fund for this purpose.

TAXATION
ASPECTS

Denmark

1. Direct Taxes

1.1. Revenue

Royalties paid by a resident licensee are treated as tax deductible business expenses provided they are on arm's length terms. A licensor is taxable on royalties it receives on an accruals basis.

1.2. Capital

A person who acquires outright or who licenses intellectual property will have to capitalise any lump sum payment made. Capital allowances are available on the expenditure spread over either the length of the user period, or where this has not been fixed, over a period of 10 years on a straight line basis.

Gains or losses realised on the disposal of intellectual property rights are treated as taxable income.

2. VAT

The transfer of ownership of intellectual property is not subject to VAT.

3. Event Organiser with Charitable Status

In general, most sports bodies have a non-profit tax status and are thus only taxable on trading profits. This is also the case for charitable event organisers. Trading profits include profits on sales of tickets or goods to non-members. Trading profits do not include payments received under a sponsorship agreement or membership fees.

TAXATION
ASPECTS

Finland

1. The Taxation of Intellectual Property Rights

Payments made by a company for the use of a trademark, copyright or design right will usually be treated as deductible business expenses. Where the owner of the intellectual property is a non-profit making charitable association they will not usually be taxed on the licence fees received.

2. Sponsorship Agreements

Where a company sponsors an athletics federation or individual athlete the payments should be allowed as marketing expenses, provided the recipient publicises the sponsor's business and the amounts are not unreasonable. Small payments made to local sports associations will generally be deductible expenses of the payer company.

If a sponsorship payment is made direct to an individual sportsperson, wage withholding tax must be deducted from the payment.

TAXATION
ASPECTS

France

1. Taxation of Intellectual Property Rights

Royalty payments are generally treated as deductible business expenses. However, excessive royalties paid between group companies may be disallowed as deductible expenses and treated as a distribution. Royalties paid to non French residents are subject to withholding tax at the rate of 33⅓ per cent, subject to reduction or exemption under the provisions of a relevant tax treaty.

2. Sponsorship

Generally, sponsorship payments made by a corporate sponsor to an event organiser or individual sportsperson are treated as allowable business expenses, provided sufficient promotional opportunities are derived from the payment. Where a sponsor makes a business asset available for use in a sports activity the depreciation on the asset will be an allowable business expense, provided adequate promotional opportunities arise from the loan of the asset. However, relief for depreciation on assets, such as passenger vehicles, holiday homes and yachts, is subject to restrictions, unless the corporate sponsor's business includes the trade of renting such assets.

A French resident sponsor, who pays remuneration to either a non French resident individual sportsperson or other legal entity in respect of sports activities carried out in France, or where benefits from the sports activity arise in France, must deduct withholding tax at the rate of 15% from the payments. This withholding is on account of the final tax liability, which will be based on net income earned taxable at the normal progressive rates, subject, in the case of non resident individuals, to a minimum of 25%. Anti-avoidance provisions state that, where payments are made for a sports activity carried out within France to a legal entity based in what is termed a tax haven, the person providing the sports activity will be assessed to tax on all such payments.

3. Event Organiser with Charitable Status

Income derived from the ordinary activities of a non-profit making organisation is exempt from tax. The investment income derived from assets, such as buildings and securities of non-profit making organisations, is subject to a reduced rate of tax of 24% or 10% depending on the nature of the income. There are a number of conditions to be satisfied by an entity to qualify for such favourable tax treatment. The objective of the organisation should not always be to achieve a surplus of income over expenditure and any surplus made should be reinvested in the organisation. The running of the organisation should not give rise to any direct or indirect material gain to the founders, senior management or members of the organisation. For the income to be exempt it must arise from the entity's defined non-profit making activities. Sports organisations and event organisers, which are commercially managed companies, are fully taxable on their income.

4. VAT

Goods and services supplied in connection with a sports activity are subject to VAT, except where the payment is remuneration paid to an individual sportsperson under an employment contract. The sale or licensing of trademarks and other intellectual property rights are treated as supplies of services for VAT purposes. Whether a transaction is subject to French VAT will depend on where the seller/licensor and the purchaser/licensee are established for VAT purposes.

Event organisers may suffer a tax disadvantage due to the low proportion of their turnover which qualifies for the purposes of reclaiming VAT on their inputs. Receipts from entrance tickets are exempt from VAT. An employer company, who is subject to VAT on less than 90% of turnover, will also be subject to a progressive payroll tax.

TAXATION
ASPECTS

Germany

1. Taxation of Intellectual Property Rights

German tax law makes no distinction between copyright, trademarks and other forms of intellectual property.

2. Direct Taxes

A German resident licensee may claim as business expenses royalty payments for the use of intellectual property provided the expenses are effectively and economically connected with the entity's business. Where a lump sum advance is paid this amount should be capitalised and expended over the period of the contract. Where an advance is received by a licensor the amount should also be capitalised and taxed over the period to which it relates.

The taxation treatment of the licensor will be determined by factors such as the residency of the licensor and, in the case of a non-resident, whether the income is classified as German source income.

A German resident licensor will usually be subject to local trade and federal income tax if the activity which creates the income is deemed to constitute a commercial business. In this context professional sportspersons are treated as being engaged in a commercial business.

A non-German resident licensor who receives royalties which are deemed to be German source income will usually be assessed to local trade and federal income tax if the income is earned through a commercial permanent establishment based in Germany. The income of a non-resident may be treated as German source income either because the royalty income is connected with sporting or similar commercial activities performed or exploited in Germany or the intellectual property is registered in Germany/exploited by a licensee who has a permanent establishment in Germany. Where the royalties are treated as German source income, the payments should be made by the licensee after deduction of withholding tax (currently at the rate of 25 per cent). Where the royalty income is connected with activities performed in Germany the rate of withholding tax is reduced (currently to 15 per cent). These rates are subject to reduction under the terms of any double tax treaty which exists.

3. VAT

The VAT treatment of royalties paid under a licence agreement for the use of intellectual property is determined by the place where the recipient carries on his enterprise. If a licensee is an enterprise located in Germany, the royalties will be subject to German VAT. For practical purposes, the 'zero-procedure' allows for no VAT to be accounted for where a foreign licensor does not issue a VAT invoice and the German licensee would have been entitled to reclaim the VAT if it had been properly invoiced.

4. Net Assets Tax

Intellectual property may be subject to net worth tax and the trade tax on capital.

5. Sponsorship

Sponsorship payments will be treated as allowable business expenses so long as they are made predominantly with a view to providing the sponsor's business with a clearly identifiable promotional benefit. If the sponsorship payment is linked to the provision of business entertainment and gifts, it will generally be disallowed for tax purposes.

A recipient of a sponsorship payment, who is resident in Germany and is not a recognised charity, will be subject to local trade tax and federal income tax (corporation income tax where the recipient is a company).

The VAT treatment of the payment will depend on the place in which the sponsor carries on his business assuming the service provided falls into the category of marketing/advertising/public-relations services. If the sponsor's place of business is in Germany the payment will be subject to VAT although the 'zero-procedure' may be applied as noted above.

6. Endorsements

The payment to a sportsperson for using the sportsperson's name and likeness will be an allowable business expense of the payer.

Where the sportsperson is a German resident, or is a non-resident with a permanent establishment in Germany, the endorsement payment will be subject to local trade tax and federal income tax. A non-resident without either a permanent establishment or permanent representative in Germany should have either 25 per cent or 15 per cent withholding tax deducted from the gross payments (subject to treaty relief). The gross payment will be the consideration including VAT even where due to the 'zero-procedure', German VAT is not charged. The VAT treatment will be the same as for sponsorship payments.

7. Event Organiser with Charitable Status

Donations to a qualifying body (this cannot include an individual sportsperson) are allowable for tax purposes provided they are within set limits.

TAXATION
ASPECTS

Greece

1. Taxation of Intellectual Property Rights

The transfer of rights connected with an enterprise, such as the right to lease or sublease or to use a patent or trademark, is taxed at 30 per cent, subject to any mitigation under a double tax treaty. The tax is withheld by the payer company.

2. Sponsorship

Greek tax legislation has no specific provisions with regard to the deductibility of sponsorship payments. Based, therefore, on the general tax provisions, only business expenses are deductible. An expense is considered as a proper business expense if it is incurred for business purposes only.

Based on the above, sponsorship payments may or may not be considered deductible based on these criteria.

Iceland

Sports clubs are generally tax exempt organisations in Iceland.

1. Sponsorship and Advertisement

For a sponsorship payment or advertisement to be tax deductible, there must be a connection between the payment made and the trading activities of the sponsor. The payment must maintain or increase the revenue of the sponsor.

Donations without an advertisement or other consideration in return could be considered not tax deductible, unless considered a gift to cultural activities or in the interests of the public. Sports activities may fall under that category regarding gifts.

2. Endorsements

Endorsement payments made to sportspersons, for the use of their names and likeness, are not common in Iceland, but would probably be tax deductible, if the payments are made to maintain or increase the revenue of the sponsor.

3. VAT

Membership fees, payment to sports clubs for participating in sports activities and tickets to sports event are free of VAT.

Sale of advertisements by sports clubs and any sale of goods or refreshments by the sports clubs are generally subject to VAT. Such activities are exempt, for income tax purposes, however, if the profit belongs to the sports club.

TAXATION ASPECTS

Republic of Ireland

1. Trademarks and Copyright

The taxation treatment of trademarks and copyright will depend on whether the specific transaction is considered to be capital or revenue. There exists a large body of Irish case law, mostly from the UK, on this subject.

1.1. Revenue

Payments for the use of trademarks and copyright are usually treated as deductible trading expenses, provided they are incurred wholly and exclusively for the purposes of the payer company's trade. There is no obligation to withhold tax on such payments.

The receipts of a licensor, where the transaction is treated as revenue in nature, will be taxed as either a trading receipt or as investment income, where the trademark/copyright is held as an investment.

1.2. Capital

Payments made for either the outright purchase of, or for an exclusive perpetual licence to use, a trademark or copyright, should be treated as capital expenditure. No capital allowances are available on this capital expenditure.

Consideration for the outright sale or grant of an exclusive perpetual licence to use a trademark or copyright will be assessable to capital gains tax where either the recipient was not the originator of the asset or where the recipient held it as an investment. Where the person receiving the payment was the originator of the copyright, the amount will be assessed as a trading receipt.

1.3. VAT

Transfers and assignments of trademarks and copyright are treated as a supply of services for VAT. For Irish VAT the supply of services is taxed where the services are received. The determination of where the services are received depends on the place of residence/establishment of the recipient and in what capacity (business or private) the person receives the supplies.

1.4. Stamp Duty

Trademarks and copyright are 'property' subject to Irish stamp duty. An outright assignment/exclusive non-revocable licence is subject to ad valorem stamp duty at rates up to 6 per cent if the assignment is made either under a conveyance or transfer on sale. If not assessable as part of a conveyance, it will be taxed at the contract or agreement stage. A non-exclusive or revocable licence to use a copyright or trademark will be subject to nominal stamp duty of £10.

2. Sponsorship

A payment under a sponsorship agreement will be a tax deductible expense of the sponsor provided the payment is incurred wholly and exclusively for the purposes of promoting the trade of the sponsor.

Business entertainment relating to the sponsorship of a sporting event is not a tax deductible expense.

3. Endorsements

Endorsement payments made to sportspersons are treated as tax deductible expenses and should be paid gross. That part of an endorsement payment which relates to the use of a sportsperson's name and likeness is treated for tax purposes like a licence to use a trademark.

4. Donations to Sportspersons/Sports Bodies

Donations where no services are received from the sportsperson/body are treated as charitable donations and are not tax deductible.

Gifts to the National Sports Council ('COSPOIR') are set off against the total profits of the donor company provided the donation is at least IR£100 with relief being restricted to a maximum payment of IR£10,000.

5. Event Organiser

Bodies which organise events whose sole purpose is to promote athletic or *amateur* games or sports will be exempt from Irish income tax. The sports body may be a particular club or an association representing a number of clubs.

TAXATION
ASPECTS

Italy

1. Taxation of Intellectual Property Rights

The same tax treatment is applied to trademarks, copyright and registered designs.

1.1. Direct Taxes

An Italian resident licensee is able to deduct payments on an accruals basis. The cost of acquiring a licence, to use intellectual property, may be amortised over the period of the licence. As regards the acquisition of intellectual property, amortisation of the cost would be deductible at a maximum of one third per accounting period.

Royalties received by an Italian resident company, or by a individual or partnership in respect of trading activities carried on in Italy, will be taxable on an accruals basis. Disposal of intellectual property by such entities gives rise to a capital gain or loss equal to the difference between the sales price and the cost which remains unamortised at sale. There is an option for the gain to be taxed in equal instalments over five accounting periods. If the company holds an intellectual property right as trading stock, its disposal gives rise to a trading profit or loss.

When royalties are paid by an Italian resident, or by a non-resident who has a permanent establishment in Italy, to a non-resident individual or company, the payer is obliged to deduct withholding tax (currently 21 per cent). This is a final tax and the recipient has no further Italian reporting requirements or Italian tax liability in respect of the royalties. An applicable tax treaty may provide a lower Italian tax rate.

The accounting treatment adopted in respect of advances received will be important in determining their taxation and this should generally follow the principle that an advance should not be booked as income until it becomes non-refundable.

1.2. VAT ('IVA')

For IVA purposes, the grant, assignment or transfer of a trademark, copyright or design is treated as a supply of services and falls within the ambit of IVA when the recipient belongs in Italy, except when the service is used outside the EC, or by a person who belongs in another EC country and it is VAT-registered there, when the supply is outside the scope of IVA. However, where a non-EC recipient pays for intellectual property rights used in Italy, IVA will, in general, be chargeable.

2. Sponsorship

No general deductibility limits exist for sponsorship payments either in money or in kind. They are regarded as publicity expenses, for which a deduction is given in the accounting period in which the expense is incurred, or in three equal instalments in the year in which it is incurred and the subsequent two accounting periods, at the option of the taxpayer.

Where the sponsorship payment is made to a non-resident group company, transfer pricing implications may arise (i.e. in the case of a sponsorship payment which is excessive in relation to the publicity thereby obtained). If the recipient group company is resident in a tax haven, the expenses will be fully disallowed unless the tax haven company is carrying on *bona fide* trading activities.

If the sponsor receives consideration in return for the sponsorship payments (e.g. tickets or entertaining facilities), the element relating to these may be treated as entertaining expenses. Entertaining expenses are only one third deductible, the deduction being given in equal instalments in the accounting period in which the expenses are paid and the subsequent two accounting periods.

A sponsorship payment received by a company resident in Italy will be taxable as a normal business profit on an accruals basis.

A non-resident individual will be taxable on a sponsorship payment if it relates to activities which he carries out in Italy. Withholding tax at 20% must generally be deducted. This is a final tax for a non-resident.

As regards the IVA treatment of sponsorship payments, some difficulty arises in analysing the nature of the supply being made. If it can be regarded as a donation, it may be possible to argue that this is not consideration for a supply received and, therefore, that IVA is not applicable. This may be a significant issue where the sponsor is not fully recovering its input IVA (e.g. a bank). However, in general, a donation will be deductible for direct tax purposes as an entertainment expense rather than as a publicity expense. It must be noted that, if the goods donated by the sponsor are goods the production of which is part of the normal activity of the sponsor, then this will be regarded for IVA purposes as a supply of goods to the sports entity.

Generally, sponsorship payments are regarded as payment for a supply of publicity or advertising services. Such services are normally regarded as taking place where the recipient belongs. When the publicity or advertising services are provided to a recipient belonging outside the EC, they are regarded as taking place where the publicity or advertising is used. For example, if a non-EC sponsor makes sponsorship payments to a sporting entity or sportsperson and the publicity is used in Italy, the supply falls into the territoriality of IVA. Thus, a sporting entity which is registered for IVA will in these circumstances be required to invoice the non-EC sponsor with IVA, which may be recoverable by the sponsor under the EC 13th VAT Directive procedures or by appointing an Italian-resident fiscal representative. Considerable delays in obtaining the repayment are likely to be experienced (currently approximately five years), making this a significant issue for non-EC sponsors. A sporting entity or sportsperson not belonging in Italy and not having an Italian IVA registration who performs services which, as above, fall within the territoriality of IVA may register and charge IVA. If he does not do so, he will not be able to recover IVA incurred on his costs in connection with making the supply.

Where the sponsorship payment is provided in kind, particular IVA problems arise. In this case, a mutual supply is regarded as taking place (i.e. of goods by the sponsor and of publicity/advertising services by the sporting entity or sportsperson) and IVA may be due on the market value of both the goods and the publicity/advertising services.

3. Endorsements

The granting by contract of the right to use the name and likeness of a sportsperson is treated for Italian tax purposes similar to the granting of a licence over a trademark, etc.

A fixed fee under the contract will be treated as the purchase price of the right and a deduction will be obtained for amortisation of the fee over the life of the contract. Any performance related element will be treated as a royalty.

4. Commissioning Agreement

The costs of commissioning the production of a logo should be deductible, but at a maximum of one third per accounting period (as with amortisation of a copyright). An aggressive but disputable interpretation suggests that, where the logo is not capitalised and costs are written-off directly to the profit and loss account, this is no longer amortisation and should accordingly be allowed as a normal expense.

The costs of commissioning advertising should be deductible as advertising expenses.

Continuing fees generally comprise two elements, being royalty payments and management fees. Management fees should be tax deductible on an accruals basis, and do not attract any withholding tax obligation.

5. Films and Videos

Where the owner of the film or video sells copies to a distributor, this is treated as a supply of goods. The place of supply is, therefore, where the copies are physically located when delivered to the customer. The IVA treatment and the particular rate applicable will depend on where the goods are located.

6. Suppliership

A sponsor purchasing the right to be the official product supplier for a sports event or series of events will obtain a tax deduction for amortisation of the cost of the right over the period of the contract. A deduction for the market value of products supplied should be available as a publicity expense.

The receipt of a payment by the event organiser for entering into the agreement will be taxable on an accruals basis. Products received under the agreement will be taxable on their market value.

TAXATION
ASPECTS

The Netherlands

1. Sponsorship

Payments derived from agreements not exceeding one year, as a rule, are classified as advertising costs and as such are fully deductible. The sponsoring of single events may lead to partly deductible expenses, e.g. food and drink provided to third parties which is 75 per cent deductible.

Sponsoring costs incurred in any given year but relating to more than one year are regarded as capital expenditure which must be amortised over the period for which the benefits of the sponsorship agreement are enjoyed. These should be capitalised and amortised in accordance with generally accepted accounting standards.

2. VAT

If the sponsor does not receive any benefits for his contribution and the party being sponsored is an entrepreneur as defined in the Dutch Turnover Act, VAT should be charged.

A distinction needs to be made between sponsoring and gifts as the latter are not subject to VAT.

TAXATION
ASPECTS

Norway

1. Trademarks, Copyrights, Registered Designs

Royalty payments are deductible on an accruals basis. Royalties received may be taxed as either revenue or capital, although the same rate of tax (28%) is applied.

There is no obligation to withhold tax on royalties paid to non-residents.

2. VAT

Services involving the transfer and/or exploitation of patents, licences and trademarks will be subject to VAT. A sale of TV rights is outside the scope of the VAT Act. Sports activities and event organising are not subject to VAT in Norway. However, sports clubs are obliged to pay VAT on marketing services, sale of merchandise and hiring out of equipment.

3. Sponsorship

Sponsorship payments will usually be deductible on an accruals basis.

Provided payments are for services (e.g. advertising) on an arm's length basis, they will be regarded as marketing costs and subject to VAT.

TAXATION
ASPECTS

Poland

1. Intellectual Property Rights

All intellectual property is afforded identical tax treatment.

1.1. Direct Taxes

From the recipient's viewpoint the Polish tax system makes no distinction between royalties received under a licence to use intellectual property and consideration for the sale of property rights. The income profits from these transactions received by foreign entities are taxable at a flat rate of 20 per cent, unless otherwise provided by a tax treaty. For domestic entities, royalties are taxable on a business profit at 40%.

A licensee who pays royalties for the use of intellectual property can claim the amounts paid as a tax deduction. Provided the intellectual property is licensed as part of a public promotion there is no limit on the amount of the payment that can be claimed as a tax deduction. Where a person acquires intellectual property outright the expenditure should be treated as capital. Tax relief can be obtained on this expenditure by amortising the cost on a straight line basis over 10 years.

The Polish system for accounting for direct taxes requires monthly advance tax payments to be made throughout the tax year. At the end of the tax year the taxpayer's actual tax liability is compared to the payments made on account and a compensating adjustment is made.

1.2. VAT

It is unclear whether the grant assignment or transfer of a trademark, copyright or registered design is a taxable supply of services. However, according to current interpretation and practice such transactions would not be subject to Polish VAT.

2. Sponsorship

Where the event organiser, as part of a sponsorship agreement, provides the sponsor with facilities, such as free tickets or hospitality boxes, the cost of this provision will be an allowable business expense for the event organiser. A sponsor, who receives free tickets or hospitality boxes, should either have the value of these facilities deducted from the sponsorship payment which is eligible for tax relief, or will have the value of the entertainment received assessed as taxable income. However, where the free tickets are distributed to employees of the sponsor the value of the tickets should be assessed on the employees and not the sponsor.

3. Commissioning Agreements/Films and Videos

The commissioning of a logo or advertisement will represent the acquisition of a copyright and will be treated as capital expenditure. Relief may be obtained by means of tax allowable amortisation.

By contrast, expenditure incurred to produce a film or video is treated as a tax deductible cost. Income received by a distributor will be subject to corporate profits tax at progressive rates, whereas income received under a licence, which grants to another party the right to distribute the film or video, will be treated as a copyright royalty and will be subject to a flat rate tax of 20 per cent.

4. Event Organiser with Charitable Status

Gifts made to bodies carrying out sports activities are tax deductible provided they do not exceed 10 per cent of the donor's profit/income. The recipient is not required to have charitable status.

TAXATION
ASPECTS

Portugal

Capital payments made by Portuguese companies to non-residents for the acquisition of a copyright or registered design should be paid gross. Payments made for the use of copyright should be paid net of withholding tax of:

- 25% when paid to a non-resident individual who is not the original owner or
- 25% when paid to a company.

Payments for the use of a registered design should be paid net of withholding tax of:

- 20% when paid to a non-resident individual or
- 15% when paid to company.

The Russian Federation

1. Taxation of Intellectual Property Rights

Profit from the sale of intellectual property will be taxed as profit from the sale of fixed assets. The initial cost is increased by an inflation index.

A deduction for amortisation of intellectual property is currently available.

Where a resident licensee pays a licence fee to a entity which does not have a permanent establishment in Russia, 20 per cent withholding will need to be retained (subject to the provision of any tax treaty between Russia and the respective country).

2. VAT

Current Russian legislation is unclear as to whether transactions involving intellectual property are supplies of goods or services, although most sports marketing transactions are likely to be regarded as supplies of services. However, it is not clear in what circumstances they would be regarded as exports which are exempt from VAT. Current legislation does not provide a clear definition of what an exported service is. The authorities seem to be interpreting an export as a service which is not only received and enjoyed overseas, but also provided overseas.

TAXATION
ASPECTS

Spain

The various sports marketing business arrangements are subject to the general principles of Spanish tax law. These are that payments for work or services provided are taxable, whether paid in cash or kind; and payments are deductible only if incurred on the generation of taxable income.

Sweden

1. Taxation of Intellectual Property Rights

All types of intellectual property receive the same kind of tax treatment; all income arising therefrom is usually treated as trading income. The deduction of royalty payments is determined by generally acceptable accounting principles.

Intellectual property is treated as depreciable property. The taxpayer may elect to depreciate the property on either a 30 per cent reducing balance or 20 per cent straight line method.

There is no requirement to withhold tax on royalties. However, royalties paid by a Swedish payer to a non-Swedish payee will give rise to a deemed permanent establishment in Sweden for the payee, if the payments are derived from the payer's permanent establishment in Sweden. Treaty relief may override this.

2. Sponsorship

For sponsorship payments to be tax deductible, there must be a connection between the payment made and the trading activities of the sponsor. The payment must maintain or increase the revenue of thc sponsor. Alternatively, the payment should result in better health for the employees.

Gifts are never tax deductible and a differentiation needs to be made between the above type of transaction and gifts.

Where the sponsorship results in business entertainment, the expenditure is deductible only if there is a very strong connection between the expenditure and the business of the sponsor.

A non-profit association is only taxable on income from business activities and income from real property.

TAXATION
ASPECTS

Switzerland

It is important to note that, besides the Swiss federal income tax, all of the 26 Swiss Cantons levy their own Cantonal income taxes and that the tax laws vary between the Cantons.

1. Direct Taxes

1.1. Revenue Transactions

Royalty payments made under a licence to use a trademark, copyright or registered design will be allowed as tax deductions, generally on an accruals basis. The receipts of the licensor will represent taxable income.

Costs incurred registering or renewing such intellectual property rights will attract tax relief, usually as business expenses, although occasionally the costs may be capitalised and tax relief given as allowable amortisation.

1.2. Capital

Where intellectual property rights are sold by a company the capital gain arising forms part of the company's normal business income and is subject to corporate income taxes.

The purchaser of intellectual property should capitalise the costs and receive tax relief through amortisation of the costs over the economic life of the asset.

2. Withholding Taxes

Payments relating to intellectual property rights are not subject to withholding tax.

3. VAT/Swiss Sales Tax

Payments relating to intellectual property rights are not subject to Swiss sales tax.

4. Sponsorship

To be able to claim a tax deduction for a sponsorship payment the payment must satisfy two tests. The sponsorship payment must result in a benefit for the sponsor and the amount must be reasonable in relation to the size of the sponsor's business.

The provision of free tickets and corporate hospitality boxes constitutes business entertainment and will be allowable business expenses, provided they meet the two tests mentioned above.

Where a sponsorship payment satisfies the two general conditions for tax allowability but is a lump sum payment and provides the sponsor with promotional benefits over an extended period of time, the payment should be capitalised. Tax relief should be obtained by amortising the lump sum over the period in which the sponsor derives benefits from the arrangement. The same treatment is accorded to initial lump sum payments made under merchandising and endorsement contracts.

The recipient of a sponsorship payment will be in receipt of taxable income from which reasonable expenses incurred in connection with the payment can be deducted. Where a lump sum is received the payment should usually be assessed to tax over the contract period, although an individual recipient may be assessed on a cash basis.

5. Commissioning Agreements/Films and Videos

Payments under commissioning agreements are usually tax deductible expenses. Where the logo or advertisement has an ongoing value the payment for the asset may have to be capitalised. As mentioned above, tax relief will be given on the amortisation of this capital expenditure. The same considerations apply to the commissioning of a promotional film or video.

6. Event Organiser with Charitable Status

Recognised charitable organisations are exempt from income tax. Furthermore, payments made by a sponsor to an event organiser with charitable status are generally considered to be tax deductible expenses.

Turkey

1. Intellectual Property Rights

No specific legislation exists in Turkey for the treatment of intellectual property and recourse must be made to general principles.

Turkish law allows expenses to be deducted where they are incurred in earning and maintaining the commercial profit.

2. Sponsorship

A payment made to a sports body or an event organiser in consideration for promotion should be an allowable business expense.

Tickets or hospitality may be granted to a sponsor. If the sponsor gives the ticket to a client then the expense is allowable, but not if given to the sponsor's staff or relatives.

Schedule of Comparative European Tax Rates

	Standard Rate of Corporation Tax (or equivalent tax) (%)	Standard Rate of VAT (or equivalent tax) (%)
United Kingdom	33[1]	17.5
Austria	30	20
Belgium	39[2]	19,5
Bulgaria		10–22[3]
≤ 1 million levs	30	
> 1 million levs	40[4]	
Denmark	34	25
France	33⅓	18.6
Germany	50[5]	15
Ireland	40	21
Italy	36[6]	19
Netherlands	35[7]	17
Norway	28	20
Poland	40	7–22

1. Small company rate of 25 per cent for profits below £250,000.
2. Companies are taxed at 39 per cent on income in excess of BF 13 million. Income below this is taxed at rates ranging from 28 per cent to 41 per cent. However, if a company is a holding company or at least 50 per cent owned by another company, then 39 per cent applies automatically.
3. The introduction of a new VAT is being debated. At present there is turnover tax of 10 per cent and 22 per cent.
4. Companies with foreign equity participation in excess of 49 per cent and US$100,000 are taxed at 30 per cent, even if profits are greater than 1 million levs.
5. 36 per cent on distributed profits. Brand tax rate is 46 per cent. Temporary 3.75 per cent surcharge is imposed on 1991 and 1992 corporation tax liabilities.
6. Also a local income tax of 16.2 per cent is due making a combined tax burden of 52.2 per cent.
7. The first Dfl. 250,000 of taxable income is taxed at 40 per cent.

	Standard Rate of Corporation Tax (or equivalent tax) (%)	Standard Rate of VAT (or equivalent tax) (%)
Portugal	36[8]	16
Russian Federation	32	20
Spain	35[9]	15
Sweden	30	25
Switzerland	10–27[10]	
Federal sales tax – sales to end users		6.2
– sales to retailers and imports		9.3
Turkey	46[11]	12

8. Applicable to resident companies and non resident companies with permanent establishments in Portugal.
9. Non resident companies operating in Spain without a permanent establishment are subject to tax at the rate of 25 per cent.
10. Varies according to Canton. Also there is a Federal Income Tax which is additional and is at a maximum rate of 9.8%.
11. Surtaxes totalling 7 per cent are levied on the corporate income tax.